CLAIMING MACEDONIA

D1607742

CLAIMING MACEDONIA

*The Struggle for the Heritage,
Territory and Name of the
Historic Hellenic Land,
1862–2004*

George C. Papavizas

McFarland & Company, Inc., Publishers
Jefferson, North Carolina, and London

LIBRARY OF CONGRESS CATALOGUING-IN-PUBLICATION DATA

Papavizas, George Constantine, 1922–
    Claiming Macedonia : the struggle for the heritage, territory
and name of the historic Hellenic land, 1862–2004 / George C.
Papavizas.
      p.   cm.
    Includes bibliographical references and index.

    ISBN 0-7864-2323-4 (softcover : 50# alkaline paper)

    1. Macedonian question.   2. Eastern question (Balkan).
3. Macedonia — Ethnic relations — History.   4. Greeks —
Macedonia — History.   5. Macedonia — Politics and government —
1912–1945.   6. Macedonia (Republic) — Politics and government —
1945–1992.   7. Macedonia (Republic) — Politics and government —
1992–   I. Title.
    DR2206.P37 2006
    949.5'607 — dc22   2005035064

British Library cataloguing data are available

Cover photograph ©2006 Pictures Now

Manufactured in the United States of America

McFarland & Company, Inc., Publishers
  Box 611, Jefferson, North Carolina 28640
    www.mcfarlandpub.com

To my grandchildren:

Michael, Sophia, Nicholas,
John, and Aidan

Acknowledgments

I owe many thanks to three friends for their careful, critical, and penetrating reviewing of the manuscript in its pre-submission form and for making many valuable comments and corrections on names and historical facts: Marcus Alexander Templar of Chicago, Spyros Petropoulos of Maryland and Panayiotis Tzimas from Canada. Special thanks are due to Mr. Templar for writing the book's appendix. I would also be remiss to not thank the following individuals for reading the manuscript in its early stage, offering comments and suggestions: Professor Nikolaos Stavrou, John Alexiou, Marina Hall, Joseph Morton and Costas Vasileiadis.

I am also indebted to the following individuals: Dr Potitsa Grigorakou-Parnassou, an expert on the Hellenistic Age, for her friendship and continuing support and encouragement of me to proceed with this project; to T. Peter Limber for allowing me to modify and use one of his many excellent color maps from his book, *Hellenika*; and to Ekthotiki Athenon of Athens for the use of a black-and-white version of a map of Provincia Macedonia, from the book, *Macedonia, History-Monuments-Museums*.

Research for this broad and timely subject would not have been possible without the help provided to me by the personnel of the following institutions in Thessaloniki, Greece: the Museum of the Macedonian Struggle, Institute of Balkan Studies, and Society of Macedonian Studies. Special thanks are due to the Museum of the Macedonian Studies for kindly providing the six photographs included in the book and for its permission to modify and use three maps of Macedonia.

My two sons, Constantine and Panos, have been marvelously supportive of this undertaking, though perhaps tired of listening to my vehement arguments about the struggle for Macedonian Hellenism through the ages. Many thanks are due to my older son Constantine, a lawyer by profession, for his keen interest in Greece's history in general, and Macedonia's in particular; and to my multi-talented son Panos, an engineer, for all the computer help he gave me.

Joanna Lawrence also deserves special attention and I offer many thanks for her skills and patience in the preparation of the maps.

Contents

Preface

When I was thirteen years old I asked my grandfather Constantine why he had joined the Greek *andartes* (freedom fighters) in 1904 and fought for four years in Macedonia against the armed Slavic bands (*komitadjides*, committee men) of the clandestine Bulgarian Komitet "Internal Macedonian Revolutionary Organization" (IMRO, *Vatreshna Makedonska Revolutionna Organizacija*). Still under the Ottomans in the early 1900s, western Macedonia and Krimini, the small village with its four hundred Greek-speaking inhabitants where I was born, were in the forefront of the so-called Macedonian Struggle (*Makedonikos Agonas*) that lasted four years. Looking at me straight in the eyes for a long time in silence, twirling his long moustache, his sixty-year-old weather-beaten face furrowed in deep pain because of the distortion of historical facts on Macedonia emanating from the Slavic north, he said softly with tears in his eyes: "To make certain that after the Turks, our Macedonia remains Hellenic and my children and grandchildren enjoy freedom as *Hellinomakedones*" (Greek Macedonians).

Always with a permanent genteel expression evincing compassion and understanding, Kotas, as he was known among his friends and relatives, was a man of genuine affability and modest demeanor, underlined by a powerful mix of genuine Hellenic Macedonian values and an unusually strong commitment to family and the Greek Orthodox Church. Representing an exclusive group of brave men with a tenacious belief in Macedonian Hellenism, Kotas, my hero grandfather, had no bigotry, hate, or chauvinism in his heart. What, then, motivated the prudent and peaceful man to become a guerrilla fighter for Macedonian Hellenism when even the official Greek government kept a cautious and ambivalent approach to

1

the Macedonian problem and a safe distance from the Macedonian Struggle in the early years? Only an intense, innate passion for Macedonian Hellenism's fate and a distaste for history's distortion could incite him to leave
his family for four years for the undeclared vicious guerrilla fight against
the Turks and Bulgarians. He died of pneumonia at sixty, leaving behind
an deep feeling of patriotism for all and an indelible, life-long Hellenic
Macedonian legacy that has had a major impact on me, his first grandson.

Sixty years later I was at my son's house for Thanksgiving dinner.
Before I sat down, my eight-year-old grandson, Aidan, ran to me and bran-
dished the *Scholastic Atlas of the World*, published by Miles Kelly Publishing Ltd. in Great Bardfield, Essex. He proudly demonstrated his geography
skills by naming several countries around the world without reading the
names, leaving his best for the end, the map of Greece. He looked at it for
a few seconds, placed his finger on the word "Macedonia," looked at me
with his intelligent blue eyes, and said: "Here, Papou [Grandfather]; I know
where Macedonia is, where you were born." Suddenly, he looked at me again
and said, disappointed, "But you told me you were born in Macedonia,
Greece."

I was not surprised that the word "Macedonia" was not on the Hellenic Macedonia, but on a small country beyond Greece's northern frontier. It was not the first time that my Macedonia, the only one that existed
when I was born, was not shown on the map. The publisher did not bother
to place the word "Macedonia" on Hellenic Macedonia, which occupies 75
percent of King Philip's historic Macedonia. I was at a loss how to explain
to my grandson why Hellenic Macedonia, the beautiful Hellenic province
engulfing the Thermaic Gulf from where the greatest military endeavor was
launched to conquer Asia and Egypt three and a half centuries before Christ,
was not shown on the map.

Not underestimating Aidan's intelligence and his precociously keen
interest in history and geography, I attempted to discuss with him the bare
elements of the Macedonian issue and how and why it has affected relations
among several Balkan and non-Balkan countries for more than a century.
He quickly comprehended my short story on Macedonia, the historic Hellenic Macedonia. But because I have learned all my life to attribute the written word with more weight than the spoken one (*verba volant, scripta
manent*), an authoritativeness that remains on paper for ever, I decided
there and then to write about a plundered legacy; a disputed identity; how
the international community (diplomats, politicians, news media, and representatives of non-governmental organizations [NGOs]) has been ensnared
in clever political-historical inaccuracies, emanated or broadcast from capitals behind the Iron Curtain in the past, from free capitals north of the
Greek frontier now; and how Greece's northern neighbors have been striv-

ing to convince the world to recognize a small breakaway republic with a name that belongs to Hellenic Macedonia and to my grandchildren's Macedonian legacy.

The nagging Hellenic Macedonian feelings in the back of my head since the serious discussion with my grandfather on this tremendously uncharted and controversial field, dormant for a long time because of life's other serious, unrelated demands, and the question raised by my grandson sixty years later, drove me into a frenzy of energy and an insatiable urge to write something compelling and accessible about Macedonia, my Hellenic Macedonia. I felt the need to express my thoughts on the people of the north who have snatched Hellenic Macedonia's name, suppressed my Hellenic Macedonian pride, and raised my anger at the distortion of historical and archaeological facts. When Balkan maps appear in newspapers and magazines, even in governmental publications, with the word "Macedonia" on the wrong place, I know that a historical transgression has been committed with Hellenic Macedonia mysteriously lifted from its original position for political expediency, compressed, and pushed northward to fit into a section of the landlocked Skopjan territory known as *Vardarska Banovina* (Vardar Province, prefecture of the River Vardar, South Serbia) till 1944, "People's Republic of Macedonia" till 1991, and *Republika Makedonija* (Republic of Macedonia, minus the word "People's" to adjust its name to the fall of communism) since 1991.

When I encounter blatant attempts by individuals or organizations to de-Hellenize the ancient Macedonians and the Hellenistic Age (the three centuries following Alexander's death), nowadays renamed the "Macedonian Period" (i.e., Slav Macedonian Period), I discover with frustration man's attempts to distort history. When I hear the Greek Macedonian city of Thessaloniki (Salonika), the city built in 316 B.C. by one of Alexander's generals, Cassandros, named after his wife, half-sister of Alexander the Great, being called "Solum," or see commemorative currency printed in Skopje depicting Thessaloniki's White Tower, my adrenaline rises. When I read that people in Vardar Macedonia speak "Macedonian," touted as the language of Alexander the Great, it offends my intelligence, my culture, and my knowledge of history behind which are Homer and Socrates, Plato and Aristotle, Euripides and Sophocles (Durant 1939). You may falsify, torch, bury, burn, ignore, forget history, but you cannot cancel it. It is always there. It will always be there. Joining the past with the future, it will always be there, because it is the learning of life. Man will always go to the books, those of the past and those of the future.

You may distort historical documents, but the coherence of Macedonian Hellenism will remain unbreakable. It is one of the characteristics defining Macedonian Hellenism. You may falsify historical documents, but you cannot quell "my liberty to be, to think, to speak — my very essence of life" (Durant 1939). You may intensely torch Hellenism's struggle, but the distillation of pain from the distortion of historical facts will last forever within pseudo-history's spurious pages. You may place historical symbols that belong to another country, another epoch, another civilization, on a national flag, but you cannot prevent me from hearing my Hellenic Macedonian ancestors' voices within me. They are language, religion, science, philosophy. Within my veins, and in the veins of millions of Hellenic Macedonians, runs the blood of Macedonian Hellenism, anxious, uneasy, creative, indestructible.

It is not my intent to add another historical book on Macedonia. It is to add a different book, one with a uniquely interpreted approach, easily read and understood by the common English-speaking people interested in the Macedonian issue and in the long political, diplomatic and military struggle for the heritage, the territory and the name of the Hellenic land. It is to show, step by step, how Greece's northern neighbors created a new state with the name "Macedonia" on the wrong footing by arbitrary government decrees. It is also to reconstruct a picture of a state-controlled "Macedonian" ethnogenesis, a Balkan political development that produced a new nationality, the "Macedonian" nationality, and how and why a polyglot conglomerate state decided to use a name belonging to its neighbor to the south, the name's derivatives, a flag symbol, and historical inaccuracies to convince the international community that its intentions were legitimate.

Why is the name so important? Because it carries along important derivatives far beyond what it says. It carries "Ghosts or real historical demons. Perhaps war or peace. Nothing and everything," wrote Leslie H. Gelb in the *New York Times* (June 12, 1992). The name, of course, is Macedonia, the land of Philip, Alexander and Aristotle; the beautiful land of Mount Olympus and the Greek gods. The rich land east and west of the bustling city of Thessaloniki with the archaeological sites of an age long gone, the Hellenic Macedonian age: Pella, Vergina (Aegae), Dion, Amphipolis, Methone, Pydna, Olynthos, Appolonia, Aianae, Philippi, Potidaea, Stagira (Aristotle's birthplace), Thessaloniki. Do any of these historical names sound Slavic to the reader? The essence of the Macedonian controversy flows from Shakespeare's spirited words: "He that filches from me my good name robs of that which not enriches him, and makes me poor indeed." Apprehending my good name does not enrich anyone, but makes me poor and unhappy indeed because it deprives me of the power of my Hellenic Macedonian ethnic pride, culture and identity, compelling me to react in writing, expressing my sadness for the alteration of Macedonia's history.

To produce an objective account of the age-old controversy, I had to begin anew — at the time of Yugoslavia's dissolution, coinciding with my retirement — a serious study of the Macedonian history that lingered in my mind since I was a youngster and lay considerable stress on the main reason, communism, responsible for the perpetuation of the Macedonian controversy since the early 1920s. I had to go to libraries, acquire new books, discuss ideas with knowledgeable people, travel to Greece to visit libraries and museums and interview some of the remaining old people in western Macedonia. Inevitably this work, done by an amateur historian, will be compared, for better or worse, with the work of accomplished scholars. I do not intend to compete with them. Neither do I intend to downgrade their scholarly accounts, or change the popular image of modern historical treatises. As an author of Hellenic descent, I may even be accused of demonstrating a strong sensitivity to and a sense of political correctness supporting Greece's views on Macedonia. On the other hand, as a scientist who explored nature's mysteries for a lifetime, and wrote hundreds of scientific publications, I believe I possess a rare attribute as a new historian: the ability to investigate objectively and judge.

As an individual born and raised in one of the hotbeds of Macedonian controversy — west Hellenic Macedonia — I perceive things differently from some modern historians who have focused on stories supported exclusively or to a large extent by Slav historiography. I was there during World War II, the occupation of Greece by foreign invaders (Germans, Italians, and Bulgarians), and the Greek Civil War of 1946–1949 when the Vardar Province (South Serbia) was named "Macedonia" by Tito's communist regime. The memory of my grandfather who fought for Macedonia's Hellenism in the early 1900s — a simple man who harbored no hatred for anyone — and the memory of my birthplace burned to the ground twice by the Germans, ravaged later by the civil war fomented and fueled by the Eastern Bloc countries, especially communist Yugoslavia, still linger in my mind. The whirlpool of painful impressions, and the injustice done to Greece that thwarted communism in the 1940s, impelled me to write a story that will be accurate but different from other accounts.

Some modern scholars do not go back far enough to trace the origin of the Macedonian problem and how it evolved to become a struggle for Macedonia under the Ottomans between two protagonists, Greeks and Bulgarians, not between Greeks and "Macedonians." Macedonianism as an independent ethnic concept had not been invented yet. It had to wait for almost seventy years to be propelled into the world. My book goes back to the origin of the Macedonian controversy, critically reviewing and analyzing the period from the appointment of the pro-Bulgarian Count Ignatieff as the Russian ambassador to the Ottoman government in Constantinople and the Treaty of San Stefano to the end of World War I (1862–1918). During the early part of this period Bulgaria became a nation and carried the relay of the struggle for Macedonia from 1878 to 1941. During those years the Macedonian Question assumed a pivotal role in the relations of four Balkan ethnicities— Greek, Bulgarian, Serbian and Turkish — with no one mentioning a "Macedonian" ethnicity.

Many modern writers disregard altogether how the Macedonian controversy was exploited by Soviet-sponsored international communism to propel into the world the unhistorical concept that the Socialist Republic of Macedonia's Slavs, Albanians, and Bulgarians were the only legitimate "Macedonians." In contrast, my book reviews the misconceptions within the analysis of the legacy of Macedonia's past, as promulgated by Soviet-sponsored international communism. It also carefully analyzes communism's role as the main protagonist instrumental in the so-called Macedonian ethnogenesis by communist government dictatorial decrees and as a pivotal source fueling the Greek Civil War of 1946–1949. The critical role played by Yugoslav communism in the struggle for Macedonia did not escape the attention of several writers who attributed the formation of a separate "Macedonian" nation of Slavs and other nationalities to the brutal force and theoretical base provided by communism.

For all the horrors and bloodshed, the Greek Civil War did not happen in a historical vacuum. It happened within the context of an unprecedented international conspiracy and grotesque violations of international law by the communist world. It was fomented and fueled throughout its duration by powerful communist organizations (Comintern, the Balkan Communist Federation, the Communist Party of the Soviet Union, and the Balkan communist parties). The main protagonists, Comintern and the BCF, keenly interested in disturbing Macedonia's status quo, threatened Greece's territorial integrity by conspiring to cede Hellenic Macedonia and attach it to a Slavic Macedonian state within a South Slav federation, a new Soviet Balkan satellite. Yet the connection of the civil war's destinies with those of Hellenic Macedonia escaped the attention of or was disregarded by several writers. The pivotal role played by international communism during the civil war on Hellenic Macedonianism was not overlooked by historian Evangelos Kofos, who wrote (1995, p. 318): "the two issues— the fate of Macedonia and the course of [the communist] revolution in Greece — would converge, interact, and shape the destinies of both."

Ever since the secession of a section of Vardar Province from Yugoslavia in 1991, its official name adopted by the United Nations and accepted by Greece and its European allies has been the Former Yugoslav Republic of Macedonia (FYROM). The cumbersome name was adopted to avoid confusing the former Yugoslav confederate republic with the historical Greek province of Macedonia until a suitable name could be negotiated. Yet, many writers rushed to recognize the small enclave as the "Republic of Macedonia" and its people as "Macedonians" immediately after its secession from Yugoslavia. While they censure the Greek writers for lack of objectivity and take a dim view of their Greek colleagues denouncing Skopje's claims of exclusive Macedonianism as historically incorrect and therefore unacceptable, they turn around and write books just as subjective as those they censure for lack of objectivity. For instance, John Shea wrote in the introduction of his book *Macedonia and Greece*: "By Greeks, I mean those people who come from or feel ties with the nation that we consider as modern Greece. By Macedonians, I mean those people who live in or feel ties with the former Yugoslav Republic of Macedonia" (FYROM 1997, p. 2).

Habitation or feelings alone do not and must not qualify a person as "Macedonian." If we accept that the FYROM Slavs, Bulgarians, and Albanians are Macedonians, because they live in FYROM and "feel" like "Macedonians," then what are the three million Greek Macedonians who live in Hellenic Macedonia, half of whom are indigenous Hellenic Macedonians (IHMs, Hellenic Macedonians speaking Greek, whose forebears lived in Macedonia for countless generations)? Are the Slav-speaking inhabitants living in FYROM more "Macedonians" than my grandfather whose ancestors lived in Macedonia before the beginning of the nineteenth century, always speaking Greek, always feeling the pulse for Hellenic Macedonia? Another modern historian placed the FYROM flag on the front cover of his book and then focused only on FYROM Slavs as the bearers of the Macedonian name. Referring to FYROM Slavs as Macedonians "would be to ignore strident and historically justified claims" that the name "Macedonia" should also refer to the large northern Greek province, wrote Cowan and Brown (2000, p. 6).

If we rush to make a premise that only the FYROM Slavs and a small percentage of the thirty-eight thousand Slav-speakers of Hellenic Macedonia are "Macedonians," we stand on the brink of accepting a historically false and unacceptable concept for which not only history, but also the people involved on both sides of the fence, will regret later. We are arbitrarily shifting Macedonianism from Hellenic-speaking Macedonians to Slav-speakers who live in a country half of which was not even part of King Philip's historic Macedonia. Carelessly using the word "Macedonians" to describe the FYROM Slavs and Albanians increased the Skopjan politicians' intransigence, arrogance, and unwillingness to cooperate in solving FYROM's name problem. Milovan Djilas, Tito's right-hand man and a Yugoslav vice president (until he was imprisoned by Tito), remarked in his book *Conversations with Stalin* (1962, p. 36): "But I do not believe that even he [Dimitrov] adhered to the view point that the Macedonians were a separate nationality."

I have tried to distinguish between obscure and controversial facts and present ideas that can be critically examined; cited international and Greek sources from which I have drawn conclusions; and expressed them in the book in a style the common English-speaking person will understand. One of the ideas, listed as a disclaimer, is the expression "Macedonia" in quotation marks versus Macedonia. The first expression refers to the way FYROM officials use the word to connote the ethnic significance of their republic (a concept disputed in this book). Without the quotations the word is a geographic, not an ethnic term, referring to the territory known as historic Macedonia by the time King Philip was assassinated (336 B.C.).

Clarifications

(A) The term **indigenous Hellenic Macedonians** (IHMs) indicates Greek citizens (and their descendants) whose tongue has been Greek and whose ancestors go back in Macedonia for many generations. They have all the characteristics, traits, sentiments, traditions, culture, inheritance, and aspirations to be considered *Ellines Makedones.*

The term **slavophone Greek Macedonians** (Greek-oriented slavophones) indicates slavophone Greek citizens whose political, ethnic, and national affiliations and sentiments are Hellenic. Most of them speak Greek also. In his book *Plundered Loyalties* (1995), the historian John S. Koliopoulos suggested that the term **slavophone Greeks** would be more accurate than the term **Slavomacedonians** (or Slav Macedonians) of Greece. The synthetic name indicates the place of abode whereas the first suggests their possible origin.

The term **Immigrant Macedonians of Greece** (prosfyges) indicates Greek citizens whose tongue is Greek and who emigrated to Greek Macedonia in the 1910s and 1920s as a result of the Treaty of Neuilly and the Treaty of Lausanne.

The term **Slavomacedonians** is used for inhabitants of Slavic descent who inhabit geographical Macedonia, whose tongue is a modified Bulgarian dialect and whose ethnic sentiments are strictly Slavic or Bulgarian.

(B) The words "Hellene" and "Greek" are used interchangeably in this book.

(C) All translations of excerpts from Greek sources are the author's.

Disclaimers

"Macedonia," in quotation marks, refers to the way the Former Yugoslav Republic of Macedonia (FYROM) officials use the word to connote the disputed ethnic significance of their republic. Without the quotations the word refers to the geographic meaning, not the ethnic.

A few selected and specially drafted excerpts were used from my book, *Blood and Tears — Greece 1940–1949 — A Story of War and Love,* published by the American Hellenic Institute Foundation of Washington, D.C., 2002.

Introduction

The precipitous decline of the Ottoman Empire at the end of the nineteenth century, coupled with the rise of the Russian Empire, were the two main causes of the so-called Macedonian Question destined to haunt the Balkans for more than a century. It began at the time when Bulgaria became a nation: first the religious restitution in 1870 (formation of the Bulgarian Autocephalous Church, the Exarchate); then the ethnic restitution in 1878 (formation of the Bulgarian Principality) by the Treaty of San Stefano, granting Bulgaria extensive areas in the Balkans. The two events, stemming from Russia's unmitigated pro–Bulgarian intervention, were the source of the Macedonian Question, not because of the events themselves, but because Bulgaria exploited its advantageous position to articulate its never-ending demands to expand into Macedonia. The events between 1870 and 1878 signaled the beginning of a vicious struggle between Bulgarism and Hellenism whose first phase lasted till 1918. The temporary increase of its size by the Treaty of San Stefano encouraged Bulgaria's dangerous imperialist policy and chauvinism in spite of the Treaty of Berlin restoring it to its pre–Stefano borders.

The Macedonian Question from 1878 to 1918 was a complex issue involving several smaller issues. It was the question of who had the historical, cultural, ethnic, and demographic rights to possess historic Macedonia with the collapse of the Ottoman Empire, the land once occupied by King Philip and his son Alexander the Great. The question inadvertently triggered a political and military struggle, leveling at the outset the fighting field between two protagonists, Bulgarism and Hellenism — two ideas and two forces— to bring the struggle for Macedonia to a successful end, victory by one or the other side. They struggled for Macedonia as Bulgarians and Greeks, not as "Macedonians" and Greeks.

Virtually from the beginning of communism's encroach into the Balkans, the Macedonian Question — and the struggle for Macedonia — took on a different meaning and new dimensions. It was, and still is, the competing claims by Greece's neighbors for Hellenic Macedonia. In simple terms, it is the coveting of Hellenic Macedonia, including its capital, the city and Aegean port of Thessaloniki. The Bulgarians first, and the Yugoslavs later, have used every means available to them to violate the Treaty of Bucharest (signed in 1913): seditious propaganda, distortion of history, anthropological and historical studies of dubious or prejudiced nature that never seriously considered the existence of millions of indigenous Hellenic Macedonians (IHMs), guerrilla warfare, and foment of war by aiding the Greek communists during the Greek Civil War of 1946–1949 to destroy historic Macedonia's Hellenism and push Greece into its pre–World War I borders. Even with the Former Yugoslav Republic of Macedonia (FYROM)'s independence from Yugoslavia, the struggle for Macedonia continues unabated on the political and diplomatic arena by Skopje's activism and the support of Slavic organizations abroad.

Marked by the blatant support of the Slavomacedonians as a separate "Macedonian" ethnicity by international communism, the two decades between the two world wars (1918–1940) saw the dynamics of the struggle for Macedonia shifting from the first period's bloody confrontation to a bloodless time interval rife with intense political manipulations and intrigue. New realities with the rise of communism in Russia and the strengthening of the Balkan communist parties prompted the revival of the struggle for Macedonia, mainly Hellenic Macedonia. Comintern (Communist International), the Balkan Communist Federation (BCF), and the Communist Party of Bulgaria carried the relay, with the small, virtually impotent Communist Party of Greece (*Kommounistiko Komma Elladas*, KKE) adrift, willingly or unwillingly dragged into the maelstrom of political intrigue.

The last period of fifty years (1941–1991) of the struggle for Macedonia is marked by the Tito-Stalin scheming relationship and intrigue and the Bulgarian communist leader Giorgi Dimitrov's frequent, but occasionally reluctant, participation. This period began with Comintern's interference in August 1941 directing Tito to assume responsibility of the Macedonian issue: "Macedonia must be attached to Yugoslavia for practical reasons and for the sake of expediency." Almost immediately, the torch was passed from Bulgaria via Comintern to Tito, who employed unusual methods to realize his goal: formation of the People's Republic of Macedonia in 1943–1944. During the last part of this period Tito's communist successors passed the responsibility to the ex-communist Kiro Gligorov, a Bulgarian and a Tito protegée. The last twenty-five years also saw multisided efforts to influence public opinion to condone the competing claims on Greek Macedonia as a movement of the "Macedonian" people to gain their autonomy and independence. To put it bluntly, the name "Macedonia" is merely a vehicle for a state-sponsored ideology that suggests the existence of a partitioned nation — with one part of it subjugated by Greece and the other by Bulgaria.

While Tito's communist regime was being laid to rest, what followed in the struggle for Macedonia was the secession from the crumbling Yugoslavia of a small landlocked country north of Greek Macedonia, whose reformed communist politicians decided to use the name "Macedonia" for the newly independent state. The multiform state, occupying a section of Vardar Province since 1944, suddenly decided that the name "Macedonia" would be appropriate to tie its Slavic past with the glorious Macedonian history. It first became the People's Republic of Macedonia in the federated state of Yugoslavia. In 1953 it changed its name to Socialist Republic of Macedonia and finally dropped the socialist mantle (almost everyone was dropping socialist and communist symbols at the same time) in 1991, becoming an independent state as *Republika Makedonija* (Republic of Macedonia). It accused its neighbor of unjustifiably using the name Macedonia for its large northern province and printed maps and schoolbooks depicting heroes and landmarks of its neighbor's cities. Its major political party threatened to hold its next congress in Solum (Thessaloniki), its neighbor's capital; rewrote its history to show the world that it had inherited the glorious history of its neighbor; resurrected the tenets of an old Bulgarian uprising (the Ilinden uprising of 1903) and embraced them to write its own new constitution's preamble; indiscriminately associated the new ethnic name "Macedonians" with the name of the wider geographic area of Macedonia to establish territorial claims on the neighbors' Macedonia; changed its language, touting it as the language spoken by its neighbor's ancient inhabitants; selected a symbol from its neighbor's past and placed it on its first national flag and public buildings; and propelled to the world a population amalgamation theory to show that its Slavic inhabitants are products of genetic blending of its ancestors and ancient Macedonians.

FYROM's people were taught by Tito's communists not to be "Serbs" or "Bulgarians"— though they used the names for hundreds of years— because these names were not glamorous enough and could not assist them in claiming their "unredeemed" brethren in Greek and Bulgarian Macedonia. After all these events, the Macedonian Question is no longer seen as a question: it has become a clever and deliberate attempt to absorb, slowly but surely, everything that belongs to a neighbor: a complete sweep of historical and archaeological values and the destruction of the neighbor's identity and pride.

The bottom-line question that needs to be asked now is which of the two groups, Hellenes or Slavs in Macedonia, is historically, culturally, and ethnically more likely to be identified as Macedonian? What are the roots, language, traditions, culture, and archaeological findings to support Macedonianism of one group versus the other? While different perceptions on the two questions are inevitable, for the sake of simplicity we must accept two possibilities for this introduction: (a) a Macedonian is an inhabitant or a former inhabitant of historic Macedonia irrespective of ethnicity; and (b) a Macedonian is an indigenous Hellene born in historic Macedonia or abroad of Greek Macedonian parents, whose forebears inhabited Hellenic Macedonia as far back as can be verified, always speaking Greek — like the ancient Macedonians did — always possessed by the power of Hellenic Macedonian ethnic identity and culture. The Slav-speakers of Macedonia could belong to either category, depending on their ethnic consciousness, not their language.

If the simplistic and unpersuasive rationale of habitation in Macedonia defines who is a Macedonian, then the two million inhabitants of South Serbia (now FYROM), Pirin (Bulgarian) Macedonia's inhabitants, and the three million inhabitants of Hellenic Macedonia are Macedonians, irrespective of ethnicity. Within this framework, we can divide historic Macedonia's inhabitants into three groups: Greek-Macedonians, Slav-Macedonians, and Bulgar-Macedonians. If habitation is the criterion of Macedonianism, FYROM's "Macedonians" would also include Albanians, Serbs, Bulgarians, Vlachs, gypsies, and Muslims of nondescript ethnicity. The Greek-Macedonian group would include the indigenous Hellenic Macedonians and Greek-speaking people who emigrated to Macedonia from Asia Minor and Eastern Rumelia during the second and third decade of the twentieth century. Therefore, if we use the word "Macedonians" for FYROM's inhabitants only, as most anthropologists and some scholars do, we discriminate against the Greek Macedonians and Bulgarian Macedonians, an overwhelming majority of Macedonian inhabitants.

Disregarding one and a half million IHMs bound by the *power of Hellenic Macedonian ethnic pride, culture, and identity*, some anthropologists insist there is only one group of people that can bear the name "Macedonian": the Slav-speaking inhabitants in the *Republika Makedonija*. If we accept this view, what name must we attach to the IHMs who always lived in Macedonia, embraced by the power of Hellenic Macedonian culture and pride? What is the ethnicity of the inhabitants of the bastions of Macedonian Hellenism such as Kozani, Siatista, Kastoria, Tsotyli, Pentalofos, Vogatsiko, Kleisura, Thessaloniki, Serres, Drama, Kavala, and hundreds of other towns and villages in Macedonia who fought during the Macedonian Struggle of 1904–1908 against the Bulgarians? In contrast, what are the historical, linguistic, cultural, anthropological, and ethnic characteristics that bear positively on a few anthropologists' views of their exclusive Macedonianism being awarded to the Slavs of *Republika Makedonija*? Why were FYROM's Slavs Bulgarians from 1870 to 1944, waiting for seventy-five years for a communist dictator to transform them into "Macedonians"? Was it not communist Realpolitik that played a decisive role in the formation of the new "Macedonian" nation, religion, and language?

FYROM's Slavs began to claim their "Macedonian" ethnicity as a result of the role Tito and communism played in their acquiring a "Macedonian" language, a "Macedonian" nationality, and a "Macedonian" country, ethnic characteristics acquired from 1941 to 1945, an ethnicity built in a remarkably short time. Old and new members of the new "Macedonian" ethnicity underwent repeated transformations: Bulgarians in 1870 when they joined the Exarchate; Bulgarian *komitadjides* later fighting against Hellenism in Macedonia; Bulgarophiles until 1943 and members of the Communist Party of Greece or the Communist Party of Yugoslavia till 1945; some of them German or Italian collaborators or IMRO and Ochrana members during Macedonia's occupation by the Germans and Italians; members of the autonomist SNOF (*Slovenomakedonski Narodno Osloboditelen Front*) later and at the same time Greek or Yugoslav communist partisans; members of the autonomist NOF (replaced SNOF) and at the same time Greek communist guerrillas fighting the Greek government's forces during the Greek Civil War; and, finally, transformed to "Macedonians" by Tito, with Stalin's advice and approval.

Some NGOs, anthropologists, and politicians awarded FYROM's inhabitants with an ethnic name and removed it from Greek Macedonians who always have been Macedonians, not Slavs one day, Bulgarians the next, Slavomacedonians later, and finally Macedonians. It is indeed instructive to assess how history's alteration done by the People's Republic of Macedonia, and later by FYROM, misled many Europeans and Americans who accepted Skopje's political and ethnic decisions as the truth. Considering these facts, history has now reached the untenable point where the small country calling itself *Republika Makedonija* (FYROM) may demand—by the power of its apprehended name, arbitrarily sanctioned by some countries and NGOs—not only to be a Macedonia, but the only Macedonia; and its people may demand not only to be some Macedonians, but the only Macedonians. That is what FYROM's recognition with a name that belongs to a neighbor has done to the legitimate recipients of the name.

With this perspective in mind, the insistence of FYROM Slavs to be called "Macedonians," a name acquired sixty years ago, clashes with the Hellenic Macedonians' right of always being Macedonians. If FYROM considers itself Macedonia, a daring step that brings the origin of its inhabitants close to Philip and Alexander the Great, then the right of these people to be called "Macedonians" stops before the freedom of others to be called "Macedonians" begins. The world knows that Philip and Alexander were Greeks, believed in Greek gods, participated in the Olympic Games, and spoke a dialect known as *koine* (common), an Aeolic (Greek) dialect modified by Philip and spread to a vast empire by Alexander the Great. The world knows that not a shred of evidence has been unearthed in Macedonia and in Alexander's vast empire that ancient Macedonians spoke a language other than Greek. The world also knows that Aristotle wrote in Greek, Euripides wrote in Greek in the Macedonian capital, Pella, and all the artifacts (statues, gravestones of common people, frescoes, coins, stelae, etc.) unearthed in Macedonia bear Greek inscriptions. The "Greek-speaking" stones and coins attest to that; and so do all the findings in places conquered by Alexander the Great from Egypt all the way to Asia Minor and the Hindu Kush.

People do not understand that the struggle for Macedonia has been an inclusive part of Hellenic history since the struggle's beginning in 1862; they have no feeling for the power of history, the power of ethnic identity, and much less for the power of Hellenic Macedonian culture and pride. They do not understand Robert Darnton's point brought forward in a recent editorial (*Washington Post*, April 4, 2003), "Burn a Country's Past and You Torch Its Future," or his point that "temples are crucial for the task of knowing who you are by knowing who you were." A good contrasting example of how history is downgraded is the *New York Times* editorial of August 25, 1993: "Macedonia's [the newspaper had already decided in 1993 that FYROM's name must be "Macedonia"] differences with Greece, though emotional, are not substantive. Like so many Balkan quarrels, they are about history—recent and ancient." the *New York Times* forgot its July 16, 1946, editorial stating that "A combined effort was made to wrest Macedonia from Greece ... the main conspiratorial activity appears to be directed from Skopje."

This kind of superficial editorialization confuses the American public and the international community. Outsiders find it hard to understand how countries can quarrel over a name, as Greece and FYROM have been doing for thirteen years. They do not understand that for three million Greek Macedonians, and eleven million Greeks in general, under whose feet lie relics of a glorious Macedonian epoch, all with Greek inscriptions, history is the learning of life. They do not understand that Hellenic Macedonia's past is its present, and the present depends on its past, on history. They fail to comprehend that Greece's history in general, and Hellenic Macedonia's in particular, depend on the development of the Macedonian issue (McNeill 1947). They fail to see that if you burn, destroy, or ignore the country's past, you torch its future. They fail to discern that history is the bridge spanning the past with the future, preserving the essence of the struggle; that the present IHMs and their descendants did not come from the steppes of the River Volga; that they are people whose ethnicity was apprehended by the Slavs who migrated to the Balkans one thousand years after Alexander's death. These people speak Bulgarian or a Bulgarian-like dialect and claim Macedonian ethnicity because a communist dictator ordered them to be "Macedonians." They have every right to live in a free and independent country, but have no right to claim a name that does not belong to them, a name linked with Hellenism since 900 B.C.

We must forgive FYROM's common people because they are decent people who behaved like most people would have done under an autocratic dictatorship: they did exactly as the communist dictators forced them to do. What is hard to condone or forgive is the disappointing stance of the fence-sitting, or even adverse-position-holding Greece's friends and allies, who approved the use of the name "Macedonia" by the small republic. Unfortunately, European and American politicians and diplomats, leading on this issue at the time, failed to see Greece's extreme importance to their national security in contrast to Skopje's unimportance and forgot the blood spilled by the Greek people to prevent communism from reaching the Aegean and Mediterranean.

The irony of the U.S. policy is that it helped Greece protect its territory in the 1940s, save Macedonia from falling into Tito's hands, and thwart Tito's and Stalin's irredentist aspirations and conspiracies, which resulted in the death of one hundred thousand Greeks and seven hundred thousand homeless, including twenty-eight thousand children kidnapped by communists and sent behind the Iron Curtain, many of them never to return; and then turned around and recognized as "Macedonian" the people against whom Greece was fighting with America's help to preserve its territorial integrity during the Greek Civil War of 1946–1949.

Equally paradoxical is the fact that when the political and military pendulum swung in the opposite direction after Greece successfully thwarted communism and prevented Soviet-sponsored communism from reaching the Aegean, Greece became the aggressor in the eyes of the West, as if Greece usurped a name that belonged to another country. It is also implausible, yet true, that the Europeans and Americans punished Greece for achieving the first substantial defeat of communism and the first major point in the post–World War II Cold War history; and then in the 1990s they decided to support the only communist country preserved intact by the fall of communism and Yugoslavia's dissolution. Greece's allies forgot that "names have a powerful significance. They may be used for territorial claims" (Gelb 1992).

The historical events of the 1940s, and those of the 1990s, showed how dangerous it was for Greece to have three communist neighbors on its northern frontier, two of them coveting Macedonia and the third Epirus. The shameless demands and unsubstantiated claims by IMRO and Ochrana terrorists, Nazi and fascist sympathizers, and former communist and Bulgarian nationalists misinformed and confused the world about their real intentions and posed a great threat to Greece's territorial integrity. It is said that their multiple ethnic disguises were so powerful and deceitful that they left an indelible lie still perpetuated.

Glossary and Abbreviations

andarte   resistance fighter

capetan   leader of a guerrilla band

CPB   Communist Party of Bulgaria

CPG   Communist Party of Greece, known by its Greek initials as KKE

CPM   Communist Party of Macedonia

CPSU   Communist Party of the Soviet Union

CPY   Communist Party of Yugoslavia

DAG   Democratic Army of Greece — the army of the Communist Party of Greece

EAM   *Ethniko Apeleftherotiko Metopo* — National Liberation Front

EDES   *Ethnikos Demokratikos Ellenikos Syndesmos* — National Republican Greek League

ELAS   *Ellenikos Laikos Apeleftherotikos Stratos* — Greek People's Liberation Army

EEC   European Economic Community

EU   European Union

FAEV   Forum Against Ethnic Violence

FYROM   Former Yugoslav Republic of Macedonia

IMRO   Internal Macedonian Revolutionary Organization — Bulgarian political and military organization seeking Macedonia's autonomy and its eventual annexation by Bulgaria

KFOR   United Nations Kosovo Force

KKE   Kommounistiko Komma Elladas (see CPG)

KLA   Kosovo Liberation Army

komitadjides   committee men — Slav-speaking guerrillas

NGO   non-governmental organization

NLA   National Liberation Army — secessionist Albanian group in FYROM

NOF   National Liberation Front — *Narodno Osloboditelen Front*, political and military organization formed by communist Slavomacedonians from Greek and Yugoslav Macedonia during the Greek Civil War

PAO   *Panhelleniki Apeleftherotiki Organosis* — Panhellenic Liberation Organization

PASOK   Panhellenic Socialist Movement

SNOF   Slavomacedonian National Liberation Front — *Slovenomakedonski Narodno Osloboditelen Front*, political and military organization formed by communist Slavomacedonians from Greece and Yugoslavia during the German and Italian occupation

VMRO   Internal Macedonian Revolutionary Organization — *Vnatresvna Makedonska Revolucionerna Organizacija* — replaced IMRO in Skopje

VMRO-DPMNE   Internal Macedonian Liberation Organization/Democratic Party of Macedonian National Unity, Skopje

1

The Origin of the
Macedonian Question

Ὄλβιος ὅστις τῆς ἱστορίας ἔσχεν μάθησιν
(Happy is the person who learned history)
—*Euripides*

Macedonia: Geography and Brief History

The history of the Macedonians began in the seventh century B.C., and Macedonia appeared for the first time on the historical scene as a geographical-political entity in the fifth century B.C., extending from the origin of the River Aliakmon and Mount Olympus to the River Strymon. The Greek tribe of the Macedons migrated from Orestis (present-day Argos Orestikon-Kastoria district, Greek western Macedonia) eastward and occupied what the historian Thucydides called "Lower Macedonia" or "Macedonia by the Sea" (present-day central Macedonia, Greece). According to the historian Peter Green (1991, p. 4), "Lower Macedonia was the old central kingdom, founded by semi-legendary cattle barons ... and ruled over by the royal dynasty of the Argeads, to which Philip himself belonged. About 700 B.C. this noble clan had migrated eastward from Orestis in the Pindus mountains, looking for arable land" (see Chapter 5 for details).

King Philip II, father of Alexander the Great, a visionary, dynamic Greek leader, ascended to Macedonia's throne in 359 B.C., and in less than four years he managed to build his broken-up country, defeat Macedonia's

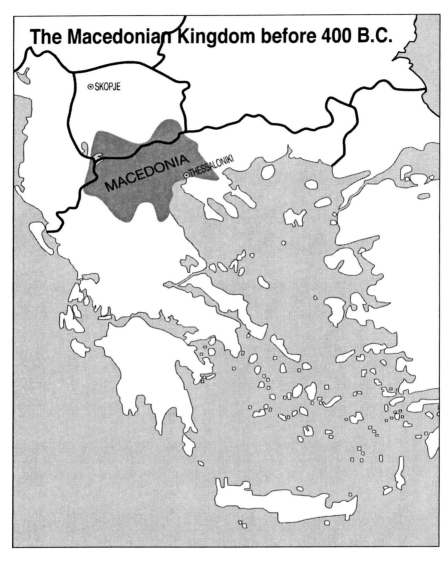

Ancient Macedonia during the Peloponnesian War (431–404 B.C.). Black and white arrangement of Map 3.0 from *Hellenika*, 1997. Courtesy of T. Peter Limber.

enemies, and enlarge his kingdom. A leading statesman in the Greek world by 342 B.C., proclaiming his devotion to Zeus, Apollo and Heracles, Philip made Macedonia the leading military power in Europe.[1] "In less than four years he transformed Macedonia from a backward and primitive kingdom to one of the most powerful states of the Greek world" (Green 1991, p. 32).

By conquests or alliances, he also united the Greek city-states into a single country, Greece. A leader with brilliant political initiative and power of persuasion, he organized the "Greek Community" (*to koinon ton Ellenon*) in which the Greek states were bound by oath to keep peace among themselves. "He brought into being the combination of a newly created Greek state, self-standing and self-governing, and a Macedonian state which was unrivaled in military power" (Hammond 1997, p. 20).

Occupying a critical geostrategic position in the Balkans, Macedonia in its tumultuous history over two millennia witnessed three multiethnic empires that ruled vast territories in three continents. It first witnessed the unification of the Greek city-states by King Philip II, followed by Alexander the Great's spread of a culturally and nationally diverse empire that extended to Egypt in Africa and the Hindu Kush in Asia and survived — divided into five smaller, distinct empires, Macedonia being one — for three centuries after his death in 323 B.C.[2] The three post-Alexander centuries, perceived as the Hellenistic Age, saw the dissemination of Greek civilization from one end to the other of Alexander's empire (Durant 1939).[3]

Then arrived the Romans, who, by 145 B.C., had conquered vast areas in Africa, Asia, and Europe. Under Aemilius Paulus, they annihilated the Macedonian army at Pydna, destroyed seventy Macedonian cities, abolished the monarchy, and split the kingdom into four tributary republics which they annexed to the Roman *Imperium* (Mitsakis 1973). The last Macedonian king, Perseus, was imprisoned in Italy and died of maltreatment. In 146 B.C., the Romans combined Macedonia, Epirus, and Illyria and formed a large province which they called "Provincia Macedonia." As the Romans consolidated their possessions in Macedonia, Latin was spoken from Danube south to a line from Durres, Albania, to Lake Ochris, Skopje, Strobo, Sofia, and east to the Black Sea. Greek predominated south of this line. Banac (1992, p. 46) placed the line for the Hellenic language farther north to Skopje and Sofia. After one more millennium in the Byzantine Empire, religiously and culturally distinct from the Western Roman Empire, Macedonia fell together with the remainder of Greece to the Ottomans and remained enslaved till the beginning of the twentieth century, when it was liberated by the armies of the Balkan Alliance (Dakin 1966; Mitsakis 1973).

Ever since Macedonia's conquest by the Romans in 168 B.C., its borders were ill-defined, depending on the political and military designs of its conquerors and the plans of the peripheral powers that attempted to influence or annex it. It is impossible to define Macedonia's frontiers, wrote Wilkinson (1951). The British historian Nicholas Hammond (1972), the first to define Macedonia as a nonpolitical area, wrote: "If we try to define Macedonia on political lines, we shall be chasing a chameleon through the centuries.... As a geographical area [ancient] Macedonia is best defined as the territory which is drained by the two great rivers Haliacmon and the Vardar [Axios] and their tributaries."

The term "historic Macedonia" in this book, not exactly coinciding with Hammond's delineation of ancient Macedonia, represents Philip's Macedonian kingdom as it existed at the time of his assassination in 336 B.C. It was closed off by the towering peaks of Mount Olympus, the Hassia mountains, and the Aegean Sea to the south; the lofty Pindus mountain range (separating today's western Macedonia from Epirus), an extension of

The Macedonian Kingdom from 335 to 168 B.C.

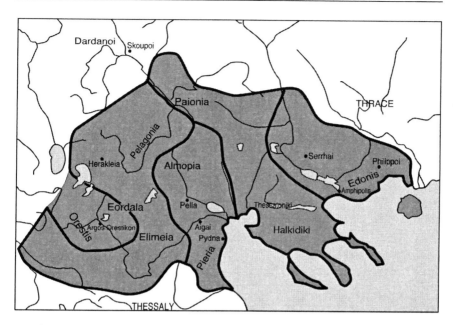

Provincia Macedonia: Macedonia according to the Romans in 146 B.C. It also included Epirus and Illyria. Skopje (Skoupoi), the capital of the Former Yugoslav Republic of Macedonia (FYROM), was outside *Provincia Macedonia*. Black and white arrangement of Map 35 from Ioannis Touratsoglou, *Macedonia: History, Monuments, Museums*. Courtesy of Ekthotiki Athenon, Athens.

the Dinaric Alps, and a line about twenty or thirty miles west of the lakes Ochrida and Prespa to the west; the Rhodope mountains to the northeast and the River Nestos to the east; and a line to the north beginning north of Lake Ochrida, passing north of the outskirts of Krushevo, south of Strobo, north of the vicinity of Strumica, reaching the northern Nestos basin, leaving almost half of the Former Yugoslav Republic of Macedonia (FYROM) outside historic Macedonia.

Paradoxically, when the Macedonian Question surfaced for the first time between 1870 and 1878, the term "Macedonia" no longer represented Philip's Macedonia, but a much larger area, the "geographical Macedonia," often confused with historic Macedonia.[4] The Ottomans considered the

Opposite: Ancient Macedonia from a year after King Philip's assassination to the year Macedonia fell to the Romans. Almost half of the area occupied by the present-day Former Yugoslav Republic of Macedonia (FYROM) was outside the Macedonian Kingdom. Black and white arrangement of Map 03 from www.-macedonian-heritage.gr. Courtesy of Macedonian Heritage, Museum of the Macedonian Struggle, Thessaloniki.

millet (religious) affiliation as an important criterion defining ethnic groups in the empire, with locality (ties to a family, village, region) even more significant (Cowan 1997). The Ottoman proclivity for retrogression was embellished by their arrogance toward the *rayahs* (infidel slaves) and by further divisive political and geographical alterations. To destroy any vestiges connecting Hellenism with history and ethnic Greek names of provinces, for instance, the Ottomans arbitrarily divided the center of the Haemus (Balkan) peninsula into three *vilayets* (provinces): Thessaloniki (Salonika), Monastir (Bitola), and Kosovo. Geographical Macedonia, as shown on Turkish maps, including the three Turkish *vilayets*, was larger than Philip's historic Macedonia (Nikoloudis 2002). Almost the entire Kosovo *vilayet* with Skopje, Tetovo and Kumanovo, important cities in present-day FYROM, were never parts of historic Macedonia. The Kosovo *vilayet* and parts of the Monastir *vilayet* were predominantly inhabited by Albanians. According to Dakin (1966), the term "geographic Macedonia," based on confused historical memories, was devoid of geographic and ethnic significance. As used in the Middle Ages, it often included areas all the way to Herzegovina.

Historic Macedonia during the Ottoman rule, more than half the size of geographical Macedonia, was inhabited mostly by Greeks (Dakin 1966). In spite of the high drain of the human element sustained under the long Ottoman occupation and the ethnological alteration that occurred by the settlement of Slavic groups and Romanian-oriented Vlachs, historic Macedonia managed to keep its main element, the Greek-speaking and Greek Orthodox–oriented population stable (Hassiotis 1992). The Greek-speaking Macedonians were a minority in geographical Macedonia because of the large provinces north of historic Macedonia populated mostly by Slavs and Albanian Muslims. The Russians and their representatives in the Balkans, the Bulgarians, exploited the historically wrong concept of geographical Macedonia at the end of the nineteenth century, because the Slavs predominated over the other ethnic groups in the northern districts of geographical Macedonia (Andriotis 1992; Army History Directorate [AHD], 1979).

Proceeding from written history's past — the only way to perceive our past — and what lessons we can derive from it, we must emphasize that the concept of a geographical Macedonia, as it was used to promote the Russian and Bulgarian geopolitical interests of the nineteenth century to achieve access to the Aegean Sea and circumvent the Dardanelles, is historically unacceptable. Philip's historic Macedonia did not extend to the northern districts of geographical Macedonia where the Slavs and Bulgarians predominated after the Slavs' descent to the Balkans. It is also unacceptable to go along with the "fantastic claims put forward by certain Bulgarians that the

Kingdom of Philip and Alexander the Great of Macedonia was not Greek and that ancient Philippi and Philippoupolis [now Plovdiv in Bulgaria] in Eastern Rumelia were not Greek cities" (Dakin 1966).[5] Not surprisingly, until 1940 the Serbs also did not recognize the concept of geographical Macedonia adopted by Russian and Bulgarian chauvinists, agreeing with the Hellenic concept of historic Macedonia.

Up until the end of the sixth century A.D., the ethnic composition in historic Macedonia did not change under the Byzantines (Koliopoulos 1995; Nikoloudis 2002). From A.D. 590 to 640, however, Slavs from the north began penetrating Macedonia as peaceful nomads or warlike invaders running through Greece marauding and destroying villages and towns (Mitsakis 1973). In short, the larger Greek-speaking element in Macedonia was fragmented by small pockets of organized Slavic groups (the Byzantines called the pockets *sklavinije*[6]), mainly Bulgarians who settled in Macedonia to work either as seasonal workers or permanent employees in large Turkish *chiftliks* (estates). The Bulgarian southward movement continued during the Turkish occupation, affecting the ethnological composition of Macedonia (Nikoloudis 2002). Most of the Bulgarians remained in the northern parts of Macedonia. Those who moved farther south learned the Greek language and were assimilated by the Greeks. Many Greeks were also affected by the Bulgarian language, becoming bilingual (Greek-Bulgarian) or monolingual (Bulgarian). Many of the Slavs living in these pockets were converted to Christianity, lived peacefully, and by the ninth century most of them were Hellenized (Dakin 1966).

As was expected, the spotty Slav penetration of the Balkans under the Ottomans in the fifteenth century brought about radical changes in the demographic and ethnic composition of historic Macedonia, virtually draining the countryside resources, adversely affecting the enslaved population. The Macedonian urban centers, already devastated by siege and looting, became pale shadows of their glorious Byzantine past. All these negative effects resulted from the Turkish westward migration and settling in fertile lands, the conversion of a number of Greeks to the Muslim religion to avoid persecutions, and the movement of Christians abroad and to less fertile, mountainous territory (Hammond 1976).

Virtually from the outset of the Ottoman occupation, many Hellenic Macedonians emigrated abroad, usually eastward or northward, and established themselves in Serbia, Bulgaria, Romania, and Austria, joining the urban class (Svoronos 1976). About one and a half million Greeks, mostly from Macedonia, emigrated in the seventeenth century to the northern Balkans and Central Europe, and even to America later, an event that had great economic effects on the poor territories inhabited by Hellenic Macedonians. Other Greeks from Macedonia emigrated mainly to the west, and to mountainous Greek territory, especially the forested areas of western Macedonia and Halkidiki, where life was expected to be harsh, but the chances of preserving traditions and family ties in isolation were favorable. The flight toward the mountainous interior also had great national significance because it preserved Macedonian Hellenism's way of life and the purity of Hellenic Macedonianism. Many mountainous villages that received Macedonian immigrants developed into thriving Hellenic centers under the Ottomans: Kozani, Siatista, Naoussa, Thessaloniki, Serres, and smaller places such as Tsotyli, Kleisura, Pentalofos, Grevena, etc. (Nystazopoulou-Pelekidou 1988). Beginning at the end of the sixteenth century, many Greek Macedonians began moving the opposite way, from the mountains to new or old commercial centers, some as far away as Constantinople (A.E. Vakalopoulos 1973).

From the early days of the Ottoman occupation, the Turks used the term *Rumeli* to designate the territory they occupied west of Constantinople (AHD 1979). *Rumeli*—country of the Rums (Romans), i.e., Greeks— included the Balkans (except Bosnia), most of which became known later as geographical Macedonia. Everything the Turks encountered in their westward advance was Greek: resistance fighters; cities they ransacked and monuments they destroyed; merchants they robbed and killed; melodies they heard when they surrounded churches with people inside singing Christian hymns, praying to God to save them from the barbarians. Everything remotely related to administration — political, civic, financial, religious— was Greek. Everything in their way west of the Hellespont was characterized by the Turks as Greek, even when they neared the northern part of the peninsula where Slavic elements predominated. Even there, the Turks could discern signs of Greek civilization in every form of human endeavor.

For the hundreds of years of darkness that followed the beginning of the Ottoman conquest, Christianity was the only beacon of light left for the *rayahs* in the Ottoman Empire (AHD 1979). The Christian religion had spread in the Balkans and won the people's hearts before the Slavs appeared in the peninsula. Two Greek monks from Thessaloniki, brothers Cyril and Methodius, taught Christianity to the Slavs in the ninth century, devised the Greek-based Cyrillic script, taught them how to read and write, and performed the liturgy in Greek in Slavic churches. In the year 865 the Bulgarian King Boris became a Christian.

A number of Slavs, including FYROM's first president, Gligorov, dispute that their religious and cultural enlightenment in the Balkan peninsula was borne from the Byzantine Christian Hellenic culture (Martis 1983). They also dispute Cyril's and Methodius's Hellenism, insisting the two brothers were Slavs. This contention was disputed by Pope John Paul II, a Slav himself, who said, "*Cirillo e Metodio, Fratelli, greci, nativi de Tessalonica.*"[7] During a visit to Czechoslovakia on April 22, 1990, the Pope also said: "The cornerstone of the United Europe is found not only at Monte Casino, where St. Benedict labored to establish Latin Europe, but also here in Moravia, where ... brothers Cyril and Methodius, Greeks from Thessaloniki in Macedonia, grafted the Greek and Byzantine tradition onto the history of Europe. We owe to them the fact we Slavs are Christians" (Martis 2001).

The Slav Byzantinist Dvornic also wrote: "All the views which in the past presented the two brothers as Slavs must be rejected. One thing is certain today, that Cyril and Methodius were Greeks" (Mitsakis 1973). Also, Professors I. Lazaroff, P. Pavloff, I. Tyutyundzijeff, and M. Palangurski of the Faculty of History of Sts. Cyril and Methodius University in Veliko Turnovo, Bulgaria, stated in their book, *Short History of the Bulgarian Nation*, pp. 36–38, that the two brothers were Greeks from Thessaloniki (Templar 2003).

The spread of Christianity to the Slavs strengthened Hellenism in Macedonia. During the long Ottoman occupation it was the Greek Orthodox Church that guarded the existence and survival of the entire Macedonian population. It was the Church that comforted the masses to endure the long, harsh slavery, caring for people's education and conditions of life. Recognized by the Sublime Porte in Constantinople (now Istanbul), the Church was the only authority representing the Christians, irrespective of ethnicity. It was the Church that kept most of the people from converting to the Muslim religion. Hellenism's survival in Macedonia depended to a large extent on the Church, officially representing the Christians in the Turkish government (Dakin 1966).

Hellenism did not survive in Macedonia during the darkest years of slavery because of faith in the Christian religion alone. Greek education was another pillar of Macedonian Hellenism. By the end of the eighteenth century there were forty schools in Macedonia teaching classical Greek and three hundred public schools. By 1902, historic Macedonia had more than one thousand schools providing Greek education to one hundred thousand pupils, irrespective of the language they were speaking at home. The schools were supported by the Greek communities, the students' parents, and Greeks living abroad. Greek education was considered fashionable and even necessary for the youngsters to advance in life.

Historic Macedonia, a crossroad between Europe and Asia for three thousand years, is a land with great economic and strategic significance. It combines fertile plains and mountain ranges. Two important river basins, the Axios and the Strymon valleys, are natural routes connecting Europe with the Aegean Sea. The old Roman *Via Egnatia* crossed Macedonia from east to west, beginning in Constantinople, passing through Thessaloniki, Edessa, and Monastir, finally reaching the Adriatic Sea.

Macedonia's economic significance was enhanced in 1871 when a railway was built connecting Thessaloniki with Skopje and in 1888 with Belgrade and Central Europe (Hassiotis 1992). A few years later Thessaloniki was connected with Florina and Monastir in the west and Alexandroupolis in western Thrace in the east. Thessaloniki, the capital of Greek Macedonia, was built in 316 B.C. by the Macedonian King Cassandros, who named it after his wife.[8] A city of great economic importance, and a major port in the Aegean Sea, Thessaloniki had a population of 120,000 in 1895 (A.E. Vakalopoulos 1997). It is no wonder that Macedonia, a rich land with an immensely important geopolitical and strategic position, became the "apple of discord" among several Balkan and non-Balkan states, not to mention the many historical falsifications of Macedonia's Hellenic history and cultural heritage. Not surprisingly, when the Ottoman Empire began to crumble during the nineteenth century's last quarter, not only the Balkan peoples, but also Russia and Austria-Hungary became interested in Macedonia and Thessaloniki for their accessibility to the Aegean Sea and the eastern Mediterranean.

By the end of the Turkish occupation (1912–1913) there were three geographic zones in Macedonia based on language preferences and ethnic affiliations. The southern zone extended between the Greco-Turkish border separating Thessaly from Macedonia and an imaginary line beginning in Micri (Small) Prespa in the west, running north of Kastoria-Edessa-Serres-Drama to the River Nestos. People speaking Greek and slavophone Greek Macedonians predominated in this zone, which also included Thessaloniki, Kozani, Siatista, Monastir, Serres, and Kavala. The northern zone, most of it outside historic Macedonia, was populated mostly by Slav-speakers who, from the middle of the nineteenth century, identified themselves mostly (but not entirely) as ethnic Bulgarians (some as Serbs) (Dakin 1966).

The middle geographic zone's northern demarcation line extended from the northern tip of Megali (Large) Prespa to Strumica, Melenikon, and the River Nestos. It was the most peculiar and controversial zone as to its language and ethnic stratification. It was inhabited by a large number of Slav-speakers of doubtful or fluid ethnicity. The ethnic consciousness of this group, more than of any other language group, was complex and wavering. Declarations of allegiance, for instance, could change rapidly and repeatedly, depending on who was applying the pressure and how forceful was this pressure for change. The struggle for Macedonia, with peaceful means at the outset, with an undeclared guerrilla war under the Ottomans later (1904–1908), was waged between pro-Bulgarian and pro-Greek factions exactly for this goal: to force the Slav-speaking Christian inhabitants of Macedonia to express their religious allegiance either to the Bulgarian

Exarchate (meaning ethnic Bulgarian consciousness) or to the Patriarchate (meaning ethnic Hellenic consciousness).

Using church affiliation (attachment to the Ecumenical Patriarchate of Constantinople) and ethnic sentiments as criteria for the xenophone elements (mostly Slav-speakers) in the middle zone, the Greeks sought to establish Hellenic ties between these people and the Macedonians of antiquity. Bulgaria, on the other hand, which did not even exist on the Balkan map until 1878, used language as the single criterion to justify a Bulgarian ethnic affiliation of the people in the middle zone. One segment of the fluid slavophone group was Hellenized together with other ethnic groups (Vlachs, Albanians, Jews), and another segment was Bulgarized. The uncommitted Slav-speakers continued to be the target of Hellenization or Bulgarization during the end of the nineteenth century and at the beginning of the twentieth century, a compelling reason for a struggle for ethnic predominance in Macedonia that lasted almost forty years (Dakin 1966; Koliopoulos 1995). Both the Greeks and Bulgarians continued to view the enslaved Macedonia as a region that one day would become part of an enlarged Greece or Bulgaria, respectively, but no one expressed interest in Macedonianism as an ethnic concept at that time. This will occur with the dawn of communism in the Balkans.

Panslavism and Bulgarian Nationalism

A perusal of most of the books on Macedonia written by Greeks and non-Greeks, except a few produced in Skopje, reveals that Macedonia's subjugated people were predominantly Greeks, Serbs, and Bulgarians (Dakin 1966).[9] The Greek-speaking Macedonians predominated in the southern zone and the Bulgarians in the northern zone. No "Macedonian" ethnicity existed then (as the term is used today in FYROM, meaning an ethnic Macedonian group), and none appeared officially till 1944. The Greek-speaking Macedonians, native in Macedonia for generations, strongly admiring their illustrious forebears, spoke Greek, though a minority had been assimilated in Slavic pockets and learned to speak a Slavic dialect. Most of these Greek-speakers did not lose their Hellenism. The Serbian courts in the pockets, for instance, were Greek in ceremony, and their titles, architecture, and literature were also Greek (Dakin 1966). Not surprisingly, having obtained their independence from Turkey earlier in the century than the Bulgarians, the Greeks' ethnic aspirations were centered entirely on Macedonia, Epirus and on the island of Crete.

The Bulgarians, a blend of Slavs and Bulgars (an Asian tribe of Turanian-Mongol origin), migrated south under King Kroum (A.D. 803–814) from north of Mount Haemus and raided Thrace. Under King Simeon (893–927), the Bulgarians entered Macedonia and advanced to near Constantinople. A Byzantine province later, greatly influenced by the presence of Greek soldiers, merchants, artisans, and Byzantine officials, Bulgaria was greatly Hellenized (Dakin 1966). Several factors hindered the development of the Bulgarian masses, the most important being their language, which was incompatible with the Greek language, the official language in Byzantium. The wealthy Bulgarians lived mostly in Russia and considered themselves Greeks. During the years that followed under the Turks, the Bulgarian Slavs exhibited very few signs of nationalism. In fact, their docility stood in such a marked contrast to the rebelliousness of the Greeks and the Serbs that the Turks openly favored and rewarded their Bulgarian subjects in many ways (Dakin 1966).

At the beginning of the nineteenth century there was no evidence yet of a national awakening among the Bulgarian masses living under the Ottomans. The first Bulgarian ethnic ferment appeared in the middle of the century, resurfacing later at its end. Seeing an excellent opportunity to obtain their own liberation, and a greater Bulgaria when chaos prevailed in the Balkans as a result of Serbia's, Romania's, and Montenegro's military attempts against the Ottomans to advance their own interests, the Bulgarians also revolted against the Ottomans. Their strong ethnic awakening was not to subside for almost half a century until Bulgaria was defeated by the Greeks and Serbs in 1913. Ignoring the enslaved Macedonia's history, the Bulgarians concentrated their efforts with respect to Macedonia based on decisions exclusively on the merits of their own interests. Their politicians and writers, ignoring Balkan history, and especially Macedonia's history, made ridiculous claims. Rakowski (1859), for instance, claimed that Olympic Zeus, Demosthenes, Alexander the Great, and the Souliot Markos Botsaris were Bulgarians. The Orphic hymns were also Bulgarian, and St. Paul preached Christianity to the Bulgarians.[10]

Given their newly awakened nationalism, the ethnic transformation, and name changes, the Bulgarian fantasies did not end with these claims. The Greek legends about Macedonia and Alexander the Great, or even those from beyond the Macedonian frontier, grew and spread among the Bulgarians in Macedonia. They discovered Hellenic Macedonian ballads about Alexander the Great and hymns to Orpheus, wrote Dakin (1966). They even fantasized that Aristotle spoke Bulgarian, but wrote in Greek for the benefit of barbarians who lived in the south; Emperor Constantine the Great and the Greek revolutionary hero Karaiskakis were Bulgarians; the monks that taught them how to write, Methodius and Cyril, were also Bulgarians and the ancient Macedonians were using the Cyrillic alphabet; and Greek Macedonian and Serbian folklore were all Bulgarian (AHD 1979). Considering

Bulgaria's late but dramatic ethnic nascency, it is perhaps easy to understand why the Bulgarians were so eager, or perhaps desperate, to adopt personalities and historical events that did not belong to them.

The Serbian state, with Belgrade as its capital, was also established early in the nineteenth century after two bloody insurrections against the Ottomans. The Serbs spoke predominantly the Serbian language of the northwestern geographical Macedonia, which differed from the Bulgarian language spoken in the Rhodope mountain district. The prevalent Slavic dialect spoken between the two regions was neither Serbian nor Bulgarian (AHD 1979). Interestingly, words of Greek origin, especially those pertaining to agriculture and home economics, as well as Turkish, Vlach, and Albanian words, could be detected easily in the dialect spoken in the upper middle sections of geographical Macedonia. This dialect was further enriched later with many Bulgarian words, giving the Bulgarians a rather unreliable criterion to unjustifiably support Macedonia's Bulgarism (Tsamis 1975).

Increasingly, the Bulgarian ideas and fantasies found credence among the Russians and European powers. Ignoring history, and that the proper use of historical principles would have promoted tolerance and peace in the enslaved Macedonia of the nineteenth century, the great European powers, Russia, Great Britain, Austria-Hungary, and Germany, made their decisions exclusively on the merits of their own interests. They had the power to settle things but lacked the will to do so because of their petty and selfish interests and rivalries. In the light of overwhelming realities and contrary to historical truths, they rushed to encourage Bulgarian chauvinism, exacerbating the simmering Macedonian problem. Their actions or inactions can be described only as pitiful negligence, and to some historians, much more than that (Vattis 2002).

The nineteenth century's last quarter was especially complicated politically and militarily in the Balkans because of conspiracies and plotting, the beginning of the so-called Macedonian Struggle, the political, diplomatic and armed phase of the Macedonian Question. The unrelentingly increasing Russian push for Panslavism, coupled with the Turkish Empire's approaching dusk, initiated the problem and triggered the conflict that has not yet been solved even after 142 years (1862–2004). Russia's blatant interference in Balkan affairs, setting in motion the creation of a large Bulgarian state, and the connivance of Austro-Hungarians, Germans, and even British and Italians, made the last twenty-five years of the century increasingly turbulent. The reasons for this state of affairs are very complex, the main being the beginning of the collapse of the Ottoman Empire. Undoubtedly, the crumbling Turkish occupation affected the subjugated peoples' dynamism and ambitions, especially in occupied Macedonia, where people of many nationalities, speaking several languages, were living. In reality, the clumsy and deplorable attempts at a solution of the Macedonian crisis in the late nineteenth century by the European powers exacerbated and perpetuated the problem.

Born when the Ottoman Empire fell into a precipitous decline and the Russian Empire was rising, and destined to plague the Balkans for more than one hundred years, what exactly was the Macedonian Question (and the struggle for Macedonia) in the early years? It was the problem of who had the historical, cultural, ethnic, and demographic rights to rule Macedonia — the land once occupied by King Philip II and his son Alexander the Great — following the simmering demise of the Ottoman Empire (Dakin 1966; Tsalouhides 1994).

It began in 1862 with the appointment of the expansionist Panslavist General Ignatieff as the new Russian ambassador to the Sublime Porte in Constantinople. Under Panslavism's aegis, Ignatieff aimed to outflank the Dardanelles and win overland access to the Aegean littoral and the Mediterranean by forcing the Ottomans out of Bulgaria (Vattis 2002). The small country was to emerge as the favored ethnic group (a satellite state) running from the Black Sea to the Albanian mountains, including all of Macedonia north of Thessaloniki. From the first days in his diplomatic assignment, Count Ignatieff set in motion a pro-Bulgarian plan directing his diplomatic skills against the Orthodox Patriarchate of Constantinople and the Patriarchate-appointed bishops. Turkey at the same time, practicing the "divide and rule" principle of controlling the multiethnic Balkans, remained neutral on the Macedonian Question. That changed in 1869. The Sultan Hamid II the Khan, considering the Bulgarians more docile and loyal subjects than the Greeks and Serbs, and pressed by Russia and Great Britain to take revenge against the Patriarchate and the Greeks, whom the Ottomans considered more rebellious than the other ethnicities, signed in March 1870 a *Firman* (Imperial Law), prepared by Ignatieff, establishing an independent Bulgarian church with an "Independent Bulgarian Exarchate" in Constantinople, a rival Orthodox Church to the Patriarchate. Any community in Macedonia with two-thirds of its population choosing to join the Exarchate was allowed to build Bulgarian schools and affiliate its church with the Exarchate. Retaliating, the Orthodox Patriarchate declared the Bulgarian Exarchate "schismatic" (AHD 1979; Nikoloudis 2002).[11]

Ignatieff's blatant interference in the Ottoman Empire's internal affairs was the first serious attempt to favor the Exarchists and ignore enslaved Macedonia's Hellenism, resurrect age-old passions and hatreds, and prepare the ground for apprehending Macedonia's identity. It was the first attempt to ignore history, depriving the Macedonian legacy from millions of indigenous Hellenic Macedonians (IHMs),[12] whose ancestors lived for generations in historic Macedonia. It was the first official recognition by the sultan of the Bulgarian ethnicity and the geographic limits where this ethnicity would prevail. It is for all of the above reasons that the consequences of the Turkish *Firman* were of special importance, because it opened new avenues to the Bulgarian irredentist propaganda to form a Greater Bulgaria, a dream never forgotten by Bulgarian chauvinists.

In addition to the unprecedented arrogance inherent in Ignatieff's diplomatic activities, the Russian Czar Alexander II, using as an excuse Turkey's refusal to improve the fate and lives of the Christians in the Balkans, declared war against Turkey in April 1877. After hard fighting, the victorious Russians, joined by Bulgarian volunteers, invaded Ottoman Bulgaria in June and moved rapidly southward to the Balkan mountains (Hupchick and Cox 2001).[13] Arriving at the gates of Constantinople in February 1878, the Russians were about to realize their age-long dream of taking the city and acquiring free access to the Mediterranean. But Britain was not inclined to allow the Russians to snatch Constantinople and acquire the Dardanelles. When the British fleet appeared near the straits, the Russians took the hint, forcing the Ottomans to seek an armistice and hastily sign the Treaty of San Stefano (March 3, 1878), granting independence to Serbia, Montenegro, and Romania.

The Treaty of San Stefano also established Bulgaria as an autonomous principality ruled by a Christian prince within the Ottoman Empire, marking the end of the Russo-Turkish War (Dakin 1966).[14] The short-lived Treaty of San Stefano, a serious event that enhanced the Bulgarian age-old dreams for a Greater Bulgaria, gave the Bulgarians the right, without the consent of the Western powers, to materialize these dreams by taking over large areas from the Danube River to the Aegean Sea, including Macedonia, and from the Black Sea to lakes Prespa and Ochrida, making Bulgaria the largest Balkan state.

The Panslavic Treaty of San Stefano, ignoring the national aspirations of Greece and Serbia, was the clearest manifestation of Russian tendencies to condemn thousands of Greeks and Serbs to Bulgarization.[15] It was a "death penalty" for Hellenism's aspirations and claims on Macedonia. If the treaty were ever enforced, certain of its articles would have irreversibly buried the Greek ethnic rights on Macedonia, also creating prerequisites for continuing demands and threats against Greece, even on its own territorial integrity (Kofos 1969). The Treaty of San Stefano revealed the Russian geopolitical and geostrategic interests and the Panslavic hypocrisy of ostensibly protecting the Christian subjects of the Sultan in the Balkans, and especially in Macedonia. With brutal irony, Russia's scheming revealed that the territorial opportunities to be created by the forthcoming disintegration of the Ottoman Empire must benefit Bulgaria only.

The Treaty of San Stefano, centered as it was on the Panslavic vision, was the brain child of Count Ignatieff, who had hoped that Bulgaria as a strong satellite would enable Russia to dominate the Balkans and the Aegean. Ignatieff's efforts, however, to obtain Austrian support for the treaty met with hostility and counterdemands, especially on the issue of allowing Bulgaria to annex Macedonia. Austria-Hungary coveted Bosnia and Herzegovina as bases for domination of the southern Balkans, also keeping an eye on the road to Thessaloniki (Dakin 1966).

Sanctioned over the last quarter of the nineteenth century by Russian Panslavism in its efforts to destabilize the Balkans and bypass the Dardanelles, Bulgaria became a nation: first the religious restitution in 1870 (formation of the Exarchate), then the ethnic restitution in 1878 (formation of the Bulgarian Principality). Within the eight-year period (1870–1878), all conditions—political, diplomatic and military—were favorable for Bulgaria's expansion into Macedonia. It acquired proximity to Macedonia, had the moral and material support of Russia, was affiliated with and supported by its own church and, on many occasions—when it was to their advantage—the support of the European powers (AHD 1979).

The two developments—the religious and ethnic restitution—coupled with the pro-Bulgarian Panslavic interference, were the reasons for the Macedonian problem of that era, not because of the events themselves, but because of Bulgaria's never-ending demands for expansion after it became a nation. Underlying Bulgaria's desire for expansion lay Panslavism's chauvinism and czarist Russia's age-old plans to descend to the Aegean Sea and the Mediterranean. In retrospect and in the unpredictable turn of events in the Balkans, it would be fair to say that the events between 1870 and 1878 signaled the beginning of a vicious struggle between Hellenism and Bulgarism in Macedonia, whose first phase lasted till 1918. Simply stated, strong pro-Hellenic sentiments clashed with equally strong pro-Bulgarian sentiments among Macedonia's people. As time passed, the Bulgarians attempted to attract Macedonia's Slav-speakers, thereby altering its demographic composition. The Greek-speaking Macedonians, on the other hand, would have to confront not only the Turks in their struggle for Macedonia, but the Bulgarians as well without even the support at the outset of the small Greek nation. Bulgarism, however, represented Slavism, not Macedonianism.

The establishment of the Bulgarian Exarchate in 1870 and the Treaty of San Stefano in 1878 were scandalous actions promulgating equally scandalous solutions to the Macedonian problem flaring under Ottoman rule. Then, as now with the problem of FYROM, the two actions imposed by Panslavism exacerbated the crisis because, simply, they disregarded history: Hellenism's deep roots in Macedonia and the certainty of a counteraction by the Greeks of historic Macedonia. Then, as now again, the competing

powers' vacillations, their diplomatic maneuvers to gain influence in territories soon to be liberated from the dying Ottoman Empire, and their inability or unwillingness to stem the Panslavic flood toward the Balkans early
in the game made the problem acute. Their indecisiveness literally and
figuratively made the Macedonian problem a Balkan "earthquake," spoil-
ing later the World War I Balkan victory, leaving the problem unresolved.
Moreover, San Stefano provided to the Bulgarians false hopes and the
propulsive force for a series of aggressive actions and made them believe
their fantastic notions of being descendants of Alexander the Great, granting them absolute privilege of inheriting his kingdom after liberation from
the Ottomans.

During the long years under the Ottomans an individual's religion,
not language or race, determined his or her nationality and the administrative status in the Empire (Danopoulos 2001).[16] In the final analysis, the
individual was either a Christian or a Muslim, and sometimes a Jew.[17] With
the establishment of the Exarchate, a Bulgarian ethnonational religious
institution, religion and language were used as the basis for creating an ethnic Bulgarian identity. The Exarchate rivaled the Patriarchate, both operating as instruments of Bulgarian and Greek nationalism, respectively, under
the Ottomans.

The scandalous Ignatieff-Bulgarian plans at Hellenic presence's expense
in the Ottoman-occupied Macedonia were soon reversed by the Austro-
Hungarian government's rebuff and Great Britain's diplomatic pressure to
deny Bulgaria the entire Macedonia, the province that was to be adminis-
tered by a Christian governor within the Ottoman Empire (AHD 1979). The
German Chancellor Otto von Bismarck, eager to show young Germany's
goodwill and international standing, invited all the European powers,
including Russia, to Berlin to formulate a new treaty, acceptable to all countries (Hupchick and Cox 2001). The hastily convened Congress of Berlin
(July 1878) isolated the Russians and opposed the formation of a large Bulgaria. The area between Rhodopi and Haemus was set as an autonomous
state, named Eastern Rumelia, heavily inhabited by Greeks and Greek-
oriented slavophones.[18] Turkey was to remove its armed forces from Eastern Rumelia and permit the use of the Greek and Bulgarian languages
together with the Turkish language. Essentially northern Thrace, Eastern
Rumelia was a distinct Greek province with about one hundred thousand
Greek inhabitants. Its Greek population was ahead of other ethnic groups
in many endeavors of life: education, civilization, commerce. The French
E. Dumont (1871, cited by Dakin 1966) wrote from Eastern Rumelia in 1866:
"The Greeks possess here prominent position. They gave to the Bulgarians
the rudiments of education they possess so far.... Their interaction with the
Greeks and the Greek energy and intelligence roused the Bulgarians."

The Congress of Berlin also reduced the size of the Bulgarian Principality with the Danube in the north and Mount Haemus in the south as its frontiers. Despite its shortcomings, the Congress of Berlin "struck a semblance of balance" in Macedonia, justifying Lord Beaconfield's characterization of it as "peace with honor" (Cappelli 1997). Without the Congress of Berlin's decisions, Macedonia would have become a Bulgarian province. The formation of an independent Bulgarian state and Eastern Rumelia's declared autonomy, combined with the Bulgarian Exarchate's proselytizing Macedonia's inhabitants, left no doubt that the new state would soon embark in a steplike program to materialize plans for a Greater Bulgaria.[19]

It became increasingly evident at the end of summer 1878 that the humiliating reversal of Ignatieff's plans for a Greater Bulgaria at the Congress of Berlin did not stabilize Macedonia. The setbacks to the Bulgarian dreams and ambitions did not discourage their irredentist plans for a Greater Bulgaria at Greece's and Serbia's expense. Under Ignatieff's influence, the Bulgarians hardened their stand and increased their activities in Macedonia (Dakin 1966). It was no longer sufficient for them to rely on the Russians and the vacillating European powers. There was now a clear and urgent need to accelerate their initiatives for the final goal, Macedonia's incorporation into their principality. Never mind that Macedonia was also inhabited by Greeks, Turks, Jews, and a few Serbs.

Though the Berlin settlement may have prevented an immediate crisis by humiliating Russia and satisfying the plans of the European powers, it created deep-rooted dissatisfactions among the small Balkan countries and struck a heavy blow to the Bulgarian irredentist ambitions, enhancing rather than decreasing their determination to win back the territories awarded to them by the Treaty of San Stefano. It soon became apparent in the summer of 1885 that the stability in Macedonia under Ottoman rule envisaged by Bismarck and Disraeli at the Congress of Berlin was to be shattered and the balance of power in the Balkans altered. The Bulgarian army moved suddenly, occupied Eastern Rumelia, and annexed it to the Bulgarian Principality (AHD 1979). The Turks offered no resistance. Russia had assiduously made certain at the Congress of Berlin that the region was free of the Turkish army. Eastern Rumelia's occupation was an unmitigated disaster for its thousands of peaceful Greek inhabitants. Most discouragingly, the Bulgarian coup d'etat was recognized and condoned at the Bucharest Conference in 1886 by the European powers, emulating each other in their pro-Bulgarian stand on Rumelia's annexation. After the annexation, all Bulgarian efforts concentrated on Macedonia.

The success of the annexationist policy in Eastern Rumelia convinced the Bulgarians that their long-term objectives in Macedonia were within easy reach and inaugurated a new period of persecutions of the Greek inhabitants in Eastern Rumelia. The Bulgarian authorities closed most of the Greek schools, expelled the teachers, abolished the Greek language previously approved by the Congress of Berlin as one of the three official languages, forced Greek pupils six to twelve years old to study in Bulgarian schools, deprived the Greek inhabitants of the right to work, and curtailed their movement in their own country. The Bulgarian actions were only the preamble for violence, ethnic cleansing, and bloodshed. When Greek communities sent representatives to Sofia to protest, many of them were murdered on their return home (Vattis 2002).

In its agonizing efforts to promote Macedonia's Bulgarization, the Bulgarian Exarchate largely rested on detaching from the Patriarchate as many Slav-speakers as possible.[20] The Exarchate's aggressive efforts to recruit Macedonia's Slav-speaking inhabitants signaled the beginning of the struggle for Macedonia between Bulgarism and Hellenism through peaceful means at the beginning. Apart from its overtones of ethnic idealism and intense passion, the struggle represented one of many sides of the so-called Eastern Question (*Anatolikon Zetema*), i.e., the question of what would happen after the impending collapse of the Ottoman Empire, and what the European powers would gain from the collapse. Austria wanted Thessaloniki and Russia Constantinople. Great Britain, on the other hand, fighting the two tendencies and striving to establish some sort of stability in Eastern Europe, formulated the doctrine of integrity of the Ottoman Empire, contrary to Russia's design to dissolve it (Notaris 1985).

The underpinning for Bulgarization as a basis toward restricting Hellenism's influence among the Balkan Orthodox Christian inhabitants attached to the Patriarchate could initially be provided by the Bulgarian Exarchate. Immediately after its formation, the Exarchate became a tool of the strong Bulgarian propaganda machine (Nikoloudis 2002). It succeeded in converting an appreciable number of villages to its wings, especially in western Macedonia. But it failed to convert all of them. The failure was due mostly to the resistance of many Patriarchist slavophone Greeks, whose stubborn attachment to Hellenism earned them the Bulgarian nickname *Grecomans* (literally, maniac Greeks), their perseverance in Hellenism unexplained by the Bulgarians.[21] Good examples of modern *Grecomans* are the people in the village of Sohos in central Greek Macedonia today, whom Jane Cowan (1997, p. 153) describes as *dopii* (local people). Though they may speak a Bulgarian dialect at home, they consider themselves *Makedones* or even *Hellinomakedones* (Greek Macedonians), vehemently rejecting suggestions that they are not Greeks.

To crown its dangerous imperialist policies and the scheming relationships in efforts to assist the Bulgarians in November 1872, the Central Panslavic Komitet (Committee) in Petrograd directed the Russian consul in Thessaloniki that the Mount Athos[22] Slavic Agency must be transformed into a committee to organize an arms cache in the so-called Romanian Monastery; send to Macedonia, Thrace, Bulgaria, and old Serbia agents assigned to distribute books and funds and recruit followers of the Slavic persuasion and volunteers for the patriotic movement; and create on Mount Athos Russian and Bulgarian colonies for the conversion of the area into Slavic territory. The organizing committee was to be funded with 50,000 rubles annually (AHD 1979).

What was more, to induce the Macedonian inhabitants to join the Exarchate, the Bulgarians flooded them with propaganda material claiming that freedom from the Ottomans could only be obtained by joining the Exarchate. Newspapers and books, mostly written in Greek, made again fantastic claims that Alexander the Great, Aristotle, the ancient Macedonians, and even Homer were the forefathers of the present-day Bulgarians. Russian agents and Bulgarian officers with civilian clothes began roaming Macedonia to proselytize the inhabitants to the Bulgarian cause. New Bulgarian schools appeared in Macedonia, and professional and technical Bulgarian personnel and tradesmen were settled in vital population centers. Agents of the Bulgarian Komitet were roving around the country collecting children of poor Greek families, peacefully or by force, to attend Bulgarian schools or study in Bulgaria. Utilizing Komitet funds, Bulgarian agents also absorbed small and large Turkish *chiftliks* (Dakin 1966).

The intense propaganda, the clandestine actions of Russian agents and Bulgarian officers, and the abundance of funds contributed by the Komitet failed to accomplish the expected results: the Macedonian Slavs did not rush to join the Exarchist movement. Many villages with Exarchists established in them failed to rush to the Exarchate. Failing to produce new religious concepts, the Exarchate managed to provoke a schism among the Macedonian Slavs. Those who joined the Bulgarian Church were simply Bulgarians. Since so many Macedonian Slavs remained faithful to the Patriarchate, it is difficult to understand why some of them bothered to change religious affiliation (Dakin 1966).

The French writer Victor Berar, who visited the area by Lake Ochrida in 1892 (Berar 1896, cited by Vattis 2002), asked a slavophone Christian about his ethnicity. "Our ancestors," he replied, "were Greeks and none spoke Bulgarian. We became Bulgarians because it is an advantage. The Turks tolerate us and the Europeans support us. Nothing will prevent us from becoming Serbs if the circumstances arise."

Bulgarian Revolutionary Committees

From the middle of the 1880s onward, especially after Greece's humiliating defeat by the Ottomans in 1897, the struggle for Macedonia between Bulgarism and Hellenism with peaceful means was about to end and a new, violent phase was about to begin. The Bulgarians concentrated their efforts on three fronts: annex Macedonian territory when possible, convince the Macedonian inhabitants that they belonged to the Bulgarian race and the Exarchate, and organize clandestine groups for propaganda purposes or to terrorize Macedonian inhabitants unwilling to join the Exarchist movement. And while the Bulgarians were planning and acting on all three initiatives, the European political leaders, overwhelmed by distorted historical views, allowed the Bulgarians to proceed with plans to Bulgarize Macedonia.

The Slavic propaganda's intensity to Bulgarize Macedonia's inhabitants under the Ottomans, the Exarchate's assistance toward that end, and the ever-present Panslavic support were not enough to prevent the Bulgarians from facing great difficulties in Macedonia. In 1885, for instance, the Bulgarian writer Offeicoff, a fanatic adherent of the concept of a Greater Bulgaria, wrote in his book *L'Etat du Bulgarism* in 1885: "The largest part of the Bulgarian population of Macedonia has not yet developed an ethnic [Bulgarian] consciousness.... If we exclude the northern sections, the people in the remaining areas are ready, with the slightest pressure, to declare for the Patriarchate and [to send their children] to Hellenic schools with Hellenic teachers. If the Great Powers were to intervene and demand a plebiscite to solve the Macedonian problem the Greeks would come out as winners" (cited by Vattis 2002). Offeicoff wrote about Bulgarians in Macedonia, not about "Macedonians."

To remedy the situation and expedite Macedonia's Bulgarization, the Central Panslavic Komitet, operating from Russia, changed its tactics on the Macedonian issue dramatically in the years 1892–1895, allowing the Bulgarian Prince Ferdinand to assume leadership of the Balkan Komitet. The appointment was significant because Ferdinand was to become King of Bulgaria. It was for the same reason — expediting the Bulgarization of Macedonia's inhabitants— that a group of young fanatic Bulgarian men, perhaps encouraged by the Central Komitet, decided on activism first and violence later as potential methods to convert the Macedonians to Bulgarism (AHD 1979). Damien Grueff, the schoolmaster of the Bulgarian school in Stip; Christo Tatarcheff, a doctor; and Gotse-Delcheff, together with others (Petroff, Tosheff, Dimitroff), founded in 1893 the Secret Macedono-Adrianople (now Edirne) Revolutionary Committee (*Tajna Makedonsko-Odrinskoa Revolucionna Organizacija*, TMORO) directed by a Central Committee (*Centralen* Komitet) (Kargakos 1992). Early in 1894 the organization's plans, formulated in a second meeting, were Macedonia's autonomy and the promotion of Bulgarian interests in a way that, if conditions became favorable, Macedonia could easily be annexed by Bulgaria. The organization's Bulgarian character — and the lack of any mention of "Macedonian ethnicity"— became known with absolute clarity (Vlasidis 1997). The Slav "Macedonians" had not been invented yet.

Because of disagreements within the TMORO ranks, the "Macedonian Brotherhoods" in Bulgaria in March 1885, composed of Bulgarian immigrants from Macedonia, formed the Supreme Committee (*Vrchornija Makedonski* Komitet, VMK) to coordinate revolutionary activities in Macedonia. The remaining TMORO members were organized in 1907 as the Internal Macedonian Revolutionary Organization (*Vatreshna Makedonska Revolutionna Organizacija*, IMRO). VMK's members became known as Vrchovists and IMRO's members as Centralists. A year later, leftist members split from IMRO and formed the Federated Popular Party, whose members became known as Federalists (Nikoloudis 2002). Both organizations, IMRO and the Federalists, discontinued their activities during World War I and resumed them at war's end.

Superficially, the Vrchovists' aims differed from those of the Centralists. In keeping with the pluralism of views expressed by the Macedonian Brotherhoods in Bulgaria, the first wanted an immediate union of Macedonia with Bulgaria (Vlasidis 1997). In contrast, IMRO and the Federalists declared support for an autonomous Macedonia, part of an eastern Slavic federation, with the Federalists preferring a socialist autonomous Macedonia within the federation. Macedonia's autonomy remained IMRO's target till 1928. In 1925 the Federalists dissolved the organization, and many of its leaders, under the Bulgarian Dimitar Vlahov's leadership, formed a new organization, IMRO United, a leftist group (to achieve formation of an independent and united Macedonia with Soviet support), an IMRO enemy from its very beginning. Not surprisingly, Vlahov was transformed to "Macedonian" in 1943, becoming a Tito collaborator in Tito's efforts to form the People's Republic of Macedonia within Yugoslavia (details in Chapter 5).

The original IMRO founders, operating from a revolutionary center (a secondary school) in Thessaloniki, began subversive activities soon destined to become full-scale guerrilla tactics against the Greek-speaking Macedonians. Considering the dissimilarities of Bulgarian and Greek aims over Macedonia, full domination in the land of King Philip II was the motive of IMRO's men under the collapsing Ottoman Empire. The cry of IMRO's fanatics was "Macedonia for the Macedonians,"[23] their activities centering around indoctrinating and training the villagers for guerrilla warfare, cementing the villages together to rise and liberate Macedonia from the

Ottomans—for the "Macedonians" (i.e., the inhabitants of Macedonia under the Turks) (Dakin 1966).

To make matters worse for the Greek-speaking Macedonians, the concept of an autonomous Macedonia was firmly established and promulgated by IMRO and the Bulgarian Principality. Theoretically, the concept of self-determination in an autonomous Macedonia would have entailed respect of all people, regardless of language, race, nationality, religion, and level of education, concepts acceptable to the European powers. However, there was never a foundation — a Macedonian nation embracing a diverse group of people such as the group that inhabited Macedonia in the nineteenth century. In antiquity, if anything, Macedonia was a state among other states in the city-state arrangement of the Greek world (Hammond 1972).

At the outset, IMRO was an embarrassment to Prince Ferdinand and his government for its violent activities. It contained individuals with strong socialist leanings as well as Marxists, anarchists, and nihilists (Vlasidis 1997). The hard core, the original IMRO (Internal) remained steadfast on the autonomy concept. The goal of the Supreme Committee in the Principality (Vrchovists), however, was Macedonia's Bulgarization under the Ottomans and its immediate annexation by Bulgaria when the Turks left the Balkans, which seemed unavoidable. Although there were shades of gray between the two committees, many IMRO adherents hated the Supreme Committee (Mihailoff 1950; Rothchild 1959). By the end of the twentieth century IMRO became known as VMRO (*Vatreshna Makedonska Revolutsionna Organizatsia*) in Skopje.

The serious crisis that occurred in Macedonia, the rich land that gave birth to Alexander the Great, following Turkey's defeat by Russia and the Panslavic Komitet's blatant interference in Balkan affairs, was exacerbated by the revolutionary actions of the two Bulgarian Komitets. The situation was complicated further by the division that occurred in the Bulgarian Macedonian movement, especially after Greece's defeat by Turkey in 1897. The two organizations, IMRO and the Vrchovists, the second less powerful than the former, especially in western Macedonia (Dakin 1966; Koliopoulos 1995), began a systematic dispatch of armed bands from outside Macedonia and distributed arms to the villagers within Macedonia. Their aims, however, were divided: IMRO believed in autonomy, not as a step toward annexation with Bulgaria, "but as an end in itself."[24]

Despite the differences and even occasional violent clashes between the two Bulgarian committees, it soon became apparent that both, genuine Panslavic instruments dominating the end of the nineteenth century in the Balkans, cooperated closely. IMRO's program for Macedonia's autonomy first was not really distant from the Vrchovists' views of annexing Macedonia to the Principality. The autonomy concept did not fool the Greek-speaking Macedonians and the common European people. The great question left unanswered by the autonomy advocates remained the fate of Macedonia after it became autonomous. Considering the fate of Eastern Rumelia, the Bulgarian strategy for autonomy could be seen as a ploy for the virtual annexation of Macedonia by Bulgaria. It also became known that IMRO, a state within the state, was adopted by Sofia, whose government was contemplating taking military action in Macedonia.[25]

Ironically, the European liberals and humanitarians were either completely ignorant of the historical truths on Macedonia or fostered gross misconceptions of the Bulgarian intentions (Dakin 1966; Vattis 2002). They were unable to discern that the aims of the two committees were identical. Within this context, IMRO's "democratic" program for the doctrine of self-determination, having the individual at the center of the concept, entitling him or her to the same rights and respect, regardless of race, color, nationality, language, and religion, would satisfy the European notion of democracy. That is why the European liberals wrongly supported those who, they believed, were the only ones to oppose the forces of the Ottoman tyranny. The European liberals, and to some extent their governments, however, were unable to understand that those struggling for autonomy in Macedonia were really fighting for territory. They selfishly placed considerable premium on the "stabilizing" nature of the Bulgarian state and on the need for a strong Balkan ally to support the democratic principles after the forthcoming collapse of the Ottoman Empire in the Balkans—a bet placed on the wrong state.

Komitadjides *and Greek* Andartes

Since the Exarchate's formation in 1870, the Bulgarian propaganda turned its attention entirely to the enslaved Macedonia, and particularly to its Slav-speaking districts. What strategies were available to the Bulgarians in their efforts to Bulgarize the Slav-speakers of Macedonia? All things being equal in the years preceding the Ottoman collapse in the Balkans, a less aggressive but more realistic approach would have been to attract the Slav-speaking inhabitants to the Exarchate by peaceful means— by the power of persuasion. Bulgaria used this approach at the beginning to convert the Slav-speakers of undetermined ethnicity, but with limited success. A more aggressive approach would have been a dual strategy, including coercion and the power of persuasion. Later in the process of conversion, the Bulgarians used the second approach, aiming at building two-thirds majorities of pro-Exarchist inhabitants in Macedonia to qualify for the new Ottoman rule whereby the majority status would grant them the prerogative, according to the Turkish *Firman*, to detach themselves from the Patriarchate, build their own schools, and acquire the right to Bulgarize the population.

The bottom line was that the Bulgarian Komitets made so many enemies using the second approach among the Greek-speakers and Greek-oriented slavophones in Macedonia that their schismatic movement, somewhat successful till 1894, never really became decisive. In spite of the Bulgarians' using the dual approach — or perhaps because of it — many Slav-speaking people steadfastly maintained their pro-Hellenic sentiments and adhered to the Patriarchate (AHD 1979). Although the Bulgarians had convinced quite a few villages to join the Exarchate, the results never met their expectations, even when the intensity of coercion increased. Because of the meager results they attained, the Bulgarians embarked on an even more aggressive approach involving persuasion, coercion, and terrorization, committed mostly by the Bulgarian Macedonian committees, especially IMRO.

The ultranationalist organization took advantage of the Greek defeat in 1897 and began sending terrorist bands into Macedonia, still under Turkish rule (Dakin 1966). Each band (*cheta*) was composed of ten men (*chetniks*) armed with Austrian rifles, a revolver, and a small bomb. The Turks called the slavophone guerrillas *komitadjis* (committee men, Slav-speaking terrorists) and the Greeks called them *komitadjides* (Tsamis 1974). At the outset, the Slav-speaking bandsmen's task was not to fight, but establish revolutionary committees in villages, but as soon as they settled in Macedonian villages a regime of terror began. The *komitadjides* terrorized only the Greek population, which constituted an overwhelming majority. They plundered villages and towns, pillaged churches, and defiled cemeteries. Greek community leaders were murdered. Docile villages were forced to join the Exarchate and swear fidelity to the Bulgarian cause. Food and other valuable items were snatched from the Greek villagers and "traitors" were rounded up and executed. But the *komitadjides* failed to despoil the Greek faith and spirit (Papavizas 2002). In the spring of 1902 the situation in Macedonia had become radically worse. Strong bands of *komitadjides* kept entering Macedonia at will, meeting no resistance, the slaughter and plundering of the Greek element increasing.

Discerning a window of opportunity in the Macedonian dispute, and seeking to emulate IMRO's forcefulness in the military arena, Bulgarian politicians submitted a memorandum to the European powers on July 1, 1899, proposing that the three *vilayets* (Thessaloniki, Monastir, Kosovo) be combined to form one *vilayet* with Thessaloniki as the capital. The governor of the new *vilayet* was to be appointed for five years from the prevailing ethnic group (Bulgarians) supported by an assembly chosen by the people (historic Macedonia had a Greek majority; the proposed new large *vilayet*, including Kosovo, had a Bulgarian majority); all employees of the new *vilayet* were to be chosen from the prevailing ethnic group; the police were to be selected by the governor, operating with officers from the prevailing majority; and the language of the prevailing ethnic group was to be equal to the Turkish language (Vattis 2002).

As it was to be expected, the Bulgarians, pursuing a narrow nationalist self-interest within the crumbling Ottoman Empire, demanded autonomy for Macedonia under their absolute control and with the Bulgarian language as the official language of an autonomous, enlarged Macedonia. The audacious Bulgarian demand, ignoring the other ethnic groups living in historic Macedonia and proposing a vast increase in Bulgaria's frontiers to include territories in the north beyond the borders of historic Macedonia (to increase the percentage of the Bulgarian inhabitants), was rejected by the European powers. No longer able to make a convincing case to the Europeans for their plan for Macedonian autonomy, the Bulgarian committees ordered the *komitadjides* to increase the intensity of terrorization of Macedonia's Greek inhabitants. New bands entered Macedonia from Bulgaria at will, and the plunder and slaughter increased in volume and frequency. One-sidedly anti-Hellenic (Dakin 1966), the struggle was between Bulgarism and Hellenism. "Macedonians" as a distinct ethnic group had not yet been invented.[26]

In April 1899 the Bulgarian commercial representative in Macedonia wrote to Prince Ferdinand (cited by Vattis 2002): "Nothing can be gained anymore with schools and peaceful means. If this situation continues, the Greeks will gain ground. Turkey has given us as much as it could. Our only aim is Macedonia's liberation."

The turbulent period following the increase in terrorization of the Hellenic element in Macedonia was described by the British general consul in Thessaloniki in 1903:

> Of the two Bulgarian committees, the one under Sarafoff's leadership [IMRO] is pushing for Macedonian autonomy, believing that sooner or later an autonomous Macedonia will be annexed by Bulgaria. Reading the papers gives you the impression that the people have risen to obtain their freedom from Turkey. This is a big lie. Nobody took up arms against Turkey. If some people followed the Bulgarian bands it was by coercion or brutal force. I want to say that the *komitadjis* is worse enemy than the Turk, and the people are squeezed between the two.... Murder is the main fighting weapon of the committees. The Greeks are mainly the victims. Thousands of them have been killed during the last few years [Vattis 2002].

The incessant efforts of the Bulgarian terrorists to convert people to the Exarchate finally ruffled the sluggish Turkish Empire's feathers, swinging the pendulum of Turkish-Bulgarian friendly relations toward violence.

For the first time Turkish villagers drew the *komitadjides'* wrath, giving Damien Grueff's macabre motto a stark, brutal reality: "Better an end with horrors than horrors without an end" (Dakin 1966). A little later in 1903, the British Blue Paper included the following on the Bulgarian committees: "Blackmail and extortions of innocent people; robberies, murders of men and women; indescribable torture of priests, doctors and dismemberments of teachers; torching of churches and dynamites against everybody who obeys the law; destruction of Orthodox Christians and Muslims; general terrorization and blood, kidnappings and slaughter" (Vattis 2002).

The Turks, sympathizing with the Bulgarians until then, turned their wrath against the Slav-speaking bands. The activities and the haphazard initial uprising by the Bulgarian revolutionary committees were easily suppressed by Turkish troops and gendarmes. The Turks informed the European powers they would take strong measures against Bulgaria if it did not curtail the activities of its terrorist organizations, withdrawing the armed bands from Macedonia (Dakin 1966; AHD 1979). The Bulgarian Council of Ministers, responding to the threat, immediately closed the offices of the two Komitets in Sofia, arrested several of their leaders, and patrolled the Bulgarian-Turkish border. The Bulgarian government, afraid of war with Turkey, arrested the agitators and prohibited the committees from raising money.

In reality, there were weighty reasons to suspect that the apparently harsh measures of the official Bulgarian government against the revolutionary committees were no more than window dressing and a camouflage of its real intentions (Vattis 2002). There was also a clear feeling among the Turks and Greeks that the Bulgarian government could not afford to suppress the Macedonian revolutionary committees. Neither could it afford to muzzle the press or public opinion clamoring for an autonomous Macedonia as a first step — the autonomy concept bode well with Article 23 of the Treaty of Berlin — or, better yet, demanding secession of Macedonia into the Bulgarian Principality. Immediate and unqualified union of Macedonia with Bulgaria could be regarded by the Europeans as a sinister plot at Macedonian Hellenism's expense.

The Ilinden Uprising

While ostensibly holding at bay the terrorist activities of the revolutionary committees, the Bulgarian government, ruminating on the idea of Macedonian autonomy, concentrated at the beginning of the twentieth century on building tensions between itself and Turkey, increasing the pressure on Macedonia's Hellenism, and promoting its dealings with the European powers.

By the end of March 1903, acting menacingly to create impressions of strength, Bulgaria dispatched new swarms of well-trained and well-armed *komitadjides* to Macedonia. While the Slav-speaking bands were applying more and more pressure on the Patriarchist and mixed villages, hoping that the Turks would look the other way, it was by now clear that an escalation of violence in Macedonia was imminent. Within a few days of the increased Slav-speaking band intrusions, on April 17, 1903, a French commercial ship was blown up in Thessaloniki (Karvelis 1996). The next day the Ottoman Bank, owned by French interests, and the German Club were also blown up. Bombs were also exploded in theaters, churches, post offices, the beer factory, and many Greek houses of the city. An attempt to blow up a train from Constantinople to Thessaloniki carrying three hundred women and children failed (Vattis 2002). A newspaper from Cologne, Germany, published the following interview with a *komitadjis* leader: "Our program is to blow up the Macedonian cities, burn the villages, destroy the agricultural products and the telephone and railroad lines, and turn Macedonia into a desert. We have plenty of dynamite and other explosives and plenty of ammunition and food" (Vattis 2002).

The bomb attacks came as little surprise to the Macedonian people who were in a state of endless revolutionary ferment for many months in 1903. Everyone, Christian or Muslim, expected a new revolt. Since 1818 at least eight revolts had been planned by Christians, and six had taken place, ending badly for the revolutionaries. Except for the Bulgarian organizers of Ilinden, all previous revolutionaries were in touch with the *Filiki Etaireia*, a major secret Greek revolutionary organization.

The failure of the massive terrorization in central Macedonia and Thessaloniki, the diplomatic defeats in the European arena — the actions of the Slav-speaking bands caused consternation even among their supporters — and the military defeats sustained between April and July 1903 in the Ottomans' hands led difficult-to-control forces into more desperately futile acts of terrorization that took the semblance of an uprising in the district of Monastir-Perlepe. The uprising began with the smoke of burning haystacks used as a signal on July 20, 1903 (the feast of the Prophet Elija).[27] The last revolt to take place in Ottoman-occupied Macedonia, it was not an organized, multiethnic, genuine popular revolution against the Ottomans. The population did not support the uprising and often betrayed the revolutionary bands to the Turks (Poulton 1995, p. 56). Simply, it was an uprising of Bulgarians instigated by IMRO's fanatic leaders and the Supreme Committee, without well-planned, well-coordinated, or well-executed strategic aims (Vlasidis 1997).

Because the uprising ostensibly represented all the enslaved Christians against the Turks, a few Greeks and other Christians also participated (C.

Vakalopoulos 1987). In reality, the uprising was no more than terrorization by an uncontrolled mob burning everything in sight, believing the czar was descending upon the Balkans to help it. In addition to the unarmed mob, forty-nine Slav-speaking bands, a total of about twelve hundred *komitadjides*, guided by Grueff and Sarafoff, also participated in the uprising,[28] which extended from Divri in the north to Kleisura in the region of Kastoria in the south and Lake Ochrida in the west. All bridges between Ochrida-Monastir were blown up, and the telegraph wires between Monastir and Thessaloniki were cut. The small Turkish military posts did not escape the mob's wrath. IMRO agents visited villages proclaiming the "revolution" and promising help from Bulgaria and Russia — including Europe's sympathy — to liberate Macedonia, end the taxation by the Ottomans, erase the debt to moneylenders, and divide the *chiftliks* among the peasants (Dakin 1966).

Besides forcing the villagers to the mountains, Ilinden's military goal ostensibly was to conduct guerrilla war against the Turks. The bands attacked Turkish troops and landowners, mostly Greek-speaking Macedonians and Vlachs, in several locations in western Macedonia, burned several Turkish villages, and destroyed several *chiftliks*. A few Patriarchist villages were also attacked, and many Greek people and Greek-oriented slavophones were killed. The terrorists also attacked the Vlach town of Krushevo, occupied the city without resistance — the Turks had dispatched their troops to Kosovo to fight Albanian revolutionaries— blew up government buildings, and established a provisional government of the Revolutionary Committee composed of IMRO's Bulgarian *komitadjides*, considered today by Skopje as the first "Macedonian" government in history (Vattis 2002). And though questions and doubts about the future goals of the revolt abounded among the Macedonian people and the European powers in 1903, in reality it was an uncoordinated uprising of a mob brandishing Bulgarian flags that hurt the Greek population more than the Ottomans. It hardly needs to be pointed out that the Krushevo provisional government was Bulgarian, not "Macedonian" (Dakin 1966; Vattis 2002).[29]

The Turkish reprisals were swift and brutal. Using undisciplined *Ilaves* (reservists), the Turks recaptured Krushevo on August 12, 1903, turning their wrath not against the Slav quarter, but against the Greek-speaking Macedonians and Hellenized Vlachs, perhaps suspecting them as the instigators of the uprising, which was not true (Dakin 1966). They destroyed hundreds of Greek houses and shops, burned all the Greek Orthodox churches, and killed several Patriarchists. Similar atrocities, almost exclusively against Greek-speaking Macedonians and Vlachs not responsible for the uprising, were perpetrated in several villages of western Macedonia. The Turks' attack against Smilevo, the center of the uprising, was brutal;

they reduced the unfortunate town to ashes with five hundred houses burned and ninety old men, women, and children killed. A total of twenty villages were destroyed, and forty thousand to fifty thousand people became homeless. By the end of August the Turks had succeeded in destroying the uprising and killing hundreds of bandits and several of their leaders. After the defeat, the surviving *komitadjides* moved south, destroying more Greek and Turkish villages in the Florina-Ptolemais-Kastoria area.

There have been repeated efforts to glorify an aimless mob uprising behind which there was no other leader than IMRO's Bulgarian Gotse-Delcheff. The political and military goals of the Ilinden uprising were not to win freedom from the Turks, but to force the villagers to the mountains, inducing some to join bands (Dakin 1966). Many villages in western Macedonia, for instance, participated voluntarily or under duress in the uprising by sheltering the bands and providing economic assistance and their own bands. Some villagers took the extra step to support the uprising actively, but no one can state unequivocally how many of the villagers' actions were done willingly. Perhaps many villagers fleeing to the mountains did so in terror of the extremists and possible Turkish reprisals. According to Dakin (1966), "the story that the rising was a widespread popular movement is entirely a myth." The flight of the peasants to the mountains was caused by terror, not by their willingness to participate in the uprising. Dakin challenged Brailsford's glorification of the uprising, widely accepted in England as "fantastic."[30]

Quite apart from its devastating human toll and destruction of property, what are we to make of the Ilinden uprising? From the scope, intensity, and achievements of the uprising, one might conclude that the shabby, unprepared, and undisciplined uprising fell short of being considered a genuine revolutionary attempt for freedom from the Turkish yoke. Men from all sides died in vain in uncoordinated mob efforts that failed to convince the European powers of Turkish insincere intentions to proceed with the promised reform program in Macedonia and take decisive measures to solve the Macedonian Question. As with the dismantling of Yugoslavia at the end of the twentieth century, the European powers were unable to accept the historical realities in Macedonia. They overlooked the window of opportunity on the Macedonian problem or purposely brushed off the overwhelming facts of the Macedonian problem by rushing to support an ethnic group whose historical roots in Macedonia were very superficial and which attempted to cover the unshaken historical facts with violence. Because this was a Balkan crisis with international ramifications, an understanding of the historical background would have enabled the Europeans, and even the Russians, to arrive at a reasonable settlement.

Thus ended the second crisis of the first period of the struggle for

Macedonia with only one winner: the Panslavic irredentists with Bulgarian extremists as the champions who exploited the destruction of Krushevo (and many other villages), touting it as the "Mesolongi of Bulgarism." Comparing the heroic Hellenic Mesolongi with Krushevo is unfortunate, to say the least. Krushevo's occupation by the mob lasted ten days, during which the perpetrators exhibited the Bulgarian flags, expropriated everything from Greek houses, and prohibited the Greek language (Vavouskos 1993). The town fell to the Turks immediately after their arrival. The Greek city of Mesolongi, in contrast, astonished the world eighty years earlier as it withstood undaunted the Turkish cannonade, the destruction and the famine, and the attacks of the besiegers for a year (Brewer 2001). But the ashes of Krushevo and of the villages awakened Hellenism in Macedonia after decades of slavery and Bulgarian abuse. A committee of important Greek citizens, springing from the ashes, dispatched the following memorandum to the European powers: "We are Greeks and will always be Greeks.... They must know we are not discouraged or afraid. We are steadfast in our beliefs on the origin of our fathers and forefathers, since we are nothing but Greeks. We speak almost all the languages in Macedonia..." (Vattis 2002).

Ilinden failed, but it gave a great push to the Bulgarian aspirations on Macedonia: it made the Slavic views on Macedonia known to the European powers and international community in general at the beginning of the century and provided information to contemporary literature and an excellent means of propaganda to the Bulgarians (and Yugoslavs later) to tout their ever-flaming aspirations for freedom and democracy that brought considerable returns. Bulgaria presented Ilinden as a unanimous Christian effort for unification of all the Bulgarians who lived in Macedonia, and IMRO's socialist line was used later as a guide during the interwar years by the Communist International (Comintern).[31]

The Ilinden uprising and its bloodbath, mostly at the expense of Hellenic Macedonians who were not responsible for it, has frequently been exploited for political purposes (Museum of the Macedonian Struggle 1993). It produced several slavophone heroes, mostly Bulgarian IMRO members, whose legacy echoes even today in three former Balkan communist countries and whose national allegiance is claimed by both FYROM and Bulgaria (Michailides 2001). Initially, the Serbs condemned the Ilinden uprising and the actions of the Bulgaro-Macedonian committees. In the early years following the occupation of Yugoslavia by the Germans, however, the Communist Party of Yugoslavia (CPY) under Josip Broz Tito assiduously cultivated the idea of an independent and united Macedonia (as perceived by the Bulgarian irredentists of the late nineteenth century) under Yugoslavia and rearranged history by reneging on the previous condemnation of the Ilinden uprising by the Serbs, recognizing it as a Slavomacedonian, not a Bulgarian achievement, a view that brought Tito opposite the Bulgarian communist leader Giorgi Dimitrov (Kouzinopoulos 1999, from Dimitrov's secret diary, translated from Bulgarian by Konstantina Koutra).[32]

Lest the slavophones of the Vardar Province not be left out of Ilinden, they grabbed the revolt's torch of the "Ilinden glory" from the Bulgarians when Cominform abandoned Bulgaria as a suitor for Macedonia in 1941, supporting Tito's claims on Macedonia (more in Chapter 5). Ilinden, according to the CPY and the FYROM politicians later, was a struggle for liberation by the "Macedonian nation," another historical misinterpretation. The Yugoslav slavophones of Vardar Province cleverly used Ilinden as a ploy to give credence to their separate ethnic identity as "Macedonians." Countless documents, published or revised in Skopje, tout the Bulgarian *komitadjides*' uprising as their own ethnic revolution against tyranny and a pillar of the birth of a new "nation," the Slavic "Macedonian nation."

Hellenism's Finest Hour (1904–1908)

The turbulent period following the Ilinden uprising drove law and order into a tailspin in the Balkans. In spite of the European pressure to proceed in a lawful manner on the Macedonian issue and the Turkish threats for intervention, IMRO and the Vrchovists continued their subversive activ-

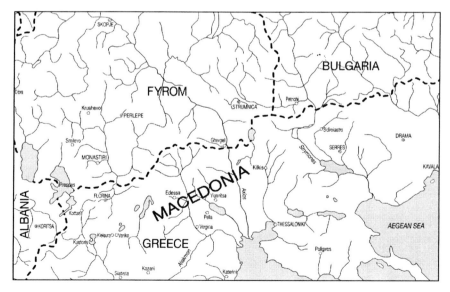

Hellenic Macedonia and parts of FYROM, Bulgaria, and Albania where most of the events of the Macedonian Struggle in 1904–1908 took place.

ities unabated, arming new bands and sending them to Macedonia at an increased rate. The third crisis of the Macedonian problem, the Macedonian Struggle of 1904–1908, as it is known in the Greek historiography, was about to begin. During this struggle, Greek-speaking Macedonians, slavophone Macedonians with strong Hellenic roots (*Grecomans*), and official Greece eventually became involved.

In 1903 the Turks dealt the Bulgarian guerrilla movement a severe blow, giving Hellenism precious time to regain ground lost from 1870 to 1903 (Dakin 1966). Slowly but gallantly, Macedonia's Hellenism began to defend itself against the Bulgarian committees. Macedonia's Greek-speakers had never forgotten the dreams and aspirations for freedom of their forefathers who had lived and prospered for countless generations in the land of Philip and Alexander. They knew that the Ilinden uprising to ostensibly liberate Macedonia from the Ottomans was no more than a camouflage and a ploy to hide the irredentist aspirations of the Bulgarian committees for a Greater Bulgaria. The claim that they were fighting for liberation from the Ottoman yoke was only a pretense to harm Hellenism. With the Ottoman Empire's days numbered, the Bulgarians feared only Hellenism, the only obstacle to their plans and aspirations.

The year 1904 was only the beginning of a struggle that lasted four years under the Turkish eyes. At the outset, three hundred slavophone Greek communities sensed the Bulgarian plot and reverted to the Patriarchate. Other villages remained openly Patriarchist. Village after village in Macedonia began to see that the Exarchists' dream of "Macedonia for the Macedonians" was a lie, a chimera, from which they had to dissociate themselves (Gounaris 1997). Quite apart from the devastating human toll, untold stories of bravery, self-sacrifice, and Hellenic patriotism took place in humble villages and communities never to be known. In hundreds of books and magazine articles the world can only read about the atrocities of the Macedonian struggle: murders of notables, burning of villages, ambushes and hanging of priests and schoolmasters, and slaughter of women and children. What the reader cannot see, but only imagine, is the greatness of a people enslaved for four hundred years who had to face not only the conqueror, but also the northern intruders, latecomers to the Balkans claiming sovereignty of the land. And although the Europeans doubted at the outset Hellenism's existence in Macedonia, the Turks knew it existed stronger than ever (AHD 1979).[33]

In 1900, during the gloom of the Bulgarian terrorization, and before the Hellenic struggle for Macedonia began in earnest, two bright rays of hope for Hellenism appeared on the horizon of historic Macedonia: Kastoria's new metropolitan, Germanos Karavangelis, and *capetan* (guerrilla leader) Kotas. Disparate in their background, education, and profession, they both played a decisive role in the Macedonian Struggle, rallying Macedonia's Hellenism.

Born on the island of Lesvos, the 34-year-old bishop Karavangelis was appointed by the Patriarch to the Metropolitan See of Kastoria in 1900 (Dakin 1966). His grandfather had fought the Turks with Kanaris and Miaoulis during the Greek War of Independence (1821–1828). As soon as he arrived in Kastoria, western Macedonia, Karavangelis compiled a report to the Greek Prime Minister Deligiannis, stressing the deplorable state of Macedonia's Hellenism, the dangers from the Bulgarian aggressiveness, and the need of armed bands to counteract the Bulgarian *komitadjides*. He never received a reply, and no action was taken by the Greek government. Mindful of frustrations and humiliations experienced during and after the disastrous Greco-Turkish War of 1897, the Greek government rejected notions of interfering in Macedonia. Using a fictitious name, Karavangelis wrote articles in Athenian newspapers and magazines always with the same slogan: "The best defense is the armed offense against the [Bulgarian] committees." Signing himself as Costas Georgios, to boost the Greek morale, he corresponded with notables in his diocese and elsewhere, including people such as the Greek ambassador in Constantinople, the distinguished Greek Macedonian Stefanos Dragoumis, his son Ion, secretary in the Greek consulate of Monastir, and Ion's sister's husband, Pavlos Melas. Later, he wrote again to the new Greek prime minister, Alexandros Zaimis, who not only did not reply but, concerned lest Turkey be offended, suggested the removal of Karavangelis from Kastoria, saying: "This metropolitan will do us great harm; he must leave Kastoria" (Vattis 2002).

Karavangelis was one of the great church leaders of the Macedonian Struggle, a courageous, dashing personality.[34] As the Greek Orthodox Church was a semi-autonomous theocracy in the Ottoman Empire, the office of a bishop or metropolitan was a political one. The higher Christian clergy were de facto Turkish officials and spiritual leaders of their flocks, and Karavangelis knew how to use his political and religious power in tumultuous Macedonia. Together with Kotas and Vangelis, another of his slavophone recruits, Karavangelis contributed to the failure and defeat of the Bulgarian committees and their armed bands in the field (Dakin 1966).

In the pantheon of Hellenism's past national achievements Metropolitan Karavangelis must be placed at the top, together with the most distinguished heroes of Hellenism. Riding armed on his white horse and disregarding the dangers looming in the valleys, the gullies, and the villages, many of which had converted to the Exarchate, he was everywhere. Many times he visited villages without guards, refusing to listen to reason and not visit Exarchist villages alone. In 1903, Karavangelis expelled the Bulgarians from a high school founded by them twenty years earlier to

Germanos Karavangelis, Metropolitan of Kastoria, western Macedonia, Greece, from 1900 to 1907. Courtesy of the Museum of the Macedonian Struggle, Thessaloniki.

Capetan Kotas with his three sons in 1904. Kotas was caught by the Ottomans, imprisoned in Monastir, and hanged on September 27, 1905. Courtesy of the Museum of the Macedonian Struggle, Thessaloniki.

accommodate Bulgarian pupils from surrounding villages (Vattis 2002). The threats of the Bulgarian committees did not daunt him. The cold, rain, and snow did not stop him from visiting the villages, forcefully opening the doors of Greek churches that had been taken over by the Exarchists, performing the liturgy in Greek with an armed pistol on the altar.

In the field of politics, Karavangelis's immediate strategy was to bring back to Hellenism those fooled by IMRO's promises of "Macedonia for the Macedonians." The immediate reward of his efforts was the recruitment of one of IMRO's key members, Kotas, from the village of Rulia (now Kotta) by the Albanian border.[35] Kotas, born and christened Orthodox, had temporarily lost his Hellenic spirit, though he lived in a Patriarchist village. Suspecting IMRO's motives and despising its high-handed methods and strict discipline, however, and convinced by Karavangelis of the Bulgarian irredentist motives, he became an implacable foe of the Macedonian committees and a deadly enemy of the *komitadjides* (Dakin 1966; Vattis 2002). A leader of Hellenism in his own right and by his own methods, Kotas with his men began his double war against the conquerors of his land, the Turks, and those conniving to grab Macedonia from the Ottomans.[36]

The metropolitan's recruiting activities did not end with Kotas. In attempting to build an organization in his diocese, he had to recruit or convert others to the Hellenic cause. In 1904, the young metropolitan, unrestrained it seems by looming dangers, embarked on such a hectic program of travel within and outside his diocese that the Bulgarian committees and the Central Panslavic Committee in Petrograd considered him the guiding force behind the blossoming Hellenic resistance in Macedonia. Almost at the same time Metropolitan Karavangelis brought back Kotas to Hellenism, he also recruited a tall, handsome, honest, devout young man, Vangelis, from the village of Strebenco (now Asprogea) in the Vitsi mountain region.[37] Enlisted in IMRO, he soon discovered he could not tolerate the killings of notables and priests. Hunted down by IMRO, Vangelis and his group fought the *komitadjides* with valor and unrestrained belief in Hellenism until 1904, when he fell into a Bulgarian ambush and was killed, together with his entire group. These were the men who fought valiantly for Hellenism and thousands of other brave and dedicated slavophones with Hellenic beliefs rooted in their hearts, branded by the Bulgarians as *Grecomans* (maniac Greeks).

During the beginning of the twentieth century, the two advocates of Hellenism, the Patriarchate and the Greek Kingdom in Athens, did not agree on many national issues, especially on the action to be taken in Macedonia to counteract the Bulgarians. Greece, devastated financially and morally by the Greco-Turkish War of 1897, not daring to ruffle feathers with Turkey again, remained quiet at best or ignored Macedonian Hellenism's plight at worst. The Greek Kingdom's myopically conservative position stemmed not only from its fear of Turkey, but also from its eagerness to please the Europeans. By doing so, it gave the Bulgarians an advantage to initiate and sustain an upheaval to reap success in Macedonia. The Patriarchate, on the other hand, reacted vigorously to the onslaught of Macedonia's Hellenism. Striving to maintain a theocracy of the Greeks, as well as Vlach-, Albanian-, and Slav-speaking inhabitants with possible Greek roots or Greek sentiments, the Patriarchate indirectly encouraged Hellenism in Macedonia. Karavangelis, Chrysostomos of Drama, and the metropolitan of Thessaloniki were good examples of church officials dedicated to Macedonia's Hellenism, with many more to appear on the scene in later years of the Macedonian Struggle, who placed their hopes on the Kingdom of Greece. The Patriarchists had to depend on Greece, and Greece needed the Patriarchists' assistance to promote Hellenism in Macedonia (Museum of the Macedonian Struggle 1993).

Virtually from the outset of the struggle for Macedonia, Karavangelis knew that victory against the Bulgarian revolutionary committees depended on the moral and material help of official Greece. The Patriarchists alone could not bring about victory in a guerrilla-type, one-sided Macedonian conflict. A powerful witches' brew of combined forces was needed. The Bulgarian relationships and support from Russia and the Europeans needed powerful alliances to be reversed. Such help began with Karavangelis's relations with Pavlos Melas and Ion Dragoumis, a military officer and a diplomat, respectively, of the Greek Kingdom.

Pavlos was the son of Michael Melas, a wealthy merchant of Epirote origin who left Marseille, France, and settled in Athens. In 1878 Michael Melas became the treasurer of the National Defense (*Ethniki Amina*), an organization supporting Hellenic aspirations in Epirus, Thessaly, and Crete.[38] Lively, sensitive, patriotic, and adventurous, Pavlos grew up in a family with strong traditions and powerful Hellenic sentiments. He graduated from the military academy (*Scholi Evelpidon*) in Athens, was commissioned as a second lieutenant in the artillery, and in 1892 he married Natalia, daughter of Stefanos Dragoumis and Ion's sister. To him, the Greek struggle in Macedonia was not a Bulgarian problem, but thoroughly Hellenic, bringing the Greek population in Macedonia against the usurpers, the Turks and Bulgarians.

Ion Dragoumis was the son of Stefanos, a politician and a diplomat, and a minister of foreign affairs in the Trikoupis government. Father and son were from Vogatsiko, a frontier village and a bastion of Hellenism in a critical section of western Macedonia. They both watched with alarm the strides and progress made by the Exarchate and the Bulgarian committees. They both became strong activists involved in Macedonian affairs, stirring

Vangelis in the early 1900s. He fell into a Bulgarian ambush in 1904 and was killed together with all his men. Courtesy of the Museum of the Macedonian Struggle, Thessaloniki.

up people and politicians on behalf of Macedonia, smuggling arms into Macedonia, communicating with Greek leaders in the region, supporting *Ethniki Amina,* and yearning for action in Macedonia.

After the Greco-Turkish War of 1897 the Greek government had serious reasons to be cautious in its dealings with Turkey, especially on issues concerning territories like Macedonia. The conservative Greek governments of Zaimis and Deligiannis were disinclined to use military power or even guerrilla warfare as primary instruments of their Macedonian policy. They knew that, historically, instability and violence in one country or territory under the Ottomans would almost certainly spread across the Balkan peninsula. While different perceptions in Athens about how to handle the Macedonian problem were inevitable, the government was afraid that a spark igniting an open revolt by the suppressed Macedonian people would inevitably hurt Greece. With this perspective, before Dragoumis left for his position in Monastir, he was instructed by the Foreign Ministry "not to raise problems."

Greece's reaction, therefore, to the events in Macedonia was slow in coming. The Greek tardiness and indecision, however, did not prevent individuals like Pavlos Melas and Ion Dragoumis from plunging with great enthusiasm into the struggle, becoming deeply involved with Macedonian affairs (Vattis 2002). As soon as he arrived in Monastir, Dragoumis began visiting both Patriarchist and Exarchist villages in western Macedonia (many times disguised as a peasant), the birthplace of his ancestors, to inspire the people to defend Macedonia's Hellenism. With the situation worsened, expecting very little or no help from the Greek government, Dragoumis conceived the idea of forming an internal Greek organization for clandestine action to thwart Macedonia's Bulgarization. From his early years, he had envisaged a clandestine war against the Bulgarians under the Ottomans. "If [the Greeks] in Macedonia work as though Greece did not exist, then Greece will help," declared Dragoumis (Dakin 1966). Many junior and senior officers of *Ethniki Amina,* like his brother-in-law Melas, Tsondos, Exadaktilos, the brothers Mazarakis, and others, supported Dragoumis's idea. Metropolitan Karavangelis and the bishops of Monastir, Edessa, and Drama, all concerned with Hellenism's deplorable strategic situation in Macedonia, also approved of Dragoumis's idea.

Unrestrained by the Greek government's indecisiveness, the young Dragoumis embarked on a hectic program of travel, undaunted by the perils looming in every step of the way outside Monastir. His idea of forming a Greek Macedonian Committee became a reality by the end of 1903 when he met in Melas's house in Athens with Demetrios Kalapothakis, owner of the newspaper *Empros,* and many young officers of the Greek army. The group decided to form the "Macedonian Committee" with Kalapothakis as

Pavlos Melas, a second lieutenant and hero of the Greek army. He was killed by the Ottomans on October 13, 1904. Courtesy of the Museum of the Macedonian Struggle, Thessaloniki.

the president. Dragoumis and Melas also kept up regular correspondence with Karavangelis, who kept them informed on the happenings in Macedonia, pressing them to send armed bands from Greece. Also, the Greek Macedonian Committee informed the new Greek government of George Theotokis about its formation and asked the prime minister to consider sending clandestine armed bands to Macedonia (Dakin 1966).

It was no accident that eleven Cretans were the first Greek *andartes* (freedom fighters) to arrive secretly in Macedonia at the end of May 1903.[39] Most new recruits from Greece in subsequent years were from the island of Crete, for whose actions the Greek government pretended not to have any responsibilities. Crete was part of the Turkish Empire during the Macedonian Struggle. Then in March 1904, four Greek officers, Pavlos

Melas, Alexandros Kondoulis, Anastasios Papoulias, and Georgios Kolokotronis, disguised as peddlers, arrived in Macedonia to study the conditions and possibilities for organizing guerrilla warfare against the Bulgarian committees. Upon their return to Athens, Melas and Kondoulis advised the Greek government that guerrilla warfare had great possibilities for success against the Bulgarian bands. The suggestion, disputed by Papoulias and Kolokotronis, was rejected by the government (AHD 1979).

The names of two other men are often associated with Hellenism's success in Macedonia: Lambros

Lambros Koromilas, Greek consul-general in the Ottoman-held Thessaloniki. Courtesy of the Museum of the Macedonian Struggle, Thessaloniki.

Koromilas and Alexandros Mazarakis. By the time these men came into the picture, Dragoumis, Karavangelis, Kotas, Vangelis, and others had already established a footing for Hellenism in Macedonia. An educated man of great vision, decisiveness, influence, and initiative, Koromilas, together with ten military officers assigned to him in 1904 by the Greek government — which no longer ignored the Macedonian problem — disguised as servants, setup the mechanism in Macedonia under the Turkish eyes to thwart the Bulgarian efforts.

Koromilas, the calm and composed consul-general in Thessaloniki, later minister of foreign affairs in Athens, was to become one of the chief organizers of the Hellenic efforts in Macedonia. The officers working with him, constantly increasing in numbers by the arrival of new ones in 1905 from Athens, included the young Second Lieutenant Alexandros Mazarakis (in later years chief of the Greek general staff), who arrived in Macedonia under the name "Ioannides." Koromilas's men were to study the Macedonian problem; learn the Slavic language; collect military, demographic, and cartographical information; observe the Turkish movements; foresee the Bulgarian plans and movements; and form local armed bands under the direction of the newly arriving military officers from Greece. The suffering of the Christian population at the hands of the Bulgarian committees finally convinced the Greek government to interfere in 1904 by sending armed bands of *andartes* to Macedonia. By the end of 1904 and the beginning of 1905, Greece was no longer the pathetic observer of the terrible events in Macedonia. The high-stakes game finally impelled Greece to intervene in its own way in the internal affairs of the crumbling Turkish Empire (Mazarakis-Ainian 1950).

To coordinate the struggle, the Central Committee in Athens divided Macedonia into three primary districts: Thessaloniki, Monastir, and Serres, with several subdistricts within the districts. This was followed by an intense recruitment of new men in Greece and Macedonia to fight as guerrillas (Museum of the Macedonian Struggle 1993).

Turkey, awakening to the clandestine guerrilla war simmering between Hellenism and Bulgarism in 1903, imposed harsh measures that took on ominous dimensions for the young Greek struggle in Macedonia. It may be revealing at this point to mention some of the Turkish measures: They prohibited the use of the Greek language during liturgy and closed the Greek schools in vlachophone and slavophone villages, despite protestations of many slavophone inhabitants; forced the Greek government to recall Koromilas, consul general in Thessaloniki; pressed the Patriarch to recall the metropolitans of Kastoria, Grevena, Drama, and Pelagonia, accusing them of supporting Hellenic causes;[40] prohibited Greek metropolitans from participating in district councils, a privilege granted almost four hundred years before; and launched a campaign of terror against the Greeks in rural areas and cities of Macedonia, confiscating properties of many Greek citizens (the Turkish prisons were filled with Greek prisoners, all of them innocent) (Papadimitriou 1991).

The successes of the Greek *andartes* in the field increased the Bulgarian brutality. An evening newspaper from Sofia wrote in 1906: "Only one race must prevail in Haemus [Balkans], the Bulgarian race. Hellenism of Eastern Rumelia and Macedonia must be uprooted, destroyed, disappear.... The destruction of Hellenism is a matter of faith for the Bulgarians" (Vattis 2002).

Determined not to be forced into submission, the life of the local Greek *andartes* was harsh. It was fraught with betrayals, ambushes, scarcity of equipment and food, plodding through snow and rain or blazing heat, mosquitos, plagues, and malaria. It was betrayal that cost Melas's young life. The dashing second lieutenant, one of the first Greeks to fight for Macedonia's Hellenism, lost his life early in the struggle. Appointed commander in chief of all Hellenic bands in the region of Kastoria and Monastir, he entered Macedonia clandestinely on August 4, 1904, as "Zezas" for his third and last trip, together with four Cretan *andartes* and several others he picked on his way to the Greek-Turkish frontier. On his way to Macedonia, he wrote to his wife Natalia: "I take up this struggle with all my heart and soul and with the idea that I am obliged to take it up. I had, and I have, the steadfast belief that we are able to work in Macedonia and save many things. Having this belief, I have the supreme duty to sacrifice everything" (Dakin 1966).

And what sacrifice he offered: his own life. On September 7 Melas and his men arrived in the village of Kostarazi, a Greek-speaking Patriarchist village that welcomed him with great patriotic exuberance. The village had been threatened to be burned for not paying dues to the Exarchists. Defying the natural vicissitudes and the threat of betrayal or ambushes, Melas and his band plodded from village to village from September 7 to October 13 to expel the *komitadjides* from the villages, encouraging the inhabitants to return to the Patriarchate after being coerced or forced to join the Exarchate. He established committees to cooperate with his men and organized new bands to defend their villages.

On October 13, 1904, Melas and his band entered the village of Statista (now Melas), not knowing that a *komitadjis* leader, with a price on his head from the Turks, had betrayed Melas to the Turks. In the skirmish that followed, Melas was killed by the Turkish contingent that encircled the village, not knowing it had killed Melas and not the marked *komitadjis*. His death was a cataclysmic earthquake for Greek society, an event that also shocked the Hellenic bands in Macedonia and the entire Greek nation. The impression caused by his death was incalculable. It touched the conscious-ness of every Greek in free Greece and reinforced the determination of the Greek people to fight for Macedonia's liberation. His death captured the nation's imagination and bolstered its determination to fight for Hellenic Macedonia. As with the death of Lord Byron, who had given his life for Greece's freedom three-quarters of a century earlier, the church bells tolled for a young man who gave his life for Macedonia's Hellenism. Although his life was short, depriving him of the opportunity to contribute his enthusi-asm to more victories in the struggle, Melas became an inspiration not only to his generation, but also to many Hellenic generations to follow. Remark-able as his short life was, he stirred the entire Hellenic nation with his brav-ery, impulsiveness (which cost him his life), and generosity. In the final analysis, he became a hero, a symbol of Hellenism whose role and untimely death prompted many others to go to Macedonia, effectively thwarting the spread of Bulgarism, preventing Macedonia's irretrievable loss.

Unlike any other event, the darkness of Melas's early death prompted the Greek government to change its position dramatically on the Macedon-ian issue to protect its unalienable rights in the land of Philip and Alexan-der the Great. His death sharply increased the awareness of the Greek government of the distinct possibility of losing Macedonia to the Bulgari-ans. That cleared the air in Athens on what to do on the burning problem. By the end of 1906 the dynamic in Macedonia had shifted dramatically from the Bulgarian committees to the Hellenic Macedonians and their clandes-tine allies from official Greece. They had captured the initiative from IMRO, induced many villages to go back to the Patriarchate, and curtailed the movements and activities of the *komitadjides*. A major split between the two Bulgarian committees (IMRO and Vchrovists) also helped the Greek effort.[41]

Finally, all the ingredients for Hellenism's success in the enslaved Mace-donia were in place. The Hellenic Kingdom of Greece decided to intervene financially and militarily: It sent armed guerrilla bands to Macedonia; organized in Athens the Macedonian Committee; and, tragic as it was, the government had a new hero in the pantheon of Greek heroes, the young Lieutenant Pavlos Melas, the leader of all Greek bands in Macedonia (Papadimitriou 1991). Scientists, intellectuals, workers, technicians, clerics, teachers, farmers, shepherds, and even students offered their services in free Greece to help their enslaved brothers in Macedonia (Papadimitriou 1995).

In spite of the Greek *andartes'* victories, or perhaps because of them, ominous clouds descending from Russia and spreading through the chan-celleries of the European powers were threatening Greece's credibility and its intentions. The Russian and Bulgarian propaganda accused the Greeks of collaborating with the Turks against the struggle for liberty of the "Macedonian people."[42] With a letter to the European courts, Prince Ferdinand of Bulgaria asked for the removal of the Greek armed bands from Macedonia (Dakin 1966). Never mind that IMRO and the Vrchovist bands had been terrorizing the Greek population of Macedonia since the Greco-Turkish War of 1897. The European politicians who expressed no compassion for Hellenism's suffering in the preceding seven years of Bulgarian atrocities in Macedonia abruptly became concerned about the "mistreatment" of the Slavs by the Greek bands.

As in previous years, it was Greece that began receiving again stern protests from the European powers for responding to the terrorist acts by Bulgarian *komitadjides*, not the Bulgarian committees terrorizing Macedonia's Greek population with impunity for years. The *Times* of London almost daily published pro-Bulgarian articles blaming the Greeks for collaborating with the Turks. It even arrived at the conclusion that a Greater Bulgaria under British influence would curtail the Russian influence in the Balkans, preventing Russia's expansion into the Aegean (Society for Macedonian Studies 1994). Only isolated individuals and some Greek-sympathizing organizations of liberal ideologues, especially French and British, who had admired the concept of democracy emanating from classical Greek writers—and had been aware of the historical truths on Macedonia — supported Greece's stand in its unequal struggle (Vattis 2002).

In spite of its sporadic and weak activities at the outset, the Greek counterorganization in Macedonia, formed to protect the Greek-speaking Macedonians from the Bulgarians and defend the Hellenic way of life, began an offensive according to a plan prepared by Constantine Mazarakis, brother of Alexander (Dakin 1966). It involved eight bands in the Thessaloniki *vilayet* and a dozen in the Monastir *vilayet*. Numerous local bands collaborated with the principal ones. While the Greek bands intensified their efforts in 1906, the Exarchist efforts were curtailed, with most of their bands lying low, being killed, or having escaped to Bulgaria. Survivors were constantly forced on the run by the Turks and by the then more numerous Greek bands of *andartes*.

Disinclined to use military power as a primary instrument in their Macedonian policies, the European powers through their ministers in Athens intensified their protestations in the summer of 1907, demanding withdrawal of the Greek bands from Macedonia, while at the same time treating Sofia gently. The European powers had forgotten who had instigated the Macedonian problem, who was the offender, and why Greece had taken those belated defensive measures. When Turkey pointed out who the culprit was, the Europeans closed their ears and eyes (Tsamis 1975). British Foreign Minister Edward Grey went so far as to suggest autonomy for the three "Macedonian" *vilayets*, a political accommodation desired by Bulgaria. The *Times* of London, reflecting the official British views on the Macedonian problem, as it was shaped after the 1906 British-Russian rapport, wrote: "Because the Greek hordes are well provided and financed in Macedonia, they are able to make more progress at the expense of others" (Vattis 2002).

In retrospect, it must be remembered that the curious thing was that the British and the Russians, and to some extent the Austrians, were alarmed only when the Greek fighting bands began to predominate over the *komitadjides*, bringing back to the Patriarchate hundreds of villages and thousands of Slav-speaking Greek Macedonians. Because of these new European political shortsighted developments, a new Bulgarian attitude emerged: lay low, hoping the European powers would reward Bulgaria for good behavior.

Disregarding European and Russian threats in 1907, the Greeks continued to dispatch armed bands into the Kastoria, Florina, and Morihovo districts of western Macedonia (C. Vakalopoulos 1987). Also, during the same year, the Greek bands, taking advantage of the temporary Bulgarian retreat — a move taken by Bulgaria to placate the Europeans — intensified their efforts, thereby further weakening the *komitadjides* during the critical spring months of 1907. At the same time, the Serb armed bands also intensified their efforts, killing Bulgarian *komitadjides* and destroying property in the Kazas of Uskub, Perlepe, Palauka, and Kupsula districts.

In the spring of 1908, the governments of England and Russia suggested that the Bulgarian government prohibit armed bands from entering Macedonia from Bulgaria. To reciprocate, the Greek government also ordered the removal of the Greek bands from Macedonia. But in May 1908, a new attempt from Bulgaria to reorganize its armed bands brought the Greek bands back to Macedonia under new and old capable leaders such as Vardas (Tsondos), Makris, Agras, Litsas, and others (Tsamis 1975). In western Macedonia, where considerable ground had been lost, the newly arrived leaders were able to tip the balance again in favor of the Greek government, despite the increased opposition from the Turks. By the beginning of the summer of 1908, the Greek bands were predominating from Lake Ostrovo to Gevgeli (present-day Gevgelija) in the center and in the Kavala, Serres, and Drama districts. The IMRO and the Vrchovist movements had almost ceased to exist.

Throughout the years 1903 to 1908 the conflict over domination in Macedonia by Bulgarians or Greeks, still under Ottoman rule, was marked by extreme brutality and gross violations of human rights by both sides. Looking back over those years one might expect exactly that. The deplorable situation was due to the fact that the Macedonian struggle was not a declared war between sovereign countries, but a guerrilla warfare between two ideas,

Hellenism and Bulgarism, reflecting two ethnic entities loathing each other under the umbrella of a foreign conqueror entrenched in the sorry land for four hundred years. It was a struggle of hidden domination, where rules of engagement did not exist, where hatreds were boiling, where both parties hated the conquerors and hated each other more, where difficult-to-control forces were unleashed in a peninsula known for its tendency for violence, and where there existed no sinew of conservatism or restraint, but only hate.

One of the inescapable misfortunes of the guerrilla war was the suffering by the civilians who experienced many casualties. In 1905 alone the *komitadjides* murdered 325 Greeks, mostly notables and elders. What was more distressing to the Greeks of Macedonia was the harsh measures taken by the Turks against the Greeks after ruthless pressure by the Russians, the Austrians, and to some extent the British government, which, beginning in 1906, openly supported the Bulgarian claims in Macedonia. The year 1906 was perhaps the hardest for Hellenism's fortunes in Macedonia.[43]

Rights and wrongs were committed by both sides of the Macedonian Struggle, but that does not absolve the Turks and the Bulgarians or, as a matter of fact, the European powers for the tragic conditions Hellenism faced in historic Macedonia: extreme poverty, pressure by the Turk *chiftlik* owners, robberies, and extreme heavy taxation (this issue incensed the Greeks more than anything else); lack of education and deplorable conditions of the Greek schools compared to the Bulgarian schools; lack of communication by the Greeks of Macedonia with free Greece and abandonment of the Macedonian Greeks by Greece; legal and illegal means used by Bulgarian propagandists (lies, bribery, denunciation, slander, terror, murder) to assist the Turks against the Greek element; and support of the Bulgarian causes by the Europeans and apathy toward the Greek misery (Museum of the Macedonian Struggle 1993). It is a miracle that a large part of the Macedonians preserved their Hellenism under those conditions, but the reasons are clear why a part of them succumbed to the pressures created by the appalling living conditions, joined the Exarchate, and eventually lost their ethnicity. Apart from those with an obvious motive for going to the Exarchate as Bulgarians and those remaining steadfast to Hellenism, there were also a large fraction of slavophones who remained neutral, paying attention only to the everyday struggle for life rather than politics.

A heavy toll of blood was paid by the Greek volunteers from Greece and the Macedonian *andartes* fighting together against the Turks and Bulgarians to preserve the spirit of Hellenism. What was the southern Greek young men's innate power that motivated them to fight away from home against terrible odds and die in the Slav-speaking pockets of western Macedonia? "What made Charilaos Trikoupis [the Greek prime minister], a man little associated with irredentism, declare in parliament in 1885 that Greece was obliged to strive for the incorporation of Macedonia, less on account of the region's strategic and economic importance than because Greece would never really achieve complete national statehood without Macedonia?... No doubt it was Greek sentiments or consciousness (*fronima*)" (Koliopoulos 1997, p. 44). It was also the intense, innate passion for Macedonian Hellenism's fate and the distaste for history's distortion that incited the Hellenic Macedonians and the volunteers from free Greece to leave their families for four years for an undeclared, vicious guerrilla war against the Turks and Bulgarians.

The Revolt of the Young Turks

The British-Russian rapprochement at the Reval, Esthonia, meeting in June 1908, suggesting the possibility of an attempt by the European powers to assume control over Macedonia, and the sultan's intentions to explore whether indeed there existed a fomenting conspiracy by young Turkish army officers, hastened the simmering Young Turks' revolt in Macedonia (Dakin 1966). The revolt, which began in Thessaloniki on July 11, 1908, quickly spread in Macedonia and all of Turkey. Sultan Abdul Hamid II was overthrown and his descendant Reat V was enthroned as a constitutional monarch. The revolt sprang from the Young Turks' liberal views of governing the Ottoman Empire's subjects and their presumed beliefs in equality, freedom, and justice. The Young Turks ostensibly sought a number of reforms in the empire, including the reinstatement of the 1876 Turkish constitution (Limber 1997). The Greeks, Bulgarians, and Serbs accepted the revolution with great relief. The Greeks and the Serbs had achieved what they had expected: defeat Bulgaria and stake their own claims on Macedonia. From 1908 to 1911 very few Greek and Bulgarian bands remained in Macedonia.

Increasingly, however, the slogans of the Young Turks for democracy, equality among the people of the empire, freedom, and justice turned into thin "icing on a hard cake that melted quickly" (Dakin 1966). The sultan's despotism was replaced by a harsher despotism, practiced by the Young Turks, who were planning to violently convert to Islam all their subjects in the multiethnic empire. The revolt further weakened the Turks and set into motion several events detrimental to the Ottoman Empire. Bulgaria, for instance, took advantage of the shaky conditions the revolt created and declared its independence, and Austria-Hungary immediately annexed Bosnia and Herzegovina (Limber 1997). Soon after the revolt, many prominent Greeks began to realize that the Young Turks would not deliver on their promises, disfavoring the Greeks as long as it suited their plans, especially after their leader, Rachmet Bey, allowed the Bulgarians to return to Thessaloniki and let it be known that he would no longer respect the old privileges of the Greeks. According to Dakin (1966), "the young Turks were fundamentally hostile to Hellenism and ... the revolution was merely a nine days' wonder." The days and months that followed showed the uncontrolled chauvinism of the Young Turks' revolt and revealed their true aims to restore the Ottoman Empire's old glory and power.

By 1908 the third crisis of the Macedonia problem ended with the Young Turks' revolt successful, the Bulgarian armed bands defeated, and their plans for an autonomous Macedonia — a first step to annexation by Bulgaria — thwarted. Most of the Greek- and Slav-speaking Greek inhabitants of Macedonia returned to Hellenic ideas and the Patriarchate, with Macedonia's Hellenism fallen this time on the Young Turks' brutal hands. At the same time a perceptible change occurred in Europe. The European people, taking a different view from their pro-Bulgarian governments on the Macedonian Question, began to reject the Slavophile sentiments of their governments, perceptibly favoring Macedonia's Hellenism and what it historically represented (Dakin 1966). Many people in the Western countries, educated in Greek and Latin, could no longer be fooled by the Slavic slogans and Bulgaria's chauvinism at Greek Macedonia's expense. They saw Greece as the birthplace of Europe and the Greeks as the promulgators of democracy and promoters of Christianity, representing Europe's rights against Islam and its "prerogative" over the eastern Mediterranean (Tsamis 1975).

By the end of 1908, with the so-called Macedonian Struggle over, Hellenism in Macedonia had again fallen into merciless Ottoman hands. But the victorious Greek bands were riding high. They had reversed an almost disastrous trend in Macedonia and restored the morale of the Greek people shattered by Greece's defeat in 1897. They had convinced the world that the Macedonian problem was no longer a Bulgarian or a Slavic problem. During the struggle, many eminent intellectual Greeks and hundreds of military officers, many of them from Crete, crossed the Greek-Turkish border and united with their Greek brothers in Macedonia.

Hellenism's Triumph in the Macedonian Struggle

The failure of Bulgaria's "unassailable" claim on Macedonia was unexpected and very dramatic because (a) the European powers had favored and supported the Bulgarian aspirations, (b) the Turks were partial to the Bulgarians, favoring them for their docility, and (c) the Bulgarians had begun the guerrilla war ahead of the Greeks. Bulgaria's defeat in its stubborn conflict with Hellenism disappointed the Europeans and defied Russian expectations. Had the Bulgarians won, the European diplomats would perhaps have sanctioned incorporating Macedonia into Bulgaria, or at least pressing for autonomy, which in the future would have meant annexation by Bulgaria. Dakin (1966, p. 475) pointed out that "the Greek victory (if such it can be called) in the armed struggle in Macedonia between 1903 and 1908 did not win Macedonia or any part of it for Greece: but it at least prevented what later became Greek Macedonia from being lost." The victory was also important because it prepared the ground and the conditions for the victory in the Balkan Wars (1912–1913).

The Greeks of Macedonia had the will and the stamina to remain Hellenes despite the odds against them. Two unlikely non-Greek sources perceived and described the spirit of Macedonian Hellenism, defining it precisely for the years of the Macedonian Struggle. Dakin (1966, p. 474) expressed this spirit in his book *The Greek Struggle in Macedonia, 1897–1913*, with a few meaningful sentences: "The Greater Bulgaria failed, for the second time, to come into existence.... It foundered in its conflict with Hellenism, which was just as natural and equally respectable as an ideal." He also argued that the Greek struggle in Macedonia "was based upon Hellenism — Hellenism [as] a way of life that existed in Macedonia among the more substantial Christian population, much of which (though not all of it) Greek by race and language and (what is more important) all of it fervently Orthodox and conservative."

The French correspondent M. Paillarès, who visited Macedonia at the beginning of the twentieth century, wrote: "Why should I care about the ethnic and glossological theories? Why should I care whether the victims of the Komitet speak Greek, Vlach, Bulgarian, or Turkish? What interests me is that all these people are Macedonians irrespective of the language they speak; they prefer to be crucified by the Bulgarians than renounce their Hellenism.... Those unimportant heroes are Hellenes, and I kneel before their supreme greatness" (Paillarès 1907, cited by Vattis 2002).[44]

The spirit of Macedonian Hellenism was also expressed by Pavlos Melas, the young Greek officer who sacrificed his life for Macedonian Hellenism. He wrote to his wife Natalia in 1904 before his death: "I do not work for the government. I work for [Macedonian] Hellenism. I do not like the government. I love Hellenism. I am in pain for Hellenism." Those few words proclaimed the spirit of Macedonian Hellenism in the early 1900s long before a "Macedonian ethnicity" was invented in the north. This spirit necessitated the classification of the Christians in Macedonia into two categories: heroes and traitors; Greeks and Bulgarians; martyrs and bloodthirsty monsters; victims and assassins (Gounaris 1997, p. 27).

The Greek leaders and their men became increasingly committed to Hellenism, a sublime ideal to them: the feeling of excitement of speaking Alexander's and Aristotle's language and the satisfaction of being able to understand Plato, Socrates, and the Apostle Paul's letters, all written in Greek, several addressed to Macedonians.[45] Hellenism survived and triumphed in Macedonia, because the Hellenic consciousness prevailed in the fighters' and civilians' psyche, because the Greek *andartes,* rich in their determination, fought for an idea, not for land, for a principle, behind which was Homer, Ulysses, Rigas Ferreos, Kolokotronis, Pavlos Melas and, yes, Alexander the Great. Bulgarism lost in Macedonia because liberty and democracy were alien to it as ideals.[46]

Hellenism won because it had young enthusiasts like Melas, Dragoumis, Metropolitan Karavangelis, Kotas, and Vangelis and excellent organizers like Consul Koromilas in Thessaloniki, Mazarakis, and others. The Greeks won in Macedonia because they were united by names and symbols: historic lineage, common land, struggle, religion, living traditions, blood spilled on their land for thousands of years. The Bulgarians were united by all these, except historic lineage and land. Macedonia was historically alien to them. In terms of historical eons, the Bulgarians were intruders, invaders from the north. The two conceptions of life — Hellenic craving for freedom from the Turks and Bulgarian lust for territory —clashed to the end, the craving for freedom predominating.

The Greeks won in Macedonia because for a century the death of heroes had inscribed with blood Macedonia's history as a preamble to the anticipated struggle. The feelings of independence, pride, and decency were always in the hearts of heroes who never bent their heads and never accepted slavery in their indomitable hearts, forced upon them by Turks, Bulgarians, or anybody else. Their desire for freedom lifted them above the circumstances, no matter how appalling, and guided them to succeed and bequeath that gem, freedom, to others. It is said the struggle for them was a command of the heart, an impulse, a brave sacrifice.

In spite of all the raids from the north and east suffered by Macedonia, Hellenism remained substantially unbreakable, unshakable. Its triumph over its rivals stemmed from a difficult-to-understand need and pride of being and remaining Hellenes: the stubborn determination to show the Europeans and Russians that Hellenism was able to survive. Hellenism survived in Macedonia because of the need and insatiable desire for liberty and democracy. Bulgarism intended to destroy Hellenism's values, culture, democratic ideas, and life itself as perceived by the Macedonian Hellenes. The European powers tolerated or condoned the Bulgarian claims and dismissed Hellenism's reverse claims. The European politicians could have solved the Macedonian problem then and there had they perceived the magnitude of

Hellenism's unity — as Paillarès did — from Haemus all the way to the island of Crete and studied Hellenism's history; had they heard "behind the turmoil of political history the voices of Solon and Socrates, of Plato and Aristotle, of Pheidias and Praxitelis, of Epicurus and Archimedes ... had they sought their company across alien centuries" (Durant Vol. 2, 1939); had they understood the important question of what would have happened in the Balkans if Hellenism lost; and had they perceived from the very beginning Russia's motives in supporting the Bulgarian claims.

There were many other reasons why the Greeks won the Macedonian Struggle, essentially over with the success of the Young Turks' revolt in 1908. One of them was the superb fighting ability and military training of the Greek bands that fought in Macedonia, both those that entered Macedonia from Greece and those formed locally. Their effectiveness was the result not only of their bravery and endurance, but also of the support received from the elaborate and extensive civilian organization. The entire Greek movement in Macedonia depended on a great number of people with a Hellenic and Christian way of life. The indigenous Hellenic Macedonians, together with the slavophone Hellenic Macedonians, far outnumbered the pro-Bulgarian slavophones, giving the Hellenic Macedonian struggle a decisive advantage over the Bulgarians in both the military and civilian sectors.

The struggle produced an outcome that was somewhat less than a total victory. It could not be a total victory unless the Ottomans were also overthrown, an unlikely event at that time. Also, the Greek movement in Macedonia was not perfect in organization or in its aims. There were divisions among the Greeks, especially between Hellenism's aims in Macedonia — to prevail over Bulgarism — and the Greek Kingdom's irredentism. But these divisions did not hurt the Hellenic movement. Hellenism's forcefulness rendered the divisions among the Greeks innocuous. In contrast, the Bulgarian movement failed to enlist considerable local support. The demands of the Bulgarian committees for help from the Exarchists did not always bring the needed help. Bulgaria failed in its conflict with Hellenism because the idea of "Macedonia for the Macedonians," music to IMRO's ears, retrogressed into a stalemate of prolonged, brutal violence.

The Bulgarian-Macedonian movement was also weakened in the field by the disastrous Bulgarian Committee's ideological and political splits and disagreements: the lack of unity between the external and internal branches of IMRO and their confused and conflicting aims; the blunder over autonomy versus annexation; the applied mixture of terrorism, religious propaganda, and social revolution combined with plundering of the villages by the *komitadjides*; and constant divisions and rivalries in the field that destroyed IMRO's credibility of the "noble" aims for freedom and democracy put forward during peaceful times.[47]

Several strong Hellenic elements — ethnological, religious, educational, linguistic, historical — synergistically antagonistic to the Exarchists constituted the moral force that defeated the Bulgarian plans for domination in Macedonia. The religious element was one of the strongest. During the last hundred years of Macedonian slavery, the predominance of Macedonia's Hellenism through the Greek Orthodox Church remained undisputed. The church had prevented the Greek-speaking Macedonians from turning to Islam. The church had founded and sustained Greek schools to keep the Greek language alive in Ottoman-dominated Macedonia. The glow of ancient Greek civilization, which continued through the years of the Byzantine Empire, was Hellenism's strength, which it derived from the Greek Orthodox Church and the Patriarchate and from the Greek schools that were mostly sustained by the Church, especially in the early years. "Hellenism was a way of life, of which the outward manifestation was the acceptance of the Greek Orthodox Church" (Dakin 1966).

The Greek Orthodox Church played a particularly important role, contributing heavily to the demise of the Bulgarian aspirations in Macedonia by its heavy involvement in the religious and political issues of the land. The Church was the only power entrusted with protecting the flock during the critical transition period (Hassiotis 1992). It kept, very often secretly, Hellenism alive from the very early days of the Ottoman occupation. During the Macedonian Struggle, the Patriarchate appointed the dynamic, dedicated young metropolitans like Germanos Karavangelis of Kastoria in sensitive areas of historic Macedonia, where they were needed the most. Also, the Mount Athos monasteries contributed to the preservation and awakening of Christian Orthodoxy and Hellenism by preserving Christian writings and promoting them by writing, teaching, icon painting, text preservation, copying, and religious information distribution. That is why by the struggle's end many priests and bishops had been removed from their congregations by Turkish demands. Many members of the Greek Orthodox clergy were also maimed, taken as prisoners to Bulgaria, or murdered by the Turks and *komitadjides*. The Greek Orthodox belief was the strongest stumbling block to Islam's making inroads among the Balkan Christians.[48]

2

The Balkan Wars and World War I (1912–1918)

The past is our present and our present depends
on the past, on history

The First Balkan War

The great dream of Macedonia's enslaved Christian people during the four centuries in the Ottoman Empire was their liberation from the harsh Turkish rule. The dreams of the *rayahs* (infidel slaves) for freedom coincided with the dreams and aspirations of the countries around Macedonia with which they had ethnic, linguistic, and religious affiliations: the enslaved Hellenic Macedonians' dream for freedom with official Greece's *Megali Idea* (Great Idea); the aspirations of the Bulgarians living in Macedonia with Bulgaria's dream for a Greater Bulgaria; and the dreams of the Serbs living in Macedonia for a Greater Serbia.

The Macedonian Christians' dreams of freedom and the aspirations of Turkey's neighbors for liberating their own enslaved nationals, while at the same time enlarging their respective territories, could not materialize if they were fighting alone or against each other, thereby assisting Turkey in its plans of dividing and conquering. The Young Turks' repressive nationalist policies and their determination to restore the Ottoman Empire's old glory and power were further factors that exacerbated the pain of slavery and acted as a catalyst for the Balkan countries to overcome their mutual animosities, push aside their rivalries, and unite against the common enemy. Turkey's neighbors needed peace among themselves, joint political and military planning, and military preparations. During the period from 1908 to 1912 Greece spent great efforts to build its economy and the armed forces. By 1912, it could mobilize two hundred thousand men and a navy capable of dominating the Aegean Sea (Mazarakis-Ainian 1950).

In spite of their intensive rivalries before 1912, Greece, Serbia, Bulgaria, and Montenegro agreed in September 1912 to combine their forces, form an anti–Turkish military alliance (Balkan League), and fight together against Turkey to liberate their compatriots (Limber 1997). The decision to join forces against the Ottomans occurred at a time when Turkey was plagued by numerous crises in the Balkans and elsewhere. Difficult-to-control forces were unleashing crisis after crisis, threatening Turkey's fate in the Balkans: the Tripolitan War; the Turkish constitutional crisis of 1912; the Albanian revolt of 1912 supported by Serbia and Montenegro; the revolt of Kosovo's Muslims and the Monastir garrison mutiny; the Albanian demands for the Monastir *vilayet* and attempts by the Turkish war minister to purge the Turkish army, a hasty effort that almost destroyed the army's effectiveness; and the Turkish-Italian War of 1911–1912, at the end of which Turkey lost the Dodecanese Islands to Italy. As if these crises were not serious enough for Turkey, on August 13, 1912, Austria-Hungary sent an alarming note to Turkey suggesting that the Turks implement the already promised decentralization policy in the occupied Balkan territories (Dakin 1966).

A plethora of ethnic, geographic, historical, and religious factors made it impossible for the new Balkan allies in 1912 to decide how they would divide the war spoils in advance, in other words the territory presumed to be liberated from the Turks, and there was no doubt that the big prize to be divided was Macedonia. The extremely complicated and sensitive, potentially explosive, issue was therefore pushed to the back burner by the Balkan League by agreeing to settle the new borders among themselves according to the territory each of the allies would liberate. England, France, and Russia would be called upon to settle disagreements if they arose on border arrangements.

The four allies deployed the following numbers for the battle: Greece 148,000 men and a strong navy to establish naval supremacy in the Aegean; Serbia 260,000 men; Bulgaria 300,000; and Montenegro 35,000. On October 7, 1912, Montenegro fired the first shot, followed by Bulgaria, and shortly thereafter by Greece and Serbia. The Greek government presented its declaration of war on October 18, three days after Turkey had signed a preliminary peace treaty with Italy. The most remarkable thing for Greece at the outset was the arrival of thousands of Greek volunteers from abroad to fight for Macedonia's, Thrace's, and Epirus's liberation, and for the union with Greece of the Aegean islands and Crete.

After Greece declared war against Turkey, Macedonia's liberation was accomplished at an astounding speed. The rapid Greek advance was due to the army's enthusiasm, determination, and aggressiveness to liberate Macedonia before the winter; underestimation of the Greek forces by the Turks and by Greece's allies; the Turkish army's shabby condition fighting four enemies on four different fronts; and the invaluable assistance behind the lines of the reorganized Greek bands that had fought so valiantly in the same area during the Macedonian Struggle of 1904–1908.

Before hostilities began, the old Greek Macedonian guerrilla forces were reactivated and armed to soften the Turkish defenses in preparation for the war by the Royal Greek Army. The guerrillas were to seize control of communications, destroy Turkish installations, seize important strong points, and provide scouts for the army.[1] In addition to their behind-the-lines clandestine operations, the Greek bands fought several skirmishes with the Turks and liberated Polygyros (the capital of Halkidiki) and several other cities in Macedonia before the Greek army arrived. Most of these sites lie within less than forty miles from Thessaloniki. Other bands under Anagnostakis ("Matapas") seized *ta Stena tis Petras* (major link between the Pierian coastal plain and the Voulstana Pass), a narrow passage south of Katerini, a quick victory which enabled the 7th Greek Infantry Division to advance rapidly and liberate Katerini after an intense skirmish with the Turks.[2]

Other bands of *andartes* under Mazarakis, rapidly moving northward, occupied the important junction of Kleidi, where they improvised building a new bridge by assembling boats and using them as pontoons—the old Loudias bridge had been blown up by the Turks—for the regular army to advance. From Kleidi, Matapas advanced to Koulakia (Chalastra), a large Greek village less than twenty miles from Thessaloniki. Other bands moved to Sindos, less than six miles from the city, and finally all bands under Mazarakis assembled in Sindos, waiting for orders to accept the city's surrender. With Bulgarian troops approaching from the northeast and east, the delay almost cost the city's surrender to the Bulgarians (Dakin 1966). Finally, the Royal Greek Army took possession of the city on October 26, 1912, with three thousand Bulgarian troops waiting at the outskirts.[3]

After October 1 events broke rapidly in other sectors of the Greek front. On October 10 Greek forces liberated Elassona, on October 12 Kozani, and on November 10 other Greek forces in Epirus had surrounded Ioannina. In the meantime, the Serbian army in the north, thanks to the Greek army in the south that immobilized considerable Turkish forces, occupied Durazzo and moved to the Adriatic Sea.

Constantine Mazarakis, second lieutenant of the Greek army. Courtesy of the
Museum of the Macedonian Struggle, Thessaloniki.

From the first days of the war the Greek navy predominated in the
Aegean Sea, denying the Turks entrance to the Aegean from the Dardanelles
(Straits), protecting the left flank of the Bulgarian army operating in Thrace
and eastern Macedonia by preventing Turkish reinforcements from crossing the Straits and landing on the Aegean shores of Thrace (Helmreich
1938). The Greek naval assistance enabled the Bulgarian army to advance
rapidly to Bunar-Hisar and Pirgos (now Burgas) and by November to the
Chataldja (Alexandroupolis) line outside Constantinople. The Bulgarian's
easy advance to near Constantinople, however, contributed to their own

misfortunes: missing the opportunity to advance as far west as possible, grabbing Macedonian territory, including the big prize, Thessaloniki, the age-old Bulgarian dream. Cholera added to their misfortunes, decimating more Bulgarian men than the Turkish guns.

On November 4, 1912, Turkey requested that the European powers intervene with the Balkan allies for an armistice. Bulgaria, Serbia, and Montenegro signed the armistice with Turkey on December 3. Greece did not enter into this agreement, continuing the sea war with Turkey and the siege of Ioannina, the capital and largest city of Epirus, which finally fell to the Greek army on February 23, 1913.

With Greece at war with Turkey, on December 16 a peace conference was organized in London with Bulgaria, Serbia, Montenegro, and Turkey participating. Greece sent representatives to attend the conference informally. It was March 22, 1913, when, finally, the European powers presented to the Turks and the Balkan allies the peace proposals: All Turkish territories (except Albania) west of the Enos-Maritsa-Ergene-Midia line were to be ceded to the allies; the Aegean islands were to be at the disposal of the European powers; Turkey was to renounce its interest in Crete; no war indemnity was to be demanded from Turkey, but the Balkan powers were to have a voice in the discussions of the International Commission for the regulation of the Ottoman debt (AHD 1979). The terms of the so-called Treaty of London were accepted by Turkey on March 30 and by the Balkan powers, including Greece, on April 21, with the preliminaries signed on March 31, 1913.

The Second Balkan War

It became apparent early in 1913 that the envisaged cooperation among the four Balkan allies could not be translated into a meaningful, profitable, and peaceful state of affairs. The spoils of victory were too enticing to be split peacefully among the three major partners. Moreover, one of the allies' proclivities for adventure were further embellished by displays of arrogance and brutal force. In the spring of 1913 the situation had changed even more rapidly than the conditions that had precipitated the first war. The Second Balkan War, and the fourth crisis of the Macedonian problem, were about to begin with a bang. In a desperate and futile effort to gain more territory in Macedonia, the Bulgarian commander in chief, General Savoff, anxious to occupy territory ceded to the Serbs and Greeks by the Treaty of London and to deploy his troops in an advantageous position for further adventures—also having been informed of the Greek-Serbian partition treaty[4]— without provocation attacked Greek and Serbian positions on June 19/20,

1913, precipitating the Second Balkan War. The Bulgarian King Ferdinand had approved the attack, hoping for Austria-Hungary's support. The Bulgarians demanded the Skopje-Monastir district, liberated by Serbia, and Thessaloniki, including western Macedonia, liberated by the Greek army and its Macedonian bands.

Bulgaria, not having learned a lesson in the 1903–1908 struggle, and still guided by an irredentist idea for a Greater Bulgaria, committed a "colossal" blunder for which it paid dearly (Poulton 1995, p. 74). Within a month of the unprovoked attack, Greeks and Serbs quickly defeated the larger Bulgarian army. On July 1 the Greek army quickly overcame the Bulgarian garrison at the outskirts of Thessaloniki and moved rapidly to liberate Serres, Drama, and Kavala, the three largest cities in eastern Macedonia. After considerable Serbian successes against the Bulgarians, Romania declared war on Bulgaria. On July 12 Turkey also entered the war against Bulgaria and quickly recaptured Adrianople.

After murderous fighting at Kilkis and Lahana, the Greek army dashed toward the north and occupied Sidirokastron and Stromnitsa. Following these decisive battles, the Greeks crashed the Bulgarians at the narrow passage of Kresna and Iraklia, aiming straight at the Bulgarian capital. Other units of the Greek army moved further eastward and liberated Alexandroupolis and Didymoteichon.

The Treaty of Bucharest

After a Romanian cease-fire proposal was submitted to the combatants on July 20, all four Second Balkan War participants gathered in Bucharest and agreed on a five-day armistice. The Treaty of Bucharest, ending the war, signed on August 10, 1913, by all the combatants of the Second Balkan War, brief as it was, settled, for a while at least, the Macedonian Question — and ended, at least for a while, the struggle for Macedonia — with Bulgaria signing away the major part of Macedonia to Greece and Serbia, relinquishing its age-old aspirations for a Greater Bulgaria. Under the terms of the Treaty of Bucharest, Greece was awarded the southern part (52 percent of Macedonia), Bulgaria a small part of northeastern Macedonia (9 percent), and Albania an even smaller part (1 percent).[5] Bulgaria was crushed, but in the end it managed to keep an important strip of territory from the River Maritsa to Alexandroupolis, giving the Bulgarians an outlet to the Aegean (Dakin 1966). The Serbs, who received 38 percent of Macedonia, called their section "South Serbia" [later *Vardarska Banovina*, a prefecture of the River Vardar (Axios)]. Serbia's section included the present-day area of the Former Yugoslav Republic of Macedonia (FYROM), part of Kosovo, and part of present-day southeastern Serbia. Among the options confronting Greece, the most difficult that arose at the conference was the fate of the city of Kavala. Austria-Hungary and Romania favored occupation of Kavala by Bulgaria. With France's and Germany's pressure, however, Kavala was finally given to Greece.

In the field of political and diplomatic endeavor during the struggle for Macedonia in the first two decades of the twentieth century, no one contributed more than Eleftherios Venizelos. Born in the Ottoman-held island of Crete, Venizelos claimed Greek nationality and transferred his political activities to Greece, where he was easily elected to the parliament, and on October 10, 1910, he became prime minister of Greece. The Balkan Wars following his elevation to the premiership were not designed by Venizelos, who believed that Greece was not adequately prepared for a war with Turkey. Even when the First Balkan War broke out in October 1912, Venizelos believed that the European powers would terminate the hostilities and force a diplomatic solution of the Turkish question (Dakin 1966, pp. 410–11, note 67, p. 442). Nonetheless, considered by others the "Architect of the Balkan Alliance," Venizelos played a pivotal role in the negotiations preceding the signing of the Bucharest Agreement, which granted Greece about 75 percent of historic Macedonia (52 percent of the liberated area). A skillful negotiator, he played off the European powers against one another, his superb diplomatic maneuvers in the Balkan Wars and in World War I having resulted in a successful outcome for Greece.

The trichotomy of Macedonia did not please the British foreign minister, Sir Edward Grey (Dakin 1966). He proposed revision of the treaty, strongly opposed by Greece, Serbia, and Romania. France and Germany also rejected Grey's proposal. In the end, Russia went along with France and Germany, with Austria-Hungary remaining uncommitted. Finally, England formally recognized the treaty in the spring of 1914.

Most analysts of Balkan foreign and military policy of the early twentieth century would agree that the signing of the Treaty of Bucharest was an event of great historical and political significance. Temporarily at least, it settled the differences among the four Balkan allies and pushed the Macedonian Question to obscurity (Institute for Balkan Studies 1990). It was a great event for Greece because it brought back a large part of Macedonia to Greece, all the way from the Pindus mountain range in the west to the River Nestos in the east. The end of the war and the withdrawal of the Bulgarian troops from sections of eastern Macedonia raised new hopes for cooperation and peace among the tired and devastated Greek Macedonian people, but the dreams were rapidly dashed. Peace was not to come soon in the land.

To the Greek people in central and eastern Macedonia and Thrace, temporarily "liberated" by the Bulgarians during the Balkan Wars, the real crisis was not the brief wars, but the Bulgarian brutalities against the Greek-speaking inhabitants and *Grecomans*. No one could restrain the Bulgarians from committing atrocities. A war was going on. Old humiliations from losing the previous crises, coupled with intense hate of the Greeks, constituted powerful motives for brutal retribution. French Prime Minister Georges Clemenceau, upon receiving reports of the atrocities in Macedonian districts occupied by the Bulgarians, declared in the French parliament: "We are witnessing the return of the years of Attila's hordes" (Vattis 2002). The British Captain Trapman wired the following from Macedonia to the newspaper *Daily Telegraph*: "Never before in the history of the world were examples given of such corrupt harshness like the one exhibited by the Bulgarians; and rarely in the History of the World a nation reached such a degree of committing slaughter, brutality, and lechery."

It was a terrible thing for people to be forced to abandon their homes, but that was a sufferable form of persecution in the Bulgarian-occupied areas of Macedonia and Thrace. First and foremost, their brutality was directed against the clergy, Greek leaders, and governing committees of villages and towns (Vattis 2002). They killed the metropolitan of Didymote-ichon and mutilated his body; occupied most of the dioceses and expelled the metropolitans of Serres, Stromnitsa, Komotini, Drama, and others; killed at least four priests and maimed others; closed Greek schools and forced the Greek parents to send their children to newly operational Bulgarian schools; exiled or imprisoned many Greek teachers and raped their women; and plundered villages and expropriated fortunes. Foreign observers estimated 40,000–50,000 inhabitants were killed in the River Strymonas basin alone.

It is doubtful whether anyone could accurately describe the atrocities suffered by the Greeks during the brief Bulgarian occupation of the lands east of Thessaloniki, all the way to the outskirts of Constantinople in 1912 and 1913. Such atrocities were mostly committed by organized, armed para-military bands (*komitadjides*), in cooperation with the regular Bulgarian army, with the intention of altering the demographic composition of the liberated areas. The Greek Orthodox Church reacted vigorously to the onslaught of the Greeks. Intense protests by the Patriarch in Constantinople to the European powers, the czar, and Russian church leaders, however, fell on deaf ears. Unrestrained it seems by the Bulgarian government, the armed hordes finished their macabre "dance" only when the Greek army pushed the Bulgarian army back to the River Nestos and terminated the fourth crisis of the Macedonian problem (AHD 1979; Museum of the Macedonian Struggle 1993).

The Bulgarians were not the only Balkan allies who perpetrated acts of violence in liberated areas of Macedonia, though their acts in the Vardar Province and in eastern Macedonia far exceeded in frequency and intensity the standards one might expect in a war where bilateral animosities surpassed the universal hate of the Ottomans. Accumulated age-old hatred brought out the worst in the enslaved people, who sought revenge against the perennial occupiers, the Ottomans and even against their allies. Greeks, for instance, burned the Bulgarian center in Kilkis and Bulgarian properties in Serres and Drama and forbade the use of the Bulgarian language (Poulton 1995, p. 75).

The Balkan Wars contributed to a temporary solution of a great historic controversy, the Macedonian Question, but did not solve it. The Treaty of Bucharest would soon be challenged and undermined by Bulgaria with its great appetite for more Macedonian land and later by the communist regimes of Yugoslavia and Bulgaria. With support from Austria-Hungary, the Bulgarians would still hold firmly the relay of the struggle for Macedonia, not as Macedonians, but as pure nationalist Bulgarians. Too many slavophones with pro–Hellenic sentiments were left in Bulgarian (Pirin) Macedonia and in Serbian Macedonia; too many slavophones of unspecified ethnicity were left in Greek Macedonia. Perhaps a final solution of the Macedonian problem could have been achieved if the Treaty of Bucharest had forced an exchange of populations among the three sections of Macedonia as was done later by the Treaty of Lausanne between Greece and Turkey. This approach might have resulted in pure Bulgarians or Bulgarian-oriented slavophones inhabiting Pirin Macedonia and Serb-oriented slavophones inhabiting the Vardar Province, with Greek Macedonia free from foreign-oriented slavophones. It would have been a painful but effective solution. After the Balkan Wars and World War I, many leaders, diplomats, groups, parties, and non-governmental organizations (NGOs) became involved with the problem, exacerbating it rather than solving it.

World War I

It soon became apparent after the fourth crisis ended in 1913 that the winds of war were approaching Macedonia again from the north with another crisis looming over the tired land. The new crisis, like the first in 1878, befell also on Greece, Greek Macedonia in particular, the result of diplomatic and military decisions of the European powers.

In spite of persistent diplomatic efforts by the *Entente Cordiale* countries of World War I (France, England and Russia), Bulgaria, the "Prussia of the Balkans" (Miller 1975), joined the Central Powers (Germany and Austria-Hungary) in 1915. Even the carrot offered to the Bulgarians by the entente at Greece's expense —concession of territory in eastern Macedonia, including Kavala— did not entice the Bulgarians to join the entente alliance. The Bulgarian irredentist aspirations were focusing on an even larger Macedonian territory than that offered by the entente, including the big prize, Thessaloniki, if the Central Powers won the war.

By September 1916, Bulgarian and German troops occupied Greek eastern Macedonia and annexed it to the Bulgarian Kingdom. Three years after the atrocities of 1913, a new wave of terrorization, more brutal than those of the past, began in the occupied territory as soon as it fell into Bulgarian hands.[6] Believing in a German victory, this time the Bulgarians decided to ethnically cleanse the Greeks of the occupied area once and for all, rapidly changing its demographic composition. Eastern Macedonia's Bulgarization by the unrestrained Bulgarians was so brutal that the Inter Allied Commission in Eastern Macedonia (Part I, London, 1919) reported the following from eastern Macedonia:

- 80,000 Greeks were kidnapped, mostly men and young girls 15–25 years. Most of the men never returned.
- 20,000 men were executed or died in prison in Macedonia or Bulgaria.
- 20,000 men were drafted for hard labor in Bulgaria. Only about 4,000 returned home.
- 30,000 people died in Macedonia from starvation and disease, mostly women and children.
- 2,000 boys under fourteen were snatched from their parents and transferred to Bulgaria to be educated in Bulgarism (Vattis 2002).

The Inter Allied Commission also reported the following numbers by city:

- Kavala: Population 69,600; only 8,000 remained.
- Serres: Population 35,000; only 5,793 were found by the committee.
- Drama: Population 28,000; only 12,000 were found. About 8,000 women and children died from starvation.[7]

The conditions in eastern Macedonia were so hideous and detestable because of the Bulgarian terrorization that even many Bulgarians protested, and the Bulgarian press wrote: "The actions [in Macedonia] stigmatize our Bulgarian civilization." Butler, a British correspondent, cabled London from Kavala in October 1918: "The rapes of young girls are numerous and it is impossible to report the hair-raising details" (Vattis 2002).

The options confronting Greece in 1916, with the war going on in the Balkans, were essentially two: fight on the side of the *Entente Cordiale* against the Central Powers, whose military efforts had been strengthened by Turkey and Bulgaria, as Prime Minister Elefterios Venizelos desired, or remain strictly neutral, as King Constantine advocated. After a tumultuous period of internal strife and disagreements, including a revolutionary movement against the Greek government by pro–Venizelist officers in Thessaloniki and the king's abdication, Greece finally declared war on the Central Powers on July 2, 1917 (Palmer 1977).

Before the Germans were finally defeated in 1918, the allied forces, including units of the Greek army, broke the Bulgaro-German front in Macedonia, and the Greek army liberated eastern Macedonia and returned it to the Greek Kingdom. After the armistice with Greece signed on September 29, 1918, King Ferdinand was dethroned and an entente friend, Malinov, became prime minister of Bulgaria. On July 25, 1920, the entire western Thrace and a sizable part of eastern Thrace were ceded to Greece by the Treaty of Sèvres. Even with a second defeat and humiliation within five years, however, Bulgaria continued claiming autonomy for Macedonia or, at least, annexation of the land around the cities of Drama and Kavala.

Greece's northern borders were by then protected by international treaties such as the Treaty of Bucharest (1913), ending the Second Balkan War, and the Treaty of Neuilly, ending hostilities between Bulgaria and the allies after World War I.[8] The Treaty of Neuilly allowed for a voluntary and reciprocal emigration between Greece and Bulgaria organized under the League of Nations' supervision. After the signing, 52,000 slavophones, considering themselves Bulgarians, moved voluntarily to Bulgaria with their fortunes in Greek Macedonia compensated by the Greek government. The slavophones that remained in Greece declared Greek ethnicity. About 46,000 Greeks and Greek-oriented slavophones left Bulgaria for Greece.[9] Many slavophones refused to leave Greece for an ethnic identity other than Greek. Many dissatisfied slavophones living in Greece considered themselves nothing else but Greeks (Ladas 1932; Pentzopoulos 1962). The Treaty of Neuilly, together with the Treaty of Lausanne (1923), stipulating a forced exchange of minorities between Greece and Turkey, drastically changed the ethnological composition of Greek Macedonia, which, under the Ottomans, was a polyglot conglomerate of people of many religions, speaking many languages and dialects.[10] The League of Nations published the following figures on the population of Greek Macedonia in 1926 after the exchanges were completed (Society for Macedonian Studies 1994):

Greeks	1,341,000	88.8 percent
Bulgarians	77,000	5.1 percent
Muslims	2,000	0.1 percent
Others (mainly Jews)	91,000	6.0 percent
Total	1,511,000	

These figures were closely corroborated by the Greek census of 1928 with 81,984 persons registered as Slav-speaking, most living in western Macedonia (Zahariadis 1994). According to the same census, 88.1 percent of the population in Greek Macedonia was Greek (Barker 1950).

E. Morgenthau, who visited Greece in 1928, wrote in his book *I Was Sent to Greece*: "After the two population exchanges, there is no Macedonian problem, and Greek Macedonia is entirely Greek."

World War I ended and with that the fifth crisis of the Macedonian problem, with Greece traumatized but victorious, and the Bulgarians defeated again, temporarily having lost momentum for a Greater Bulgaria. The Macedonian problem was solved for Greece by the Treaty of Bucharest, but not for Bulgaria and Yugoslavia. After World War I Greece never demanded any territory from its northern neighbors. The irredentist nationalist groups in Bulgaria like IMRO, however, never really accepted the Treaty of Bucharest and never stopped agitating for Macedonian autonomy or Macedonia's annexation by Bulgaria. Raising the Macedonian issue over and over in the ninety years after World War I, Slav chauvinists were determined to create problems, instigating new Macedonian crises. The outbreak of earthshaking events elsewhere that resulted in the rise of communism in Russia, and eventually in the Balkans, was to bring the Macedonian problem repeatedly back to the front. The pervasive interconnections between the Balkan communists and those of Russia impelled Greece to continue the struggle to support its age-old rights on Macedonia over and over, even after the fall of communism in Europe.

3

The Rise of Communism and the Macedonian Question

Τα γιγνόμενα τα τε γενησόμενα
τοις γεγονόσι συνήρτηται
(Today's events and those of the future
are related to those of the past)
—*Plutarch*

The Interim Period (1918–1940)

Bulgaria

After the signing of the Treaty of Lausanne in 1923, Greek diplomacy's main aim was to protect the country's independence and territorial integrity. That was not an easy task. Twice-defeated Bulgaria never abandoned its dreams and plans for Greece's Macedonia and western Thrace. Disregarding the well-known fact that 52,000 slavophones voluntarily left Greece for Bulgaria according to the Treaty of Neuilly, and the majority of those remaining in Greece harbored Hellenic sentiments, Bulgaria, as was repeatedly demonstrated during the struggle for Macedonia, insisted that all slavophones in Greek Macedonia must be granted minority status as Bulgarians, not as Macedonians. Though a misleading measure, Bulgaria always considered language as the criterion of nationality (Koliopoulos 1995).

There seems to be little doubt of repeated Bulgarian attempts to Bulgarize Macedonia's inhabitants or annex Macedonia or parts of it between 1878 and 1918. But the Bulgarians never really intended to use the name "Macedonia" or create a false Macedonian nation. To the Bulgarians and the Greeks alike, there never existed a Macedonian nation embracing all groups living in Macedonia.[1] If anything, it was only the city-state of ancient Macedonians, all of Greek descent. Apprehending Macedonia's name for chauvinist purposes would come much later, in the 1940s, as a result of Stalin's strong-arm tactics on Yugoslavia, aiming to destabilize capitalist regimes in the Balkans. During the period between the two world wars, Bulgaria struggled to heal its wounds without admitting that the Macedonian Question had been resolved by the Treaty of Bucharest and the Treaty of Neuilly. It never stopped dreaming that territories ceded to Serbia and Greece in 1913 would eventually be annexed by Bulgaria. If the Bulgarians had accepted the meaning of the Treaty of Bucharest, it would no longer be a Macedonian Question, complicating relations among neighbors for almost a century after Bucharest. Greece's northern neighbors, Bulgaria and Serbia (later Yugoslavia), never really accepted the unequal but correct trichotomy of Macedonia by the Treaty of Bucharest. They never accepted historical facts: that the past in Macedonia is Greece's present, and its present depends on the Macedonian past, on history, and in this case, on the Hellenic Macedonian history.

Because of two consecutive military defeats and the expenditures for three wars in a decade, for its part Bulgaria remained bogged down in economic stagnation for a long time. Immediately after 1918, the Bulgarian leaders in general, and Prime Minister Stamboliiski in particular, concentrated on building the sinuses of power and solving the pressing economic problems of the defeated and financially depleted country. The premier, temporarily ignoring IMRO's *komitadjides*, pursued a policy of rapprochement with Greece and Serbia (Vattis 2002).

Bulgaria's attempted reconciliation with its neighbors notwithstanding, it became painfully apparent again in 1919 that, even without government support, IMRO was still alive and kicking. Reorganized on a new platform, it secretly engaged in planning and recruiting new members within Bulgaria and outside the country. More tangibly, undeterred by the collapse of their dreams and the mounting world opinion against their motives and methods, IMRO's irredentist conspirators, who led many Bulgarians to fight and perish during the Macedonian Struggle and in the Second Balkan War, promulgated new ideas, resurrected old slogans, and created new ones to attract young people into their fold, especially in foreign countries such as the United States, Canada, and Australia. New organizations sprang up, and IMRO subcommittees with new financial resources began vicious propaganda against Greece (Vattis 2002). It is uncertain how many men and women joined these committees outside Bulgaria at the outset and how many members remain faithful and active today; but one thing is certain: it never occurred to IMRO's leaders to pursue stability in the Balkans according to the 1913 and 1919 treaties. This was particularly true of Bulgaria's endeavor to enunciate and practice rapprochement with its neighbors being greatly jeopardized by IMRO's leaders' fanaticism and intransigence. Beginning in 1919 many small organizations known as "brotherhoods" were formed in Bulgaria from native Bulgarians and Bulgarians who had left Greece and Serbia during the Balkan wars (Vattis 2002). Camouflaged as philanthropic organizations, the brotherhoods were IMRO's clandestine auxiliary groups. Unrestrained by the government, and generously financed from inside the country and abroad, IMRO and its small groups plunged again into action involving recruitment in the country and abroad for the brotherhoods. IMRO also dispatched agents abroad to attend conferences, propagandize for Macedonian autonomy, support its nationalist adventures, assist the *komitadjides* with men, materiel, and funds, and influence the direction of the country toward a policy favorable to their irredentist ideas.

Government restrictions, adverse world opinion, and three defeats from 1870 to 1918 did not curtail IMRO's plans or deter its activities. On the basis of available sources (Vattis 2002), it is now known that the territories in Greek and Yugoslav Macedonia, considered by Bulgarian nationalists as belonging to Bulgaria, were clandestinely divided by IMRO into six districts: Thessaloniki, Serres, Drama, Stromnitsa, Skopje, and Monastir (Bitola), each district under a super-secret administrative committee. All six committees were guided secretly from the center (Sofia) by absolutely trusted special agents. One of those secret agents was Alexopoulos, who later, during the German and Bulgarian occupation of Greece, joined Kaltsev's terrorist organization Ochrana and several Slavomacedonian communist organizations closely cooperating with the Greek communists.[2] Meanwhile, *komitadjides* were recruited with full government knowledge from Bulgarians who were born in Macedonia and emigrated to Bulgaria when the revolutionary committees began losing the Macedonian struggle. Organization, grouping, and training took place in Bulgaria, from which the *komitadjides* were dispatched to Greek and Yugoslav Macedonia (Vattis 2002).

Below are excerpts of IMRO's 1919 charter:

> IMRO aspires and works for a free and independent Macedonia with its border framework and its conversion into an independent political unit, an equal member of the future Balkan Federation. The independent Macedonian state will be formed on the basis of complete ethnic, political, civic, and educational equality of all people [of Macedonia].

To realize these goals, IMRO must set up a General Revolutionary Organization to encompass the people of the three sections of Macedonia (Serbian, Greek, Bulgarian), including the Macedonians who emigrated to other countries; organize, educate, and prepare the people toward a General National Revolution; unite all the ethnic Macedonian forces and attract all persons and groups, irrespective of ethnicity, sex, religion, and citizenship, all people that accept IMRO's ideals, principles, and methods; establish close relations with all ethnic revolutionary organizations and committees in the Balkans that support the idea of an independent Macedonia. IMRO promises to work hard for freedom of education and language for all ethnic groups in Macedonia and for land distribution among the peasants. Because of the projected goals, this organization [IMRO] is a revolutionary organization. It acts revolutionarily, but it also acts by the law, depending on the place and circumstances. IMRO will attain these goals by the following means: propaganda to wake up the ethnic and revolutionary consciousness of the Macedonian masses; and preparation and education for the ethnic revolution. The propaganda will be organized both by legal and illegal means and by arming the Macedonian masses for a successful general ethnic uprising [Vattis 2002].

Its irredentist ideas and clandestine actions, "legal and illegal," aided IMRO to emerge stronger than ever as a reclothed politico-revolutionary constellation in Bulgaria and abroad. Because of its super-nationalist ideas and goals for Macedonia, IMRO echoed the public sentiment in Bulgaria, while opposing the official peace-inspiring government intentions. Its influence spread rapidly among the country's nationalist elements for which IMRO was a perfect outlet for their frustrations, capable of embracing the nationalist aspirations of the thrice-defeated Bulgarians within fifteen years. Its strong influence following its regeneration in the early 1920s eventually impelled the government to alter its cautious foreign policy, adopting many of IMRO's extreme positions on the Macedonian problem.

With IMRO in the background, no solution of the ongoing Macedonian Question between Greece and Bulgaria could have been attained since slavophones with Bulgarian ethnicity remained in Greek Macedonia and Greeks and slavophone Greek Macedonians remained in Bulgaria. A radical solution of this problem could only have been accomplished by forceful population exchanges. This was not done by the Treaty of Neuilly signed by Greece and Bulgaria on November 27, 1919, which stipulated a voluntary emigration on both sides. In retrospect, two interesting questions must be asked: Would enforcing a compulsory population emigration between the two countries have perhaps resolved the Macedonian Question? Was the decision of the Bulgarophile or neutral Slav-speakers to remain in Greece after the signing of the Treaty of Neuilly their own or were they coerced to remain in Greece as a Slav-speaking, Bulgarian-oriented nucleus for future political reasons? No one can risk an answer to the first question. To address the second question, it is important to look carefully at the question's context because the answer may lie in IMRO's ultranationalism and its clandestine decisions and actions to impose its revolutionary views on the Bulgarian government and its people.

Serbia

During the long Ottoman occupation of the Balkans, many pure Greek settlements were on friendly terms with the Serbs. Like the Greeks, the Serbs never accepted the Turkish occupation, repeatedly revolting to obtain their independence. The relations between the Greek people and the Serbs continued to be friendly, with the Greeks considering the Serbs close supporters during difficult periods of history. Deprived of Russian support, the Serbian government had no quarrels with Greece. Weakened by numerous problems (internecine strife; the problem with Bosnia, Herzegovina, and Novi Pazar, coveted by Austria-Hungary; the massive Albanian migration into Kosovo, the old Serbia), the small country turned its attention away from Macedonia. The first strain between free Greece and autonomous Serbia occurred during Charilaos Trikoupis's premiership. His attempts to strengthen Greece's relations with Serbia were met by Belgrade's outrageous demands: Serbia must be granted a zone of influence beyond its frontiers, including Korytsa, Kastoria, Monastir, and the northern section of the Thessaloniki *vilayet*.

The first Serbian attempt to proselytize the slavophone inhabitants of Macedonia began in 1887 in the Kosovo *vilayet* and north of the Perlepe-Krushevo-Stromnitsa line. Later, the Serbian attempts spread to Monastir, Thessaloniki, Serres, and Halkidiki. By 1889 there seemed to be little doubt of Serbia's renewed interest in Macedonia, as it began pursuing an outlet to the Aegean through Thessaloniki. Serbia appointed Serb teachers and priests and performed the liturgy in the Serbian language. Serbia's interest in Macedonia intensified in 1912 with Albania's declaration of independence (Giannakos 1992).

There was, however, a remarkable contradiction in the methods used by Serbs and Bulgarians to proselytize Macedonia's slavophone inhabitants. Bulgaria employed violent methods as far south in Macedonia as possible. Most of the slavophones joining the Exarchate also converted to Bulgarism, and almost never returned to Hellenism. In contrast, the Serbs employed milder means of persuasion without severing the country's ties with the Patriarchate. To Greece's mild protests and attempted rapprochement on the subject of slavophone indoctrination the Serbian prime minister replied bluntly that his country had the obligation to proselytize the

slavophone inhabitants of Macedonia with the same zeal whether they were
Serbs or pure Bulgarians (Vattis 2002).

Underlying the continuing demands for a zone of influence in Greek
Macedonia lay Serbia's determination to begin a serious Serbianization
process outside its frontiers laid down by the Treaty of Bucharest. From 1913
to 1915, for instance, all Slav-speakers in Vardar Macedonia (South Serbia)
were characterized as Serbs. Serbia also made great efforts to move Serbs
to Macedonia to Serbianize the local slavophone population. Thus, fifty
thousand Serb soldiers and gendarmes, including 4,200 families from Serbia, were relocated in Vardar Macedonia to expedite Serbianization. All
inhabitants were forced to change their names. For example, Stankov
became Stankovic, and Atanasov became Atanasovic (Kofos 1974). But
Serbia's efforts to Serbianize the uncommitted slavophones in occupied
Macedonia met with great difficulties, because the local Slavs remained
stubbornly attached to Bulgarian nationalism and the Exarchate (Palmer
and King 1971). Also, the slavophone inhabitants in areas claimed by Serbia spoke a dialect resembling the Bulgarian dialect, making communication between teachers and people difficult. The imposition of teachers and
priests on the slavophones of Hellenic ethnicity (*Grecomans*) was more
difficult than the imposition of Bulgarian Exarchists who were recognized
by the sultan and protected by the Ottomans. Interestingly, the Serbian government in 1913 to 1915 was struggling to Serbianize, not Macedonize, the
Vardar Province's inhabitants.[3]

There were other reasons for the failure of Serbia's efforts. The building of Bulgarian schools had been agreed upon by the sultan and the European powers, including Russia. Similar agreement between the Ottomans
and the Serbs did not exist. Also, until 1896, Serbia had no support from
Russia, because Serbia had signed an agreement with Austria, a country
frequently at loggerheads with Russia. After the Greco-Turkish War of 1897,
however, the sultan, succumbing to renewed Russian interest in Serbia and
Russia's increased pressure, granted extensive privileges to the Serbs in the
Ochris-Monastir district and in Thessaloniki (Vattis 2002).

Greek-Serb relations improved from 1897 on because of Bulgarian
pressure on both the Serbs and the Greeks. During the Balkan Wars and
World War I, Greece remained a true and trusted friend and ally of Serbia,
despite obvious Serbian aspirations on Greek Macedonia and especially
Thessaloniki. The Serbian ambitions for Macedonia, and occasional occurrences of anti–Hellenic propaganda, distressed but did not mar the pro–Serbian feelings of the Greek people. During Greece's neutrality in the first two
years of World War I, Greece allowed Serbia to use the port of Thessaloniki
for supplying its army fighting the Bulgarians and the Germans. In 1915,
when the Serbian resistance collapsed under the overwhelming military

pressure by Bulgarians, Germans, and Austrians, Greece offered to Serbia the island of Corfu as a base to assemble and rearm the remnants of its army and as a temporary seat for the Serbian king, his entourage, and the Serbian government in exile. From Corfu the Serbian army returned to Serbia, counterattacked, brought victory to the Serbs, and reinstated the government in Belgrade.[4]

Whereas the overwhelming majority of the Serbian people harbored sincere friendly sentiments toward the Greek people, the Serbian political leadership pursued a loggerheads policy toward Greece before and after World War II, never satisfied with the part of Macedonia it had received from the Treaty of Bucharest. Many Greek families, for instance, suffered greatly when the Serbian army occupied Krushevo from 1912 to 1913, because they refused to give Slavic names to their children (Brown 2000). Utilizing the flimsiest of excuses while a guest in Corfu, the Serbian government hardened its line even further and sought to convince the French commander general on the Balkan front, Marshall Saraij, to take away the political administration of Thessaloniki from Greece, transferring it to Serbia (Vattis 2002). To give away its sovereign rights over Thessaloniki — a significant part of Greece's history and a major coordinating center for the whole Balkan Peninsula — would have had disastrous consequences for Greece with respect to other sections and cities of Macedonia and to the Greek economy and pride. The French general turned down the Serbian proposal.

To this familiar, vexing problem between the two countries must be added the Serbian government's ingratitude that continued even after the end of World War I despite the sacrifices of Greek soldiers for the liberation of Serbia from the Bulgarian occupation. To gain favor with Italy during the distribution of the war's spoils from the defeated Austria-Hungary, for instance, Serbia did not even hesitate to cooperate with the Italians, who emboldened the Serbian aspirations on Macedonia and Thessaloniki (Vattis 2002).

As the Ottoman Empire continued to decay, and the Habsburg Empire was dissolved during the second decade of the twentieth century, the South Slavs, including the Serbs, decided to unite, and the State of Yugoslavia was born on December 1, 1918. The original agreement to bring the Serbs, Croats, and Slovenes together to form the Kingdom of the Yugoslavs, known as the Corfu Declaration (the agreement was signed on the Greek island of Corfu), did not include Macedonia (Dragnich 1992). In fact, even after 1915, the Serbian government continued to embark on its ambitious program of Serbianization of the Slav-speakers of Yugoslav Macedonia (Banac 1984).

Ironically, the Yugoslav demands on Greece during the years between the two major wars were heavier than those made by Bulgaria. Often allied

with the Bulgarians, the Yugoslavs demanded from Greece (a) a free operation zone in the Thessaloniki harbor with complete Yugoslav domination
and zone administration, (b) sovereign concession on the Greek land along
the lines of the railroad connecting Thessaloniki with Gevgeli (a town by
the Greek-Yugoslav border), and (c) characterization of the Greek Macedonian slavophones as a Serb minority (not as a Macedonian minority).
Greece granted the first two demands to Yugoslavia (Vattis 2002).

As if these demands did not infringe strongly enough on Greece's sovereignty, the Belgrade elite launched an unbelievably slanderous campaign
against Greece and its people. For almost ten years, the Yugoslavs, without
provocation, circulated reports, magazines, and fliers overflowing with
anti–Hellenic propaganda, stigmatizing the Greek army for cowardice and
the Greek people as incapable peddlers and untruthful merchants (Vattis
2002). In retrospect, it is very difficult even to guess why a government
showed so much ingratitude and bad faith for its neighbor, in spite of the
well-known fact that it was spared the humiliation of a major defeat by
being sheltered on a Greek island to compose itself and reorganize its army
before returning to reclaim Serbia. And, as we shall see in subsequent chapters, the official Yugoslavia became even more inimical to Greece, plotting
in the early 1940s to dismember its neighbor to the south by the secession
of parts or of the entire Greek Macedonia.

Communism and the Struggle
for Macedonia — Early Attempts

The end of World War I found Russia defeated and under a totalitarian Bolshevik system. Foundering economically, the new communist system was immersed in immense political, military, and economic problems.
By 1920, its right-hand authority and executive group, Comintern, had not
yet become involved in the struggle for Macedonia. Because of the ensuing
initial weakness of the Bolshevik system, the Balkans received low prior-
ity, and the Macedonian problem was temporarily ignored. It did not take
long, however, for the imperial policies of the czars to resurface reclothed
in new red garments to participate in the struggle for Macedonia. The communist slogan for internationalism appeared to be compatible with Russia's expansionism and its plans to enlarge the Soviet Empire with new
countries and satellites. A "Free and Independent Macedonia" would qualify as a Bolshevik satellite in the Balkans under a Bulgarian or Yugoslav
umbrella, especially because Macedonia was strategically situated at the
crossroads between Europe and Asia, an excellent promontory to dominate
the Aegean and eastern Mediterranean (Woodhouse 1976).

Toward the beginning of the 1920s, the old Russian nationalist sentiments, reinforced by radical Bolshevik ideas and Comintern's unprecedented international manipulations, plunged again into Balkan politics to increase the Soviet Union's influence. The Communist Party of Bulgaria (CPB), the strongest in the Balkans in the early years of communism, was to be Comintern's right-hand instrument to spearhead the efforts on the Macedonian Question under the eyes of the noncommunist Bulgarian government. Drawing on the lessons of the Macedonian Struggle of 1904–1908, and the unprovoked Bulgarian aggression on its allies in 1913, the Soviets inaugurated in 1921 a policy to accomplish a Balkan fragmentation as it was conceived by Leon Trotsky and commissar Dmitri Manuilski and — what the Bulgarians had failed to achieve during the first five crises of the Macedonian problem — an autonomous Macedonia.

To reach this goal, the Soviets engaged four weapons, much more sophisticated and powerful than those previously used by Bulgarians: Comintern (an adjunct of the Soviet foreign policy), the small but dynamic Balkan communist parties, the Ilinden "uprising of the Slavs" as a moral weapon, and the Balkan Communist Federation (BCF).[5] Assiduously cultivating BCF's irredentist aspirations for an autonomous Macedonia (to be followed by secession into Bulgaria), the Soviets cleverly engaged the fledgling Balkan communist parties, including the Communist Party of Greece (known by its Greek initials as the KKE, *Kommounistiko Komma Elladas*), to attain the age-old goal, a warm-sea port in the Aegean, a goal the czars had failed to accomplish. The CPB was therefore ordered by the Communist Party of the Soviet Union (CPSU) to assume leadership in the Balkans under Comintern in the ongoing struggle to achieve an autonomous Macedonia (Averoff-Tossizza 1978). With the benefit of hindsight into how communism operated, it takes little imagination to figure out that Bulgaria's endorsement as a suitor for Macedonia would not last forever.

While actively engaged in promoting its revolutionary policies outside the Bulgarian government in the early 1920s, the CPB, whose platform on the Macedonian issue coincided with BCF's line, scored a great victory at the BCF's Sixth Congress in Moscow (Zotiadis 1961). The Bulgarian communist leaders, with Moscow's support, were able to secure a majority vote on a proposal for an "autonomous and independent Macedonia and Thrace" written by Kolarov, CPB's general secretary (Averoff-Tossizza 1978; Kofos 1964). Looking back over the years from the early 1920s to 1870, it was the first politically motivated mention of Macedonia, the land of King Philip and Alexander the Great, as an autonomous and independent state. The proposal, a fantastic conglomeration of illusions and a mosaic of historic inaccuracies, included the following: "Macedonia (Greek, Serb, Bulgarian) and Thrace (Turkish, Greek, Bulgarian) are inhabited by people who are neither Greeks, Serbs, Bulgarians, or Albanians but Macedonians, with Macedonian consciousness (Macedonian race); and the Thracians with Thracian consciousness (Thracian race). Consequently, these people have unalienable rights for autonomy and independence" (Nikoloudis 2002). In keeping with the pluralism of views expressed at the congress, and without instructions from the KKE Central Committee, the Greek representative Nikos Sargopoulos also voted for the Bulgarian proposal, immediately ratified by Comintern (Averoff-Tossizza 1978; Vattis 2002).

BCF's decision at its Sixth Congress, spelling Greece's future territorial mutilation, caused international shock and forced the Seventh BCF Congress in Moscow in July 1924, under Comintern's direction, to change the autonomy-for-Macedonia platform. While broad generalizations are always hazardous, especially regarding secretive Soviet policies, available information today suggests that Stalin, whose seal was on Comintern's functions and goals, was determined to create a new "Macedonian" nation, a new satellite in the Balkans (Kouzinopoulos 1999, from Dimitrov's diary). An inclination of what was to happen was amply demonstrated during Comintern's Fifth Congress in Moscow held concurrently with the Seventh BCF Congress. Russian comrades, in keeping with Stalin's wishes, suddenly dropped the autonomy-for-Macedonia platform and proposed formation of an "Independent Macedonian State" in the Balkans. Not a sincere departure from previous plans for Macedonia, it was a well-thought-out strategy to avoid alarming the Balkan communist parties, mollify their suspicions that the Soviets were in a sinister conspiracy with the CPB to harm Greek Macedonia and Yugoslav Macedonia, placate the noncommunist elements in Macedonia, and prevent adverse European reaction to the autonomy-for-Macedonia concept. The KKE delegates Pouliopoulos and Maximos voted again in favor of the new proposal. Unlike the Bulgarian and Greek delegates, the Yugoslav representative of the Communist Party of Yugoslavia (CPY) voted against the new platform. The CPY never accepted Macedonia's autonomy outside its boundaries and never lobbied for a "Macedonian" nation outside Yugoslavia (Papaconstantinou 1992).

Assumptions expressed elsewhere (Poulton 1995, p. 98) that the Greeks, Bulgarians, and Serbs unjustifiably blamed the Comintern line for inventing the idea of a Macedonian nation are refuted by revelations in Dimitrov's diary, and by the proceedings of BCF's Sixth Congress and Comintern's Fifth Congress in Moscow (see also the section titled "Bulgarian-Yugoslav Rivalry Over Macedonia," Chapter 4). The Soviet-dictated decisions of Comintern's Fifth Congress were summarized as follows: "Because the Macedonian people are suppressed by the Greek, Bulgarian, and Yugoslav bourgeoisie, the communist parties of the three countries, according to the Marxist-Leninist principles for self-determination ... must help the Macedonian people struggling for freedom and self-rule to obtain their independence.... After obtaining their independence, the Macedonian people will have the right to select by the ballot the way to be governed" (Vattis 2002).[6]

By 1928 new conditions emerged that prompted the Soviet Union and Comintern to reevaluate the Balkan situation and refocus on the Macedonian Question. In an effort to avoid friction among the southern Balkan states, especially between Bulgaria and Yugoslavia, and promote the spread of communism, the Soviet Union named for the first time Macedonia's Slav-speaking inhabitants as a "Macedonian ethnicity" and allowed formation of the Communist Party of Macedonia (CPM) (Vlasidis 1997). With these initiatives, Stalin abandoned the Soviet Union's previous position of forming a Balkan communist federation, with an autonomous Macedonia included, and adopted the doctrine of self-determination of the "Macedonian ethnicity" as a first step toward its elevation to an independent and united nation-state. Contrary to its ultranationalist policies, IMRO undertook the task of promoting the new Soviet policies on Macedonia in cooperation with the CPB. IMRO's new position, however, involving cooperation with the communists, jeopardized its standing with the Bulgarian government, a decision that spelled its approaching doom. The noncommunist Balkan governments declared IMRO's position illegal and unleashed a wave of persecutions against it.

Surprisingly, even in the face of such a favorable turn of events on the Macedonian issue — the naming of Slav-speaking inhabitants of Macedonia (mostly Bulgarians) as a separate "Macedonian ethnicity"— the Yugoslav communists rejected the Soviet plan. The pre–Tito communist leaders of Yugoslavia were not ready to embrace the idea of a separate Macedonian nation, insisting that only linguistic differences existed among Macedonia's people. Ironically, it was Tito later who used the label "Macedonian" to create a new nationality, contrasting the "Macedonians" with Greeks, Bulgarians, and Serbs (Giannakos 1992). On the seesaw of World War II and the Balkan partisan wars of liberation against the occupation forces, blatant falsification of history was very common to "solve" ethnic problems.

Just as the Soviet Union continued interfering in Bulgaria's foreign policy and in the struggle for Macedonia in the 1920s through the emerging CPB (under Vasil Kolarov and Giorgi Dimitrov), IMRO became a clandestine state within the official Bulgarian state, with Stamboliiski's government unable to control it (Vattis 2002). Not surprisingly, the premier's reluctance to support IMRO contributed to his fall from power on June 8, 1923, the rise to power of a dictator supported by IMRO, and Stamboliiski's execution by firing squad.[7] IMRO's ups and downs continued till May 1924, but its adherence to the autonomy-for-Macedonia concept remained unaltered till 1928 (Vlasidis 1997).[8]

After Stamboliiski's execution, political agitations, anarchy, and IMRO's terrorism increased in Bulgaria, with IMRO stepping up its terrorist raids into Greek and Yugoslav Macedonia in 1923. Southwest Bulgaria was practically in IMRO's hands. But it was eventually worn out by internal friction among autonomists, annexationists, and new IMRO communists, a condition that eventually degenerated into an internal civil war. More than four hundred people died from 1924 to 1934. The 1934 one-year dictatorship established by progressive intellectuals dealt such a heavy blow to IMRO that it never really recovered.

In the wake of severe pressures by emerging Balkan strategic alliances and the Soviet Union's blatant interference with the Macedonian Question, IMRO approached the Soviet Union, the Balkan communist parties, and rival forces within the Bulgarian committees (Federalists, etc.). After hard negotiations, IMRO's Central Committee declared that its aim was the formation of an independent Macedonia within a union of Balkan democratic states, a sharp departure from its pre–World War I autonomy-for-Macedonia platform (Rothchild 1959), and this goal could only be realized with the cooperation of all the Balkan people and the "progressive" forces. Further negotiations between IMRO's Alexandrov and CPB's Kolarov sealed the agreement and "wiped out" the differences between the CPB and the nationalist IMRO on Macedonia's future (Barker 1950). From 1924 to 1927, the ultranationalist IMRO had practically become another Soviet Union satellite without a country.[9]

Within the framework of the decisions of Comintern's Fifth Congress was also the decision to win over IMRO in the struggle for Macedonian autonomy. BCF did not have to work hard for this. Considerable cooperation already existed between Comintern's and BCF's communist leaders with the nationalist IMRO. Notwithstanding their ideological differences, the common goal for autonomy or independence of Macedonia tied the three organizations together, impelling them to cooperate. The extreme ethnic Macedonian views of IMRO's leaders did not contradict Comintern's long-term Balkan policies. Moreover, both Comintern and BCF needed IMRO's strong arm and its penchant for terrorism in the field (Vlasidis 1997).

Early KKE Involvement with the Macedonian Question (1920–1940)

At this point, we must go back chronologically to review briefly the involvement of the Communist Party of Greece (KKE) with the Macedonian problem and its policies on the issue. It was founded in 1918 in Piraeus as the "Socialist Party of Greece." In 1920, after the success of the Bolshevik revolution in Russia, the small party replaced in its name the word *socialist* with the word *communist*. During the same year, the party of the Greek proletariat was awarded full membership in the Comintern (Averoff-Tossizza 1978).

The first attempt to press the fledgling KKE into forming an "Independent Macedonia" occurred in 1921 during the Third Comintern Congress in Moscow (Averoff-Tossizza 1978). The leader of the Greek delegation, Ioannis Georgiadis, general secretary of the KKE, was approached by Kolarov, leader of the Bulgarian delegation, and asked to opt for a united and independent Macedonia. Georgiadis took up the matter with Lenin, pointing out that Kolarov's proposal for a united and independent Macedonia encompassing all three sections of Macedonia would mutilate Greece and offend the Greek people, adversely affecting the party's growth. With cold civility, but cold-hearted irony, Lenin explained to Georgiadis how the BCF and Comintern were planning Greece's territorial dismemberment: Macedonia's autonomy had been decided by Comintern and no one could change the decision; the task was to be achieved with Bulgaria's initiative (Averoff-Tossizza 1978; Vattis 2002).

Georgiadis, who correctly discerned a pattern of anti–Hellenic Slavic machinations at Greek Macedonia's expense, depressingly similar to the age-old Panslavic ambitions, opposed Kolarov's idea. He was then dismissed from the KKE when he returned to Athens (Averoff-Tossizza 1978). After his dismissal, Georgiadis declared that he was convinced of the unpatriotic motives of his party. On the face of it, Georgiadis's sobering assessment of the Macedonian problem did not alter the pro–Bulgarian position of the KKE's leadership. Similar proposals for Macedonian autonomy were submitted by Kolarov at BCF's Fourth Congress in Sofia, but were tabled.[10]

The Macedonian Question, a complex issue involving several smaller issues, greatly influenced the mentality and development of the Communist Party of Greece, and its anti–Hellenic position on such a vital ethnic issue for Greece greatly curtailed its growth. To prepare its cadres on the anti–Hellenic decisions made by BCF and Comintern conspirators, the KKE's Central Committee wrote in the second issue of the *Communist Review* in February 1924: "The Macedonian people lost their unity because of the 1912 war. The people were liberated from the Turks to be enslaved by the Greek, Bulgarian, and Serb merchants, industrialists, and *chiftlik* owners" (Vattis 2002).

To the Greek people the *Communist Review* article, imitating the Sixth BCF Congress's proposal that Greek Macedonia and Thrace are inhabited by people with "Macedonian consciousness," was seditious, or even treasonous. It was the first time that an official KKE publication suggested that all the Slav-speaking people living within the borders of Hellenic Macedonia were "Macedonians." The only people in Macedonia who were not Macedonians, according to Kolarov's BCF and Dimitrov's Comintern, were the Greek Macedonians, pure descendants of families with strong and long roots in Macedonia, whose forefathers were Greeks from the time of Alexander the Great, living in historic Macedonia for countless generations (Averoff-Tossizza 1978). Why, exactly, the KKE went astray in dealing with this vital ethnic Greek issue is unanswerable. While international communism was setting the foundations for the greatest falsification of history, where were the bleeding hearts for democracy and equality in Europe when such a distortion of history was taking place? Were there no more men left like Byron of England, Normann of Germany, or Tarella of Italy (Brewer 2001)?

Comintern's pressure on the fledgling KKE with respect to the Macedonian problem was ruthless. Shortly after its Fifth Congress in Moscow in November 1924, Commissar D. Manouilsky, a Comintern leader, arrived in Athens to attend the KKE's Third Special Congress on December 12. His official assignment was to obtain approval by the attendees of the decisions on Macedonia approved by the Fifth Comintern Congress. But Manouilsky went beyond that. He accused the CPY and KKE of opposition to BCF's views on the Macedonian issue and rejecting Comintern's directives to cooperate with IMRO. He insisted there was a strong movement in Macedonia to form an independent state and asked the delegates to align their decisions with BCF's and Comintern's objectives (Tsaparas 1996). He convinced KKE comrades to expel from the party two leaders, Kordatos and Apostolides, vocal opponents of the decision for an "Independent Macedonian Nation" and reinstate Maximos and Pouliopoulos.[11] The KKE, by then captured by the BCF's deft manipulations of the Macedonian issue, endorsed the BCF plan with the following resolution published in the official party newspaper *Rhizospastis* on December 14, 1924: "The Congress unanimously accepted the decision of the ... Communist International.... As long as the division and oppression of Macedonia and Thrace continues, we cannot avoid an imperialist war. That is why we are fighting for the unification and independence of the three sections of Macedonia and Thrace" (Averoff-Tossizza 1978).

In doing so, the KKE thoughtlessly embraced the irredentist plans of a foreign organization assiduously promoting malicious relationships in the Balkans at Greece's expense. In retrospect, it is difficult to say precisely why a party that could have enjoyed solid support and popular following among the poor Greek masses opted to go along with deceitful conspiracies to hurt its own country. More than half a century later, it appears a miscalculation of historic proportions that dogged the KKE, tarnishing its national reputation for a long time. Adherence by a Greek party to the Marxist-Stalinist views on the Macedonian issue could be nothing but treason.

The KKE's adherence to the BCF's intrigue on the fate of Macedonia became a serious issue for the party in the Greek parliament in 1927. Accused of treason, the party of the proletariat was confronted with a dilemma: repudiate BCF's demand for Macedonian autonomy, a decision that would have certainly invited a stinging rebuff— to say the least —from the BCF and Comintern, or accept BCF's demand and face charges for sedition and even treason by the Greek parliament and the people for giving away Greece's sovereign rights over Macedonia (Mavrogordatos 1983). The KKE leader and deputy Maximos defended the party so cleverly in the parliamentary censorship discussions that, temporarily at least, the party was exonerated of the charges of treason.

From 1921 to 1950 the KKE faithfully obeyed Comintern's and BCF's directives on Macedonia whose name was propelled to the world as Autonomous Macedonia, Federated Macedonian State, United and Independent Macedonia, and even United and Independent Macedonia and Thrace (Kyrou 1950). The names and projected future affiliations were adjusted according to which communist party had Moscow's favor. Not surprisingly, it made no difference to the Soviets which of the two Slavic countries, Bulgaria or Yugoslavia, would rule Macedonia as long as the Aegean (Greek) Macedonia was detached from Greece. The Soviet Union would have achieved its dream of acquiring an outlet to the Aegean Sea.

Although the Macedonian Question evolved in unexpected ways because of the Tito-Stalin split in 1948, the basic elements of the Soviet policy remained unaltered: (a) Aegean Macedonia must be detached from Greece, a nation which, because of its freedom-loving people, can never accept communism; (b) Bulgarian communism's and Yugoslav communism's imperialism and the intention to annex Macedonia will remain unaltered through the ages; and (c) the KKE will always be obedient and eager to serve the expansionist plans of Greece's enemies. These plans and policies were also in complete agreement with IMRO's nationalist objectives.

The Soviet pressure on the Balkan communist parties in relation to the Macedonian issue, and especially on the KKE, and the brazen disregard of Greece and the Greek Macedonians' aspirations and wishes continued. In 1930, Comintern's unprecedented interference in the affairs of a foreign political party resulted in removing the KKE's leadership and installing a new group of leaders, among them a young communist, Nikos Zachariadis, who emerged later as the absolute KKE leader and played the most controversial and destructive role in his party over the next twenty years (Averoff-Tossizza 1978). At the same time, in keeping with a strategy of intimidation orchestrated by the Kremlin, Comintern sent the following rebuff to the KKE leaders and cadres: "The KKE did not actively participate in the revolutionary ethnic liberation struggle of the peoples suppressed by the Greeks. It failed ... to stabilize with organized measures the huge sympathies of the suppressed ethnicities of Macedonia for the communist movement.... The party must, without delay ... fight for freedom and self-determination [of Macedonia], even its secession" (Vattis 2002).

Ironically, by giving away Greece's sovereign rights over Macedonia — a significant, rich part of its territory — the KKE automatically sacrificed its own independence. It also irreparably damaged its reputation as a trusted Hellenic party, allowing itself to be seen by the Greek people as a foreign agent determined to sever Macedonia from the country. If the party of the Greek proletariat refused to go along with the master's wishes, it would have brought BCF's and Comintern's condemnation and rebuff, not a very pleasant situation for a young party and its leaders. Rather than untangling itself from the BCF's tentacles and its anti–Hellenic policies, the KKE plunged even more decisively for a second time into supporting the BCF's position for an independent Macedonia. The plenum of the KKE's Central Committee unanimously approved the following resolution in Athens in December 1931: "Greece is an imperialist country which has conquered by force whole regions populated by other nationalities. In the name of the fundamental principles of Bolshevism the KKE declares for Macedonia and Thrace the principle of self-determination, which includes the right to separate themselves from Greece, and the party actively sustains the revolutionary efforts of the people of these regions directed toward their own national liberation" (Averoff-Tossizza 1978, from the KKE Archives).

The capstone of BCF's strategy for an "Independent Macedonian State" failed. Contrary to Comintern's expectations for an easy and rapid victory, the slogans for an autonomous or independent Macedonia not only fell on deaf ears from 1924 to 1934, but also threatened the KKE's deployment and growth, and even the growth of the Communist Party of Yugoslavia. BCF's revolutionary policy was not received favorably by the slavophones who still retained their ethnic Hellenic consciousness (Vattis 2002). To align itself with the new Comintern platform and gain some of the popularity lost because of its stand on the Macedonian issue, the KKE leadership finally gathered sufficient courage to disregard Comintern's directives and undertake to diminish the impact of the Third Special Congress's December 1924 decision for an "Independent Macedonia and Thrace" and the tough resolution of the Central Committee's plenum of December 1931 that "Greece is an imperialist country" (Kofos 1995). To accomplish this, the party reneged on "the principle of self-determination," which included the right of Macedonia and Thrace "to separate themselves from Greece." Instead, it adopted Comintern's new 1935 platform promoting the idea of "full equality for the minorities" within Greece (Averoff-Tossizza 1978; Rallis 1993). The anti–Hellenic spirit of the tough 1931 resolution, set aside for eighteen years, would be resurrected in 1949 in the Grammos mountains during the Greek Civil War (see Chapter 6).

The KKE's activities were not limited to its interconnections with the Communist Party of Bulgaria (Vattis 2002). It also established connections (willingly or unwillingly) with IMRO. Convinced that its cooperation with Comintern served its nationalist plans for Macedonia, IMRO dispatched one of its fanatic leaders, Panitsa, to Thessaloniki in 1924 (Vattis 2002). Under extreme secrecy, with the help of Slav agents, Panitsa met with the KKE's General Secretary E. Stavrides and attempted to convince him of the easiest and safest way to settle the Macedonian problem, also informing Stavrides of the Comintern-IMRO cooperation. From Thessaloniki, Panitsa went to Athens under a fictitious name where he continued his contacts with the KKE leaders without any interference by the police, managing to convince them to agree with Comintern's plans on Macedonia. The KKE became increasingly committed to the Comintern-IMRO cooperative plan.

To improve its influence on the KKE, from 1930 to 1934 IMRO assisted the KKE with hard currency pouring into IMRO's coffers from its subsidiaries in Canada, Australia, and the United States. The communist newspaper *Rhizospastis* on April 25, 1934, expressed the party's gratitude to IMRO for the financial assistance: "In the revolutionary movement to assist the ethnic minorities, the workers and farmers of Greece can find a true ally ... in the Macedonian movement that has organized IMRO.... The party must help IMRO's movement and its efforts to be organized" (Vattis 2002).

In ten years, the bourgeoisie would die in the Balkans (except in Greece), and communism would prevail; with that, the Macedonian Question would again emerge into the forefront more complicated and dangerous for Greek Macedonia than ever before.

4

World War II and the Struggle for Macedonia

The proper teaching of history can be crucial
in promoting tolerance and peace
—John Brademas

Because of its geographic and strategic significance, Greek Macedonia became the center of important political and military events during the 1940s. Decisive fighting took place in Macedonia and Epirus during the Greek-Italian War of 1940–1941. Greek Macedonia suffered a triple occupation — German, Italian, and Bulgarian, the last being the most brutal. The Germans established the *Wehrmacht*'s headquarters from 1941 to 1944 in Thessaloniki, central Macedonia, the most important junction of communication lines in the Balkans. The Greek people experienced the darkest period of their lives (famine, financial ruin, population movements, exiles, concentration camps, torture, and executions) in Macedonia and western Thrace, the German and Bulgarian zones of occupation. People experienced terrible events instigated by Bulgarian- and Yugoslav-oriented slavophones in western Macedonia. The world witnessed with horror the annihilation of the law-abiding Jewish population in Thessaloniki (Mazower 1993).

The Communist Party of Greece (KKE) exercised a vacillating and often seditious "Macedonian" policy for Macedonia, aligning itself with Comintern's anti–Hellenic position, undermining its own unity and its leaders' credibility. The KKE was compelled to cooperate with Bulgarian autonomists, such as Gotse, and Tito's partisan leaders, such as Paschali Mitrofsky (Mitropoulos before he changed his name) in western and central Macedonia. It also compromised with the Slavic demands in western Macedonia again, accepting the Yugoslav-oriented Slavomacedonians as "Macedonians." Because of such anti–Hellenic policies, the KKE was also accused of echoing the secessionist demands or condoning the irredentist designs of Greece's communist neighbors over Macedonia.

During the Greek Civil War of 1946–1949 all of Greece suffered. But the war reached a climax in Macedonia and Epirus, the two critical frontier battlefields. In the bloody conflict between the Greek national army and the communist Democratic Army of Greece (DAG), Macedonia became the focus of interest of the Yugoslav partisans and Tito's manipulations. The bloody struggle in Macedonia took place not only between democracy and communism, but also between communism and Hellenism, the latter endeavoring to defend Hellenic Macedonia's territorial integrity.

The KKE and the Greek-Italian War (1940–1941)

It all began in Hellenic Macedonia and Epirus on October 28, 1940, when Italy attacked Greece from Albania without provocation. Suddenly, Greece's 7.5 million people were at war with Italy's 45 million. Italy's dictator, Benito Mussolini, had allied with Nazi Germany, which by October 1940 had quickly overrun Austria, Czechoslovakia, Poland, France, Holland, Belgium, Denmark, and Norway. Although the Greek people were apprehensive about the outcome of the war, they were firmly united in their belief that no one had the right to invade their country and enslave its people. It was a magnificent time for the Greek nation, its finest hour. From that day till May 1941 only two countries in Europe stood up to the Axis powers— Great Britain and Greece. It was a great spectacle for the world to witness the magnificent patriotic fervor in Macedonia and Epirus and the instantaneous arousal of an entire nation when Mussolini unleashed his unprovoked attack; the patriotism and euphoria that gripped the nation, not seen in generations; the miracle of a small country defeating and humiliating a great power; and the Greek exuberance of victory over the foreign invaders.

Three days after the Italian army attacked Greece, Nikos Zachariadis, general secretary of the Communist Party of Greece (KKE), defined the official position of the party in his "open letter to the Greek people" from the Corfu prison where the Metaxas dictatorship had incarcerated him.[1] The letter, which received great publicity in the Greek press, extolled the working class for its resistance to the fascists and appealed for a unified front to resist the invaders to a final victory. Zachariadis's letter gave greater apparent unanimity in the determination to fight a foreign aggressor than the Greeks had ever before experienced in their long history.

The Zachariadis letter of October 30, 1940, shocked the KKE's Central Committee in Athens because the Soviet Union had signed an agreement with Nazi Germany on August 23, 1939, and Italy, Greece's enemy, was Germany's partner in the Axis Alliance. In the opinion of high-echelon communists, offending Italy was tantamount to offending the Soviet-German pact. The letter drove the Central Committee to such an awkward position that it questioned its authenticity and denounced it as a "fabrication" of the Metaxas Ministry of National Security (Averoff-Tossizza 1978).

Twenty-six days later, in a second letter published by the KKE's official newspaper *Rhizospastis,* Zachariadis forgot his patriotic exuberance, branded the war "imperialistic," advocated an "honorable peace," and plotted a new line for the KKE compatible with the Soviet Union's policies: "After expelling the Italians beyond the Greek-Albanian border the struggle ceased to be defensive; it is an imperialistic war; Greece could have asked the Soviet Union to intervene for peace."

In addition to the tremendous arrogance of branding the Greek people's titanic struggle to defend their freedom an "imperialist war," other KKE leaders committed a big error, which did not endear the communists in the Greek people's hearts. Because the Soviet Union was on friendly terms with Nazi Germany, the communists made an abrupt political turn, adopting a line that seemed to favor the Axis powers, rather than the Greek forces fighting in Albania. The KKE's Central Committee manifesto of December 7, 1940, just thirty-seven days after Zachariadis's first letter was published, called upon the people of Greece and Greek soldiers to stop fighting beyond the Greek border: "The war was brought about on Greece by the King-Metaxas gang, ordered by the British imperialists.... This war has nothing to do with our country's defense; that is why we call our fighters to refuse to fight beyond the borders of our fatherland. What are we doing in Albania? The people do not want another Sangarius! When they make this decision, our fighters should submit terms to the opponents without demanding territorial recompense or other compensation" (Averoff-Tossizza 1978).

The KKE's favorable disposition toward the German-Soviet pact and the party's manifesto calling on Greek fighters to refuse to fight beyond the borders were not all that offended the public. While the country was at war with a numerically superior invader, party members circulated pamphlets among the Greek men fighting in Albania, urging them to refuse to fight beyond the Greek-Albanian border. Simply stated, they asked the victorious Greek men to abandon the liberated areas in Albania and return to the Greek border. Why the KKE flip-flopped on such an important national issue, merely because the Soviet Union had signed a temporary agreement with the devil, is beyond comprehension.

Hitler and the Macedonian Question

As early as November 12, 1940, Hitler, forced by the unexpected and humiliating defeat of Mussolini's vaunted army by the Greek army in the Albanian mountains, addressed his generals to prepare for the invasion of Greece from Bulgaria if Mussolini failed to occupy the country. To speed his operations with minimal effort, Hitler needed Bulgaria (Miller 1975). First, he informed Molotov, the Soviet foreign minister, of his plans to attack Greece from Bulgaria. Hitler said he had no territorial ambitions in Greece. He simply wanted to expel the British from the Greek bases they had occupied after the Greek-Italian War began. Molotov agreed with Hitler's argument and submitted to Hitler several Soviet demands: dominate the Dardanelles, the "gate of every contemplated attack against Russia," especially after Great Britain set bases in Greece; strengthen the ties between the Soviet Union and Bulgaria; offer guarantees for Bulgaria's independence and territorial integrity, without changing its political system; and guarantee Bulgaria's opening to the Aegean littoral (Miller 1975).

In his eagerness to attract Bulgaria to his plans, Hitler invited Filov, the Bulgarian prime minister, to Obersalzberg and offered him Macedonia and Thrace, the price given to Bulgaria with the 1878 Treaty of San Stefano. The conflict with Greece was deplorable, Hitler said, but it gave Bulgaria an opportunity to satisfy its Aegean aspirations (Miller 1975). In return, Bulgaria would have to sign the Tripartite Pact and allow German troops to use its soil as a base.[2] Bulgaria signed the agreement on March 1, 1941. On the same day von Ribbentrop, the German foreign minister, informed Filov that his country would be rewarded with an outlet to the Aegean between the rivers Strymon and Evros. Immediately after Bulgaria signed the Tripartite Pact, Germany moved its 12th Army of fifteen divisions, four of which were Panzer divisions, alongside the Greek border to the south and the Yugoslav border to the west.

Lest Hitler's plan not be threatening enough to Greece's territorial integrity, he simultaneously promised to fulfill the age-old Yugoslav dream of an outlet to the Aegean Sea, including complete control of Thessaloniki. He did this fully knowing that the Bulgarian aspirations for Macedonia were in direct conflict with the Yugoslav dreams. Under pressure, the Yugoslav government of Drasiga Cvetkoviae capitulated to the German "carrot and stick" tactics and signed the Tripartite Pact in Vienna on March 25, 1941.[3] The German-Yugoslav plan, however, lasted only two days until demonstrations and riots toppled the government of Prince Paul and Cvetkoviae. Hitler became so enraged with the anti–Nazi coup that he remarked to von Ribbentrop that the Macedonian Question could be settled only in favor of Bulgaria (Miller 1975).

The blitzkrieg against Greece and Yugoslavia, beginning on April 6, 1941, brought the two countries down rapidly with *Wehrmacht* troops entering Athens on April 27. The German invasion abruptly and sadly reversed the incredible victory of the Greek army against the Italians in Albania, in spite of the overwhelming odds the Greeks faced from the beginning. Greek rejoicing was short-lived and the occupation of the country by the Germans, Italians, and Bulgarians began. On April 23, 1941, the German Marshall List and the Greek General George Tsolacoglou, with the defeated Italians participating, signed a surrender document, which included the Italians, without the consent of the Greek government, which had escaped to Egypt. Hitler dismembered Greece into three occupation zones, with the Bulgarians occupying eastern Macedonia and western Thrace (Mazower 1993).

Italy's defeat by the Greek army had given Great Britain and Greece, the only two Allies in 1940 and early 1941, the first taste of victory against the Axis. Mussolini and his army became the objects of ridicule by the free world and Germans alike. Hitler had planned on a rapid victory over the Soviet Union before the Russian winter arrived, and perhaps he would have accomplished his plan if he had been able to launch his massive attack in May as he had originally planned. But he was forced to delay *Barbarossa* (code name for the attack against the Soviet Union) for more than a month, a critical change in plan that may have cost him the war in Russia.

Regrettably, the Greek contributions to the Allied cause in World War II have been minimized or ignored in the modern pages of history. Waller's (1996) remarks on the subject are a good example. He wrote: "The Yugoslav upheaval [against Hitler] was a nasty fly in the *Barbarossa* ointment, a fly that had to be swatted even if it meant postponing Germany's invasion of Russia, scheduled for May 15." He ignored the Greek contribution altogether.

There would have been no Yugoslav "nasty fly," if Greece had surrendered to Mussolini on October 28, 1940. To support this contention, we must assume a plausible, alternate scenario of events that would have occurred if Greece had surrendered on October 28: The Italians would have occupied Greece during the last week of October 1940; the Italians would have surrounded Yugoslavia from Albania in the west and from Greece in the south. German troops were already in Austria and Hungary. Bulgaria, a traditional German ally, accepted the *Wehrmacht* without a fight, surrounding Yugoslavia from the east. Romania had already offered its territory to Germany on September 4, 1940. The thoroughly surrounded Yugoslavia, with a pro–German prime minister, would have surrendered without a fight. Greece was the nasty fly that upset the Axis plans in the Balkans and Eastern Europe, a fact that Anthony Eden, the British foreign minister, implied in a telegram from Cairo to Churchill dated February 21, 1941: "If we fail to help the Greeks there is no hope of action in Yugoslavia" (Churchill 1950).

Hitler's alliance with Filov in 1941 rekindled the hibernating irredentist motives of ethnic groups and committees in Bulgaria and stimulated the revolutionary activities of IMRO, which had never really forsaken its claims on Greece's Macedonia and western Thrace. Bulgarian and Yugoslav nationalists and communists later exploited the artificial resurgence of the Macedonian problem through Hitler's promises to the fascist government of Filov during the Balkan occupation.[4]

Hitler's dallying with the Macedonian problem did not worry the Greek communists or upset their long-term objectives. The KKE circulated the following resolution on March 18, 1941: "The KKE Central Committee invites the working class ... to organize a united anti-war front ... using demonstrations, work stoppage ... to do everything possible to stop the war brought to the country by the pro–British clique, causing the Italian invasion.... The Greek people should emulate their brethren, the heroic people of Bulgaria, and do everything possible for the restoration of peace in the Balkans" (Vattis 2002).

Ironically, the resolution was released eighteen days after Bulgaria and the "heroic people of Bulgaria" had signed the Tripartite Pact, bringing the German army behind the Greek frontier to attack Greece on April 6, a fact perhaps unknown to the KKE. While the Greek people were spilling their blood in the mountains of Albania, a Greek political party, blinded by its adherence to the erroneous, doctrinaire policies of its master (Stalin), was urging the Greek people to emulate Filov's malign alliance with Hitler, only because the Soviet Union had signed an agreement of "friendship" with Nazi Germany. Then to everyone's further surprise, the KKE reversed its position on March 18, praising the "heroic people of Bulgaria," and declared war against the Germans, Bulgarians, and Italians.

Bulgarian Occupation of Greek Eastern Macedonia and Western Thrace

To fulfill his promises to the Bulgarians, Hitler turned over the fertile plains of eastern Macedonia and western Thrace, including the thriving cities of Serres, Drama, Kavala, and Xanthi, to his Bulgarian allies, who

Zones of occupation in Greece from 1941 to 1944. From *Blood and Tears: Greece 1940–1949*, by George Papavizas.

quickly grabbed the spoils without firing a shot (Papavizas 2002). It was Hitler's ultimate ethnic punishment of the Greeks, who had fought so many battles against the Bulgarians to keep those areas Greek. Hitler's gift to the Bulgarians was a worse punishment for Greece than if he had taken as prisoners of war the "bleeding and bandaged men," the heroes of the frontier battle against the *Wehrmacht*, the men the German army had saluted for their heroic resistance.[5]

The Bulgarian occupation of eastern Macedonia and western Thrace began in May 1941. The Bulgarian King Boris reassured the Greeks of Drama that they had nothing to be afraid of from the Bulgarian occupation,

WORLD WAR II
Greek and Yugoslav provinces under Bulgarian occupation (1941–1944)

Greek and Yugoslav provinces under Bulgarian occupation in 1941–1944. Black and white arrangement of Map 3. Courtesy of Macedonian Heritage, Museum of the Macedonian Struggle, Thessaloniki.

"because [their] life and belongings will be respected by the Bulgarians." But the king's words rang a hollow note, a false promise. Annexation of the entire Greek Macedonia and western Thrace was in the plans of King Boris's fascist Bulgarian government; annexation could only be accomplished by suppressing or exterminating the Greek population in the occupied zone. History knew better (Amperiadis 1998).

Predicating their strategic planning on the assumption that Nazi Germany would win the war, the Bulgarian Nazis settled in the occupied districts and, utilizing the flimsiest of pretexts, plunged into a brutal effort to exterminate Hellenism. What the Bulgarians failed to do— de-Hellenize Macedonia — in the nineteenth century and at the beginning of the twentieth century, they attempted to do during the occupation by setting up an extermination mechanism to achieve their goal in a very short time (Miller 1975). At the peace conference, with Germans as victors, they would not have any difficulties in convincing the world of Bulgarism's prevalence in Macedonia. To put this issue in perspective, the Bulgarians were not interested in appropriating the Macedonian name to form an independent country with the name "Macedonia," as others were at the end of the twentieth century; they were planning to annex Macedonia as a province of Bulgaria.

If Germany had won the war, they would have accomplished it (Amperiadis 1998).

Losing the sovereign rights over eastern Macedonia and western
Thrace, a rich part of Greece's territory, had great repercussions on the
country and beyond. First, it brought the Bulgarians to the shores of the
Aegean. Second, thousands of families from the occupied provinces abandoned their homes and belongings to the Bulgarians and spent their sav-
ings and other tangible assets to hire boats for nighttime flights to safety in
the German zone of occupation. More than one hundred thousand refugees
secretly fled from the Bulgarian-occupied areas to Halkidiki and Thessaloniki, creating crowded conditions all over and exacerbating the chaotic
situation in the German occupation zone by reducing the already dwin-
dling food supplies.

For people from the Bulgarian-occupied zone, it was worth everything
they had to reach the German zone. Cold and efficient Bulgarian fascist
brutality exceeded even the harshest barbarian standards of the other two
occupying forces. Ethnic cleansing was invented in the Bulgarian occupation zone. The official policy was to forcibly Bulgarize the Aegean littoral
that the Nazis had bestowed on the Bulgarians (Miller 1975). Bulgarian
Nazis expropriated fortunes, stole and plundered properties, confiscated
food and animals, and tyrannized the people. Their secret organizations
attempted to Bulgarize as many Greek inhabitants as possible and expel or
exterminate the rest. To change the demographic composition of the occupied area, they encouraged Bulgarian colonists to settle on land forcibly
taken from Greek inhabitants, hoping to ensure permanent control by
demonstrating that the region was inhabited by a Bulgarian majority. Bulgarian authorities closed the Greek schools and expelled the teachers, established Bulgarian schools and suppressed the Greek language, replaced Greek
clergymen with Bulgarian priests, and deprived the Greek inhabitants of
the right to work (Amperiadis 1998; Miller 1975).

Allied with various military and paramilitary organizations, the Bulgarian fascist government rapidly pursued its sinister plans in the occupied
Greek territories. The prime goal on its agenda of the territory's de–Hellenization was to wipe out every trace of the Greek administration. More
tangibly, whereas the Germans and Italians did nothing to disturb the local
Greek administration, the Bulgarians in their zone did everything to destroy
it: they closed the Greek administrative offices, replaced the Greek teachers and the clergy, closed the Greek banks or expropriated them, and forced
the people to admit in writing they were Bulgarians, not Greeks. Exiles,
dismissals, arrests, murders, and rapes of women were everyday atrocities
aimed at forcing the Greek population to migrate to the German zone of
occupation. The entire ordeal, the fifth (and most violent) ordeal suffered

by Hellenism, was aiming at demolishing it in the occupied districts once and for all (Amperiadis 1998).[6]

Events in Drama and the "Doxato Massacre"

For all the fascist Bulgarian brutality aimed at dismembering Greece at the end of World War II, the evil plan was a failure. A hard core of Greeks remained in towns and villages, in spite of the terror, with only a few succumbing to pressure, changing their names and ethnic affiliation for the record. Hellenism prevailed again: the Greeks remained steadfast to their ethnic roots and principles despite the harsh treatment they received at the hands of the Bulgarian fascists (Amperiadis 1998). It would have been a historical reversal and a rebuff to Hellenism's long history, if the Greeks in the Bulgarian zone of occupation had succumbed to terror. Hellenism remained steadfast in 1878–1908 and again in 1912–1913. Nothing could defeat Hellenism's spirit now, not even the Bulgarian fascist brutality. But the Bulgarian brutalities did not end with expulsions, suppressions, or even executions of hundreds of prominent citizens.

What they failed to accomplish with terrorization, the Bulgarians attempted to bring about with treachery preceding a wholesale massacre. On September 27, 1941, the Bulgarians claimed that a revolt by the Greek population broke out in Drama and spread through the occupied territory. On September 28, Bulgarian troops, accompanied by terrorist *checkists* (local bulgarophone inhabitants), quickly and bloodily suppressed the "rebellion," killing fifteen thousand Greeks in what is known as the Drama uprising and the "Doxato Massacre" (Amperiadis 1998; Vafeiadis 1985).[7] In the city of Drama alone, more than three thousand civilians were killed during the first few days of the massacre, with rivers of blood running in the city streets (Miller 1975). In the town of Doxato, Bulgarian soldiers, gendarmes, and *checkists* ordered the people to concentrate in the square, selected four hundred men and executed them *en masse* in front of horrified women and children.[8] The Bulgarian atrocities spread to Serres, Sidirocastron, Zihni, Prosotsiani, and Tzoumayia. The material damage was incalculable. Entire villages were looted and machine-gunned. The massacre produced a new torrent of refugees from the Bulgarian zone to Thessaloniki and Halkidiki.

According to Amperiadis (1998), several other sources reported 23,000 to 48,000 massacred in the Bulgarian occupation zone; the losses reported by the War Criminals Service were underestimated. Foreign embassies estimated 30,000 dead, 50,000 exiled to Bulgaria, and 100,000 sent to forced labor camps (Amperiadis 1998). The exiled Greek government in Egypt estimated that 55,000 were victims during the entire Bulgarian occupation

(1941–1944). The Bulgarians lost 178 men. This was the official Bulgarian announcement of the massacre: "Greek guerrilla bands crossing the border of eastern Macedonia attempted to arouse the Greek population to revolt. Bulgarian troops counterattacked and pushed them out of the territory after a prolonged skirmish" (Daskalov 1992).

The terrible disaster that befell the Bulgarian-occupied territory was the responsibility of the local KKE leaders, who acted without authorization from the KKE Macedonian Central Committee in Thessaloniki (Amperiadis 1998). Bramos (1953) directly accused the Thessaloniki KKE for unintentionally informing the Bulgarian Club about the pending "revolt" in eastern Macedonia and western Thrace. In September 1941, about a month before the so-called revolt broke out, villages around Drama were visited by Bulgarian employees and military officers accompanied by local Greek communists who were attempting to convince people hiding in the mountains to take part in the forthcoming uprising purported to be followed immediately by a general revolt in Bulgaria (Amperiadis 1998). Chrysochoou (1952) believed that the Bulgarian terrorist organization Ochrana organized the conspiracy, inciting a few Greek communists hiding in the mountains to revolt, thus giving the Bulgarians an opportunity and an excuse to bloodily suppress it.

Chatzis, a member of the KKE Central Committee, pointed out in his book, *The Victorious Revolution That Was Lost (1977)*, that the responsibility for starting the uncoordinated uprising lay with the KKE Central Committee which had failed to establish satisfactory communication lines with the Macedonian organization, leaving it without guidance. The predicament was exacerbated by the underground activities of Bulgarian agents that had infiltrated the KKE in eastern Macedonia and by the extreme position assumed by the Macedonian KKE, incapable of coordinating or preventing events. Chatzis also claimed that the Drama KKE was aware of the Bulgarian authorities' knowledge of the forthcoming uprising. He pointed out that Hamalides, the KKE leader in Drama, had made contacts with Bulgarian anti-fascist agents, possibly Bulgarian terrorist agents of Ochrana. Another KKE leader in the area, Michaslis, believed that some of the Bulgarian agents had pushed Hamalides to start the uprising, believing that assistance was forthcoming from the Bulgarian Left. Though Hamalides had been told in writing to discontinue the contacts, he failed to do so. The Drama organization went ahead with the uprising despite the warnings. According to Michaslis, Hamalides fell into an Ochrana trap, and for that reason he was responsible for the disaster.

The ghastly memory of the massacre and the doubts of who was responsible for it still linger in the Greek national consciousness, including the lies fabricated by the official Bulgarian government to justify it. The true story of the KKE's careless involvement, if any, may never be known. It is now known that the uprising that cost so much Greek blood was purposely instigated by Bulgarian provocateurs looking for an excuse to escalate the level of persecutions and bloodily suppress the revolt, thereby exterminating the Greek population of the occupied territory (Miller 1975).

By the end of the terrible year 1941, the Bulgarians had accomplished what they had set their minds to do: indiscriminate killings, thousands of arrests and exiles, an increased number of people fleeing the Bulgarian zone of occupation, seizure of countless Greek properties and transferring thousands of Bulgarian farmers to settle in the occupied territory, and destruction of the last vestiges of the Greek administration. Even inscriptions on Greek graves were changed to the Bulgarian language. Some of the newly established civilians from Bulgaria belonged to the group of slavophones that had voluntarily left Greece between 1919 and 1932 after the signing of the Treaty of Neuilly.

Meanwhile, instead of arming themselves to fight the Germans, as the Yugoslav and Greek communists did, the Bulgarian communists opted to remain docile. There was no resistance in Bulgaria to speak of during the German presence in the country. Strangely, the Bulgarian communists did not even fight when Germany attacked the Soviet Union. Perhaps the Nazi Balkan policies served the CPB's long-range plans and, indirectly, the Soviet plans. An article published in the CPB newspaper *Novo Breme* supports this view; the CPB called on Bulgarian communists not to be convinced by the other Balkan communist parties to participate in a war for freedom against the Germans, because they (the Germans) gave to Bulgaria the largest part of Macedonia (Vattis 2002).

Bulgarian Activities in Greek Western and Central Macedonia

Virtually from the outset of Greece's occupation by German, Italian, and Bulgarian troops, Hellenic Macedonia became a land of vileness and viciousness: betrayals, burnings, plundering, and executions appeared to have something to do with pervasive interconnections fermented between elements that defected to the conquerors and sinister new occupation forces emerging in Vardar Province (southern Yugoslavia) adjacent to Greece's western Macedonia. To begin with, within a few days of the German army's occupation of Yugoslavia, the Germans allowed the Bulgarian army to move into the Vardar Province, grabbing the spoils without firing a shot, just as it had in Greek eastern Macedonia and western Thrace. The Bulgarian General Marinov, a secret IMRO operative, was named military commander in

Skopje, the capital of Vardar Macedonia, to coordinate IMRO's activities in Bulgarizing both Yugoslav Macedonia and Greek Macedonia (Vattis 2002). Marinov, working closely with the Nazis, set up an office in Monastir (Bitola), near the Greek-Yugoslav border, staffed with high-echelon IMRO leaders to coordinate activities in western Macedonia.[9]

Foremost among the results of these interconnections were betrayals by and defections of many slavophone inhabitants in Macedonia, especially in the Kastoria and Florina provinces, who came out openly for Bulgaria and cooperated with the Italians, and after Italy's capitulation to the Allies in September 1943, with the Germans. Throughout the first two years of the occupation (1941–1943), a group of Macedonia's Slav-speakers believed the Axis would win the war, spelling the Greek state's demise in their districts and signaling Bulgaria's chance to annex all of Macedonia (Koliopoulos 1995). It hardly needs to be stressed that the slavophones who defected to the conquerors considered themselves nothing but Bulgarians.

There was more to come in the spring of 1941. The Bulgarian fascist government convinced the German occupation authorities to allow posting of Bulgarian officers to the German garrisons in central and western Macedonia (Koliopoulos 1994; Vattis 2002). The Italians granted similar permission. The Bulgarian officers stationed in German and Italian garrisons were under the newly established Bulgarian Communications Office in Thessaloniki, where the *Wehrmacht*'s high command was also located (Mazower 1993). The unprecedented arrangement helped the Bulgarians to spread their tentacles in rural Greek western and central Macedonia, under the protection of the Nazis and fascists, to prepare the ground for Macedonia's annexation at war's end. The Bulgarians had not forgotten Hitler's promises to Filov in March 1941. The pattern was historically and depressingly similar throughout Macedonia to previous Macedonian crises. The times had changed, but IMRO's methods remained unaltered, first under the Turks, now under the Germans and Italians.

In addition to their role as instruments of terrorization and protectors of Bulgarian interests, the Bulgarian liaison officers rapidly succeeded in establishing close rapport with German and Italian officers and with the troops manning the garrisons. Bribing the Germans and Italians with golden sovereigns, bestowing on them Bulgarian medals, or providing them with women for sex, the Bulgarians succeeded in establishing intriguing connections with the occupation authorities used in many ways against the Hellenic population.

While the fascist Bulgarian officers were in position in the Italian and German garrisons, the Communist Party of Bulgaria (CPB) clandestinely called on Bulgarian and Slavomacedonian communists to refrain from attacking the Italians and Germans. The Bulgarian people must be satisfied, the CPB declared, with the German territorial concessions to Bulgaria and the freedom and independence gained by the people in the Bulgarian-controlled territories. It was becoming increasingly apparent that Bulgarian communism was soft on the fascists and Nazis. The CPB had forgotten that the Germans were the implacable enemies of the Soviet Union, using all their might to destroy it (Koliopoulos 1995).

At the same time, the Bulgarians were also allowed to organize their own club in the German-held Thessaloniki, another concession to them by the Germans that strengthened their power to abuse people as well as their capabilities of rewarding those willing to go along with their plans. Whatever its policies, the club became a place for meetings, a center for Bulgarian propaganda. The club's hidden aim was to proselytize the rural inhabitants to Bulgarism. Those who were convinced to obtain Bulgarian identification cards from the club were allowed free food (scarce during the occupation), medical care, easy traveling arrangements, immunity to persecution by the occupying authorities, free education in Bulgaria, and several other amenities (Koliopoulos 1995). Bulgarian club members and officers were able to recruit about 16,000 men and women, but in western Macedonia, most of the 75,000 slavophone inhabitants and the overwhelming Greek majority refused to succumb to the enemy bait.

Shortly after the occupation began, a Bulgarian mission of political and military leaders arrived in German-held Athens ostensibly to serve as liaison officers between the German and the Bulgarian governments. In reality, the mission's members (mostly IMRO agents) had two goals: establish contacts with the KKE and convince the Gestapo to release local KKE leaders from Acronafplia, where the Metaxas dictatorship had incarcerated them (Vattis 2002). In June 1941, twenty-seven communists, most of them Slavomacedonians, chosen by the concentration camp's communist leadership, were freed. Most of the freed communists played a crucial role in the events to follow. Among the nonslavophones was Andreas Tzimas ("Samariniotis," a Vlach from Samarina settled in Kastoria),[10] a member of the KKE Central Committee, later appointed as the number two man in ELAS's supreme three-member committee, together with Aris Velouhiotis and General Stephanos Sarafis.[11]

It has been difficult even to guess how and why the Gestapo was persuaded to free some of the most fanatic pro–Bulgarian communists from one of the most infamous Greek incarceration camps. Difficult as it may have been to believe it, twenty-seven important KKE members were indeed set free eight days after Germany invaded the Soviet Union. The liberation of such important communist leaders became a mystery after 1941 and remained so for a long time. Not surprisingly, the episode created serious tensions among the KKE leaders who harbored unfriendly feelings toward

Bulgarian sympathizers. It is now historically correct that the prisoners were freed after they had signed or silently accepted the Bulgarian nationality, promising to support Bulgarian claims that all Slav-speakers in Greece were Bulgarians and to aid the age-old Bulgarian dream for a Greater Bulgaria. The releases left no doubt about the clandestine cooperation of Filov's fascist government with IMRO, the CPB, and the KKE (Vattis 2002). In retrospect, it is difficult to say why the KKE, a party that had so many capable Greek leaders, selected Tzimas in 1942, a declared Bulgarian sympathizer, as ELAS's political commissar, a position loaded with great political and administrative responsibilities.

After Macedonia's occupation began in May 1941, expert Bulgarian agents and officers began roaming all over Greek Macedonia, especially in western Macedonia. The most notorious was Anton Kaltsev, born of Bulgarian parents near Kastoria before Macedonia's liberation from the Ottomans. Kaltsev served in Thessaloniki and later in 1941 was transferred to the Edessa garrison, and from there to the German garrison in Florina, his influence spreading to Kastoria, where he established close cooperation with the Italian First Lieutenant Jovanni Ravali. Exploiting the Metaxas government's unfriendly treatment of the slavophones in Greece and lecturing to individuals persecuted for their language and customs, Kaltsev convinced many slavophones that Macedonia was Bulgarian and induced or forced them to take up arms in support of the occupation authorities.[12] Closely cooperating with other Bulgarian agents, he began imprisoning and murdering Greek-oriented slavophone Macedonians (Vafeiadis 1992).

Ravali, a fanatic Italian fascist who hated the Greeks more than he liked the Bulgarians, was director of the Kastoria garrison's information office. A powerful man in Mussolini's Fascist Party, he exercised great power over his superiors. Kaltsev and Ravali, an odd couple indeed, became close friends, with Ravali receiving appreciable bribes in gold from Kaltsev. They began a dual strategy, orchestrated by Kaltsev, by gathering around them many anti–Hellenic individuals— Bulgarizing slavophones, Albanian vlachophones, and Ochrana members— and guiding their energy and hatred toward exterminating the Hellenic population.[13] But their respective plans for the future of the Kastoria and Florina provinces were not in alignment. Ravali's plans included exterminating or imprisoning the territory's Greek leaders using Albanians, Slavomacedonians, or vlachophones to replace them. His brutality at exterminating Hellenism in the area aimed at expanding Mussolini's Albanian enclave into western Macedonia, exploiting the mineral wealth of the territory, and enlarging the Roman *Imperium* (Miller 1975).

Kaltsev and his friends, more brutal to the Greeks than Ravali, were not interested in promoting Ravali's and Mussolini's plans for a new Roman

Empire. They were in the midst of their greatest opportunity to annex Hellenic Macedonia if the Axis won the war and were not about to annihilate Macedonian Hellenism for Ravali's sake. If the Axis won and Ravali's plans succeeded, Ravali's victory would constitute a historical disaster, not only for IMRO, but also for the Bulgarian government and the CPB.[14] Ironically, both the vaunted Italian and Bulgarian fascists "conquered" Greek Macedonia not by the force of their arms, but by grabbing the crumbs falling behind the German Panzers.

There is little doubt that the shameless, brazen cooperation between the CPB and organizations of the right (IMRO, Ochrana, Italian fascists, Filov's fascist government) was the harbinger of mass terrorization of the Greek inhabitants to achieve the territory's Bulgarization and Greece's mutilation. The blatant disregard of Greece and the Greek Macedonians' aspirations and wishes—and the terrorization of the people by IMRO's and Ochrana's operatives with Italian and German approval or participation — forced many Greek civilians and former army officers to take up arms and join ELAS or form independent armed bands to fight the Italians and the Bulgarian terrorists (Koliopoulos 1995). Anticipating danger from the Greek reaction, Ravali strengthened the conspiratorial connections between the Italians, IMRO agents, and officers of the Bulgarian army (e.g., Kaltsev) acting officially as liaison officers with Bulgarian army units occupying southern Yugoslavia. The new fascist group, the so-called Axonomacedonian Bulgarian Committee of Kastoria (Komitet), organized several *komitadjides,* composed of young slavophone pro–Bulgarian villagers under the leadership of a mixture of older pro–Bulgarian fanatic individuals, some of them IMRO agents (Papathanasiou 1950).

A number of educated individuals from the younger generation of pro–Bulgarian Slav-speakers (high school or teacher's academy graduates and others), exposed to communist indoctrination and propaganda and well informed of Comintern's 1941 position on the Macedonian issue, began exploring various other possibilities and interconnections to accomplish their ultimate goal, the snatching away of Hellenic Macedonia and its incorporation into the Bulgarian Kingdom. Some of these individuals became involved with the KKE and ELAS at one time or another and later formed the communist SNOF organization (see the end of this chapter for details).

Together with the Italians, Kaltsev's *komitadjides* unleashed a wave of terrorization resembling or even surpassing in brutality the terrorization of the previous Macedonian crises against the Greeks. Not surprisingly, the Komitet called on the Slav-speakers to close the Greek schools and expel the teachers; occupy the churches; expel the Asia Minor refugees who had settled in western and central Macedonia after 1923; and divide the land among the Bulgarophile Slavomacedonians. Greeks were arrested on spurious investigations or from catalogs prepared by the Komitet, and several of them were executed. Others were transferred to concentration camps. Villages were sacked, and the town of Argos Orestikon was burned to the ground. Kaltsev's arms-collecting *komitadjides* (*tagmata erevnis,* search battalions) accompanied the Italians in their searches for guns and ammunition in the villages. They guarded bridges and roads and formed temporary garrisons to protect the Italians. When the Italians raided Greek villages west of the River Aliakmon, where ELAS predominated, the accompanying *komitadjides* sacked the villages, looting food, house utensils, animals, and even honeycombs (Koliopoulos 1995; Papavizas 2002). Use of false witnesses, informers, betrayals, lies, and false accusations were everyday occurrences against the Greek population and the slavophone Greek Macedonians. To complicate matters further and increase the occupiers' suspicions, the *komitadjides* hid arms in or around villages and then brought the Italians or Germans to "discover" them.

An event that set off one of the most macabre incidences of terrorization of Hellenic Macedonians in western Macedonia is the provocation of the Nazis orchestrated against the inhabitants of the Greek village of Kleisura. An ELAS guerrilla group under Ypsilantis (Alecos Rosios) attacked a German convoy in the morning hours at "Daouli" on the Kastoria-Amynteon-Florina road and killed two motorcyclist advance soldiers. As in previous attacks by ELAS freedom fighters, *komitadjides* from the nearby villages of Vasiliada, Verga, and Variko rushed to the Nazis' help. After a brief skirmish, Ypsilantis and his men left in a hurry through Kleisura, located near the road where the skirmish occurred. The Bulgarian *komitadjides* approached the battlefield, dismembered the bodies of the two German soldiers, and invited the German commander, who arrived in the afternoon from Kastoria with reinforcements and Kaltsev's *komitadjides,* to witness the horror "perpetrated by the Greeks." The Germans and *komitadjides,* with revenge on their minds, massacred every living soul in Kleisura, mostly women, children, and old inhabitants (277 total), and burned the town to the ground (Gregoriadis 1984; Haritopoulos 2001).[15] Macedonia's history of the 1940s abounds with atrocities perpetrated by Germans, Italians, Bulgarians, and Bulgarian irregulars.[16]

In the spring of 1943, before Mussolini's overthrow, the impudent leaders of the Komitet and IMRO submitted a memorandum to Rome through Ravali demanding secession to Bulgaria or autonomy of the Kastoria district, removal of all Greek authorities and replacement with Bulgarian authorities, and compensation of the Komitet's men by the Italians (Vattis 2002). Rome's rejection of the requests strengthened the Komitet's resolve and its membership. By June 1943 it was under the complete control of Bulgarians and IMRO, with the Italians unable to control the course of events.

Even German officers, succumbing to Kaltsev's gold and closing their eyes, refused to see the injustice and atrocities perpetrated by official Bulgarians and Kaltsev's armed bands against the Greeks and Greek-oriented slavophones.[17]

Occupation, Resistance and the Macedonian Question

Without apologizing for the hasty manifesto of December 7, 1940, urging the Greek troops "to refuse to fight beyond the borders of the fatherland," the KKE abruptly reversed its position again when Hitler attacked the Soviet Union on June 22, 1941. The communist leaders urged the Greek people to fight the Nazis and fascists, foreign and domestic. The new manifesto of the party's Sixth Plenum defined the goals well: "The duty of every Greek communist is to organize the struggle for the defense of the Soviet Union and the overthrow of the foreign fascist yoke" (Averoff-Tossizza 1978; Fleischer 1995).

The new decision to fight "for the defense of the Soviet Union" coincided with the hopes and aspirations of the Greek people for freedom. The Greek people had to fight for freedom, and the KKE cadres had to fight for "the overthrow of the foreign fascist yoke" and "for the defense of the Soviet Union." The unprovoked Nazi attack against the Soviet Union and Greece's occupation by the same superpower furnished the right conditions, as well as an ideal political and moral justification, for the KKE to commence organizing the resistance in Greece. The decision alone to organize the resistance was not enough. The other ingredients needed for the operation to start were disciplined leaders and cadres, tough high-echelon leadership, and underground conspiratorial organization. The Metaxas dictatorship and the foreign occupation assured that the three ingredients for a successful beginning would become available to the party.

The imprisonment and exile of the communist cadres by the Metaxas dictatorship hardened their resolve and taught them how to survive underground as small, super-secret cells of three to five members each. Moreover, the Metaxas dictatorship left the country in a political and economic mess of unresolved problems and wrecked its democratic institutions. The occupation exacerbated the problems by bringing a scarcity of food and other goods, super-inflation, a black market, a shift in wealth, diving incomes, disruption of education at all levels, cruelty and villainy, and an early humiliating submissiveness of the Greek masses. These unrelentingly adverse conditions inevitably helped the KKE, the only party clandestinely organized during Greece's occupation. The KKE was capable of eliminating all domestic competition and appreciated that grabbing power at the bottom was the only worthy approach to eventually seizing the state apparatus, and ultimately the government in Athens (Stassinopoulos 1997).

The occupation found the KKE smaller than before the Metaxas persecutions, but what remained was tough, disciplined, and well organized. Most of the KKE cadres who suffered greatly under the dictatorship were ready and eager for new struggles, convinced they had the right and the will to assume power in Athens. The KKE leadership could see light at the end of a narrow tunnel, a distinct possibility of seizing power at the end of the foreign occupation. When the Germans occupied Greece, many of the imprisoned communists, including Zachariadis, were herded to Nazi concentration camps in Greece, Germany, and other occupied northern European countries. Not all of the KKE's leaders, however, were imprisoned or exiled. There remained a hard core of communist stalwarts who saw the possibilities for victorious resistance against the enemies. To achieve the ultimate goal, the stalwarts took upon themselves the initiative to organize a guerrilla war, the *Andartico*, against the occupation forces. Success in the struggle against the enemy would automatically propel the KKE to the forefront of the struggle toward the ultimate goal, political or military victory in Greece. So they moved with alacrity from the problems of persecutions and quiescence into the forefront of resistance.

In 1941, the disciplined KKE was under Giorgos Siantos, who served as general secretary of the party until Zachariadis returned to Greece in 1945 from Dachau. Siantos, a genuine communist who craved power and was ruthless in his treatment of subordinates, realized that no military resistance and no military organization could be sustained for long in a country under triple occupation without a political front or a single party behind it. Such an organization would eventually embody the popular will, especially if the resistance succeeded against the occupation forces, uniquely positioning itself to found a people's social republic (*laocratia*) in Greece. With this in mind, the KKE leadership called on all the Greek people at the party's Sixth Plenary Session to raise in unison the banner of revolt against the foreign oppressors occupying the country. On September 27, 1941, the KKE, together with three minor parties of the Left or leaning toward it (the Popular Democratic Union, Socialist Party of Greece, and Agrarian Party of Greece), formed the National Liberation Front (*Ethniko Apeleftherotiko Metopo*, EAM).[18] The historic document that underlined the goals of EAM called for the formation of a provisional government by EAM after liberation, which was to proclaim elections by a constitutional national assembly, based on proportional representation, "in which the people will rule on the form of government" they desired (Fleischer 1995).

Siantos was unwilling to reveal that the KKE was planning to exploit for its own ends the burning desire of the Greek people for liberation and the political gain that would ensue: monopoly of power and a Bolshevik government in Athens. To avoid the impression that EAM was dominated by the KKE, he invited other groups of fellow travelers to join the movement, adopted a policy promoting patriotic ideals aiming at boosting the morale of the Greek people and their determination for liberation from the Nazis and fascists, and disguised as much as possible Marxist ideas and the ultimate aim of the movement. EAM rapidly emerged as a national coalition with no other aims except liberation of the country (Papavizas 2002). EAM, the political organization, founded the Greek People's Liberation Army (*Ellenikos Laikos Apeleftherotikos Stratos*, ELAS) April 10, 1942 (Fleischer 1995).

The people of Greece knew from the very beginning of the resistance movement that EAM/ELAS was the most powerful group, that it was expected to determine the postwar political and economic system in the country, and that it was under the undisputed control of the Communist Party of Greece. EAM/ELAS had the outward appearance of a solid, national coalition encompassing small noncommunist parties and noncommunist individuals, but there was no doubt that behind every decision, every action, political or military, was the KKE.[19] After the beginning of 1943, any group in the country with political beliefs disparate from those of the KKE that stood as an obstacle to the party of the proletariat's ultimate goals of dominating the country and establishing a Bolshevik government in Athens was crushed with astonishing speed and stark brutality (Averoff-Tossizza 1978; Stassininopoulos 1997).[20]

Not everyone in Greece agrees that EAM/ELAS was the only organization that staged a fierce and meaningful resistance against the Axis forces. Other organizations blossomed in Macedonia and Epirus. Former officers of the Greek army, veterans of the victorious war against Mussolini's fascists in Albania, obeying the wishes and aspirations of the Greek people, formed on July 10, 1941, a patriotic organization in Macedonia, the Defenders of Northern Greece (*Yperaspiste Voreiou Ellados*, YVE) (Papathanasiou 1997). The resistance movement changed its name later to Panhellenic Liberation Organization (*Panelleniki Apeleftherotiki Organosis*, PAO). PAO's goals were the country's liberation and Macedonia's protection from the irredentist aspirations of its northern neighbors, especially the Bulgarians, and from communism's territorial demands over Macedonia. PAO fought valiantly against the Germans, Italians and Bulgarians in many locations in northern Greece: Fardykampos in 1943, in the Kastoria province, and in several other locations in central Greek Macedonia. During the occupation, and immediately after the Germans and Bulgarians evacuated the country,

PAO's brave men continued their fighting against the Greek communist and Slavomacedonian autonomists.

At the outset, the broad-based resistance movement by EAM/ELAS and the KKE concentrated on fighting the Germans, Italians, Bulgarians, and their internal enemies. It soon became apparent, however, that interference with the Macedonian problem by the neighboring communist parties, especially the Communist Party of Yugoslavia (CPY), would not be long in coming; the new reality would certainly entangle the KKE in the Macedonian labyrinth for years to come. In 1937, with Tito taking the reins of the CPY, a new Macedonian line surfaced, depressingly similar to that sponsored by IMRO and Bulgaria, aiming at Greece's territorial dismemberment by the secession of Greek Macedonia (Woodhouse 1948, 1976). From that year till his death, Tito had only one goal with respect to Macedonia: formation of a "United and Independent Macedonia" under his hegemony. The fact that Serbia had signed the Treaty of Bucharest in 1913 on Macedonia's trichotomy was old history that should not interfere with his megalomaniac schemes.

The new Balkan realities became apparent in the early 1940s when the Macedonian Question resurfaced, now more complex than ever before. New powerful players with strong connections in Moscow pressed for immediate solutions of the problem at Greece's expense even before the Germans left the Balkans (Averoff-Tossizza 1978; Woodhouse 1976). Considering the age-old dissimilarities of Yugoslavia's and Bulgaria's aims on Macedonia, it is not surprising that Tito, Moscow's favored protégé, would attempt to take the initiative in the battle for Macedonia and the city of Thessaloniki. With his leadership, the powerful communist leaders of the Yugoslav resistance movement arbitrarily decided that all the Slav-speaking inhabitants in the three sections of Macedonia — Serbian Macedonia, Pirin (Bulgarian) Macedonia, and Aegean (Greek) Macedonia — were a separate ethnic group: they were "Macedonians," Slavs who differed from Serbs and Bulgarians (Kofos 1995).[21] These "Macedonians" also included gypsies, Romanians, Turks, Vlachs, Bulgarians, Albanians, Serbs, and Muslims of nondescript ethnicity. The Kremlin master had not yet professed his explicit desire or nodded to the Yugoslav communists to assume a unilateral responsibility in handling the Macedonian issue. That would come in August 1941.

Considering the simmering animosity between the Bulgarian and Yugoslav claims on Macedonia, it is not surprising that it took another year before Moscow decided to change its policy, openly supporting the Yugoslav claims on Macedonia. Thus, the state-controlled ethnogenesis of the new "Macedonians" began with Comintern's dispatching the following directive to the Bulgarian and Yugoslav communists in August 1941: "*Macedonia must be attached to Yugoslavia for practical reasons and for the sake of expediency. The two parties must take up the stand of the self-determination of the*

Macedonian people" (Dragojceva 1979; Pavlowitch 1992, p. 42).[22] Stalin's endorsement of Tito's plans for Macedonia through Comintern was a great victory for the ruler of Yugoslavia.[23] The decisive Comintern directive, tipping the balance in the Yugoslav-Bulgarian rivalry, may explain Dimitrov's ambivalence on the issue, discussed in the next subsection. Ignoring Greece, Comintern decisively shifted the burden and responsibility of how to conduct the struggle for Macedonia from Bulgaria to Yugoslavia. To put it bluntly, Comintern and the BCF reversed the seventy-year-old Bulgarian momentum of the struggle for Macedonia and ruled for an "Independent Macedonia and Thrace" under Yugoslav hegemony (Kofos 1995, pp. 281–82; Poulton 1995, p. 102). Under pressure from Moscow and Belgrade, Dimitrov sacrificed the Bulgarian ambitions on the altar of Yugoslav-Bulgarian "friendship," a decision that temporarily suppressed Bulgaria's irredentist plans on Macedonia.

While Comintern's initiative of August 1941 might not be surprising, it is remarkable by any measure because it rapidly precipitated dramatic, secretive events on the Macedonian issue. From late December 1943 to early January 1944, representatives of the KKE, CPY, and CPB met in a village near the Greek city of Edessa. Andreas Tzimas, one of the three leaders of the EAM troika, represented the KKE, and Vasiliev, a pro–Bulgarian Slavomacedonian, represented the CPB (Vattis 2002). The three delegations decided that the KKE would grant the territories around the Greek cities of Kastoria, Edessa, Giannitsa, Kilkis, and Florina as zones of operation to CPY, a major concession to the pro–Tito communist Slavomacedonians. In large part it explains why the Bulgarian communists began as early as 1943 to tone down quietly their claims on Macedonia.

In many ways, this inadvertently brings up the question of the Slav-speaking inhabitants in Macedonia, who descended from the slavophone pockets during the Byzantine and Ottoman years and included slavophones with pro–Tito sentiments and slavophones with Hellenic sentiments.[24] There were three factions of slavophones in the three sections of Macedonia (Greek, Yugoslav, and Bulgarian), whose declaration of allegiance could rapidly change as a result of pressures from one or another established ethnic group (Hellenic, Bulgarian, or Slav). Their division emerged from the efforts of Greece, Bulgaria, and Serbia to assimilate them (Koliopoulos 1995). From 1943 to the end of 1944, the three factions turned Greek Macedonia into a battleground of opposing ideological and nationalist groups under the Axis occupation. The majority of Slavomacedonians spoke Greek and, together with the Vlach-speakers, Pontian-Greeks, Albanian-speakers, and other Greeks, were integral parts of the Greek state.

Kofos (1995) described how the groups surfaced after World War I. After the mass exodus of Slavs from Greece in the late 1910s and 1920s, a small slavophone minority remained in western Macedonia around Lake Prespa and in the border districts of central Macedonia. By the 1930s there were two opposing ideological and nationalist Slav-speaking groups: the Slav-oriented faction (favoring Bulgaria), and the Greek-oriented slavophones (*Grecomans*). The Bulgarian-oriented slavophones, many of them former fascists or members of terrorist organizations during the occupation, commanded by Bulgarian officers, turned their hatred against the Greek slavophones. They still loathed the *Grecomans* for the role they had played in defeating the Bulgarians during the Macedonian Struggle of 1904–1908 and for their allegiance to Greece.

A third smaller group, the Skopje-oriented faction, surfaced in the multilingual republic of Vardar Province. This group clashed with the other two, the Bulgarian-oriented and the Greek-oriented slavophone factions. Later, the Skopje-oriented group, the strongest lobby within the KKE and EAM, sought the support of the Bulgarian-oriented slavophones, most of whom joined the Skopje-oriented Slavomacedonians after the Germans abandoned Greece.[25] The encouragement of the Skopje-oriented slavophones by the KKE was the result of its 1935 platform promoting the idea of "full equality for the minorities" within Greece. Considerable opposition developed, however, within the EAM/ELAS ranks about accepting Slavomacedonians in the resistance organization.

Predicating his strategic planning of the Macedonian issue on the certainty that Comintern had given him the green light, Tito turned his attention south and east, to the other two sections of Macedonia outside Yugoslavia. In February 1943, he dispatched a leading Yugoslav communist, the troubleshooter Svetozar Vukmanovic-Tempo, a member of the CPY Central Committee, to the Vardar Province (south Yugoslavia) to begin organizing the area as "Macedonia" under Tito's hegemony (Kofos 1989). After organizing the first guerrilla groups of Yugoslav communists, Tempo visited Greek Macedonia and met with KKE and EAM/ELAS leaders to persuade them to participate in the organization of a permanent headquarters of Balkan resistance movements (joint Balkan headquarters). The headquarters was to lead the Balkan partisan armies to their national liberation from the Nazis, securing popular democratic governments in all Balkan countries (Banac 1995).

What was more, Tempo also briefed the Greek resistance leaders in western Macedonia about the Yugoslav views of the postwar solution of the Macedonia Question. The maximum Yugoslav objective was the formation of a unified Macedonian state composed of the three parts of Macedonia. As a minimum objective Yugoslavia would accept annexation of certain areas of Greek Macedonia adjacent to the Yugoslav border, including Thessaloniki (Kofos 1995). The British legation in Sofia learned that Thessaloniki was indeed to be included in the South Slav federation to be dominated by Yugoslavia, a plan also endorsed by the Soviet Union (McNeill 1947). Regardless of the validity of these proposals, it initially appeared that Tempo's ideas behind the joint Balkan headquarters and his suggestions on the Macedonian Question reflected the "megalomaniacal and hegemonistic" intentions of the Communist Party of Yugoslavia.[26]

Even more than Tempo's outrageous demands, public speeches by prominent Yugoslav communist leaders (Dimitar Vlahov, Milovan Djilas, etc.) reaffirmed the Yugoslav view of an independent and united Macedonia to include Greek Macedonia under Yugoslavia. Some leaders in the Vardar Province and in the CPY favored military action to take Greek Macedonia by force. During the critical weeks between the liberation of Greece (October 12, 1944) and the commencement of the *Dekemvriana* (December 3, 1944), the Second Round of the Greek internecine fighting in Athens between the Greek forces and the British against ELAS, "Yugoslavs and Bulgarians were in agreement on detaching, in one way or another, Greek Macedonia from the Greek state" (Kofos 1995, p. 293). It is not known, however, whether the Yugoslav and Bulgarian communists would have used force to accomplish their plan. Such a solution could have been attempted if ELAS won the battle of Athens.[27]

It is impossible to give a precise picture of Tempo's accomplishments and failures because information on his meetings with KKE and EAM/ELAS leaders is confusing (Nicoloudis 2002). One thing is certain: ELAS's leaders did not agree with Tempo's proposal to discuss the subject of Macedonia's autonomy (Vukmanovic-Tempo 1981). In a report to Tito, Tempo ignored the disastrous meeting with ELAS leaders in Tsotyli and his second meeting in Pentalofos, western Macedonia, with ELAS leaders and the British liaison officer Nicholas Hammond, also known as "Mr. Eggs."[28] He only reported his apparently successful meetings with ELAS's top leadership (Velouhiotis, Tzimas and Sarafis) on July 6 and 9, 1943. According to Tempo, ELAS was to participate in the joint Balkan headquarters, cooperate with Albanian and "Macedonian" guerrillas during joint military operations against the occupiers, and allow entrance of "Macedonian" guerrilla groups into Greek Macedonia to proselytize "Macedonian" civilians (many of whom had collaborated with the enemies) (Shoup 1968).The Yugoslav irredentist plans were also rejected by the KKE's General Secretary Giorgos Siantos. While Tempo was on his way back to Yugoslavia, he was told to return to central Greece, where he met Siantos. The latter abruptly rejected the plans for a joint Balkan headquarters and informed Tempo about Greece's unalienable rights on Macedonia (Haritopoulos 2001). However vehement the opposition was to his proposals, Tempo did not waver in asserting later that EAM/ELAS's leadership had actually consented to the ultimate right of Slavomacedonians to self-determination and secession.[29]

Tempo's ultimatum-like demands in Greek Macedonia ended with his departure without accomplishing anything favorable to the Yugoslav side. Perhaps under pressure by Stalin and Dimitrov, Tito ordered Tempo in September 1943 to abandon the plan of establishing a joint Balkan headquarters and return to Yugoslavia (Barker 1976).[30] After he returned from occupied Greece, Tempo said in Monastir: "Whether Greeks want it or not, Macedonia will become autonomous and will be in the federated Yugoslav state. If the Greeks do not want it peacefully, we will achieve it with guns" (Antonakeas 1993).

With ELAS's claiming more and more territory as time went by in 1943, especially when many Slavomacedonians joined ELAS, the remaining fanatics concentrated in villages and towns controlled by the Italians first and Germans later (Kofos 1989). The villages in the Kastoria-Florina districts could be divided into three categories: (a) villages faithful to the Komitet; (b) villages that joined ELAS; and (c) villages faithful to ELAS from the beginning. The inhabitants of the first category were fanatic Bulgarians who voluntarily took up arms from the Italians. The inhabitants of the second category were gradually convinced by the anti–Metaxas and anti-monarchy communist slogans of EAM/ELAS. Those of the last category refused to accept Italian arms from the beginning (Hammond 1991).

Beginning early in 1944, the *komitadjides* became targets of the reorganized ELAS units, an action that displeased a few KKE leaders such as the general secretary of the Macedonian office, Leonidas Stringos, and Tzimas. They both believed the KKE and EAM/ELAS policies toward the Slavomacedonians must be "correct": treat the Slavomacedonians correctly before all join Kaltsev (Koliopoulos 1995). Tzimas evaluated the situation like the genuine communist he was: "We must press the Slavomacedonians to join us; and this is very easy in the Kastoria district where we exercise great influence.... The Slavomacedonians who are not our regular followers are not necessarily our enemies."

Contrary to Stringos's and Tzimas's naïve or calculated favoritism toward all the Slavomacedonians, the pro–Bulgarian armed irregulars were organized into "groups," with German approval, under the most notorious leaders Macedonia will never forget: Gotse (Elias Demakis), Paschali Mitrofsky (Paschalis Mitropoulos), Naoum Pejov, Keramitziev (Kalimanis), and others. We will meet these German collaborators later as leaders cooperating with EAM/ELAS, some of them even much later fighting with the communist Democratic Army of Greece (DAG) against the Greek National Army during the Greek Civil War of 1946–1949.

It hardly needs to be pointed out that people west of the River Aliakmon, where EAM/ELAS predominated, were not better off than the people of the Kastoria and Florina districts from the radical approaches to everyday life imposed by the resistance organization under the KKE's guidance. By April 1943, with the exception of the Bulgarian-oriented groups, any individual or group in Macedonia that opposed EAM/ELAS was brutally crushed. The entire area west of the River Aliakmon was incorporated into the so-called Free Greece. The Bulgarian-oriented groups were treated at the outset by EAM/ELAS as allies, not surprisingly since many active EAM leaders were Bulgarian-oriented Slavomacedonians. Even the notorious Kaltsev with a group of Bulgarian officers and newly drafted *komitadjides* joined the ELAS guerrillas for a while in March 1943 (Koliopoulos 1995).

To attract as many Slavomacedonians as possible into their ranks, EAM/ELAS leaders acted more like internationalists and less like ethnic Greeks. The general secretary of the KKE Macedonian office, Leonidas Stringos, reported to the KKE Central Committee complaints by Tito's partisans that ELAS's attitude in Macedonia provoked the Slavomacedonian partisans to abandon Greece. He wrote: "It is the policy of our party [KKE] to support the right of the Slavomacedonians. We condemned to death three Greek officers for rousing the Greeks against the Slavomacedonians" (Koliopoulos 1995). What followed the party's attitude (behind the EAM/ELAS façade) was a bloodbath. Several noncommunist Greek officers were arrested, tried by the people's courts, and executed (e.g., Zisis, Kiourtsidakis, Portis, and others). Others, like Sidiropoulos, were caught in battle and executed (Papavizas 2002). Still others repented and joined ELAS, to be executed later during the Greek Civil War (e.g., Giorgis Giannoulis) (Papaioannou 1990). Most of the executed men were former officers of the victorious Greek army who had fought the Italian army in Albania and later as PAO members the German Nazis and the Bulgarian occupiers (Papathanasiou 1997).

By the fall of 1943, ELAS's 9th Division controlled the entire Aliakmon basin. The ELAS guerrillas and EAM's numerous committees (*epagrypnisi*, vigilance, the most dreaded of all committees) had placed the rudiments of communism into practice in the entire area. A small Iron Curtain had been imposed on the inhabitants without their will. While they were struggling for survival, working in their small plots to raise food, KKE and EAM operatives struggled to indoctrinate the villagers in Marxist ideology and dialectics while coercing them to turn against all other beliefs, rapidly consolidating their stranglehold on every aspect of life, including life itself. With their brainwashing and propaganda, the communists began to control people's minds. This way, slowly but steadily, step by step, a miniature communist system was established throughout western Macedonia, which was to stay until spring of 1945.

The tribulations of everyday life under the undeclared but well-entrenched rudiments of communism included secretive methods; revolutionary people's committees; heinous people's courts; incessant and hollow Marxist dialectics; propaganda and brainwashing; spying and suspicion of every movement; loss of individual freedom within "Free Greece"; extreme difficulties imposed on travel, even from one village to the next; continuing pressure to join ELAS as "volunteers"; liquidation of rival organizations that did not share the Marxist ideology; paranoia; and sudden knocks at the door at night to drag "reactionaries" and "enemies of the people" to court or, worse, to *boudroumi* (jail) with no explanation or trial.[31]

The Bulgarian-Yugoslav Rivalry Over Macedonia

The rivalry between Serbia and Bulgaria dates back to the last part of the nineteenth century, when Serbia's first attempt to Serbianize the Slav-speakers of geographic Macedonia met with great resistance by Bulgaria and its supporter, czarist Russia (Anastasoff 1938). The rivalry between the two countries in modern times began when the Bulgarian army occupied the Vardar Province (South Serbia) in April 1941 after Bulgaria's allies, the Germans, defeated the Yugoslavs. The dissimilarity of the Bulgarian and Yugoslav aims on Macedonia was also exacerbated by Comintern's directive of August 1941 granting Tito *carte blanche* on how to handle the Macedonian Question and how to manipulate Giorgi Dimitrov, the Bulgarian communist leader, into accepting Comintern's pro–Yugoslav solution of the Macedonian Question.

There was another factor intrinsically connected with Tito's *carte blanche* that added to the difficulties in the relations between Bulgaria and Yugoslavia. When Tempo suggested the unification of Macedonia during his clandestine visit to occupied Greece in 1943, he was insinuating an independent Macedonian republic within the federated state of Yugoslavia (Papaconstantinou 1992). Not surprisingly, the CPB disagreed with Tempo's demands, suggesting that his arguments were unacceptable, because the Yugoslavs did not take into account the critical fact that there never existed a Macedonian ethnicity, with Vardarska's "Macedonians" always having been Bulgarians, not Macedonians. In a desperate but futile effort, the CPB was aiming at an independent, large Macedonia, with close ties to Bulgaria; as a minimum, Bulgaria would keep Pirin Macedonia outside Tito's grasp. As expected, Tito was angry with CPB's demands and refused to accept the existence of a Bulgarian minority in South Serbia — actually a majority.

While they thus quarreled, the Skopjan propaganda machine saw the CPB's interference as an excellent opportunity for verbal revenge against Bulgaria, insisting that the Bulgarian influence in Macedonia was ephemeral and superficial, with the Bulgarians being unable to Bulgarize the "Macedonians" who remained true Slavs. Even the state of King Samouil, a genuine Bulgarian hero, was a "Macedonian" state, according to Skopje, unrelated to the Bulgarians (Nystazopoulou-Pelekidou 1988).

It is important here to place events in sequence within the context of the traditional Yugoslav-Bulgarian antagonism and the acrimonious Tito-Dimitrov rivalry. Beginning in December 1941, the Bulgarian Patriotic Front adopted IMRO's old motto, "Macedonia for the Macedonians." To counteract this move, Tito organized the Communist Party of Macedonia (CPM), which immediately called on all "Macedonians" to unite within Yugoslavia. From then on there were ups and downs in Bulgarian-Yugoslav relations, but one thing remained constant: the Bulgarians always considered the Slavs in Vardar Province Bulgarians, while Tito considered them "Macedonians," a new ethnicity manufactured behind closed doors in Belgrade and Skopje (see Chapter 5 for details). During World War II, friction between Tito and Dimitrov on the Macedonian issue was so common that it brought Stalin into the picture again (Stalin's first interference was in 1940 when he supported the Bulgarian fascist government's claims on Macedonia), this time favoring Yugoslavia. Stalin ordered the CPY and CPB to begin negotiations on the Macedonian issue and find an amicable solution. A shaken Dimitrov, trying hard to agree with Stalin, wrote to Tito on July 26, 1944, saying that he would do everything possible to support the new Yugoslav Federation's policy on Macedonia, granting the "Macedonians" self-determination and the right to secession. From 1944 to 1948, Dimitrov's relationship with Tito moved from an equal comradeship to subordination on the Macedonian issue (Kouzinopoulos 1999, from Dimitrov's secret diary).

Specific talks on the Macedonian issue between the CPY and CPB began in September 1944 in Sofia. The CPY representatives demanded approval from the Bulgarians for a unified Macedonia, including Yugoslav Macedonia, Greek Macedonia, and Pirin Macedonia, under Yugoslav hegemony (Vattis 2002). The Bulgarian communists were also forced to submit to self-criticism, admitting they had deviated from the "correct" Marxist line on the Macedonian issue by pushing hard for a Greater Bulgaria and not resisting the Germans. Finally, Tito succeeded in forcing Dimitrov into a humiliating compliance because of not only his overwhelming posture with the World War II allies, but also his ability to manipulate certain Bulgarian leaders behind Dimitrov's back (Kouzinopoulos 1999).

The tension between the two communist leaders intensified in December 1943, almost at the time Tempo clandestinely visited occupied Greece. It was when Tito began manipulating people to attain his goals on Macedonia at both Bulgaria's and Greece's expense. After naming Dimitar

Vlahov and Tomov, two Bulgarian communist leaders, as "Macedonians," Tito placed them in the Anti-Fascist Council for the National Liberation of Yugoslavia (AVNOJ), the former as president. When Dimitrov learned of the appointments, he informed Stalin that Vlahov and Tomov were known as Bulgarian communists. Vlahov was for many years a high-echelon Bulgarian government employee and Tomov a CPB deputy in the Bulgarian parliament. They had nothing to do with Macedonia. He also stressed that it was not politically wise for the two Bulgarian leaders to be members of the Yugoslav Anti-Fascist Council. It was the first time two prominent Bulgarians were officially transformed into "Macedonians" (Kouzinopoulos 1999, p. 19).

The tension between the two leaders increased further, impelling Dimitrov to protest vehemently to Stalin and Molotov, accusing Tito of treating the Bulgarian communist leaders shabbily, neglecting to correct the error with Vlahov and Tomov.[32] He also expressed doubts on what was going to happen in Macedonia after the war. The most desirable arrangement for the Balkans and the Soviet Union, according to Dimitrov's view, would be formation of a federation of South Slavs, including Bulgarians, Serbs, Croats, Slovenes, and Macedonians, with equality as the basis.[33] Within this federation, Macedonia could find its ethnic and national existence and cease being the apple of discord among the Balkan people (Kouzinopoulos 1999, p. 21).

In 1943 Tito had created the first two "Macedonian" leaders, converting by magic the Bulgarian genes into "Macedonian" genes (Kofos 1987) (see also Chapter 5). It was the genesis of a "new" ethnicity that fooled the world then and will continue to fool it as long as the world does not accept that the present depends on the past, on history, and that the glamour of a communist war hero against the Nazis, Tito, does not necessarily go hand in hand with the truth, in this case, the historical truth. As we shall see in the next section, thousands of Slav and Bulgarian fascist and Nazi collaborators during World War II and the ensuing occupation, former fascist and Nazi collaborators (as *komitadjides* and Ochrana terrorists), turned into Yugoslav partisans, and finally "Macedonians," descendants of King Philip II and Alexander the Great. The worst thing for Greece, Bulgaria, and Macedonia's history was Stalin's refusal to support Dimitrov.

In spite of these drawbacks, and in a desperate effort to harmonize his position with his mentor's wishes, the still-wavering Dimitrov asked the CPB Central Committee to approve his decision to support the Macedonian policy of the new Federated Yugoslavia, granting autonomy to the Pirin Macedonians. He also asked the CPB to consent to the secession of parts of Macedonia to Yugoslavia that belonged to it before 1913 if the population agreed. If a federation was to be formed, United Macedonia would be included (Kouzinopoulos 1999). Dimitrov's reluctant agreement on the Macedonian issue encouraged the Yugoslav leader and the Skopjan nationalists to work even harder to materialize their dream for a "Greater Macedonia." Though Tito was facing his country's occupation by the Nazis at the time, he never stopped scheming to form a Greater Yugoslavia, extending from the Adriatic to the Black Sea and from the Austrian border to the Aegean; his plan involved the truncation of Greece and Bulgaria by the separation of Greek Macedonia and Pirin Macedonia, respectively.

Dimitrov's capitulation was complete and final, foreshadowing all other points in Yugoslav-Bulgarian relations. On June 7, 1946, Stalin met with Molotov and Zhdanov representing the Soviet Union; Tito, Rankoviv, and Nescovic representing Yugoslavia; and Dimitrov, Kolarov, and Kostov representing Bulgaria (Tsalouhides 1994). Stalin advised the Bulgarian communist leaders to declare autonomy for Pirin Macedonia, a strongly needed initial step for the unification of the three parts of Macedonia. When Dimitrov expressed doubts about the Pirin inhabitants' Macedonianism, Stalin rushed to explain to Dimitrov how state building — even if it is a fabrication — leads to acceptable nation building. His remarks to Dimitrov on nation building were revealing indeed:

> You must ask for an outlet to the Aegean Sea.... You have every right to ask for an edaphic approach, but it is difficult to believe you can achieve it today. Such a request can only be achieved by force. You must be prepared for the future.... Pirin Macedonia must become autonomous within Bulgaria.... *Whether there is a Macedonian nation or not, and whether its population has not yet developed a Macedonian consciousness, makes no difference. Such consciousness did not exist in Byelorussia either when, after the October revolution, we proclaimed it as a Soviet republic.*[34] Later, however, it was shown [to people] that a Byelorussian people did in fact exist [Martis 2001; Kouzinopoulos 1999, p. 22].

The Byelorussians, who always considered themselves Russian, had been forced to embrace a new ethnicity after their state was forced to separate from Russia and accept a new name. Tito, using Stalin's miraculous prescription, also created a new "nation," the "Macedonian Nation," encompassing many ethnic groups, most of them never having heard the word "Macedonia" before.[35]

The disparate position on the Macedonian issue adopted by Bulgaria and Yugoslavia demonstrated how artificial the problem was and how seriously it was manipulated by Bulgaria, Yugoslavia, and the Soviet Union after the beginning of World War II to fulfill their irredentist claims on Macedonia. To the three communist Slavic countries, Greece, the recipient of 75 percent of historic Macedonia, was irrelevant; the only thing that mattered to them was how they would annex all of Macedonia or parts of it, and who would be the major beneficiary. Both the Bulgarians and Yugoslavs made valiant efforts to compromise their Marxist internationalist philosophy with Moscow's un-Marxist chauvinism and their own nationalist pressures and priorities.

Unquestionably, the KKE played a secondary role in the ideological and nationalist conflict between the CPY and CPB. Much recent literature examines how the KKE's virtual prewar insignificance in the communist world was exacerbated by the loss of support by the Greek people for its anti–Hellenic stand on the Macedonian issue. It was becoming increasingly apparent to a few KKE leaders, for example, that international communism was laying a trap for their party, but the KKE leadership at the top could not see it or master enough courage to object to the CPY's, CPB's, and Comintern's demands on Greek Macedonia (Kordatos 2001).

A trap was indeed laid by the Yugoslav communists before the fighting began in Athens in December 1944. New evidence suggests that as early as 1942 the KKE's high-echelon leadership had made military plans to seize Athens as soon as the Germans left (Farakos 2000). A little before the battle of Athens, the so-called Second Round (*Dekemvriana*) of the Greek fratricide between ELAS on the one hand and the Greek government forces allied with the British on the other, Tito encouraged the KKE leadership's revolutionary aspirations, promising help and urging the KKE to seize Athens by force, although he knew that his policy was bound to clash with Stalin's to live up to the agreement he had made in Moscow with Churchill in October 1944 (90 percent British influence in Greece); and that such action would definitely be opposed by the British (Banac 1995, p. 263). As the fighting in the Greek capital intensified, the KKE leadership asked for Tito's support, but Tito refused to oblige and began preparing new guerrilla units to invade Greek Macedonia and Epirus, ostensibly to confront the EDES partisans, ELAS's archenemies.[36] Dimitrov gave the same negative reply for assistance during the *Dekemvriana* as Tito, indicating they both had the same instructions from the same source. Tito, in the meantime, assured the British he did not intend to force the Macedonian problem, but he would raise the issue at the peace conference (Kondis 1984). After ELAS's defeat in Athens, Dimitrov, reflecting Stalin's views, advised the KKE leaders to avoid future confrontation with the British.

Events in Western Macedonia
After the Italian Surrender

Dramatic events in the European theater of war at the end of July 1943 changed the occupation zones in Greece and brought the Germans to western Macedonia. Mussolini's overthrow by Marshall Badoglio shocked the Germans so profoundly they frantically began preparing to disarm the Italian army of occupation just in case the Italian "allies" decided to become neutral or join the resistance (Mazower 1993). It was a toss-up in western Macedonia who would be able to convince the Kastoria garrison, eight hundred men strong, to surrender. The ELAS leaders tried hard, but the Germans won out (Papavizas 2002).

After Italy's surrender in September 1943, more turmoil was to come in the form of terrorization of the Greek people and slavophone Greek Macedonians. Kaltsev and other Komitet leaders, working with the Germans, unleashed a new wave of terrorization just as brutal as that practiced by the Bulgarian authorities in occupied eastern Macedonia and western Thrace. The Bulgarians and Kaltsev's *komitadjides* practiced the same harsh methods as those unleashed by their predecessors from 1902 to 1908, with Germans overseeing the actions this time. At the outset, EAM/ELAS was unwilling or unable to stop the terrorization against the Greeks and slavophone Greek Macedonians. Its reluctance to intervene was exacerbated by the pressure from Slavomacedonian leaders on the KKE's leadership to form separate slavophone bands, ostensibly to cooperate with ELAS against the Germans. This reflected the behind-the-scenes pressure by the powerful communist leaders of the Yugoslav resistance movement under Tito, whose armed partisans entered Greece at will, ostensibly to regroup after battles or skirmishes with the Germans. Many partisans, uninvited in Greek Macedonia in 1943, proselytized the slavophone inhabitants with the familiar ideas of a "Macedonian nation" and a "United and Independent Macedonia."

Early in 1943 the KKE faced a serious dilemma: maintain friendly relations with Tito and his partisans, tolerating the "Macedonian" indoctrination of the Greek and slavophone population by Slav ideologues and running the risk of offending the ethnic Greeks, or sever its relations with the Yugoslavs, extolling at the same time EAM's Hellenic patriotism to hold the Greeks in its grip, a policy certain to offend Tito and his partisans (Koliopoulos 1995). The Greek party of the proletariat attempted the impossible: please the autocratic dictator next door and avoid offending the patriotic feelings of the Greek people. To accomplish the first, the KKE unwisely and hastily recognized the Slav-speaking minority in Greece as Slavomacedonians, courting the slavophones irrespective of ethnic affiliation to join ELAS. To give the impression that EAM was an organization encompassing most of the Greeks and that EAM was not dominated by the KKE, the party adopted a policy promoting patriotic ideals aimed at boosting the morale of the Greek people and their determination for liberation from the Nazis and fascists and disguised as much as possible Marxist ideas and the ultimate aim of the movement (Averoff-Tossizza 1978).

To please Tito and his partisans further, the KKE took one more giant, fateful step. It allowed formation of an independent political slavophone organization in Greek Macedonia within the ranks of the resistance movement, the Slavomacedonian National Liberation Front (*Slovenomakedonski Narodno Osloboditelen Front*, SNOF), the EAM of the Slavs, with its own special armed bands within ELAS (Hammond 1991). Part of its motivation to allow SNOF's formation was surely the desire to enhance the party's standing with the Slav-speakers in Greece, especially because this approach was compatible with the conservative position adopted by the KKE at its Sixth Party Congress in December 1935 for the "complete equality of minorities" within Greece (Kofos 1995). The KKE justified this act as a necessary move to attract the slavophones to ELAS. Joint Greek-Yugoslav armed detachments were also allowed by ELAS to operate on both sides of the frontier. In May 1943, for instance, the first slavophone guerrillas appeared within Greece near Florina wearing a communist red star on their caps, the flag of the nationalist IMRO on their sleeves, and the initials NOB (*Narodno Osloboditelen Boiska*, National Liberation Army).[37] Yugoslav political instructors were also allowed to cross into Greek Macedonia at will to inculcate in Macedonia's slavophones the idea of a "Macedonian nation" and present Yugoslav plans for a solution to the Macedonian Question. The proposed "solution" included self-determination of the Slav-speakers and the right of secession from Greece.

SNOF's formation in 1943 with KKE's consent was tantamount to an official party statement of unequivocal support of Tito's Slavomacedonians and partisans. Lest this entanglement not be enough, the KKE adopted a parallel strategy, orchestrated by Yiannis Ioannides, Politburo member, to strengthen its ties with the CPB (Kyrou 1950). One of the most convincing documents of such cooperation is the agreement signed on July 12, 1943, in New Petritsi, in Bulgarian-occupied eastern Macedonia. Immediately following SNOF's formation, the KKE and its secret information media had assured the Greek people that EAM and its allies were working to safeguard Greece's territorial integrity. Yet, Yiannis Ioannides, the strongman behind the KKE's general secretary, Giorgos Siantos, openly defying the KKE's official line, signed an agreement with CPB's Dusan Daskalov, consenting to BCF's plans for detaching Macedonia from Greece to form an autonomous Macedonia, the nucleus of a new communist Macedonian state.[38] Following are excerpts of the agreement:

> The KKE and the CPB ... having in mind the last Comintern instructions before its dissolution ... decide with the representatives who sign this agreement, Yiannis Ioannides from the KKE and Dusan Daskalov from the CPB, that the final aim of both parties is the establishment in the Balkans of a Union of Soviet Republics, which will include Greece,

Bulgaria, Macedonia, and Serbia. The communist parties of Greece and Bulgaria are free to act accordingly to reach the goal.... An outlet to the Aegean will be given to Bulgaria.... The Aegean, Pirin, and Serb Macedonia will become an autonomous Soviet Republic within the Balkan union. The official language will be Greek and Bulgarian [Vattis 2002].

By allowing the Slavomacedonians to form SNOF, giving it equal status with EAM, the KKE unintentionally or by design allowed difficult-to-control forces to operate in a critical section of Macedonia to stir up new problems, a major episode for criticism for the party of the proletariat. Mertzos (1984) described what he thought were the "ten deadly sins" perpetrated by the KKE, some pertaining to the Macedonian issue. He also expressed great concern over how the KKE failed to take a strategic retreat from ideological precepts and to initiate policies to avoid agreements bound to hurt Greece: tolerating SNOF's Slavomacedonians favoring Tito's Yugoslavia while signing an agreement with the Communist Party of Bulgaria to allow incorporation of Greek Macedonia, together with Pirin Macedonia and Vardar Macedonia, to form an autonomous Soviet-type republic of Macedonia.

Evidence appears to support the view that the SNOF leaders, at least at the beginning, did not belong to IMRO's separatists, but to Tito's agents in Macedonia (Koliopoulos 1995).[39] As soon as SNOF was formed, its operatives attempted to replace the Bulgarians' and IMRO's influence on the Slavomacedonians, challenging them to join the maelstrom leading toward a Yugoslav-oriented autonomous Macedonia. Interestingly, the Slavomacedonian leaders did not seem to be burdened by qualms about abandoning Bulgaria and siding with Yugoslavia. After all, Dimitrov had capitulated to Stalin's demands and Tito's intrigue, disqualifying Bulgaria's claim on Macedonia. Not surprisingly, none of all the persons and organizations involved with the Macedonian issue — Stalin, Tito, Dimitrov, SNOF, Comintern, BCF, KKE, CPB, and CPY — bothered to ask what the Hellenic people of Macedonia, two and a half million strong in the 1940s, would prefer to do with their Macedonia.

A first glance at Tzimas's and Stringos's unexplained tolerance of the pro–Bulgarian or pro–Tito Slavomacedonians would suggest that the entire EAM and the KKE structure harbored the same pro–Slavic sentiments. This was far from the truth in 1943–1944. ELAS's leadership never officially accepted the Yugoslav position on Macedonia. This was amply demonstrated from the KKE's rather blunt reply to Tempo in 1943 about forming a joint Balkan headquarters and Siantos's abrupt rebuffing of Tempo's blatant demands at Greek Macedonia's expense. Offering Macedonia on a platter to the Slavs would come in 1949 by despair-consumed Zachariadis during DAG's last rites. In retrospect, considering the unpredictable turn of events, one would wonder why a group of KKE and EAM/ELAS leaders tried so hard to maintain friendly relations with the Yugoslav partisans and the pro–Tito SNOF leaders operating on Greek soil while at the same time encouraging Bulgarian aspirations on Macedonia.

One explanation is the KKE's desire to maintain good relations with Tito, hoping for his support if ELAS decided to take Greece by force or if EAM/ELAS needed his protection in the event of a failure. Another explanation is the KKE's and ELAS's desire to attract undecided slavophones and slavophone autonomists of unknown affiliation to EAM, as they did indeed.[40] It was a risky policy to say the least: placate the Yugoslav leader for future benefits by grafting pro–Yugoslav elements into ELAS's center of power while at the same time signing a cooperative agreement with the Bulgarian communists. It soon became apparent to the KKE leadership, however, that the envisaged cooperation could not and would not benefit Greece's views on the Macedonian Question, because the Slavomacedonians misunderstood EAM/ELAS's goodwill for cooperation as a silent promise to advance their plans for autonomy.[41]

With Italy's capitulation, the Bulgarian liaison officers attached to the German garrisons formed a new paramilitary Slavomacedonian organization, replacing the Italian-supported Komitet. The new group, named "Voluntary Battalion" by the Germans, a Slav-speaking terrorist group headed by Kaltsev and manned by the most fanatic Slavomacedonians, became widely known as Ochrana.[42] As with the old Ochrana, the new Slavomacedonian Ochrana members were cooperating with the Germans for Macedonian autonomy and eventual annexation of Macedonia by Bulgaria (Troebst 1989). To make matters more confusing, the Slavomacedonians could join any of these organizations— Komitet, Ochrana, ELAS, or SNOF— and then leap from one to the other according to the circumstances (Koliopoulos 1995).[43]

Several accounts from the same period help us understand SNOF's pretentiously inimical attitude toward Kaltsev's new pro–German Ochrana, accusing it of being an instrument of the fascist Bulgarian bourgeoisie. In reality, there was close cooperation between the communist SNOF, Ochrana and IMRO, the ultranationalist Bulgarian organization, all aiming at destroying Macedonia's Hellenism. Ochrana's leaders were urging their members to join SNOF-EAM, a line also advocated by the Nazi-serving puppet government in Sofia (Koliopoulos 1995). Mitrofsky, Gotse, Pejov, and others were among the first to transform themselves from Ochrana-Nazis to SNOF-communists. Some of Ochrana's methods, besides terrorization, were similar to those of SNOF: (a) demand that the Slavomacedonians openly declare their ethnic identity; (b) proselytize the KKE leaders sympathizing with the Bulgarian dreams and plans; and (c) cooperate, when feasible, with pro–Bulgarian ELAS leaders.

At the outset, the KKE assumed it could control SNOF because its leaders, old and tried communists, some of them freed from Akronafplia, were believed to be trustful Marxist comrades. Most of them, however, did not perform as the KKE expected. The first indication that something was not going according to KKE's expectations was a meeting of SNOF leaders on January 28, 1944, who expressed the view that after the war Greece must become a "federated people's democracy" like Yugoslavia, composed of two republics, the "People's Republic of Greece" and the "People's Republic of Aegean Macedonia" (Nikoloudis 2002). This view, however, was rejected by the slavophones of the Florina district with the justification that Greece was not a multiethnic conglomerate like Yugoslavia. From then on SNOF split into two parts. The Kastoria's SNOF, the strongest of the two, worked for Macedonian autonomy; the Florina's SNOF followed the KKE's official policy of equality for the minorities in Greece. Later they were united and turned their wrath against the Bulgarian propaganda and the slavophone *Grecomans* who remained attached to Hellenism.

The political challenges to the KKE's leadership by SNOF's clearly defined pro–Yugoslav proclivities were further exacerbated by some ambitious individuals of the party's high-echelon leadership. The KKE leadership, for instance, did not take immediate measures against the SNOF autonomists because of the disagreements among its high-echelon leaders on how to handle SNOF autonomist tendencies and the KKE's desires to recruit as many Slav-speakers as possible. Farakos (2000), who served as general secretary of the KKE, attributed the party's indecisions to the incompetence of its leadership, composed of old communists, incapable of responding to new challenges. The leadership's vacillation and the arrogant nationalist-autonomist propaganda by SNOF leaders did not escape the attention of ELAS's military leaders from Greek western Macedonia, former officers of the victorious Greek army. Eventually, most of the EAM/ELAS leaders realized that SNOF had plunged into a frenzy of nationalist separatist propaganda, clandestinely antagonizing EAM's aims published in its founding proclamation. SNOF became a "Trojan horse of Yugoslav partisans" within the Greek resistance movement in Macedonia, as Koliopoulos pointed out (1995). It became a Yugoslav vehicle for transferring wavering Slavomacedonians from ELAS to the Yugoslav partisans and to the autonomy-for-Macedonia concept, a blatantly inimical intention against Greece.

Alarmed by SNOF's aims at Greece's expense, Giorgos Siantos, the KKE's general secretary, wrote to Stringos in September 1944: "Be very careful with the ethnic Macedonian problem and the movements of the Slavomacedonian elements, but keep brotherly relations with Tito's forces" (Koliopoulos 1995). How naïve was the KKE! Nothing can excuse its tolerance toward the provocations by Yugoslav partisans operating on Greek soil without the consent of Greek Macedonians and the Greek people in general. What, given all this, was the motive behind the SNOF leaders' provocative behavior? And what would have happened to Greek Macedonia and Greece if Tito's claims on western and central Macedonia (with Thessaloniki) were materialized? The Serbs and Greeks were friends, but the glaring reality was that Tito, a Croat, and his comrades were incapable or unwilling to honor the age-old Greek-Serbian friendship.

To serve their own political ambitions, certain key KKE and ELAS leaders tolerated, and even supported, Slav-speaking mercenaries to join ELAS units, ready to turn against Greece at the first opportunity. But SNOF's unprecedented scale of provocative and disruptive actions could not be tolerated forever, especially by ELAS officers born and raised in western Macedonia, whose motivation was surely the desire to keep Macedonia's Hellenism intact. As expected, the first open rift between ELAS's leadership and SNOF's Slavomacedonian autonomists occurred in May 1944. The local Greek communist leadership reacted immediately, arresting a few SNOF leaders such as Naum Pejov and Mitrofsky for promoting Macedonian autonomy (Koliopoulos 1995). Other SNOF leaders were expelled to Yugoslavia. Drawing on the lessons of previous perceptions of deceitful Tito-prone slavophones, the KKE Central Committee decided to dissolve SNOF and notified the party's Provisional Committee in Kastoria to proceed carefully with the task. It did not take long, however, after these events for the imprisoned irredentist-prone SNOF leaders to be freed by ELAS's leadership.

No other slavophone individual played as great a role in the events of the tumultuous 1940s in western Macedonia as Paschal Mitrofsky (Koliopoulos 1995). The colorful, fanatic Mitrofsky, from a village near Kastoria, with a law degree from the Aristotelian University of Thessaloniki, had been invited by the KKE local committee to join the communist mechanism behind the ELAS façade.[44] A clever individual for political manipulation and intrigue, he was instrumental in SNOF's formation, together with other autonomists. After ELAS freed him from prison, he joined the Yugoslav partisans, and with SNOF's demise, he and other SNOF leaders formed the "Provisional Revolutionary Committee of Macedonia Occupied by Greece."

Last, but not least, among the controversial Slavomacedonian communists was Gotse (Elias Demakis) from the village of Melas, north of Kastoria. He repeatedly served time in prison for theft, and later the Metaxas dictatorship incarcerated him for his communist beliefs, which he had acquired while in prison for theft. Released from prison after he signed a declaration of repentance, he flirted with the *komitadjides* and later as an ELAS leader pretending to work for Macedonian autonomy (Koliopoulos

1995). He remained a Bulgarian to his core, but in the end he joined the Yugoslav partisans.

Although there had been a few efforts for reconciliation, as the 1944 autumn was approaching, the ELAS-SNOF and ELAS-Yugoslav partisan relations deteriorated, a harbinger of more turmoil to follow. In November ELAS had learned that strong Yugoslav partisan units were moving toward the Greek border. This was confirmed later by Skopje Commander Petso Tsaikov, who in 1949 revealed that an organized plan existed for the "forceful annexation of Aegean Macedonia and Pirin Macedonia." An order of the Soviet General Birgiuzov prevented such action (Farakos 2000). This was also confirmed by Mitsopoulos, a DAG *capetan* in the Paiko mountains: "When after the *Dekemvriana* the role of England became known, the Skopje chauvinists ... told us they were ready to protect Macedonia's independence, going forcefully all the way to Mount Olympus!" (Makris 2000).

Before discussing SNOF's demise, it is indeed interesting to see at this point what happened to the *komitadjides* of western Macedonia. Many of them defected from the Germans in 1943 and 1944. The war pendulum in Europe had swung against Germany, and they were rushing to join the winners.[45] ELAS and, later, the Greek government arrested and executed some of them. Looking the other way, the KKE had no qualms in approving the *komitadjides*' abandoning the Italians and the Germans to join ELAS. Not knowing whether Bulgaria had ordered their defection, ELAS continued recruiting *komitadjides* by the end of 1943, unconcerned about the consequences. Some of the *komitadjides* even assumed responsible positions in ELAS units (Chrysochoou 1952). Even those that had been arrested were soon released with SNOF leaders' intervention. Pejov, Gotse, and Mitrofsky, all active again in western Macedonia, tried hard to convince the wavering *komitadjides* to defect and join ELAS. Many escaped to Yugoslavia and joined the armed bands of the Bulgarian fascist Vancho Mihailov of IMRO. Some joined the Yugoslav partisans, whose leadership did not care whether they were *komitadjides* or Ochranists. Kaltsev approached the KKE and offered to work in the resistance as an ELAS volunteer, but he was not accepted (Kofos 1989).[46] Many *komitadjides*, afraid they might be punished after the war, suddenly became "Macedonians" and joined the Yugoslav partisans, their motivation surely being the desire to dissociate themselves from the crimes they had committed and the treasonous acts perpetrated against their country (Nikoloudis 2002).

As the *komitadjides* defected from the country's occupiers and joined ELAS, a dangerous witches' brew of Bulgarian fascist irredentism passed into ELAS's ranks. Yet, not many voices of protest were raised by the KKE and EAM/ELAS leaders for harboring war criminals, enemy collaborators, and traitors. After the war, the KKE strongly accused the Tsaldaris government of harboring German and Italian collaborators, a grave mistake committed first by the KKE. It appeared that the KKE and EAM/ELAS leadership in western Macedonia did not consider harboring pro–Bulgarian or pro–Yugoslav war criminals a violation. *Rhizospastis*, the official KKE newspaper, wrote a year later (July 1945): "Because of our right policy with EAM, the great majority of the Slavomacedonians [*komitadjides*] joined EAM. More than 3,000 joined ELAS.... Applying the right policy of equality for minorities, EAM was able to detach them from Bulgarian, Italian, and German influence." Utilizing the flimsiest of pretexts, the party forgot that these Slavomacedonians (not the majority of the slavophones) were *dosilogoi* (enemy collaborators) and many of them war criminals and traitors, conniving to turn over western Macedonia to Bulgaria or Yugoslavia (Vattis 2002).

Lest the KKE had not made enough unwise and hasty decisions to characterize the slavophone minority in Greece as Slavomacedonians, allow SNOF's formation, and finally recruit *komitadjides* into ELAS's ranks, the party of the Greek proletariat committed another error: It allowed formation of the "Slavomacedonian Battalion," with Gotse as its political commissar, to absorb the *komitadjides* defecting from the Germans.[47] In less than a month, the battalion doubled its strength, incorporating many German or Bulgarian collaborators. The battalion became the salvation for many desperate individuals attempting to avoid reprisals at war's end: *komitadjides*, Ochranists, Slavomacedonian adventurers, Bulgarian and Yugoslav agents, and autonomists guided by communists freed from Akronafplia by the Germans, struggling to bury their Bulgarian past (Koliopoulos 1995). It did not take long for Gotse to assume firm command of the Slavomacedonian Battalion, eventually guiding it to Tito's partisans. The journey from Bulgaria to SNOF, to western Macedonia, and then to Yugoslavia was completed. Gotse had assumed four nationalities: Greek, Bulgarian, Slavomacedonian, and finally communist Yugoslavian; were he alive today, he would certainly have been "Macedonian" in FYROM, a direct blood connection to Alexander the Great!

Before it finally crossed the border to Yugoslavia, Gotse's battalion had become independent of ELAS's 9th Division's 28th Regiment, a threat to ELAS's aims in the region, and an effective propaganda machine pressing hard for extreme Macedonian positions favoring the Yugoslav partisans and Tito's aims on Greek Macedonia. The KKE leadership had not taken such dangers into account when it allowed the battalion's formation. Neither had such dangers been foreseen by the local EAM and ELAS leaders who, in their haste to increase their numbers, recruited or accepted every slavophone individual who chose to join ELAS.

The relations between Gotse's battalion and ELAS deteriorated further when he refused to obey ELAS's order to attack a German convoy and move his battalion to Siatista, a pure Greek patriotic town in western Macedonia. Disobeying the two orders, Gotse invited the demise of his unit. ELAS immediately ordered its 28th Regiment to suppress militarily the rebellion of the Slavomacedonian conglomerate battalion, forcing it out of Greece. In Yugoslavia, where it escaped, Gotse's group was renamed the "First Aegean Macedonian Brigade" (Kofos 1989).

A more serious reason for attacking and expelling Gotse's battalion was that the KKE, under pressure, finally and honestly abandoned the autonomy-for-Macedonia concept and returned to its 1935 policy on the equality of the minorities within Greece. This policy, which the Bulgarian- or Yugoslav-oriented Slavomacedonians seriously abused, caused considerable opposition to KKE's leadership by party cadres and high-echelon ELAS officers of western Macedonian descent. The opposition increased when it became evident that the Skopje-oriented slavophones were at work undermining ELAS's goals, indoctrinating the villagers of western Macedonia that all slavophones were "Macedonians"; the Greeks of western Macedonia, the overwhelming majority, were not really Macedonians; and Gotse's and Mitrofsky's "Macedonians" had the right to self-determination and secession from Greece to form their "Macedonian" state within the Yugoslav federation.

With Gotse's "Macedonian" battalion expelled from western Macedonia to Yugoslavia in October 1944, the KKE, ELAS, and the majority of the peaceful, family-oriented, pro–Hellenic slavophones were relieved. How mistaken they were! Many of Gotse's men would return to Greece in 1947–1949 to assist the KKE in fighting the civil war.

A hard-nosed examination of the events in Macedonia during the occupation, especially in Greek western Macedonia, should lead the world to conclude that Greece's northern neighbors attempted by illegal means, including cooperation with the common enemy, deceit, terrorization, and brutality, to impose on innocent people the reinterpretation of Macedonian history, construct an artificial nationality distinct from Greeks, Serbs, and Bulgarians, and propel to the world the myth of a "Macedonian nation" (see next chapter). They never informed the world that the so-called "Macedonian nation" was founded by people who changed ethnic affiliations several times during the tumultuous 1940s. The world does not know that several of the individuals who underwent repeated ethnic transformations before and during World War II were later awarded high government positions in the People's Republic of Macedonia and FYROM. History was repeating itself for the fourth time under the eyes of another conqueror.

The brazen demands of adventurers, Nazi and fascist sympathizers, communists, reformed communists, redressed Bulgarian nationalists,

German-loving Ochranists, and terrorists (*komitadjides*) posed a major threat to Greece's territorial integrity. Greece's heteromorphic enemies cleverly misinformed and confused unsuspecting foreign observers, who were unable to distinguish between the historical truth, the myth, and history's alteration; discern the multitude of affiliations and loyalties; and see how Greece's connection to a collective past would be morally devastated if the conspiracies by its enemies severed the nation's past from contributing to its present and future civil spirit. Their multiple ethnic disguises were so powerful that they left an indelible lie still perpetuated.

5

State-Controlled "Macedonian" Ethnogenesis

Who steals my purse steals trash;' tis something, nothing;
'Twas mine, 'tis his, and has been slave to thousands;
But he that filches from me my good name
Robs of that which not enriches him,
And makes me poor indeed.
—*Shakespeare*

By meddling in the affairs of Macedonia to protect and support Bulgaria, its favored Balkan nation still under Ottoman rule in the second half of the nineteenth century, and to use Bulgaria as a corridor to descend to the Dardanelles, Russian Panslavism, the articulator of the great Bulgarian dreams, essentially created the Macedonian problem. But Russia was not the only power implicated in the historical blunder. Because of vacillations and shabby "solutions" and the inability to understand history, or the political pressures to disregard it, the European powers also contributed greatly to the perpetuation of a problem that could have been satisfactorily resolved a long time ago. In the early phases of the problem, the Europeans had the power and the means to settle things in Macedonia but lacked the will to do so for political and diplomatic reasons and for their own selfish interests. It is thus not surprising that because of the actions of power blocks competing for influence in southeast Europe, the Bulgarians first and the Yugoslavs later perpetuated and exploited the Macedonian Question. But it is doubtful that the Yugoslavs and Bulgarians ever deluded themselves into believing they were fighting on history's right side.

The author will attempt in this chapter, at the risk of being considered a polemic anticommunist, a serious historical review of the misconceptions pertaining to the analysis of the legacy of Macedonia's past, promulgated by Soviet-sponsored international communism; and an equally careful analysis of the Macedonian controversy's infrastructure, with emphasis on the history that now lies in dead communism's shadow and in Tito's defunct socialist imperialism. What is the Macedonian Question (or Macedonian controversy), and how did the struggle for Macedonia change from the late 1800s to the tumultuous 1940s?

It was originally a conflict among Bulgaria, Greece, and Serbia. Their aspirations for possession of Macedonia, the rich land under the Ottomans with its seditious mix of nationalities and its great prize, the city of Thessaloniki, a precious gateway to the Aegean littoral, had been frustrated one way or another or ignored by the European powers at the Berlin gathering in 1878. Bulgaria received almost the entire Macedonia by the Russian-dictated Treaty of San Stefano only to lose most of it a few months later by the Treaty of Berlin (see Chapter 1 for details). Serbia, losing some territories won in the 1877–1878 Russo-Turkish War, was forced to accept Austria-Hungary's occupation of Bosnia-Herzegovina. The Greeks felt isolated from the events and negotiations on the fate of the waning Ottoman Empire in the Balkans. All these events set the stage for confrontation among the three Balkan countries. Against this old, grim backdrop after Berlin, the three countries turned their attention to Macedonia, eventuating a rivalry still reverberating today.

There can be no doubt that from 1870 to 1912 the problem of who had the historical, cultural, ethnic, and demographic rights to possess Macedonia mostly involved Hellenism and Bulgarism, two ideas—and two forces—that fought with ethnic idealism for Macedonia with peaceful means at the outset, guerrilla war later. The two ideas, Hellenism and Bulgarism, clashed for Macedonia, embodied as Bulgarians and Greeks, not as "Macedonians" and Greeks. With the onset of communism in the Balkans, however, the Macedonian Question — and the struggle for Macedonia — took on a different meaning and new dimensions.

As the World War II occupation was changing into a prolonged period of internecine struggle and civil war in Greece, the old Greek-Bulgarian and Bulgarian-Yugoslav enmity for Macedonia was reignited with the German authority in the Balkans waning, leaving no doubt that the Macedonian controversy was to resurface stronger than ever. For this book, the Macedonian controversy in the 1940s was the competing claims by Greece's northern communist neighbors for Hellenic Macedonia. In simple terms, it was the snatching away of Greek Macedonia, including its capital, the sprawling city and Aegean port of Thessaloniki. The Bulgarians first, and the

Yugoslavs later, have used every means available to them to violate the Treaty of Bucharest signed in 1913 to acquire Macedonia or parts of it. They used propaganda, guerrilla warfare, distortion of history, anthropological and historical studies of dubious or prejudiced nature that never seriously considered history or the existence of millions of indigenous Hellenic Macedonians, and indirectly civil war (aiding the Greek communists during the civil war of 1946–1949) to destroy historic Macedonia's Hellenism, truncate Greece by separating its Macedonia, and push Greece to its pre–World War I frontiers. Even with FYROM's independence from Yugoslavia, the Macedonian Question continues unabated, thanks to Skopje's activism, the Aegean Refugee Association's undiminished propaganda, and the support of Slavic organizations abroad (Michailides 2000).

It is sobering to reflect that the Macedonian controversy was revived almost immediately after the Treaty of Bucharest was signed in 1913 with the intent to settle the conflict in Macedonia. It is not a coincidence that its revival went hand in hand with communism's genesis in the Balkan peninsula. Any doubts concerning communism's unorthodox involvement with an ethnic problem of paramount Balkan significance would have been dissipated early in the game were it known that Comintern, Stalin's right-hand instrument, was involved from its very early inception with the Macedonian Question. During the first quarter of the twentieth century, the Communist Party of Bulgaria (CPB), acting as Comintern's political instrument, whose efforts the thoughtless and often revolutionary decisions of the Communist Party of Greece (KKE)'s leadership first tolerated and later sustained, undertook forming a Greater Macedonia dominated by Bulgarians, to the detriment of Greece's territorial integrity. The small party of the Greek proletariat willingly or unwillingly tolerated or encouraged the agitations of the insignificant Slavo-Bulgarian communist minority in Greece, allowing their nationalist aspirations to flourish at Greece's expense (Papavizas 2002; Woodhouse 1948).

The late 1930s and early 1940s saw the Macedonian Question remaining dormant for awhile, but not in the propaganda mills of the Yugoslav, Bulgarian, and Greek communist parties or in the plotting halls of the Communist Party of the Soviet Union (CPSU). During World War II and the Greek Civil War of 1946–1949, a period of ten years (1940–1950), the Balkan socialist states continued to press for an independent or autonomous Macedonia dominated by the Slavs. With the Germans still in Yugoslavia, the early part of the 1940s saw Tito taking over the initiative on the struggle for Macedonia from Bulgaria with Stalin's and Comintern's support, managing to exploit Stalin's favoritism by quickly, but shabbily, presenting the world with a *fait accompli*: creation of a new "Macedonian" republic.

From Vardarska to "Macedonia"

The first clue that Tito's Yugoslavia would manipulate the Macedonian issue, assuming leadership and exploiting the situation created by war and occupation, surfaced when Stalin — through Comintern — directed the Yugoslavs to assume responsibility in rearranging Macedonia's frontier. Comintern's directive to the CPY and CPB in August 1941 that "Macedonia must be attached to Yugoslavia for practical reasons and for the sake of expediency," reflecting the Kremlin's predilections, was a clear message that Yugoslavia must grab the struggle's relay for Macedonia from Bulgaria. More than anything else, it had been Comintern's decision that decisively shifted the burden and responsibility of how to handle the Macedonian problem from Bulgaria to Yugoslavia. To put it bluntly, the Soviet-sponsored Macedonian designs arrogated the rights of the citizens of Greece that owned 75 percent of King Philip's historic Macedonia and infringed specifically upon the rights of Hellenic Macedonians whose Macedonianism had become an integral component of their ethnic identity.

The rapid flow of events that followed Comintern's directive proved again how rapidly history, especially Balkan history, was swinging on its hinges. It was into this setting that the Yugoslav communist leadership, effectively grasping the window of opportunity on the Macedonian dispute, deliberately and cleverly chose polarizing strategies, regardless of whether such strategies were ethically correct, to set the stage for eventually acquiring Greek Macedonia, or parts of it, including Thessaloniki.

With the Germans still in Yugoslavia, on November 29, 1943, the Anti-Fascist Council for the National Liberation of Yugoslavia (AVNOJ) proclaimed the formation of a new republic, the People's Republic of Macedonia, equal in status with the other five republics of the federated state of Yugoslavia. On August 4, 1944, the first Anti-Fascist Assembly of National Liberation of Macedonia (ASNOM) at the monastery of Prohor Pcinjsky proclaimed "Macedonia as a federal state in the new Democratic Federation of Yugoslavia" (Poulton 1995, pp. 103–105; Vattis 2002). The founding declaration said: "You will succeed to unite all parts of Macedonia that the Balkan imperialists [Serbs, Greeks, Bulgarians] occupied in 1913 and 1918." With these words, the Macedonian Question was revived stronger than ever, with the struggle for Macedonia assuming dangerous dimensions for the stability of the Balkan peninsula. As the new republic became one of the six constituent republics in the federated state of Yugoslavia, the question naturally arose: would Tito and the Yugoslavs plunge into an undeclared war to accomplish the unification of Macedonia, parts of which were "occupied" by the "Balkan imperialists"?[1]

There is increasing evidence (Woodhouse 1976) that the People's

Republic of Macedonia was founded on political criteria only, since its population, a polyglot conglomeration of nationalities, had no relation to ancient Macedonians.[2] Tito's Macedonia, with Skopje as its capital, created in the same manner as Stalin's Byelorussia after the end of the Bolshevik revolution, had been a part of Vardar Province, which also included Kosovo.[3] Knowledgeable people knew at the time that the small republic named "Macedonia," occupying about one half of the Vardar Province, was formed as a ploy to serve as a bridgehead for the virtual annexation of Hellenic Macedonia and the mutilation of Greece (Giannakos 1992; Iatrides 1995).[4]

Over a period of more than half a century, between 1878 and 1940, before the People's Republic of Macedonia was formed, the Bulgarians also attempted to alter Macedonian history. Witnessing the Yugoslav machinations, however, and correctly perceiving that a veil of deception had effectively camouflaged them, the Bulgarians dissociated themselves from the claim that there had ever been a separate "Macedonian nation." After the formation of the People's Republic of Macedonia, mindful of the frustrations and doubts experienced by Dimitrov on the existence of a separate Macedonian ethnicity, Stalin met the Bulgarian communist leader in Moscow, where he advised him to declare autonomy in Pirin Macedonia as a first step toward unification with the new republic (Martis 2001). An extremely distinctive, revealing, and pertinent feature of Dimitrov's diary on the issue is his personal doubt regarding the way the Yugoslav communists were handling the Macedonian problem and his angered admonition of the renegade Bulgarian Dimitar Vlahov, the man who organized IMRO United, one of the first Bulgarians transformed to "Macedonian" by Tito.[5] Dimitrov asked questions reflecting not only his personal views, but also his worries about where the Skopjan irredentism would lead: "Are we talking about a Macedonian nation or a Macedonian population made up of Bulgarians, Greeks, and Serbs? Does a Macedonian nation exist, and if so, where and how? Can Macedonia exist as a separate state or find freedom and statehood within the South Slav federation, regardless of the ethnic conglomerate of which it is composed?" (Kouzinopoulos 1999, from Dimitrov's secret diary, p. 21).[6]

Eight months later, however, Dimitrov capitulated to Stalin's unrelenting pressure, forgetting about the "ethnic conglomerate." On December 21, 1944, he accepted inclusion of the following sentence in the text of the Yugoslav-Bulgarian agreement: "Bulgaria agrees to the secession of the territories that belonged to Bulgaria before 1913 [before the Treaty of Bucharest] to the Yugoslav Macedonia, if the population desires it." But Tito's interest extended to the Greek Macedonia (*Aegeska Makedonija*), beyond Pirin Macedonia, even if his irredentist ambitions put him at loggerheads with the British and American policy.

Defying history, Tito adopted the name "Macedonia" to legitimize the new federated Yugoslav republic, a daring act historically and ethnologically unsupportable. Even the strongest nationalist advocates' resolve to link the Macedonians of antiquity with the Slavs, propelling into the world unsupportable theories, must admit there are no similarities between the two groups, only a plethora of dissimilarities. Chronologically, linguistically, or in any other respect, the bloodlines of the new Macedonia's Slavic inhabitants cannot possibly be linked to those of ancient Macedonians. If historians, politicians, and NGOs cannot accept this persuasive rationale, they must find it even more difficult to secure international legitimacy and accept that the republic's polyglot conglomerate is actually a *separate* Macedonian ethnicity. The term "Macedonia," wrongly used first by the Slavic movement during the interwar years to symbolize the national character of Slavonic people (Zahariadis 1994), has a geographic, not an ethnic connotation. Even the term "Slavomacedonians" is incorrect (Kargakos 1992). Jovan Svijics, a Serb living in Vardar Province, first coined the term in 1918. The Serbian government, however, immediately rejected the idea with the justification that Vardarska's inhabitants lacked a "clearly defined national [Macedonian] character of their own" (Zotiadis 1961).

Creating the "Macedonian" Language

In the March 1996 issue of *National Geographic* magazine, Priit J. Vesilind wrote: "Today's Macedonians know who they are. They trace their name to the empire of Alexander the Great in the fourth century B.C. They trace their ethnicity to the Slavs who migrated into the southern Balkans a thousand years later and their faith to the Byzantine Empire that brought them into the Eastern Orthodox Church" (124). The article also reported that 67 percent of the inhabitants in Macedonia speak a Macedonian language. Most of the historically educated people in the world, even those whose works or thoughts have evolved in support of Tito's ethnic transformation of Vardar Province, would dispute the transparency of these statements and admit there is no such thing as a Macedonian language. Since the language spoken in Vardar Province is a Bulgarian dialect, it cannot be Macedonian. A Slavonic dialect did not exist in ancient Macedonia when Alexander the Great was alive, simply because no Slavs or Bulgarians existed in the Balkans at that time (Andriotis 1991).[7]

For a reputable news medium such as *National Geographic* to perpetuate historic inaccuracies on the language spoken in the People's Republic of Macedonia, spread by Skopje's propaganda, is inexcusable.[8] The claims about the language's origin, however, have not fooled astute reporters, including Hitchens (1994) writing in the *Nation* in 1994 from Skopje: "Bear in mind that the language spoken in Skopje is essentially Bulgarian, which is called Macedonian for convenience, and that the most powerful political minority is led by IMRO, the Internal Macedonian Revolutionary Organization, which historically favors a greater Bulgaria.... The largest national minority is Albanian and Muslim, and does not care what the republic is called as long as a part of it is one day denominated as either Illyria or Greater Albania."

Bulgarian officials who fled Vardar Province before Tito named part of it the People's Republic of Macedonia declared that its inhabitants could not be Macedonians because no such ethnicity existed; simply, they are Bulgarians and speak Bulgarian. These serious allegations, coming from Bulgaria, a country greatly involved with the Macedonian issue for more than a century, created a stumbling block to Tito's plans to Macedonize the new republic and its inhabitants. To remedy the problem, he created a separate Slavomacedonian ethnicity (see the next subsection of this chapter) that differed from Bulgarians and Serbs. In promoting the new ethnicity, however, he could easily falsify history and traditions, but not the spoken language, difficult to conceal in the historical books of the Skopjan revisionist historians. After all, very few people would read history books, but everyone visiting the new republic would hear the inhabitants speaking their native language.[9]

To sever the linguistic bonds between the "Macedonians" and Serbs and Bulgarians, a new language was fabricated and touted as a separate Macedonian language, the language, it was said, of Alexander the Great (Nystazopoulou-Pelekidou 1988). In contrast to Alexander's language, which had an alphabet (Greek), the present "Macedonian" language did not have an alphabet until 1945. To complete the deception, Tito commissioned the linguist Blago Konev (he changed his name later to Blaze Koneski) to devise an alphabet. Koneski modified the Serbian version of the Cyrillic alphabet and called it the "Macedonian alphabet" (Templar 2002). Koneski and his glossologists also modified the old church Slavonic, used by Cyril and Methodius (now named "old Macedonian"), and fabricated the lexicon of the "Macedonian" language from a mixture of Bulgarian, Serb, Croat, Slovenian, and other Slavonic languages.

In subsequent years, painstaking efforts were also made to camouflage the language's fabricated origin, but nonetheless it remains an offshoot of Bulgarian and is spoken in villages and towns of what is now known as the Former Yugoslav Republic of Macedonia (FYROM).[10] The new dialect was carefully cleansed of glossic elements betraying its Bulgarian origin, replaced by "Macedonian" neologisms, and forced on the pupils from above for political reasons (Koneski 1993; Nystazopoulou-Pelekidou 1988). These comments are not meant to denigrate the language spoken in FYROM today, but simply to insist that this most impressive new language must not be touted as "Macedonian," which it is not, but simply as a new Slavonic dialect based on the Bulgarian language.

What was more, creation of the "Macedonian" language and its imposition on the mostly Bulgarian inhabitants of the new republic was not the end of the glossological experiment. In the years preceding FYROM's secession from Yugoslavia, the Yugoslavs established chairs of "Macedonian" language in Yugoslavia and abroad, trained teachers in the language, and sent glossologists to America, Canada, and Australia to teach the language and present lectures on the existence of a special Slavic race related to ancient Macedonians (Vattis 2002).

Converting the Slavs and Bulgarians to "Macedonians"

Yugoslavia was always known as the land of the South Slavs, composed of three nations— Serbs, Croats, and Muslims. Carter-Norris (1996) characterized the slavophones of geographical Macedonia as a "shapeless mass of Slavs with no particular ethnicity." Myrivilis (1977) made a similar observation when, as a soldier during World War I, he visited a village inside present-day FYROM: "These people speak a language understood by both Serbs and Bulgarians. They hate the Serbs because they [the Serbs] treat them as Bulgarians; and they hate the Bulgarians because they draft their sons to the army.... They accept us [the Greeks] with some compromising curiosity for the only reason we represent 'Patric,' the Patriarchate."

It is uncertain how many men and women among the Slavomacedonians felt hate for the Serbs and Bulgarians and a "compromising curiosity" for the Greeks in Tito's newly created People's Republic of Macedonia. One thing, however, is certain: ethnologically, Tito's new "Macedonian" republic was always a fluid country inhabited by six or seven ideologically contentious groups with ties to Albania, Bulgaria, or Serbia (Gage 1992). The 1940 official Yugoslav census recognized only two large ethnic groups in Vardar Province, Slavs at 66 percent and Muslims at 31 percent. In 1945, three years after the formation of the People's Republic of Macedonia, the Slavs disappeared from the census which showed 66 percent "Macedonians." Was this remarkable transformation process an en masse genetic mutation or a census falsification?[11] How could a group of people (Bulgarians and Slavs) change ethnicity, becoming "Macedonians" in five years? The Bulgarians insisted that the so-called Macedonians in the People's Republic of Macedonia — and in FYROM later — are actually Bulgarians, except for the

Albanians. Tito forcefully created an artificial nationality, a 66 percent majority, with the remainder assigned to Muslims (Albanians and Turks).

The difficulty of ascertaining the real ethnicity of the 66 percent majority in the People's Republic of Macedonia contributes to an uncertainty as to the long prospects for the small republic's survival. Nevertheless, the republic's multilingual conglomerate, wittingly or unwittingly, became the primary "Macedonian" component that distinguished it from the people of the other Yugoslav republics and from Bulgaria. Virtually by default, the new "Macedonians" were forced to bend to the restorative visions of genuine "Macedonian" grandeur invoked by Tito to heal Yugoslavia's wounds inflicted by communist promises and to make them believe they were the only true descendants of ancient Macedonians and the only people in the Balkans entitled to the Macedonian legacy. To them, the Greek-speakers of Macedonia, whose fathers and forefathers lived in Macedonia, and who had bequeathed to their Greek-speaking descendants the Macedonian legacy, are usurpers of the "Macedonian" heritage. An interested and perceptive observer, however, would know that the newcomers descended upon the Balkans almost a thousand years after Alexander died, apprehending in modern times a name and an identity that did not belong to them (Martis 1983).

To put the state-controlled ethnogenesis in perspective, we need to go back to 1913 and trace the origin of the slavophones who were transformed into "Macedonians" in the People's Republic of Macedonia. Many of them underwent several primary transformatins before their final ethnic conversion (Koliopoulos 1995): South Slavs or Serbianized Slavs till the German army occupied Yugoslavia in 1941; Bulgarians when the fascist Bulgarian army occupied South Serbia (a Hitler gift to Bulgaria for signing the Tripartite Pact during World War II);[12] Yugoslav communist partisans during the occupation; some of them Ochranists or IMRO cadres and communist Macedonians by 1943 with new roots, history, traditions, and language; and upon the passing of Tito's epoch, centered as it was on the inherent megalomaniac charisma of a single man, reformed communist "Macedonians" in FYROM, harboring irredentist aspirations at their neighbors' expense (see Skopje's constitution, Chapter 7).

Their "enslaved" brothers in some sections of northern Greece, especially in western Macedonia, also underwent similar transformations (see Chapter 4): slavophone-Greeks or slavophone-Bulgarians before Greek Macedonia's occupation in 1941 by the German army; the slavophone-Bulgarians became Slavomacedonians or IMRO cadres collaborating with the Germans and Italians during the occupation; communists later during the occupation (members of EAM/ELAS or Tito partisans); DAG fighters during the Greek Civil War; and finally, self-exiled or expelled to Yugoslavia, many appointed to official positions later as "Macedonians" in the People's Republic of Macedonia (1944–1991) or FYROM.[13]

Looking now at this backdrop from a historical perspective, and with Macedonia as our primary concern, how did Tito and Yugoslavia manage to create a new ethnicity from a polyglot conglomerate of Slavs, Bulgarians, Albanians, Romanians, gypsies, Turks, and others? More interestingly, how did Tito manage to deceive the world of the Skopjan Macedonian ethnicity's legitimacy? Simply stated, how did he manage to subordinate the polyglot conglomerate to the state's demands and convince the world at the same time that his methods and reasons for creating a new ethnicity out of an artificial concoction of nationalities were legitimate?

The answer to the questions is simple. Using Stalin's advice on how to create a new nation, as Lenin and Stalin had done in the 1920s with Byelorussia (Kouzinopoulos 1999), Tito proceeded to create his "Macedonian ethnicity" in three steps and in such a clever way that the world did not question the World War II hero's deeds: (a) convert a part of Vardar Province to the People's Republic of Macedonia within the Yugoslav federation, using the geographic name "Macedonia" as an ethnic name; (b) give the people in the new republic a new language, the so-called "Macedonian" language; and (c) create an artificial nationality by transforming the Slavs, Bulgarians and Albanians of the new republic to "Macedonians." Within a short time, Tito, procreating new nationalist sentiments blended with radical socialist ideas for a conglomeration of people with no firm ethnicity, had a land with the name "Macedonia" attached to it, a new "Macedonian" language for the multiethnic group of people, and "Macedonians" living on the land.

To legitimize these steps and strengthen their position, Tito and the Yugoslavs had to do considerable related peripheral work within the two-odd years that intervened between the decision to form a new republic with the name "Macedonia" and the day the decision was officially announced to the world: assert that the ancient Macedonians were not Greek and attempt to establish new links to connect the modern "Macedonians" (Slavs) with the ancient Macedonians. If the world could be convinced that Alexander the Great was not Greek, that he spoke a language similar to the present-day "Macedonian" language, and that the Greek philosopher Aristotle's student only learned Greek to debate Demosthenes of Athens, as the Skopjan propaganda insists, half of the game would be won.

Let us now return to the center of the Macedonian Question and ask a few serious questions about the Slavic "Macedonian" society's history lying in the shadow of Tito's dead imperialism and Cominform's manipulations and intrigue. If the slavophones without Hellenic consciousness in the People's Republic of Macedonia were really "Macedonians," as the world calls them today, why did they not assert their "Macedonian" identity before a communist dictator officially transformed them to "Macedonians" in 1943–1944? What are the millions of Greek-speakers whose ancestors always lived in Greek Macedonia, and whose Greek Macedonian history, heroes, myths, culture, civilization, customs, language, all go back three thousand years? Why has the world decided to escape history, ignoring the Greek Macedonians, embracing the polyglot conglomerate of the People's Republic of Macedonia [later FYROM] as "Macedonians"? To put it more bluntly, does a three-thousand-year history carry less weight than the spur-of-the-moment elevation of a Slavic group of people to the status of history-laden Macedonians?

Disregarding the shrill campaign about the Macedonianism of the People's Republic of Macedonia, who was responsible for the transformation of the Slavs and Bulgarians into "Macedonians" and the appropriation of the Macedonian name belonging to a neighbor? How did the egregious political decision to create a new Macedonian ethnicity emerge? There are many documents available now leading to an indisputable conclusion (Kofos 1995): Tito's ideologically Marxist authoritarian regime was responsible. The Marxist revolutionary theory on ethnic minorities, cleverly adjusted by Lenin and Stalin to compromise communist internationalism with their own nationalist aspirations, was also responsible. Given a limited nationalist pride and self-determination within a larger political system, ethnic minorities could become revolutionary cadres against the bourgeoisie. Comintern established the basis for interpreting Marxism's theory on minorities in its Second Congress of 1920: "Every communist party has the obligation to consider the interests of the suppressed minorities.... The proletariat struggle must submit to the interests of the world revolution. The communists must be able and ready to make big 'ethnic sacrifices' if the wider strategy dictates it. The ethnic minorities must have the 'right of self-government' that may go as far as splitting from the nation to which they belong" (Papakonstantinou 1992).

Tito's Yugoslavia was not the only authority responsible for the falsification. Others also played a role: Comintern (Cominform later) for undertaking in the dark the task of coordinating the most successful historical alteration; Stalin behind Comintern's directive of 1941 and his admonitions to Tito and Dimitrov to solve the Macedonian problem, brandishing the Soviet Byelorussian example;[14] and the communist parties of Yugoslavia and Macedonia, in cooperation with the communist parties of Bulgaria and Greece, all in the forefront to assist in the transformation. The most disappointing side of it was the behavior of eager Europeans who, enmeshed in a major world war, paid no attention to Tito's manipulations (Tsalouhides 1994).

In light of the momentous events of the early 1940s pertaining to Macedonia, who actually invented and promoted the new "Macedonian" ethnicity? Slavism and communism invented it, because it is indeed an invention. It did not exist before the onset of communism. New ethnicities are borne over hundreds and thousands of years, not in a few years. "Ethnicities do not appear for the first time during the epoch we live in" (Papakonstantinou 1992). In Europe, new ones appeared in the nineteenth century, but those were suppressed ethnicities that had always existed. The new "Macedonian" ethnicity was created to discredit and suppress the Hellenic-Macedonian ethnicity that has lived in Greek Macedonia for three thousand years. The western politicians allowed the new "Macedonian" ethnicity to establish itself firmly for the last fifty-nine years because of their political expediency and historical ignorance or disregard of historical facts. History, however, cannot allow the people who came to the Balkans one thousand years after Alexander's death to break suddenly into the world of historic Macedonian Hellenism, attempting to discredit its existence.

The unrelenting pressure from the Soviet Union also played an important role, forcing the transformation. The CPY, ruthlessly pressed by Stalin through Comintern, elevated the geographic term "Macedonia" to a concept with nationalist implications, i.e., people living in geographic Macedonia are by necessity Macedonians, irrespective of ethnicity. Tito named the Vardar Province slavophones "Macedonians" in 1943–1944 with their own traditions and "Macedonian" language, a separate ethnic entity that had nothing to do with the Greeks, Bulgarians, or Serbs (Kofos 1974, 1986). Seeing an excellent opportunity—created by the formidable war instability—to become the new Balkan master, and aided by Comintern's directive of August 1941 to the Yugoslavs to assume responsibility to "solve" the Macedonian problem, Tito created the new nationality, beginning with granting "Macedonian" ethnicity to two Bulgarian communist leaders, Vlahov and Tomov.

During the seventy-three years from 1870, the year the Bulgarian Exarchate was established, to 1943, no other ethnicity in Macedonia amounted to much except Turks, Greeks, and Bulgarians. No ethnicity existed calling itself "Macedonian" (Dakin 1966). It is true that rivalries surfaced for the first time among populations in Macedonia with the Exarchate's formation, but those were clashes between two Christian ethnicities, the Greeks and the Bulgarians (Tsaparas 1996). With the Exarchate's formation, Vardar Province slavophones were identified only as Bulgarians and remained Bulgarians till 1943.

The demographic picture above, favoring Bulgaria's assertion of Vardar Province's inhabitants being Bulgarians, begs the question as to what interrelated reasons were at work in the conversion of the Bulgarians to

"Macedonians." People in the Balkans and elsewhere knew that South Serbia's slavophones were not really Macedonians. If the new republic were to become credible, stable, and recognizable as such by the world, Tito needed "Macedonian" inhabitants. The Slavs and Bulgarians had to acquire a new identity, the "Macedonian" identity. No state could survive for long with the name "Macedonia" if its inhabitants were Slavs or Bulgarians. How to transform the Slavs and Bulgarians into "Macedonians" was difficult but not unresolvable. While it was natural for the Greeks of Macedonia to be Hellenic Macedonians, it was difficult for the newly named "Macedonians" to adapt to the new name because they had to become accustomed to their new ethnicity. To accomplish this, the new republic needed, in addition to the new language, a history to connect it with the past; it needed new school textbooks, maps, archives, everything from the beginning (Poulton 1995, p. 117). Someone had to create a historical background for the new republic, severing the links between the new "Macedonians" in the People's Republic of Macedonia and the Bulgarians and Serbs. Someone had to invent a new Macedonian history or revise the existing history.[15]

The Yugoslavs also created the "Macedonian" ethnicity for economic reasons— to snatch the Aegean Macedonia from Greece — and at the same time place another obstacle to the free world during the clash between democracies and communist totalitarianism (Tsalouhides 1994; C. Vakalopoulos 1987, 1989). Macedonia, a rich country, situated in a critical Balkan area, always has been the "apple of discord," because, in addition to being rich in minerals and agricultural products, it is also the crossroad between Asia and Europe, East and West, which offers an opening to the Aegean and Mediterranean (Woodhouse 1948). It was worth it to the Slavs to create a new ethnicity with territorial claims on the entire Macedonia, including the city and port of Thessaloniki. But Tito and his commissars faced one serious obstacle in their struggle for Macedonia: Greece, which possessed not only historic but also demographic, commercial, and educational superiority over Macedonia. "Serbia had no titles and only a small demographic participation. Bulgaria had the title of the defunct Treaty of San Stefano and small pockets of slavophones which it considered Bulgarian, although a good percentage of them were Greeks" (Papakonstantinou 1992).

To de–Hellenize Macedonia's ancient history and cross out or reduce ancient Macedonia's Hellenism, the Skopje history revisionists of the "Foundation of Ethnic History" were given the daunting task of altering history. They had to revise old historical documents, collect new ambiguous material, destroy or disregard authentic material damaging to their "Macedonian" hypothesis, and propel to the world the news that the slavophones living in the three sections of Macedonia are indeed "Macedonians," true descendants of King Philip and Alexander the Great; that there exists a distinct continuity from ancient Macedonians to the Slav "Macedonian people," a fact justifying considering them as members of a separate "Macedonian" ethnicity; the ancient Macedonians were not Greek, and, with the exception of the Macedonian elite, they did not speak Greek; and that the common people were speaking a language resembling the Bulgarian-"Macedonian" dialect spoken in FYROM today (Nystazopoulou-Pelekidou 1988, pp. 9–11).

Establishing a "connection" between the inhabitants of the People's Republic of Macedonia and ancient Macedonians was not enough. The Skopjan historians had to sever all the links that connected the Slav-speakers of Vardar Province with Bulgarians and Serbs, inculcating in the inhabitants of the People's Republic of Macedonia a feeling of pride that they belonged to a separate ethnicity, the "Macedonian" ethnicity, with all its glorious past and rich history. To accomplish this, all Bulgarian and Serb documents connected with the People's Republic of Macedonia had to be renamed "Macedonian" to fit the "Macedonian" model. If the documents were incompatible, they were discarded (Nystazopoulou-Pelekidou 1988, p. 9).[16] Also, the revisionist historians had to de-Hellenize Macedonia and its history by minimizing or deleting everything Hellenic associated with Macedonia; to misinterpret the role of the Macedonians during the so-called Hellenistic Age, the two centuries following Alexander's death;[17] and to project to the world the historical revolution of the "Macedonian people" and their ethnic identity, including their connection with the ancient Macedonians. Within this framework, the Skopjan history revisionists embarked on an extensive propaganda effort to teach the world that the three sections of Macedonia (Greek, Bulgarian, and Yugoslav) must be united into one Macedonia on the basis of their "common historical and ethnic characteristics."

To name a section of Vardar Province "Macedonia" and its polyglot inhabitants "Macedonians," irrespective of ethnicity and language, Tito and the Yugoslav communists treated history with indifference and contempt. The formation of the People's Republic of Macedonia with a historical name that belonged to another nation for three millennia revived the Macedonian Question — dormant in the early 1940s because of the war and occupation — and exacerbated the ethnic differences and animosities in the Balkans. It resurrected an old controversy and helped Skopje use the name "Macedonia" and all its derivatives. It may not even be happenstance that the beginning of the Greek Civil War coincided with the resurrection of the Macedonian problem, a notion supported by Vafiadis (1985), the Greek communist army's commander.

Creating a new ethnicity was not enough for the communist ruler of Yugoslavia. After World War II, a revised, radical Yugoslav policy emerged with a new platform on the Macedonian issue: formation of a separate "Macedonian Nation." The new official position was presented in several publications by Skopje's "Institute of National History" in a three-volume work entitled *Istorija na Makedonskiot Narod* (History of the Macedonian Nation 1969) (Kofos 1974, 1986). The formation of the People's Republic of Macedonia and the advancement of the concept of a new nation aimed precisely at strengthening southern Yugoslavia to remove any vestiges of Bulgarian influence and aspirations. Studies critical of Greece's policies on Macedonia categorically assert, however, that the terms "Macedonia" and "Macedonians" were never used to describe a separate ethnicity (Perry 1988).

The Amalgamation Theory

Because historical facts and archaeological findings in Macedonia, Egypt, and Asia revealed no connection between the ancient Macedonians and the Slavs and Bulgarians of Tito's new republic, Slavic organizations around the world, especially in Australia and Canada, promulgated the so-called amalgamation theory to establish such a connection. The theory attracted a few followers abroad, especially among Slavs in the United States, Canada, and Australia (Nystazopoulou-Pelekidou 1988). According to this theory, during the Middle Ages the Slavs annihilated many local people in Macedonia and absorbed the remainder (Anarhistov 1982). From the blend of the Slavic element and the indigenous descendants of ancient Macedonians a new "Macedonian" nation emerged related to ancient Macedonians. Therefore, a Macedonian, according to this concept, is a "completely modern product" of racial amalgamation between the Slavs of the Middle Ages and a mixture of ancient Macedonians and other inhabitants of ancient Macedonia (Martis 1983).[18]

Vlasidis (2003, pp. 346–47) reported recently that this theory is part of the regular curriculum in FYROM's schools today. According to the theory, despite contacts with Greeks, Romans, and other people, the ancient Macedonians remained ethnically unchanged till the Slavs descended to the Balkans. First, the Slavs and Macedonians coexisted, but eventually they were amalgamated, producing the present "Macedonian nation" by the tenth century A.D. This theory does not agree with Marxist Dusan Taskofski's theory that the "Macedonian" people appeared during the period of capitalism's explosion, about the nineteenth century. Both theories purposely overlook a critical point: Why did the Macedonians wait one thousand years to be amalgamated with the Slavs? The Greeks were always there, speaking the same language.

To support this theory, history revisionists speak about "local people" (not Greek Macedonians) being annihilated by Slavs, thus propelling the notion again that the Macedonians were not Greeks (more in the next subsection of this chapter). If we temporarily accept that this assumption is correct, who were the local people of Macedonia at the end of the nineteenth century and at the beginning of the twentieth century who fought valiantly for Hellenism against Bulgarism, winning the Macedonian Struggle? What were the thousands of Greek-speakers and slavophones with Hellenic consciousness (*Grecomans*) who helped defeat and chase the Bulgarian bands out of Macedonia from 1904 to 1908? What are the Greek-speakers in Macedonia today (not those who migrated from Asia Minor) whose forefathers lived in Macedonia for centuries, surviving the harsh Ottoman occupation? History showed that the Greek Macedonian people with strong genetic and ethnic constitution and deep Hellenic convictions were unlikely subjects to be amalgamated with Slavs or any other invaders. The Greek-speaking Macedonians with their long Hellenic history, deep-rooted traditions, stubborn attachment to Hellenism, and indomitable spirit were unlikely candidates to support the obsessed eugenics of the amalgamation theory and the model of weak people being absorbed by the "strong" Slavic people.

The amalgamation theory is based on serious historical and technical errors. With all the new findings, especially in Vergina of Greek Macedonia, exhibited at the Archaeological Museum of Thessaloniki and in Vergina, the Skopje historians have no grounds to support their theory. On the basis of old and new findings, Greek and foreign historians (Durant 1939; Grant 1988; Hammond 1987) insist that the ancient Macedonians were Greek. Under the influence of the new common language, the *koine*, the ancient Macedonians were amalgamated with the rest of the Hellenes (Hammond 1989, 1997) and modern Greeks were produced (Templar 2002). To this important challenge we must also add the familiar fact that Alexander the Great died in 323 B.C., and the Slavs migrated to the Balkan peninsula around A.D. 650, almost one thousand years later. If we accept the historically unaccepted view that the Macedonians were not Greeks, as the Skopje historians claim, then the ancient Macedonians, whatever ethnicity they were, had better chances, a common language, and a thousand-year span to blend with other Greeks and Romans than wait all those long years for the new Slav-speaking "suitors" from the north. It is useless for Skopjan historians to attempt to prove differences between ancient Macedonians and the other Greeks. Even if they existed, such differences disappeared in the thousand years before the Slavs arrived in the Balkans.[19]

There is also insurmountable difficulty in ascertaining the validity of the ancient Macedonian-Slav amalgamation model because the emotional justification provided by its proponents is unconvincing. Given the seriousness of this dispute and the unsustainable assertions by the theory's proponents, two important questions must be answered convincingly if there is a slim chance for this theory to be considered seriously. Why had the Slavs not considered themselves "Macedonians" for seventy-five years (1870–1944)? Why during all these years did they consider themselves Bulgarians, fighting to incorporate Macedonia into Bulgaria? The answers given by Skopje historians are rife with obvious shortcomings: they insist that the people, being illiterate during the early years of the Macedonian controversy, did not know what their ethnicity was, an unconvincing explanation, especially because the founders of the Internal Macedonian Revolutionary Organization (IMRO) in 1893, a Bulgarian group, were not illiterate. Damien Grueff was a schoolmaster and Tatarcheff a doctor (Dakin 1966). Skopje's superficial answer to the second question is that the Macedonian Slavs affiliated themselves with Bulgaria because of its activist policy and dynamic handling of the Macedonian Question. Eventually, they eradicated the Bulgarian sentiments and became Macedonians (Kofos 1962)!

Other serious problems with this theory remain. For example, an important methodological error is the extension in place and time of a locally restricted group of people, i.e., Slavomacedonians, and how difficult it is to extrapolate from a relatively small area (People's Republic of Macedonia) the entire historic Macedonia through the centuries, formulating population genetics theories without those being affected by historic events, localities, and types of people involved (Nystazopoulou-Pelekidou 1988). Interestingly, the Skopje historians admit the prevalence of Hellenism in certain areas of Macedonia at certain times, but they do not account for what subsequently happened to the Hellenic population.

Who Were the Macedonians?

The question of the ancient Macedonians' ethnicity has received great notoriety among historians and anthropologists, especially after World War II, simply because it is linked with the national identities of people living in Macedonia and in a more specific way with the ethnicity debates and competing perspectives offered on the Macedonian issue by Greece, Bulgaria, and FYROM. Because old sources of information on this sensitive subject may not be reliable or complete, and contemporary sources may be dysfunctional or influenced by political and nationalist prejudices, determining the ethnicity of a group of people instrumental in an old glorious civilization is an arduous, complicated and often controversial task. The question of whether it is necessary to define the ancient Macedonians' ethnicity prompted Borza (1990, p. 96) to state from his own perspective:

"Who were the Macedonians? As an ethnic question it is best avoided, since the mainly modern political overtones tend to obscure the fact that it really is not a very important issue. That they may or may not have been Greek in whole or in part — while an interesting anthropological sidelight — is really not crucial to our understanding of their history."

Given the fact that the ancient Macedonians' Hellenism and use of a Hellenic dialect by them have been challenged by a few scholars (Badian 1982; Poulton 1995; Shea 1997), and by a few former communist countries, it is very important to determine the ancient Macedonians' ethnicity. Their ethnicity cannot be separated from the Hellenic history because it did not evolve in a vacuum, but within the broader limits of the Hellenic civilization. It is inexorably linked with Greece's *total* history. When their historical achievements and their name are both perceived and used as propulsive forces to create and sustain — with heavy-handedness— a new ethnic model with the Macedonian name, forcefully embedded within the glorious Macedonian past, it is important that we connect history with ethnicity. Also, it needs to be remembered that since the contemporary misleading rhetoric disputing the ancient Macedonians' Hellenism, emanating from Skopje — and more acrimoniously from organizations of the Slavic diaspora — has been greatly elevated after FYROM's secession from Yugoslavia, it would be thoroughly justified to continue emphasizing this very important issue dealing with the ancient Macedonians' ethnicity. Challenging the ancient Macedonians' Hellenism — and Droysen's *Hellenismus*— has been very persistent and too controversial to be ignored, especially because the unwonted challenge is related to communism's establishment in the Balkans with its implacable malice thrust upon the people.[20]

Virtually from the beginning of the twentieth century scholars have studied the ancient Macedonians' origin and their ethnicity, arriving at different conclusions, often contradicting each other. To understand the Macedonians' ethnicity we must first and foremost study their history — and even mythology — of their origin, migrations, interactions with other tribes, and places where they settled. We must also determine from available historical and archaeological information what language one of the most important city-states of antiquity spoke. It is generally believed, though it may not always be true, that language is indeed one of the most important characteristics determining a group's ethnicity.[21] To bind all these perceptions together simply and efficiently and to draw meaningful conclusions, we must go back in time to the Greek Dark Ages before the reign of the Macedonian King Perdiccas I, and even farther back.[22]

The beginning of the Middle Bronze Age (ca. 1900 B.C.) saw the migrations and invasions of the so-called Indo-European people from Central Europe, who eventually descended into Greece, bringing with them their weapons and horse-drawn carriages, giving rise to the earliest forms of the proto-Hellenic (proto = first) language (Hammond 1976). Three groups of proto-Hellenic–speaking people are distinguished: the Western, Eastern, and Southeastern groups. In terms of the time when the migrations occurred, the Western group is subdivided by some historians and archaeologists into four subgroups.[23] The first subgroup (known as *Makednoi* = tall mountain men) colonized the Pindus mountain range, spreading to Orestis (present-day Argos Orestikon–Kastoria district), Elimeia (near Kozani), and Lyncestis (Florina-Bitola). Some of the tribes colonized several areas as far south as Servia and Vergina in western and central Macedonia, respectively, maintaining their tribal dialects, the origins of the Greek language. According to legends that came to us from Herodotus, the "father of history," Pindar, the poet, and the historian Hesiod (I.56), the *Makednoi* were the earlier ancestors of the Dorians, the second subgroup that eventually migrated southward from Pindus to Doris and took the name "Dorians" after Doris's colonization. The *Makednoi*, known also as Proto-Dorians, also established themselves in the foothills of Mount Olympus and in northeastern Thessaly, a region important to the development of early Macedonian history. The early settlement of a tribe of the Western group near Olympus was also confirmed by the historian Thucydides (mentioned by Pausanias 9.40, 7–8). The third subgroup established itself in Thessaly, and the fourth migrated from Doris and central Greece all the way to Peloponnesus.

While broad generalizations are always hazardous, particularly regarding population movements and linguistic developments of the early Macedonian times that occurred three to four millennia ago, we have to depend on what is available, which often is not enough or lies in a gray area between history and legend. This is true not only of groups and tribes of people, but also of persons who presumably played significant roles during early Macedonian times. Thus a legend (mentioned by Hesiod), also discussed by Hammond (1989, pp. 12–13), has it that Zeus and Thyia, daughter of Deukalion, had two sons, Magnes and Makedon, who loved horses and lived in the Pieria region and in the southeast vertiginous slopes and foothills of Olympus and Mount Ossa. Hessiod also mentioned that the war-loving Doric King Hellen fathered three sons— Dorus, Xouthus, and Aeolus— who settled in various parts of Greece and became the founders of the three dialects of the Hellenic speech — Doric, Ionic, and Aeolic. Hellen's three sons were referred to by Hesiod as cousins of Makedon and Magnes.[24]

In the latter part of the fifth century B.C., the historian Hellanicus visited Macedonia and modified Hesiod's genealogy, making Makedon not a cousin, but the son of Aeolus, thus bringing Makedon and his descendants firmly into the Aeolic branch of the Greek-speaking family. According to Hammond (1989), Hesiod and Hellanicus had no motive for making false statements about the language of the Macedonians, who were then obscure and not a powerful people. It is therefore prudent to compare a contemporary hypothesis promulgated by some historians about the Macedonians not speaking Greek with the two ancient historians' views who had no reason to be biased. "Their independent testimonies [on the Macedonians' language] should be accepted as conclusive" (Hammond 1989).

The Indo-European tribes that descended to Peloponnesus from Pindus and Doris were given the name "Dorians," with their violent descent and settlement known in the Greek and foreign historiography as the "Dorian invasion." The Dorians were originally a barbaric northern tribe that descended south and wrested control of most of Greece. They are even considered responsible for destroying the Mycenaean civilization sometime after ca. 1100 B.C., a view disputed by Borza (p. 67), who also (p. 65) disputed the term "Dorian invasions" based on Herodotus (9.26) and Thucydides (I.12) as an "invention of nineteenth-century historiography ... otherwise unsupported by either archaeological or linguistic evidence." He mentioned later (p. 69), however, that he considers the Dorians because they were probably connected with the earliest Macedonians.

Herodotus (I.56) gives a story about the descent of the Classical Dorians from an early tribe called "Makednon" [tall Macedonian race (Proto-Dorians)], which was violently expelled by the Cadmeians from the Pieria-Olympus territory to the Pindus mountains of Upper (western) Macedonia at the late Bronze Age, ca. 1000 B.C. Later the group moved to Dryopsis and Peloponnesus, where it took the name "Dorian," presumably from the Doris province or from Dorus, son of King Hellen. Pindar (Pyth. I.65) also mentioned the temporary home of the Dorians.[25]

The connection between the Macedonians and Dorians was disputed by Borza (1990, p. 71) on the grounds that we lack sufficient archaeological and linguistic evidence to support it. On the same page, however, he wrote: "It is to suggest that the ancestors of both the historical Macedonians and those who later were called Dorians may have co-existed along the slopes of Pindus in the middle Haliacmon basin during the transition from the Bronze to the Dark Age." There is no evidence to suggest that the Dorians and the Macedonians were separate tribes coexisting in Pindus. If they were not of the same group, one group would probably have eliminated the other. Also, Herodotus (8.43) described some unknown Spartan allies as *Dorikon te kai Makednon ethnos* (Dorian and Macedonian nation).

There is no other point in the ancient Macedonians' history more intriguing — and more controversial — than the Macedonian-Temenidae (also referred to as Macedonian-Heracleidae) connection. Was there a Macedonian-Temenidae connection? Did the Macedonian dynasty, the so-called Argeads or Argeadae, descend from the Temenidae, the royal family of Argos in Peloponnesus, whose illustrious ancestor was Heracles (Hercules)? The Heracleidae of Argos, themselves not Dorian, were Heracles's descendants who had been exiled from Argos and from all areas of Mycenaean rule (Pandermali-Poulaki 2003). Granted refuge by Dorian tribes in return for Heracles's assistance in the fight against the Lapiths (a tribe between myth and reality), several Heracleidae were first encountered in the Olympus region. Perhaps this event explains the finding of Mycenaean artifacts in Macedonia. According to Pandermali-Poulaki, the Heracleidae led the so-called descent of the Dorians in their own return to Peloponnesus.

Herodotous (H.37) in his own way established a connection between the Macedonian dynasty and the Argeo-Temenids by reporting that three brothers—Perdiccas, Aeropus, and Gauanis—descendants from the Heracleid Temenos, founder of the Argead royal dynasty, took refuge in Illyria and then moved to upper Macedonia. Eventually, Gauanis ruled in Elimeia, Aeropus in Lyncestis, and Perdiccas, the founder of the Macedonian dynasty, in Lower Macedonia from 670 to 652 B.C.[26] Borza (1990, p. 78) dismissed the Temenidae-Macedonian connection, but he admitted that "*the 'Macedones' or 'highlanders' of mountainous western Macedonia may have been derived from northwest Greek stock. That is, northwest Greece provided a pool of Indo-European speakers of proto-Greek from which emerged the tribes who were later known by different names as they established their regional identities in separate parts of the country.*"[27] Borza (p. 84) also hypothesized that if we accept Herodotus's story of the three Argeo-Temenid brothers—Perdiccas, Aeropus, Gauanis—and that the "Makedones" of western Macedonia may have been derived from northwestern Greek stock, then at least three groups of ancient Macedonians could "trace" their origin to an eastward movement of the Argeads in the seventh century B.C. Herodotus's and Thucydides's stories—excluding the Macedonian-Temenidae connection—portray the Macedonians' traditions and beliefs of their origin.

"The descent of the Dorians and the return of the Heracleidae was for antiquity one of the most important, if not the most important, events of the early history of the Greek world. Even today it still remains a provocative mystery of antiquity, the interpretation of which creates disagreement among scholars," pointed out Pandermali-Poulaki (2003). Should the Dorians' descent and the Heracleidae's return be proven to be a fact, it will verify the Macedonian dynasty's Mycenaean tradition and Peloponnesian origin, explain the existence of Mycenaean elements in the Macedonian dialect, and strengthen the pro–Hellenic historiography's interpretation that the royal dynasty of Lower Macedonia descended from Temenos of Argos, son of Heracles.

Let us now leave behind events, legends, and myths of the Greek Dark Ages and proceed to the seventh century B.C. when the history of the Macedonians began (Green 1991, p. 4). As already suggested by Borza above, "at least three related branches of the Makedones" moved eastward at the beginning of the seventh century. The dynamic Greek-speaking Orestis clan, the Argeads, migrated eastward out of the Aliakmon basin, went through the Petra Pass north of Olympus, and settled in the Piedmont of northern Pieria and east of Olympus, looking for arable land and grazing pastures for their cattle, sheep, and goats. On their way to Lower Macedonia, they subdued the local chieftains and dispossessed the Pieres out of the area to Mount Pangaeum, the Bottiaiei out of Bottiaia, the Eordi from Eordaia, the Almopes from Almopia, and all tribes (Tracians, Paeonians, and Illyrians) found in Anthemus, Crestonia, Bysaltia, and other lands (Templar 2003).

Some historians dispute the suggestion that the eastward migration involved both the Macedonians as a Greek ethnic group and the ruling dynasty. With the benefit of hindsight, knowing now that hostile groups were expelled by the Argeads from Lower Macedonia, it is logical to assume that a ruling dynasty would not have traveled alone. Together with their domesticated animals, the Argeads introduced their own language, believed to be a dialect of the Greek tongue (Daskalakis 1965). "The name [*Makedones*] itself is Greek in root and in ethnic termination. It probably means 'highlanders,' and it is comparable to Greek tribal names such as 'Orestai' and 'Oreitai' (oros = mountain), meaning mountain-men" (Hammond 1989, pp. 12–13).[28] Though disputed by some historians (Badian 1982), Hammond's and Daskalakis's contention is not unusual or difficult to accept.

More than anything else, the language of the ancient Macedonians became the subject of strenuous disagreements among scholars. Analyzing this issue carefully before we draw any conclusions necessitates looking into two important facts related to linguistics and the Macedonians' ethnicity: the existence of hundreds of Hellenic tribes, subtribes, and families of the Hellenic nation; and the lack of linguistic homogeneity — or to put it in a different way, the polyglot forms of the Greek language encountered — among the Greek tribes. There were more than 230 Hellenic tribes, including the Macedonians, that spoke more than 200 dialects (Templar 2003). These are facts of great significance, but also sources of perplexity to a few doubting scholars.[29] The great linguistic diversity resulted from the excessive fragmentation of the Greek nation into many city-states (Attica, Lacedaemon, Corinth, etc.), and larger states (Molossia, Macedonia, Thesprotia, Aetolia, etc.).[30] Their inhabitants spoke variations of the same language, whose structure and mechanism had been adjusted to the level of knowledge and civilization of each tribe. Also, the nomad inhabitants of a monarchical regime like that of archaic Macedonia would hardly be expected to speak Athens's refined dialect.

Three dialects of the Greek language were best known: Doric, Ionic, and Aeolic.[31] According to Hammond (1989, p. 193) and Templar (2003), the Macedonians of antiquity spoke an Aeolic dialect of the Western Greek language that was later modified by Philip and spread to Asia by Alexander. The Macedonians' dialect maintained peculiarities of the Homeric times, retaining the nominative cases of the first declension without an "s," a characteristic distinguishing it from the *koine* mentioned by Hammond (1997, p. 100).[32] The language's Hellenic character is also shown by the fact that the majority of the early names of both the Macedonian elite and the common people are formed from Greek roots.[33] The Macedonian Hellenic language preserved features that had disappeared from the other Hellenic dialects, shown by the fact that Roman and Byzantine lexicographers and grammarians used examples from the Macedonian dialect to interpret difficult features of the Homeric poems.[34]

Borza (1990, p. 94), less certain about the dialect spoken by the ancient Macedonians, speculated that perhaps a variety of dialects were spoken by them. The written language was in standard Greek dialect, with the common people speaking an unknown idiom of a language or dialect now beyond recovery. He also speculated that the common people's dialect declined with time and was replaced by the standard *koine* (common) Greek. By the fourth century B.C., official communications in the Macedonian kingdom were conducted in Greek. Borza also pointed out (p. 92) that "standard Attic Greek was used by the court for personal matters and by the king for official business from at least the time of Archaelaus at the end of the fifth century B.C. The use of Greek may be the result of the process of hellenization.... The evidence suggests that Macedonian [dialect] was distinct from the ordinary Attic Greek used as the language of the court and diplomacy." It is commonly accepted that two dialects were used by the Macedonians of antiquity, the official for formal discourse and communication and a second idiomatic dialect used for ceremonies, rituals, or "rough soldiers' talk," but there is no evidence to suggest that the secondary (unofficial) dialect was not Greek. In fact, the evidence presented in previous paragraphs on the multitude of dialects and idioms used by the ancient Greeks leaves no doubt that the Macedonian dialect was Hellenic. Also, it is more logical to assume that the Macedonian dialect had many similarities with the official Greek dialect than to assume that the Macedonian officials were speaking Greek and the remainder of the population with Greek names, using Greek-inscribed coins, statues, gravestones and frescoes, spoke an incomprehensible, alien dialect.[35]

Such political and historical challenges on the ancient Macedonians' ethnicity and language were further compounded by a few insignificant incidences or misinterpretations of events in the Macedonian elites' lives. A few historians, for instance, use an incident in Alexander's life to suggest that the Macedonian dialect was incomprehensible to the other Greeks and therefore it was not Hellenic. This argument is based on the mention by Plutarch that Alexander the Great spoke *makedonisti* (= in a Macedonian manner) to his men in Asia during a crisis. Borza (1990, p. 92) also mentioned in a footnote that Eumenes, secretary to Alexander the Great, dispatched the Macedonian-speaking Xennias to negotiate with a Macedonian commander and concluded that the incident "leads one to suspect that more than a style of speaking is meant." The commander in question could have been non-Macedonian (Illyrian, Thracian, etc.). It is a well-known fact that Alexander recruited capable men to his army irrespective of ethnicity or language (Hammond 1997). The hypothesis of the Macedonian dialect being a separate, non-Greek dialect ignores again two well-known facts: (a) the Greek language was spoken in many dialects and idioms indicated by names describing the manner of speaking: *doristi, atticisti, ionisti, laconisti, makedonisti*, etc.; and (b) even today, the Greek language is characterized by inexhaustible capabilities for "mutational" or locally accepted idiomatic transformations. For instance, Greeks from the mainland of Greece may have some difficulties understanding thoroughly the Greek-speakers from some Aegean islands and mountainous districts of the country.

Thomas Cahill, discussing the controversy on the ancient Macedonians' language in his book *Sailing the Wine-Dark Sea: Why the Greeks Matter* (2003, p. 221), remarked: "I imagine the situation was somewhat parallel to a Scottish movie needing to be distributed with subtitles even in the English-speaking world." To crown this with another reputable quotation, we must go to the book of Paul Cartledge, *Alexander the Great (2004)*, who wrote: "But were the Macedonians themselves Greek? This may seem an astonishing question, especially in light of the recent international brouhaha over the (Former Yugoslav) Republic of Macedonia. But actually many Greek in Alexander's day were of the view that the Macedonians were either not very, or not entirely, or not at all Greek. In so far as there was any historical base for that view, it rested on the perception of the Macedonians' language, often incomprehensible to standard Greek-speakers. Against it, however, was the symbolic language of shared and accepted myth, which spoke firmly for the inclusion of the Macedonians in the Hellenic family — both all of them as descendants of the eponymous Macedon, and royal family, the Argeadae in particular" (p. 45).

Another point of controversy is the date of the Macedonian Hellenization. Borza's suggestion of a possible date (middle of the fifth century B.C.) is true enough as far as it goes. But there is no evidence to preclude the possibility that Hellenization began before 500 B.C., in the seventh century — before, during, or after the age of Perdiccas I.[36] In view of the fact that the Indo-Europeans carried with them the essential elements of a proto-Hellenic dialect, and Perdiccas's Macedonians were of Indo-European stock, it is again reasonable to assume that Hellenization may never have occurred in the true meaning of the word; after all, these people belonged to Hellenic tribes to begin with, and, therefore, only evolution of the Archaic (Aeolic) Macedonian dialect occurred, not Hellenization in a true sense. The process of evolution of the proto-Hellenic linguistic elements took place, successfully, simply because the ancient Macedonians, even those before King Perdiccas II (ca. 454–413), were prone to gradually embracing the linguistic refinements that brought their archaic western-type Hellenic dialect to a level close to the Attic dialect, climaxing with the formation of a final product, the *koine*, in Philip's and Alexander's time. Nothing like that occurred with the non–Hellenic Illyrians and Thracians, despite their proximity to the Greek world, simply because their tongue had no linguistic affinity to the Hellenic dialects. Even Borza (1990, p. 3), who expressed doubts whether the Macedonians spoke a Hellenic dialect before the middle of the fifth century, concluded: "This is not, however, to insist that the Macedonian is Illyrian or Thracian. It is only to say that there is an insufficient sample of words to show exactly what the Macedonian language was. It must be emphasized that this is not to say that it was not Greek; it is only to suggest that, from the linguists' point of view, it is impossible to know."[37]

The language is not the only criterion used in the disputes between nations to define ethnicity. Archaeology plays an important role in projecting ethnic claims over history and civilization on earth (Danforth 1995). By digging, the archaeologists discover the past of a nation and can expose it to the public's admiration in archaeological museums. In the dispute between the Greeks and the Slavs on what was the ethnicity of ancient Macedonians, the new spectacular archaeological findings in Vergina, Pella, Dion, and other locations in Hellenic Macedonia, and even as far north as Skopje, unambivalently prove the ancient Macedonians' Hellenism. Archaeology legitimizes the Greek ethnic position on the Macedonian Question. Manolis Andronikos, the eminent archaeologist who headed the excavations in Vergina, wrote with respect to the epigraphic evidence of the stones discovered in Vergina: "In the most convincing way the evidence confirms the opinion of the historians who maintain that the ancient Macedonians were a Greek tribe ... and shows that the theory they were of Illyrian or Thracian origin and were Hellenized by Philip and Alexander rests on no objective criteria" (Andronikos 1984).[38]

The spectacular archaeological findings are also disputed by some historians who support the Slavic contention that the ancient Macedonians were not Greek. Badian (1982), for instance, dismisses the contention that there was a connection between the ancient Macedonians and the other Greeks before the Persian War of 480–479 B.C.[39] Borza (1990, p. 91), discussing the ancient Macedonians' ethnicity based on linguistics, wrote: "The 'Greek' position, put simply, is that the meagre literary and archaeological evidence — the latter presented by inscriptions — points to the use of the Greek language by Macedonians." What Borza considers "meagre" (the inscription in Greek on the stones, coins, and funeral stelae) and Badian considers lack of evidence for a connection before about 500 B.C. are considered by others as the greatest archaeological discoveries in Macedonia, providing historical and archaeological evidence to countenance the idea that the Macedonians of antiquity rightly and justifiably considered themselves descendants from Greek Argos in Peloponnesus.

Customs and culture can also be used as indicators to determine a population's ethnicity. The new archaeological discoveries and the lifelong studies of the Hellenic Macedonian civilization by eminent scholars demonstrated many more behavioral and cultural similarities than dissimilarities between the ancient Macedonians and the other people of Greece. The Macedonians, for instance, worshiped the same gods as the other Greeks who had placed their gods on Mount Olympus situated in Macedonia and participated in Panhellenic events. Their arts and customs were strongly influenced by the Greek city-states. More importantly, the differences between the Macedonians and the other Greeks were not greater than the differences between the Athenians and Spartans, for example, or the Athenians and the Molossians. Yet, no historian ever considered the Spartans or the Molossians non-Greek. But the preponderance of similarities versus differences in many aspects of life did not alter the perception of the Macedonians' not being of Hellenic stock by a few historians, including Borza, who wrote (1990, p. 95): "In brief, one must conclude that the similarity between some Macedonian and Greek customs and objects are not of themselves proof that the Macedonians were a Greek tribe, even though it is undeniable that on certain levels Greek cultural influences eventually became pervasive."[40] Considering the less numerous differences more important and the more numerous similarities unjustifiably less important constitutes a rather unfair evaluation system negatively affecting the Macedonians' Hellenic ethnicity. More than anything else, one often wonders what exactly it would take to alter the perceptions of a few contemporary scholars about the ancient Macedonians' ethnicity and convince them to grant the Macedonians of antiquity what historically belongs to them: recognition of their Macedonian Hellenism.

Differing perceptions of the ancient Macedonians' Hellenism are inevitable, and so is the significance attributed by some historians to the accusations by other Greeks of antiquity that the Macedonians were "barbarians." The name-calling began in Athens as a result of political fabrications based not on ethnicity or language but on the Macedonian way of life (Casson 1971, p. 158) and also because Philip II and Alexander the Great incurred the enmity of the Athenians, specifically Demosthenes, the orator who shamelessly castigated the Macedonians. When the winds of war were approaching from the north — Macedonia — it was natural that some people, especially orators, would call the Macedonians barbarians. The Athenian way of life differed profoundly not only from the Macedonian, but also from the Spartan and other city-states' way of life.[41] Even Badian (1982), an opponent of Macedonia's Hellenism, concluded that name-calling might have been no more than invective by angry orators unrelated to historical facts.[42]

Not all the Athenian orators and writers were against King Philip and the Macedonians. The conservative educator Isocrates insisted that the Greek city-states must unite. For four decades he urged the Greeks to abandon their petty quarrels, advocating a Panhellenic crusade against Greece's archenemy, the Persian Empire (Borza 1990, p. 224). He even campaigned on the issue during the Olympic Games of 380 B.C. When his pleas fell on deaf ears, he turned his attention to a strong leader, Philip, and urged him in his oration *Philip*, and with three letters to Philip, to unite the Hellenic city-states and guide them against the Persians. The question we must ask now is this: Would a renowned Athenian pedagogue like Isocrates, who remained for almost fifty years the most famous, successful, and influential Athenian, favor Philip to unite the Greeks if the Macedonians were considered non-Greek? Nobody has accused Isocrates of a lack of patriotism.

Over the past fifty years, much scholarly effort has been devoted to the study of ancient Macedonia and its people. A perusal and careful analysis of articles and books on Macedonia, however, would reveal many obvious shortcomings resulting from bias, disregard of evidence, misconceptions, doubts, or plain lack of good evidence. Scholars are reluctant to be convinced especially by archaeological discoveries. Borza concluded (1990):

> Their [the ancient Macedonians'] adoption of some aspects of Hellenism over a long period of time is more important than the genetic structure of either the Macedonian population or their royal house in particular.... Once freed from the constraints of modern Balkan political rhetoric, the issue of the ethnic identity of the ancient Macedonians and their royal house recedes into its proper historical significance: the bloodlines of ancient people are notoriously difficult to trace [pp. 96–97].

True, the ethnicity of ancient people is difficult to trace. However, the evidence presented by ancient historians and by renowned contemporary scholars leaves no doubt of the ancient Macedonians' pure Hellenism. As new cogent historical information on the ethnicity of the ancient Macedonians is unlikely to be forthcoming, scholars of Macedonian history are challenged to peruse carefully and weigh without bias the existing Hellenic, international, and Slavic historiography and formulate an objective opinion of both the contributions of the ancient Macedonians to the world civilization and their ethnicity.

Discrediting the ancient Macedonians' Hellenism, a key flash point that some writers, politicians, and NGOs espouse to break the connection between the present-day Hellenic Macedonia and ancient Macedonia and to establish a connection between FYROM's Slavs and ancient Macedonians, necessitates intellectual and civilized discussions. As these seem not to be forthcoming, we must turn to what is currently available. The Skopjan nationalist historiography, for instance, rejects the notion that modern Hellenic Macedonians are related to ancient Macedonians, but admits that contemporary "Macedonians" (i.e., FYROM's Slavs) are descendants of the Slavs whose ancestors arrived in the Balkans in the sixth century A.D. and that the ancient Macedonians were not Slavs. Kofos (1994) and Andonovski (1978) characterized the ancient Macedonian state as the "First Macedonian State," both suggesting there is continuity between ancient and contemporary Macedonia. The agreement between the two historians, however, ends on this note. For Kofos, Greek Macedonia is the continuation of ancient Macedonia; for Andonovski, the Republic of Macedonia (FYROM) is. Kofos's numerous scholarly publications support his contentions. If Andonovski persists with his idea, on the other hand, he must provide evidence to prove it and enumerate the characteristics of the present FYROM Slavs that match similar characteristics of the Macedonians of antiquity, including language, culture, names, customs, traditions, history, and supporting archaeological findings.[43]

To crown its proclivity in using distorted historical facts, the Yugoslav communist propaganda attempted to discredit everything announcing to the world the pure, unadulterated Macedonian Hellenism. They embarked on an intense propaganda barrage against the so-called "speaking stones," the hundreds of monuments and crafts (marble statues, gravestones, coins, frescoes, etc.) unearthed in Macedonia, Egypt, and all the way to India, bearing Greek inscriptions ("speaking Greek").[44] Though Alexander's and his descendants' Hellenism is well known to the world, the Skopje messengers proclaimed that the ancient Macedonians were not Greek but an Illyrian group;[45] the Macedonian kings were not Greek, but "Philhellenes";[46] the ruling class was Hellenized, but the common people remained "Macedonians";

and during the Hellenistic Age, slaves and Greek mercenaries transmitted the Greek civilization in Asia, not the Macedonian elite (Nystazopoulou-Pelekidou 1988). Not surprisingly, the Skopje history revisionists are offering not one iota of evidence to support these claims; not one statue, coin, monument, gravestone, or any other evidence has ever been discovered in Alexander's kingdom supporting Skopje's contentions; not a shred of evidence has ever been unearthed that a language other than Greek ever existed.

Who Are the Macedonians Now?

Perceptions on the question of who the Macedonians are now — or to put it in a different way, what the historical, cultural, linguistic, and ethnic characteristics are defining Macedonianism of the Hellenic Macedonians versus all the other inhabitants of historic Macedonia — are inevitably complicated. While the clash between Hellenism and Bulgarism over who was entitled to Philip's and Alexander's Macedonia has been laid to rest since the Treaty of Bucharest (signed in 1913), questions and doubts on the Macedonian problem and whether there exists a separate Macedonian ethnicity abound among government officials, academics, politicians, NGOs, diplomats, and especially anthropologists. In November 1994, three years after FYROM declared its independence from Yugoslavia, for instance, the Forum Against Ethnic Violence (FAEV), a group of anthropologists, held a conference on Macedonia at University College, London (Cowan 2000). The conference's theme was "the 'Macedonian Controversy' (the question of who had the right to call themselves, or others, Macedonians) and the question of diversity within and between communities residing in a territory so named."

The FAEV conference also raised the question of who is a Macedonian and suggested that the word may be used "for an inhabitant, or former inhabitant, of a region called Macedonia, irrespective of ethnicity; for a citizen of the Republic of Macedonia (FYROM), irrespective of ethnicity; or for a member of the Macedonian nation or ethnic group. It is the third, apparently most 'natural' usage, which is most controversial" (Cowan 2000, p. xiv).

If the simplistic and unpersuasive rationale, habitation in Macedonia, defines who is a Macedonian, then the two million FYROM inhabitants (formerly a part of Vardar Province), Pirin (Bulgarian) Macedonia's inhabitants, and the three million inhabitants of Hellenic Macedonia are Macedonians, irrespective of ethnicity. Within this framework, on the basis of habitation, a nonethnic characteristic, we can divide the present inhabitants of historic Macedonia into three groups: Greek-Macedonians, Slav-Macedonians, and

Bulgar-Macedonians. Therefore, if we use the word "Macedonians" exclusively for FYROM's inhabitants, as most anthropologists do, we are committing political and ethnic discrimination: we deprive the inhabitants of Greek Macedonia (75 percent of historic Macedonia) and Bulgarian Macedonia (9 percent of historic Macedonia) of their ethnic and cultural identity, a serious and unjustifiable political, historical, and ethnic violation.[47]

The second suggestion is also discriminatory because it grants the prerogative (and the glorious Macedonian heritage) to the Slavs and Albanians of FYROM, almost half of which was not even inside King Philip's historic Macedonia, while depriving the Macedonian ethnicity from the inhabitants of Greek Macedonia and Pirin Macedonia. Unfortunately, this scenario is also preferred by some historians, anthropologists, sociologists, and NGOs. This scenario is also at odds with itself because it automatically converts the large Albanian minority to "Macedonian," a concept arraying itself against the Albanians' well-publicized distaste for being called Macedonians. A fitting epilogue to this concept would be that it is not a concept at all.

If we support the third suggestion, a Macedonian is a "member of the Macedonian nation or ethnic group," we stand on the brink of accepting a historically incorrect concept. Speaking of a Macedonian nation is as false as speaking of an "Athenian nation," a "Peloponnesian nation," or a "Thessalian nation." There was never a Macedonian nation. Philip's and Alexander's Macedonia was a Greek state among the quarreling (and often warring) Greek states that eventually predominated over the others with the Macedonian victory at Chaeronea in 338 B.C. and united Greece for the first time (Green 1991; Hammond 1972). Virtually by default, and by communist decree, this scenario arbitrarily shifts Macedonianism from the legitimate Greek-speaking beneficiaries to Slav-speaking newcomers.

Who are the Macedonians now? Any person versed in Greece's history, as outlined by scholars before or after the establishment of communism in the Balkans (Durant 1939; Hammond 1972–1988, 1976, 1989), would agree that the indigenous Hellenic Macedonians (IHMs) are the only people who can be called Macedonians. Because this claim is bound to be characterized as biased, a brief attempt will be made here to support the IHMs' Macedonianism. They have all the characteristics and traits not only to describe themselves, but also to be described by others as Macedonians. Generation after generation of IHMs has lived in Hellenic Macedonia — 75 percent of King Philip's historic Macedonia — the rich land east and west of Thessaloniki with the existing archaeological and historical sites of an age long gone, the Hellenic Macedonian age: Pella, Vergina, Dion, Aegae, Pydna, Olynthos, Aiane, Appolonia, Philippi, Stagira (Aristotle's birthplace), Thessaloniki. Does any of these historical names near the IHMs' abode sound

Slavic to the reader? The IHMs' features are Greek and the soil they tread is Greek, hiding under their feet coins, statues, gravestones, frescoes, monuments, all inscribed in Greek (Dakin 1966).

The IHMs have spoken Greek — as the ancient Macedonians did — for as many ancestral generations as it can be ascertained. They possess cultural traits together, have Greek names, and have used Hellenic Macedonian first names for generations (Alexander, Alketas, Philip, Parmenion, Kleopatra, Eurydice, Filotas, Aristotle, etc.). The Greek state did not have to grant the IHMs visions of grandeur and a glorious, fascinating history to force them to express their Macedonian Hellenism, an innate characteristic among them. They are the backbone of Hellenic Macedonia. Their fathers and forefathers fought the Romans, Ottomans, and the Bulgarian guerrillas (*komitadjides*) and won the Macedonian Struggle of 1904–1908. They all share the same Hellenic Macedonian dreams and aspirations. To the IHMs Macedonia is the collective place of glory, myth, Hellenic pride, achievement, Aristotle's philosophy, Alexander's greatness and vision, and the spirit of the Hellenic language's triumph. To them Macedonia is the domestic place where the essence of Hellenic Macedonian life was formulated and blended with the rest of Greek life and culture.

A brief mention of a few other characteristics of the Hellenic Macedonians will suffice: enduring attachment to the land and its history and culture; unaltered patriotism of Macedonian Hellenism as perceived directly or indirectly by unlikely non-Greek sources connecting modern Macedonia's Hellenism with that of ancient Macedonians (Durant 1939; Grant 1988; Hammond 1949);[48] continuing attachment to the customs and special ritualized events of the forebears by the contemporary indigenous Hellenic Macedonians; a plethora of Greek Macedonian vernacular understood by the IHMs; and most importantly, possession of the *power of Hellenic Macedonian ethnic pride, culture and identity.*

The IHMs are a good example of self-ascription to Hellenic Macedonianism, fitting well with Barth's (1969) critical features of ethnic identity. He defined ethnic groups as "categories of ascription and identification" (pp. 10–13). The critical aspect of ethnic identity, according to him, is the characteristic of self-ascription and ascription (identification) by others. As a good example of self-ascription to Hellenic Macedonianism, the IHMs are unjustifiably ignored, bypassed, or disregarded by anthropologists in their research to understand who the Macedonians are and draw conclusions on ethnicity based on examples from certain limited areas of Hellenic Macedonia where slavophone inhabitants exist (Danforth 2000). The IHMs and their descendants living in Macedonia and abroad never vacillated from one ascription to another. Their self-ascribed and ascribed-by-others national identity is a permanent, unaltered characteristic. No one forced upon them the glorious Macedonian history or coerced them to express their Macedonianism, an innate characteristic perpetuated naturally from generation to generation. Their aspirations, songs, ballads, and dreams always have been Hellenic; they read Homer, Plato, Thucydides, Herodotus, and Aristotle in original Greek when they attend high school; and they can also read the inscriptions on the "speaking stones and coins" found under their feet in Macedonia, unshakable evidence of ancient Macedonia's Hellenism.[49]

In keeping with the majority of views expressed by scholars on ancient Macedonia, it could be argued that Philip's historic Macedonia had been situated not on Yugoslav territory, but within modern Greece's borders. It would also be argued convincingly that Philip's Macedonians, on the other side of the historical spectrum, had all the characteristics and traits to describe themselves as Greeks: The names of their cities were Greek (Pella, Aigae, Dion, Heracleia, Olynthos, etc.) and so were the names of their months (Dios, Apellaios, Artemisios, Panaimos, etc.) (Mitsakis 1973). They had a single alphabet, the alphabet used by Aristotle, Alexander's teacher, and Euripides, who wrote his plays in Greek in Pella, the capital of ancient Macedonia; they had a single religion (they believed in the Greek gods) and participated in the Olympic Games;[50] and they left buried in the ground a plethora of gravestones of common people, statues, frescoes, stelae, and coins inscribed in Greek, dated as far back as 480 B.C.[51] Alexander the Great claimed ancestry on his mother's side from Achilles and on his father's from Heracles (Hercules) and read Homer's *Iliad* (written in Greek), which he considered his most treasured possession. Alexander's Macedonians spoke "Greek in root and in ethnic termination" (Hammond 1989) and wrote in the same language, as can be attested by the thousands of artifacts discovered in Macedonia and all the way to Egypt and India (Martis 1985). The early struggle of ancient Macedonians to prove their Hellenism blends somewhere through the centuries with the modern Hellenic Macedonians' Macedonianism.

In the past few years and in the light of recent Balkan events with FYROM's secession from Yugoslavia, some historians and anthropologists believe that the word "Macedonians" may be used only for members of the "Macedonian nation" or ethnic group — implying the Slavic "Macedonian nation," Tito's creation (Bacid 1997; Poulton 1995).[52] This view, within the constraints of the present Balkan rhetoric, is potentially explosive, in both the short and long term, and highly controversial. Given the evidence presented thus far in this book, based on the writings of eminent historians and anthropologists supported by historical facts and archaeological findings, and by the fact that the Macedonians of antiquity spoke a Greek dialect as far back as at least seven hundred years before Christ, it is hard to comprehend why the word "Macedonians" must be used for the FYROM Slavs, Bulgarians, and Albanians. It is even more remarkable to read historical treatises ensnared in the dysfunctional and unhistorical pronouncements propelled into the world by the Skopjan historical elite. These proclivities are further embellished by FYROM's displays of arrogance and recalcitrance to negotiate in good faith a reasonable compromise on the name taken from a neighbor without permission.

Poulton, for instance, focused in his book *Who Are the Macedonians?* (1995) only on FYROM's citizens as the bearers of the Macedonian name. Why Poulton was so generous, granting the FYROM Slavs, Bulgarians, and Albanians the privilege of being Macedonians while ignoring the existence of millions of Hellenic Macedonians, is not known. Referring to FYROM Slavs as Macedonians "would be to ignore strident and historically justified claims" that the name "Macedonia" should also refer to the large northern Greek province, wrote Cowan and Brown (2000, p. 6). Powerful political, social, economic and cultural forces, with the dictatorial power of a totalitarian state being the most forceful, are forces instrumental in shaping or structuring ethnic identities, wrote Danforth (2000, p. 87). Neither Poulton nor the NGOs take into account this crucially important point — or the point brought forward by Cowan and Brown of ignoring three million Greek Macedonians — both concepts applying chapter and verse to the small republic's formation by Tito's dictatorial powers. Against these well-known events, which downgrade the concept of ethnic identity to no more than another communist experiment, there remains also the problem of the Skopje political leadership's not considering the Albanians "Macedonians." According to FAEV's scenario, the Albanians are "Macedonians" because they inhabit "Macedonia." Therefore, assuming the name "Macedonia" does not help to keep their country united with the large Albanian minority excluded. A neutral name acceptable by all ethnic groups must be adopted, as in the case of multiethnic countries, such as Canada and the United States. Otherwise it is natural for the Albanians to desire independence or to join Kosovo.[53]

In the light of compellingly arbitrary or biased suggestions that only the FYROM citizens are Macedonians, the two terms "Hellene" and "Macedonian" are therefore mutually exclusive, with the term "Macedonian" arbitrarily transferred through the ages from the Macedonians of antiquity not to the legitimate descendants but to the Slavs, Albanians, and Bulgarians of FYROM, almost half the area of which did not even belong to Philip's historic Macedonia. The unjustifiable suggestion of a few historians is problematic, because by depriving the IHMs of the right to be called Macedonians, it grants virtually by default the exclusive right to FYROM's Slavs and other nationalities to be "Macedonians" and raises many interesting conceptual questions: What characteristics (historical, cultural, genetic, linguistic, or anthropological) does the FYROM population possess— besides inhabiting a section of the former Vardar Province — to be described by communists first, by anthropologists later, as "Macedonian"? Why did the Slav "Macedonians" describe themselves as Bulgarians from 1870 to 1943 — and many do so today — waiting for almost seventy-five years to be transformed into "Macedonians" by the dictatorial powers of a communist state? Given the ethnic transformation of FYROM's Slavs into "Macedonians," can anyone describe without bias a single characteristic of FYROM's inhabitants that reflects a similar characteristic possessed by the Macedonians of antiquity? What are the other criteria used to elevate the Slavs to the status of being Macedonians? "In what sense are Danforth's [1995] 'ethnic Macedonians' more indigenous than people of Greek, Vlach, or Albanian origin who inhabited Greek Macedonia?" (Mackridge and Yannakakis 1997, p. 21).

Fundamentally, history knows that the "Macedonianism" of Vardar Province's slavophone inhabitants and Albanians is exclusively based on the role played by external factors of paramount importance when in the early 1940s they were transformed into "Macedonians" for political reasons by communist dictators (Tito, Stalin, and Dimitrov) and infamous communist organizations (Comintern and the Balkan Communist Federation).[54] In reality, it was not even a self-ascription or ascription by others and assignment of a cause, but a dictatorial order, a forceful conversion that preceded the FYROM Slavs' self-ascription as "Macedonians," resulting in an unorthodox and scandalous creation of a new artificial ethnicity in a manner similar to Byelorussia's formation by Lenin and Stalin. As Danforth (2000) pointed out, "Given the common nationalist view of the immutability of identity, conversion from one identity to another [by ascription by others] is bound to raise serious questions of authenticity and legitimacy. He also pointed out (p. 100) that "It is possible precisely because Greeks and Macedonians are not born, they are *made*. National identities, in other words, are not biologically given, they are socially constructed" (p. 87). That is what happened to the Slavs of the People's Republic of Macedonia. They were not born Macedonians; their Macedonian ethnicity was constructed by the state in 1943–1945. In contrast, the IHMs, whose forebears always lived in Hellenic Macedonia, always spoke Greek, were not made Macedonians by a totalitarian communist system; they were born Macedonians.[55]

The strong force binding the Hellenic Macedonians together is history, the learning of life, the bridge connecting the past with the future. History may be irrelevant to NGOs and politicians, but not to the people of Greece. It played a great part in the politics of the Macedonian Question and the struggle for Macedonia, fueling the Greek people's Hellenic Macedonian pride, strengthening the sense of Macedonian identity. History has given the Greeks of Macedonia a strong sense of Hellenic Macedonian pride. History to the Greeks "is not merely a warning reminder of man's follies and crimes, but also an encouraging resemblance of generative souls ... a spacious country of mind, wherein a thousand saints, statesmen, inventors, scientists, poets, artists, musicians, lovers, and philosophers still live and speak, teach and carve, and sing" (Durant and Durant 1968).

The sense of a Greek cultural identity, developed among the Hellenic Macedonians and the immigrant Macedonians of Greece *(prosfyges*, refugees) in Macedonia together is another strong reason for the intensification of the Hellenic Macedonians' pride, defining together with other characteristics Macedonian Hellenism. The sense of belonging to a distinct cultural and ethnic group, the IHM group, enhanced the sense of belonging to Hellenic Macedonia among the *prosfyges*, the Greeks who arrived in Macedonia in the first quarter of the twentieth century, helping the assimilation policy of the refugees in Hellenic Macedonia.[56] These Hellenes have every right to be in Macedonia, as they arrived through a legal exchange under international law, to replace the Muslims who were legal residents of Hellenic Macedonia. The Greek cultural identity resulted from the demographic changes that occurred in Macedonia, the scrutinized exploration of the Greek historical past, the socioeconomic developments, and the sustained mentality of the area. All these traits reinforced the Hellenic Macedonian pride and assisted in developing the process of nation-building since Greece became independent from the Ottoman Empire.

6

The Greek Civil War and the Struggle for Macedonia

Ἔστιν μεν οὖν Ἑλλάς και η Μακεδονία
(Macedonia is also a part of Greece)
—*Strabo, 1st century B.C.*

Even before major combat operations ceased in the Balkans, the Greek people expected the liberation of the country in the early fall of 1944 with great exhilaration. They watched the Nazis loading their trucks and trains to leave the country, anticipating with longing the elusive gem, freedom, after almost four years of slavery by some of the most brutal conquerors the country had ever seen. This pleasant perspective, however, was not in the people's hearts in Macedonia. Hungry and apprehensive in their improvised shacks or ransacked houses, barely making a living on what the multiform invaders and the local fanatic elements had left, the people were asking the same questions over and over: What would happen to their villages and themselves if the clever revolutionaries continued their struggle for power? What would happen to their freedom if the yoke imposed on them during the occupation by the Germans and Bulgarians settled permanently? What would the Bulgarian Komitet men, Tito's partisans, the Bulgarian occupation army, and the Slav-speaking autonomists do? Would the leaders of any color and persuasion attempt to exploit the fluidity of the conditions to impose by force the political and economic system of their preference? Would Tito's partisans invade western Macedonia, snatching it from Greece by force before the Greek government could establish its authority?

Looking at Macedonia's tumultuous past from a broad perspective, exacerbated in the early 1940s by precarious conditions resulting from World War II, resistance against the conquerors (Germans, Italians, Bulgarians), and a new, powerful force, communism, all these assumptions were not too far-fetched. Stalin intended to abide by the percentages agreement on the Balkans—favorable to Greece—he had made with Churchill in Moscow (Churchill 1953).[1] But the dramatic events of the fall of 1944—defeat of the SNOF Slav-speaking partisans and of the Slavomacedonian autonomists—did not alter the trajectory of Tito's strategy on the Macedonian issue. He was still making plans at Greek Macedonia's expense. Immediately after liberation, he turned his attention again southward and began preparing new partisan groups near Greece's northern frontier to infiltrate Greek Macedonia.

It is important to place the events of the early 1940s in the proper perspective and discuss in more details further factors and the percentages agreement on the Balkans that added to Tito's difficulties in his continuing plans at Hellenic Macedonia's expense. Dramatic forces beyond Tito's spectrum of influence and events in Moscow and Yalta, external to the Balkans and beyond the control of the communist parties of Yugoslavia and Bulgaria, had a decisive—but temporary—impact on the Macedonian Question. On October 9, 1944, three days before the Germans abandoned Athens, Winston Churchill and Joseph Stalin met in Moscow and decided how they would divide their influence in the Balkans after Germany's defeat: 90 percent British predominance in Greece, 90 percent Russian predominance in Romania, and 50–50 in Yugoslavia (Churchill 1953, pp. 227–28). At the ensuing Yalta Conference with Churchill and Roosevelt, Stalin offered no objection to British intervention in Greece (Banak 1995).

Looking upon the Moscow Agreement in another way, the questions to ask are: (a) what would Tito have done if there was no agreement? (b) What would the situation have been in Macedonia, especially in Greek eastern Macedonia and western Thrace, if the two World War II leaders had made no agreement? The Soviet army could easily cross the Greek-Bulgarian frontier in September or October 1944, to support the territories' occupation by the Bulgarians; or even worse, the Soviets could occupy the entire Hellenic Macedonia and remain there indefinitely.

The occupation's end found Greek western Macedonia with EAM/ELAS in firm control. It was about the middle of April 1945, six months after liberation, when the Greek government was finally able to establish its authority in the region, especially in the Kastoria and Florina districts. The majority of Slav-speaking inhabitants in these districts and elsewhere in Macedonia were faithful to Greece and remained in the country; but blended with them also remained in Greek Macedonia a number of

Slav-speaking autonomists and *komitadjides*. In fact, Greek-speaking inhabitants and Greek-oriented slavophones in the two districts were shocked watching known *komitadjides*, who had elected to stay in Greece, parading in city streets, celebrating with the regular ELAS troops the country's liberation, wearing the brand-new red insignia of liberators. They had already undergone their first transformation from Bulgarian autonomists, *komitadjis* terrorists, and German or Italian collaborators to Slav-speaking ELAS liberators. At the time of liberation, questions of identity did not come to the attention of the EAM/ELAS and KKE leaders.

Even from its relatively early stage, the gross distortion of history could not last forever. With ELAS's defeat in Athens by the British and the loyal Greek government forces and the signing of the Varkiza Agreement between EAM/ELAS and the Plastiras government (February 12, 1945), ELAS began losing its grip on Macedonia. If the Athens defeat was a humiliating blow to ELAS guerrillas, who would not enjoy their dreamed-for political system anytime soon, to the villagers returning home from the ELAS reserve units it meant the end of a long, devastating storm. For the first time in more than three years they would be free from the fascists and Nazis, free from the communists, free from Kaltsev's *komitadjides* and Gotse's Bulgarian autonomists, free from Tito's irredentism for a "united and independent Macedonia" under Yugoslav hegemony.

Looking back over those terrible years, it is difficult to say precisely what the majority of the Slav-speakers would have done before or immediately after liberation if ELAS had won the battle of Athens. Would they have sacrificed everything for an autonomous Macedonia promised by SNOF leaders (Koliopoulos 1995)? Would they have abandoned their previous, not always perfect life under the Greek government, to live in an autonomous country with Komitet's or Ochrana's fanatics? Would they have sacrificed a relatively known quality of life in Greece to live under Gotse, Kaltsev, Mitrofsky, Peyov, and other individuals who changed affiliations several times during the occupation? Perhaps they would have been fooled by the autonomy-for-Macedonia slogans promulgated by Gotse and his *komitadjides*. Even Patrick Evans, a British liaison officer with ELAS, was deceived and convinced that all Slav-speaking individuals were genuine "Macedonians."[2] But for how long would they remain outside Yugoslavia's or Bulgaria's communism?

The Bulgarian Withdrawal from Greece

The problem in Bulgarian-occupied eastern Macedonia and western Thrace was different from the remainder of Macedonia. The difficulty of ascertaining the precise conditions and the Bulgarian intentions from the beginning of eastern Macedonia's and western Thrace's occupation virtually contributed to an uncertainty of what they would do in the bloody territories when the Germans withdrew from the Balkans. Would they use military power to protect their "liberated" area? Would the approaching victorious Red Army support the Bulgarian age-old ambitions, allowing them to remain in the occupied territory? The Greek population's apprehension of the Red Army's intentions was unjustified. When the Red Army reached the Bulgarian-Romanian border, the Soviet Union declared war on Bulgaria on September 4, 1944 (Vattis 2002).[3] Seeing an excellent opportunity to erase the Nazi stigma, Bulgaria asked for an armistice with the Soviet Union and declared war against Germany. By one minute to midnight, the Bulgarian Janus exhibited its pleasant face, hoping for magnanimity and forgiveness from the World War II Allies. Before the Bulgarian people had a chance to enjoy freedom, however, a communist regime assumed power in Sofia on September 9, 1944 (Karvelis 1996). Bulgaria, now a Soviet satellite with thousands of Soviet troops occupying the country, remained in the Soviet orbit till communism fell in Europe near the end of the twentieth century (1989–1991).

It soon became apparent, even after the Soviet Red Army moved into Bulgaria and the communists ascended to power in Sofia, that the Bulgarian authorities and the fascist troops were reluctant to withdraw from occupied eastern Macedonia and western Thrace. Bulgaria's wish for absolution by the Allies notwithstanding, the Bulgarian army and its paramilitary organizations continued terrorizing the Greek population of the occupied areas (Amperiadis 1998). Perhaps relying on Russian support, the Bulgarians turned the fall of 1944 into a bloody period: hanging, shooting, and burning people alive in their houses. Most of these atrocities were committed by the new ally of the Soviets and, by extension, an ally of the British and Americans. Bulgaria had unmounted the tired Nazi horse and climbed a fresh red one.

After the initial flare of diplomatic activities, war declarations, and terrorization of the Greek population, the new Bulgarian communist government assured the representatives of the Middle East Allied headquarters they would discontinue all inimical acts against the Greek population, soon withdrawing from the occupied territories.[4] While making these promises, they were fabricating all kinds of excuses to delay their departure from Greece as long as they could, audaciously hoping the allies would allow them to keep the occupied territories granted to them by Hitler (Kofos 1989). Given the fact that the Bulgarians were now communists and friends of the Red Army, one way to accomplish that — keep the occupied territories — was to cooperate with the KKE forces in the occupied territories against armed bands of nationalist Greeks who hated the communists just as much as the Bulgarians (Karvelis 1996).[5] On September 20, 1944, in the village of Melissohorion, representatives of the CPB (mostly from the Bulgarian army of occupation), ELAS, and the Political Committee for National Liberation (*Politiki Epitropi Ethnikis Apeleftherosis*, PEEA) signed the infamous Melissohorion Agreement to "strengthen the mutual liberation struggle and future cooperation."[6] Never mind that the Bulgarian signatories were Nazi collaborators and occupiers of the Greek land (Vattis 2002). The text included the following articles (not all cited):

1. The Bulgarian army will offer immediate support of ELAS with war material.
2. The Bulgarian army will support ELAS's operations against the government forces and nationalist groups.
3. During the Anglo-American landings in Greece ELAS is obliged to include Bulgarian troops for support.
4. In the event of defeat, ELAS is obliged to support Bulgarian troops in their effort to retreat.
5. All the Bulgarian war material in Macedonia and Thrace will go to ELAS.
6. ELAS will protect the Bulgarian minority and their belongings and assist it in moving to Bulgaria if it desires it.
7. EAM, KKE, ELAS, and CPB will undertake the task of forming an independent Macedonia after the war, abolishing the border between Greece, Bulgaria, and Yugoslavia.

All these concessions were made by EAM and KKE to the Bulgarian fascists-turned-communists for promising to support ELAS in the event of British and American landings in Greece (Vattis 2002).[7] To repay ELAS for the concessions made at Melissohorion, the Bulgarian army assisted ELAS's VII Division to take control of areas occupied by Greek nationalist groups.

While actively engaged in some areas in violating the Greek-Bulgarian armistice signed on October 25, 1944, by cooperating with Bulgarian units against PAO, ELAS units violently expelled the Bulgarians from others (Karvelis 1996). On some occasions, after fierce fighting, ELAS forced several Bulgarian units to abandon their posts and escape to Bulgaria or surrender. For instance, on September 12, 1944, the 26th ELAS Regiment annihilated the Bulgarian garrison in the outskirts of Alexandroupolis, and a Bulgarian army unit in the village of Proti surrounded the city and forced the Bulgarians to surrender. After three years of occupation, the Greek flag was raised in the Alexandroupolis mayoral building with great public jubilation. Many Bulgarian soldiers were killed by ELAS and several Ochranists were arrested. Similar events occurred throughout the Bulgarian-occupied zone (Karvelis 1996).

Ignoring the armistice signed between Greece and Bulgaria on October 25, 1944, the Bulgarian army remained in the occupied territory for another three and a half months. After ELAS's capitulation in Athens, the signing of the Varkiza Agreement, and the pressure applied by the British and the Americans on the new Bulgarian government, the remnants of the Bulgarian army finally trickled out from the occupied territories into their country, dragging with them Bulgarian criminals and KKE fanatics who settled in camps within Bulgaria to prepare for the so-called Third Round, the Greek Civil War of 1946–1949.

Thus ended three and a half years of unquestionably the harshest occupation of Greek land in generations, a bloody tragedy in eastern Macedonia and western Thrace with the Bulgarian army disgraced, abandoning the Hellenic territory in shambles: more than fifty thousand Greek people were killed, and thousands more were tortured, deported or imprisoned in the occupied area or in Bulgaria. Thousands of refugees from the area crowded the already stressed neighborhoods in Thessaloniki and in other cities in the German zone of occupation. Hundreds of villages were destroyed or burned to the ground, and hundreds of women and girls were raped. Many priests were deposed or imprisoned, and hundreds of Greek teachers lost their jobs. When the Bulgarians finally withdrew from the occupied territory, they left behind a Greek population in numb silence and shock. The four-century-long Turkish occupation did not leave as many deep scars on the Greeks of eastern Macedonia and western Thrace as did the four-year-long occupation by the Bulgarian fascists, redressed later as communists (Amperiadis 1998; Miller 1975).

Civil War

Several motives have impelled independent countries to intervene in the internal affairs of neighboring states. But the massive aid in war equipment, supplies, bases, and instructors provided by Greece's communist neighbors, especially Yugoslavia, from 1945 to 1949 to the Communist Party of Greece (KKE) was unprecedented and beyond anything described in recent world history (Papavizas 2002). Much has been written on this unique event of international conspiracy and violation of international law by the communist world, with great attention focused on the extraordinary danger Greece faced of losing its freedom, not to mention the envisaged detachment of Hellenic Macedonia and its annexation by Tito's People's Republic of Macedonia. Initially, the Greek government arrived at some simplistic views on its communist neighbors' involvement in the Greek fratricide, ignoring the intricacies of the problem and the threat to Greece's territorial integrity, misinterpreting the sinister policies of its adversaries (Zafeiropoulos 1956). Slowly, but better late than never, the Greek government correctly and justifiably perceived the imminent threat to Macedonia in the 1940s, emanating from the Yugoslav-supported secessionist plans of the Slavomacedonians and Tito's irredentist territorial designs.

Despite the stresses and strains on bilateral relations between the two totalitarian communist Balkan regimes, the Bulgarian-supported secessionist activities of a group of Slav-speakers first, and similar activities by Yugoslav-supported Slav-speakers later, were real. The sense of imminent threat to Greece's territory from the communist North was alive, known from repeated Yugoslav references to or demands for the unification of the three sections of Macedonia. Also, the basically ambivalent agreements betweenTito and Dimitrov later revealed a thinly veiled conspiracy to snatch Greek Macedonia and attach it to a unified federated Macedonian state within a South Slav federation (the new phase of the Macedonian Question) (Kouzinopoulos 1999; Woodhouse 1976). Unfortunately, from the onset of its existence, the KKE leadership accepted the massive aid from the Balkan communists to support its war against the government, tolerating the irredentist plans of the Eastern Bloc for reasons the party deemed advantageous to its development, thoroughly submitting itself to Moscow's and Comintern's directives. The Greek government and the people finally were able to discern that a naked conspiracy was in the making. They saw the Greek communists and a group of Slavomacedonians as seditious foreign agents determined to assist their Yugoslav comrades in detaching Macedonia from Greece (Averoff-Tossizza 1978).

The author does not intend to discuss here the reasons for the Greek Civil War of 1946–1949 and the tumultuous war events unless they are related to or impinge upon the Macedonian Question. Reasons and events were covered extensively elsewhere (AHD 1980; Averoff-Tossizza 1978; Koliopoulos 1995; Margaritis 2002).

Even if public opinion exculpates the KKE of being solely responsible or co-responsible for triggering the civil war, it would be most difficult to excuse it for its leadership's thoughtless decision to tolerate the agitations and plans of the Slavo-Bulgarian communists, allowing their nationalist aspirations to flourish at Greece's expense. Neither must the Greek people forget the disruptive actions of a fraction of the slavophone minority in Greece that attempted to project the Greeks as usurpers of the Macedonian name and illegal occupiers of their "ancestral" land. Even if the KKE is not identified as a tool of Soviet expansion and Balkan communist irredentism at Greece's expense — a notion accepted by some historians— the indirect role played by the Soviet Union and its satellite Balkan communist countries in the Greek Civil War was decisive (Koliopoulos 1995).[8]

Unlike previous historical challenges, Greece was very close indeed to losing its territorial integrity during the civil war if the Left had won it. Even if public opinion accepts that the Right's reprisals against the Left were the most important reason triggering the civil war — overwhelming evidence and new disclosures point toward the opposite — it must accept that Macedonia, the historically bloodstained region, would have been reduced to bondage under Greece's red enemies and Greece would be truncated to its pre–Balkan War size. And even if we admit that the country contributed to the civil war by errors committed by both the Left and the Right, especially by the inability of both sides to control extreme elements, we must admit that the communist parties of Albania, Bulgaria, and Yugoslavia were blatantly responsible for fueling the civil war for their own reasons.

It is no secret now that Yugoslavia especially played a pivotal role in Zachariadis's decision to initiate the civil war.[9] It assisted the KKE in its revolt against the Greek government not only by providing material aid (war material, bases, instructors, etc.), but also by manipulating a militant group of Slavomacedonians, especially in western Macedonia, against Greece. Many of the secessionist-prone Slavomacedonians, hostile to Greece, allied themselves with Bulgaria first and Yugoslavia later to achieve their age-old dream of creating an autonomous Macedonia, including Greek Macedonia, under Bulgarian or Yugoslav hegemony (Iatrides 1995).

During the brief period of peace from the Varkiza Agreement[10] to the day general elections were held in Greece (March 31, 1946), two events destined to impinge on the Macedonian Question later took place. Nikos Zachariadis, the KKE's general secretary and Stalin's man in Greece, returned to Greece from Dachau, the Nazi concentration camp, on March 30, 1945. Blameless for the KKE's past mistakes during the occupation and resistance years, not wavering a moment in asserting absolute control of the party's apparatus, Zachariadis was the propulsive force in a series of events whose climax was DAG's defeat by the Greek national army and the annihilation of his party. The second event, a change in Yugoslavia destined to have serious repercussions on the Macedonian issue, occurred shortly before Zachariadis's return to Greece. Tito had placed his communist seal on the official documents renaming the largest part of Vardar Province the People's Republic of Macedonia. Other significant events also occurred: formation of a new organization, the National Liberation Front (NOF), and the Bled Agreement; organization of bases and camps in the Eastern Bloc countries for training and indoctrinating Greek communists before Greece entered the war; and Tito's expulsion from Cominform. Some of these events took place only before or during the Greek Civil War. Other events continued after the war. All were connected with the Macedonian isue and Greece's planned mutilation by its northern neighbors (Woodhouse 1976).

Born in Asia Minor, Nikos Zachariadis became a communist when he was seventeen. He studied at Moscow's KOUTB (Communist University of the East for the Working Class) from 1921 to 1930 and became a member of the Communist Party of the Soviet Union (CPSU) in 1922, an interesting fact unknown to KKE cadres until 1957, eight years after the civil war's end.[11] According to Rodakis (1986), a KKE leader, the party had a double leadership during the resistance and the civil war years: the formal leadership elected by the cadres and the hidden one composed of three individuals. The secret leaders were appointed by and reported to the CPSU, to which they belonged. Nikos Zachariadis, Yiannis Ioannides, and Petros Roussos were the powerful members of the secret committee. The three members of the shadow leadership group were also members of the KKE's Politburo (Gagoulias 2001).[12] Zachariadis's ascension to the highest communist party post in Greece was a remarkable achievement, especially by the party's standards with leaders rising to high-echelon posts at older ages. Except for a period of almost four years when he was a German prisoner in Dachau, Zachariadis served as the powerful KKE general secretary from 1931 to 1957, during which time he had frequent personal contacts with Lavrenti Beria, the KGB leader and a consummate embodiment of evil in the Soviet citizens' minds, before Beria was overthrown and killed by Nikita Khrushchev's group.[13]

Zachariadis was a fanatic, doctrinaire, paranoid leader, suspecting everyone within the party. Gagoulias (2001), the political commissar of DAG's 7th Division during the civil war, wrote that one of the curses crippling the KKE was *epagrypnisi* (vigilance). Simply, the comrades did not trust each other. The evil practice sprang from Zachariadis's dictum: "Search for the enemy with the red identification card." After the defeat, half of the exiled comrades were watching the other half. Thousands of communists became victims of this practice. Some were expelled from the party; others were followed constantly for their entire lives. Some were not allowed to pursue their education in the Eastern Bloc countries where they lived in exile for thirty years or more after DAG's defeat. Many were imprisoned, tortured, or even killed. Yiannis Ioannides, a KKE Politburo member and a member of the CPSU, bragged that he had ten thousand dossiers on KKE cadres (Gagoulias 2001; Yiatroudakis 1998).

Before he arrived in Greece, Zachariadis met with Soviet representatives in Paris, where he received instructions on his party's actions. The political situation in Greece had changed during his incarceration in Dachau, and even more radically after the party's and ELAS's defeat in Athens. Polarization between the Left and Right gradually sharpened after Varkiza and rallied the opposite camps (Margaritis 2002). When Zachariadis returned to Greece, the country was hopelessly and tangibly divided into two sections without borders, loathing each other. The national government had unleashed a wave of terror (White Terror) against the Left, and the extreme Left had methodically prepared the country during the occupation for collectivization and Marxism. Not surprisingly, the party's image was also hopelessly tarnished by its anti–Hellenic stance on the Macedonian issue, exacerbated by its repeated vacillations on the issue and its favoritism of an autonomous Macedonia promulgated by Greece's Eastern Bloc neighbors.

Aspiring to demonstrate its ideological and political superiority over the older high-echelon party leaders as soon as he set foot in Greece, Zachariadis began taking tough, uncompromising stands in leftist newspapers on critical national and international issues. His fierce activism was not confined to inflaming the political situation in Greece. There were clear-cut objectives behind his political and military activity: destroy the bourgeoisie and win absolute power in Athens. To accomplish these objectives he had to move simultaneously on two fronts: (a) activate a military nucleus with the many ELAS commanders who had never surrendered after Varkiza and the radical ELAS and KKE veterans who never accepted the Varkiza Agreement; (b) secure the political and military support from the KKE's foreign ideological brothers who were already frenziedly embroiled in efforts to fan the flames of war in neighboring Greece.

A short time after he arrived in Greece, Zachariadis began frantic efforts to secure political and military support from Greece's neighbors in the Eastern Bloc. He did not have to work very hard to extract lavish promises for help. But at what price? To the dark forces behind the Iron Curtain, conspiring to detach Macedonia, including Thessaloniki, from Greece, the civil war in Greece was a stroke of good luck. The war maelstrom south of the borders could easily justify their meddling in the internal affairs of their noncommunist neighbor (Smith 1995). Besides helping their ideological brothers in Greece, the war also presented a big challenge to the Bulgarians and Yugoslavs on the Macedonian issue since the *Dekemvriana* (the fighting in Athens in December of 1944) two years earlier. It simply gave them additional opportunities, political and military, to manage events in Greece, and especially in Macedonia.

One such opportunity was a clandestine meeting of high-echelon members of the KKE Central Committee with Yugoslav and Bulgarian military leaders in the Bulgarian village of Petric on December 17, 1945, ten months after the Varkiza Agreement. The three participants decided that an armed insurrection by the KKE was needed to achieve the goal of establishing a Bolshevik government in Athens. Averoff-Tossizza (1978) cited in his book *By Fire and Axe* the Petric meeting held three months before the Greek general elections as more important than the decisions taken by the

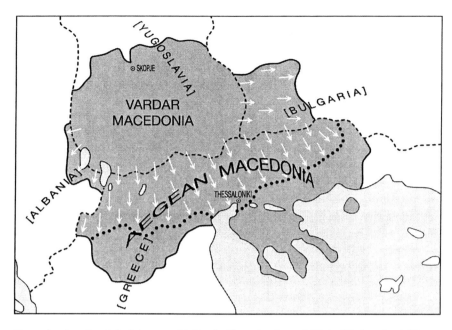

Yugoslav territorial claims on Hellenic Macedonia and Pirin (Bulgarian) Macedonia (indicated by arrows) in 1946. Black and white arrangement of Map 4 from www.macedonian-heritage.gr. Courtesy of Macedonian Heritage, Museum of the Macedonian Struggle, Thessaloniki.

KKE's Second Plenum of its Central Committee on February 16, 1946.[14] Important, secret, warlike decisions were made at Petric between the KKE and Yugoslavia and Bulgaria, two suitors for Macedonia. The communist leaders present from the three countries decided that the time had arrived for the KKE to reorganize Greece's communist partisans into an army to fight new battles to achieve what ELAS had failed to do: impose a communist regime in Greece.[15]

The Greek people did not know of the Petric agreement to form a joint Balkan headquarters or that DAG had been placed in a communist organization under Yugoslav protection. To keep the promises given to DAG at Petric (and later at Bled), the leaders of the three Eastern Bloc countries — Albania, Bulgaria, and Yugoslavia — supported the KKE with materiel, instructors, and huge quantities of arms and supplies, fueling a destructive civil war to form a new communist state (an autonomous or independent Macedonia) as the northern neighbor of a mutilated, Stalinist Greece (Averoff-Tossizza 1978; Kofos 1995).

A few military bases in the Eastern Bloc countries had been organized by the KKE for the Third Round (the civil war) before reprisals by the Right

Supply bases and training camps of the communist Democratic Army of Greece (DAG) in the Eastern Bloc countries and routes of movement into Greek Macedonia and Epirus during the Greek Civil War of 1946–1949. From *Blood and Tears: Greece 1940–1949* by George Papavizas.

against the Left intensified. Bulkes north of Belgrade (in Vojvodina), DAG's first and most important base, was the indoctrination camp and school for KKE cadres.[16] About 5,500 communists were in the camp at the beginning of 1946. Most of them were undesirable communists and fanatics from

Greece who never accepted the Varkiza Agreement. The men and women were organized into five-person cells to inform on one another (Banac 1995). The smallest violation of camp discipline was considered treason. Markos, before leaving the camp for Greece in 1946 to assume command of the communist guerrilla forces, had extensive consultations with high-ranking members of the CPY who promised to supply DAG with German arms, ammunition, food, instructors, and hospital supplies.[17]

The aid given to the KKE by the ideological brothers of the Eastern Bloc was not restricted to arms and instructions. The three communist countries offered DAG numerous bases on their own soil. In Yugoslavia, Bulkes, Tetovo, Kumanovo, Strumica, Ochris, Stip, and Skopje were some of the best training camps, supply bases, and routes into Greek Macedonia and the remainder of Greece. In Albania, Rubig north of Tirana and bases close to the Greek border such as Valona, Korytsa, Argyrokastron, and Permet constituted an easily accessible complex of bases and supply routes. In Bulgaria, Berkovitsa, Sofia, Nevrokop, Petric, and Ortakiot completed the excellent network of bases easily accessible by DAG but inaccessible by the Greek national forces. The huge quantities of armaments and materiel captured from the retreating Germans in Yugoslavia and Bulgaria also became available to DAG. Markos in the meantime had set in motion the mechanism to roll the supplies southward to DAG bases in Greece (Averoff-Tossizza 1978; Howard 1987).

The decision to interfere in Greece's affairs formulated under conspiratorial wraps at Petric by the neighboring communists was only the beginning of a great conspiracy to expunge the Hellenic Macedonian legacy. Much more was to come. In the spring of 1946, as the storm clouds of the approaching civil war had gathered over much of Greece, especially over Macedonia, Zachariadis visited Prague on March 3 to attend the Eighth Congress of the Czechoslovakian Communist Party (Averoff-Tossizza 1978). There he met with Soviet leaders, including Georgi Malenkov and Andrei Zhdanov, and European communist representatives, including the Bulgarian communist leader Dimitrov, who raised the question of "liberation of the Slavomacedonians of the Aegean Macedonia" (Smith 1995). Zachariadis received lavish promises for help, "material and moral," from the Czechoslovakian communist leader and from the Russians and Yugoslavs (Kofos 1995, p. 298, note 64; Koutsonikos 2000).

The critical decision for armed struggle in Greece was made during a Stalin-Zachariadis meeting in early April 1946 in Moscow (Smith 1995). According to Gagoulias (2001), Stalin instructed Zachariadis: "You will move from the villages to the cities gradually so that you will not provoke the British, having also in mind the route of compromise." Zachariadis did not like the vacillation. From Moscow he went to Crimea where he met again with Stalin and Molotov. According to Kofos (1995, p. 298), in Crimea Stalin finally approved the KKE's decision to escalate the war, assigning its coordination in Greece to Tito. Zachariadis later admitted that the final decision to enlarge the war was made in Crimea. On May 20, 1947, Zachariadis had another private meeting with Stalin and, according to a Russian source, "War materials and diplomatic backing were guaranteed by Moscow" (Vattis 2002). Hot on the heels of his problems, Zachariadis returned from Crimea to Belgrade and met secretly with Tito to make arrangements on the promised help. There is no written evidence on what the two leaders discussed or agreed upon. Even after the acrimonious break between the KKE and CPY, neither of the two parties or their leaders ever revealed the contents of their so-called "unwritten agreement" (Vattis 2000).

The conspiratorial relations between two neighboring communist parties (CPY and CPB) at Greek Macedonia's expense do not seem to support the notion that the Slav-speaking autonomists were solely responsible for entangling the KKE leadership into a provocatively seditious and anti–Hellenic policy on Macedonia (Koliopoulos 1995). For their part, the Slav-speakers and the Greek communists were only instruments in a bigger game played by strong communist leaders behind the Iron Curtain. Both had become instruments of Soviet-sponsored international communism in its continuing struggle for complete domination in the Balkans and the Eastern Mediterranean. As long as it was obvious that Stalin was not the agitator, for example, it was in his interest to embroil Greece in a civil war to distract his former allies and exhaust their resources. Many observers agreed that Stalin tacitly approved the conflict in Greece. They speak of three possible scenarios (Yiatroudakis 1998, p. 275): (a) Zachariadis asked Stalin to allow him to begin the conflict, which Stalin approved at the Crimea meeting; (b) Stalin urged Zachariadis to begin the conflict; or (c) Stalin ordered Zachariadis to begin the war for the Soviet Union's foreign policy reasons.

Stalin's interest in Macedonia, revealed by his trust in Tito to handle the KKE's actions in nearby Greek Macedonia, was not new. In November 1940, with Soviet-German relations characterized as "polite," to attract Bulgaria to the Soviet Union, Stalin informed the Bulgarian fascist government of his intentions to support its claims on eastern Macedonia and western Thrace (Kouzinopoulos 1999). After the German attack on the Soviet Union, however, Stalin reneged on his promises to Bulgaria and sent a note to both Tito and Dimitrov, clearly favoring a solution favorable to Yugoslavia after the war (Kouzinopoulos 1999, p. 20). Stalin's view was identical with Comintern's directive of August 1941 favoring Yugoslavia over Bulgaria for the "solution" of the Macedonian Question.

After the KKE's defeat in 1949, Zachariadis wrote in his book *New Conditions, New Tasks* that "Tito and his clique promised great help to us to fight the war, which was an important factor for us to decide for war" (cited in Antonakeas 1993). Zachariadis, however, failed to say why Tito promised great help to the KKE. He also failed to mention the shady deal between the two leaders as part of which Zachariadis conceded Greek Macedonia to the People's Republic of Macedonia. In his memoirs, Markos Vafiadis verified Zachariadis's "donation" of Greek Macedonia in 1946 to Tito and Paschali Mitrofsky. He wrote in 1992: "The other thing with Zachariadis is that in 1946 he agrees with Tito and Paschali and gives them Greek Macedonia with Thessaloniki, just as the Fifth Plenum had decided [later] for a united and independent Macedonia."[18] The reaction among many KKE and EAM leaders was so strongly against Zachariadis's decisions that a party conference held five months later condemned the "selling" of Macedonia.

Predicating his strategic planning on the assumption that he would soon have another opportunity to interfere in the affairs of Greek Macedonia, especially because the CPY had orchestrated conditions favorable for the winds of war to blow again in Greece, Tito ordered the formation of a "new" organization to replace the defunct SNOF. The slavophones who escaped to Yugoslavia from Greece (most of them communists), slavophones from the People's Republic of Macedonia, and former Yugoslav-trained slavophone officers promptly formed the National Liberation Front (*Narodno Osloboditele Front*, NOF) in the People's Republic of Macedonia, a reincarnation of the old SNOF without the word *Slovenomakedonski*. Not surprisingly, its underlying goal was the unification of the three sections of Macedonia under Yugoslavia's hegemony (Kofos 1964). Destined to play a significant role during the Greek Civil War, NOF disapproved of the Varkiza Agreement, and in the beginning of 1945 its special armed bands moved to Greek territory and began sporadic guerrilla attacks against the first Greek government's forces and gendarmes that arrived in border districts to impose its rule. Functioning initially as the Aegean Macedonian Committee of the Communist Party of Macedonia (CPM), NOF was indeed entrusted with the goal of unifying the three parts of Macedonia (Kofos 1995, p. 296). In the meantime, the Yugoslav propaganda machine, free from the burden of efforts to justify its actions to the international community where Tito's World War II heroics ran high, continued hammering for the secession of Greek Macedonia and training NOF bands to return to Greece to participate in the Third Round of the Greek fratricide, the civil war.

To a neutral observer, NOF's formation in 1945 posed two serious questions: Because both Greece and Yugoslavia were free in April 1945, what was the reason behind the phony "liberation" promises that motivated Tito and the Bulgarians Keramitziev and Gotse, turned Macedonian communists, to form a new liberation front? And why was the Slavic word *Slovenomakedonski* omitted from the new organization's name? After ELAS lost the battle of Athens, shattering Tito's plans for a united Macedonia under Yugoslav hegemony, Tito placed all his bets on the new, non–*Slovenomake-donski* front to entice DAG into a new trap during its forthcoming "liberation" struggle of the working class from the "monarcho-fascist" Greek government. He almost succeeded, given the fact that by 1949 almost half of DAG's fighting force was composed of Tito-prone slavophones, a fact admitted by Vafiadis (Kofos 1989, pp. 20–22; Vafiadis 1992).

In keeping with appearances, at the outset (1945) the KKE condemned NOF's formation and its activities as "autonomist," "chauvinist, "and "provocatory" (Kofos 1995, p. 296). Given Yugoslavia's pivotal role in Zachariadis's decision to begin the civil war, however, it is not surprising that he would soon reverse his position. Nor is it surprising, given Zachariadis's desperation for allies in his forthcoming military struggle against the Greek government, that he practically would hand almost everything to Tito's Yugoslavs. In December 1945 secret meetings took place in Thessaloniki between NOF's leaders and members of the KKE's Central Committee, including Zachariadis. After the meetings, Zachariadis reversed his position, characterizing NOF as a "democratic" and "antifascist" group fighting "for the common cause" (Kofos 1995, p. 297–98). A new rapprochement was quickly established, and an agreement was reached between the KKE and NOF in November 1946, including the following terms: NOF would be incorporated into the KKE, severing its links with the Communist Party of Macedonia (CPM), and would form a central organ under Keramitziev and Mitrofsky reporting directly to the KKE's Regional Committee for Macedonia and Thrace, desisting attempts to inculcate secessionist ideas to the Slavomacedonians. It would have its own youth organization and press, including special units within DAG, and would run educational networks promoting "Macedonian" schools and cultural educational institutes (Kofos 1964, 1993). The NOF partisans in Aegean Macedonia and Greece would have complete organizational and political unity, and no special "Macedonian" units would function separately. After the agreement was signed, NOF's armed bands advanced to Greece to participate in the battle against the Greek government (Nikoloudis 2002). Zachariadis's new blunder, establishing a cooperative relationship with the "Macedonian" slavophone separatists over the objections of several communist leaders, brought the fanatic elements of Gotse and Mitrofsky back to Greek Macedonia.

None of NOF's features and goals were new and distinctive from SNOF's. It was the old SNOF with the old separatist-prone communist Slavomacedonians and Bulgarians, many of whom had cooperated with the Germans and Italians, turned communists when the conquerors left Greece. Mitrofsky was NOF's general secretary, with Gotse collaborating. In a meeting between DAG and NOF leaders in January 1947, pretending good behavior, NOF finally broke its ties with the CPM, dissolved its armed bands, and merged with the KKE and DAG, with NOF's leaders assuming new leadership positions in DAG and KKE. Indeed, at the beginning, NOF discontinued activities for autonomy or secession of Greek Macedonia. With this arrangement, and "good" behavior, most of the old SNOF leaders and cadres, expelled by ELAS a year earlier, returned to the KKE. Everything was forgiven and forgotten. In his remarks published by the Belgrade newspaper *Borba* on March 22, 1947, Vafiadis lavishly praised NOF's Slavomacedonians (Vattis 2002): "NOF is the People's Liberation Front, a political organization of Macedonians in Greece, just like the EAM of the Greek people. It is represented in EAM and today the Macedonians are fighting together with the Greek people for their ethnic and political rights."[19]

The Slavomacedonian NOF was essentially composed of two groups: the KKE allies, controlled by the party's Macedonian mechanism, and NOF's pro–Yugoslav wing under Gotse, Keramitziev, and others, controlled by Skopje, struggling hard for the secession of Greek Macedonia and its annexation by the Yugoslav federation. The KKE vigorously attempted at the beginning to control NOF, but its intent to recruit as many slavophones to DAG as possible for the hard fight ahead against the ever-increasing Greek national forces forced it into an inescapable dilemma: curtail the chauvinist propaganda by the pro–Yugoslav NOF elements, losing thousands of recruits for DAG, or tolerate the pro–Yugoslav elements' influence on DAG and allow their irredentist plans to flourish at Greece's expense. Unfortunately for the KKE cadres, its leadership chose the second approach (Banac 1995; Kontis and Sfetas 1999).

In retrospect, it is difficult to say precisely why Zachariadis, who knew that military and political cooperation with the autonomist Slavomacedonians would eventually force him to make concessions on Macedonia unacceptable to the Greek people, cooperated with the new organization. And why did he tolerate Tito's pressure through NOF on his decisions and actions? One explanation is that he desperately needed recruits for DAG.[20] NOF's cadres could help him take over the triangle of Kastoria-Florina-Edessa in western Macedonia, perhaps as a base and a seat for a future KKE provisional government. His broader plans to impose a government of the Left in Athens could only be achieved with Yugoslavia's military support and Tito's cooperation and friendship. To put it more bluntly, if Zachariadis won the civil war with Tito's assistance, he would have established a Bolshevik regime in Athens.

The plan of embracing the pro–Tito Slavomacedonians was prone to severe criticism from within and outside the KKE ranks. The KKE was already under severe criticism by revengeful nationalists unwilling to forgive and forget and by uncommitted people for conniving with secessionist-prone slavophones previously linked with NOF's predecessor, SNOF, and for calling NOF's activities "autonomist" and "chauvinistic" and then shaking hands and praising the "patriotic" and "democratic" qualities of the new organization (Kofos 1995). Accepting NOF as a "Trojan horse" in its ranks, as Koliopoulos (1995) pointed out, the KKE tacitly tolerated its secessionist activities, as had happened from 1943 to 1944 with the SNOF, and granted the Slavomacedonians full equality within the party, with proportional representation in the KKE and DAG units. Compounding this problem was the party's idea of allowing the Slavomacedonians to disseminate the "Macedonian" idea, but not publicly conceding Greek Macedonia or parts of it to the Slavs. Simply stated, the KKE seeded the dragon's teeth, but did not want the product to flourish.

By embracing NOF without reservations, the KKE helped the Yugoslavs snatch the relay of the Macedonian problem from the Bulgarians and eventually pass it on to the younger generations of reformed communists in Skopje. To show good behavior, in May 1945 NOF declared that its members were not affiliated with Ochrana or the Macedonian autonomists (favoring Bulgaria). Not surprisingly, the reformed NOF leaders, previously SNOF leaders, rejected the Bulgarian-inspired autonomy-for-Macedonia concept, pretending their aims within DAG were only to fight the "monarchofascist" Greek government. Even with their camouflage, however, they were unable to hide their irredentist aspirations for a unified People's Republic of Macedonia, including Greek Macedonia, within Tito's empire.

Vafiadis, DAG's commander, was aware of NOF's conspiracies behind the scenes at Greek Macedonia's expense but refused to admit that Tito and Skopje formed NOF, with Mitrofsky as its president, to fight for the secession of Macedonia from Greece and its annexation by the People's Republic of Macedonia. As time went by, NOF's operatives within DAG and KKE continued surreptitiously their propaganda to unify Greek Macedonia with the Skopjan republic. This was amply revealed by the contents of an NOF bulletin (Vattis 2002): "We are not Ochrana members or autonomists because this [these affiliations] will push the Macedonian people to the cliff, to permanent slavery [subjugation to Bulgaria], and because autonomy is the platform of international reactionaries that intend to break the unity of the Yugoslav people. The Macedonians have expressed their will to live with the peoples of Yugoslavia ... because the Macedonian people under Marshall Tito's guidance ... will realize for the first time their ethnic freedom." The encomium to Tito's leadership, however, could not be counted on to convince the Hellenic Macedonians, the overwhelming majority of Macedonians in the Balkans, of Yugoslavia's sincere intentions with respect to Greece.

To put it bluntly, autonomy for Macedonia was no longer an option for Tito and NOF in 1945. Nor was it certain that self-determination of the minorities in Greece, a platform with the individual at its center, adopted by the KKE in 1935, or the old Bulgarian concept of autonomy with the territory at its center, would satisfy the Yugoslav dictator who actively sought to damage and dismember Greece, with the pretext of forming an independent Macedonia. Tito's ambitions were simple and blunt: *annexation of Greek and Bulgarian Macedonia, including the sprawling city of Thessaloniki, into the People's Republic of Macedonia* (i.e., Yugoslavia).[21] Zachariadis also repudiated the autonomy-for-Macedonia concept in 1946, but he refrained from openly agreeing with NOF's statement that "the Macedonian people under Marshall Tito's wise guidance ... will realize for the first time their ethnic freedom."

Dimitrov's concessions to the Yugoslavs on the Macedonian issue, the result of Stalin's unrelenting pressure, coupled with Zachariadis's compromising stand on the same issue, encouraged Tito and the Skopjan chauvinists, who were dreaming and assiduously plotting for a "Greater Macedonia," to make increasing demands. Bilateral talks between the two communist leaders continued in December 1944 in Sofia and in January 1945 in Moscow. Finally, a secret meeting between Tito and Dimitrov took place in Bled, Slovenia, in August 1947. Bulgaria was forced in Bled to recognize the existence of the artificial concoction, the so-called "Macedonian nation." There is no doubt today that the two top communists also agreed on at least two additional important points (Kofos 1995, p. 307): secession of Pirin Macedonia to the People's Republic of Macedonia (Yugoslavia) and the fate of Greek Macedonia (secession of Greek Macedonia to Yugoslavia if DAG won the civil war). In exchange for the Bulgarian sacrifice, Tito promised to back Bulgarian claims on Greek Thrace and return to Bulgaria a region annexed by Serbia after World War I. On August 3, 1949, two years after the Bled meeting, *Borba* published Dimitrov's comments to western journalists coinciding with his views he had expressed previously at the Tenth Plenum of the CPB in August 1946: "It is not right to use the phrases '*Vardarska Makedonija,*' '*Pirinska Makedonija,*' and '*Egejska Makedonija.*' There are not three Macedonias. There is only one Macedonia."[22]

Immediately after the Bled Agreement was signed, the Yugoslavs infiltrated Pirin Macedonia as a first step toward incorporating the region into Yugoslavia, and Bulgarian communists in Pirin supported the idea of unification with Skopje as a first step toward unifying all Macedonia. Also, Belgrade and Sofia began negotiations to form a South Slav federation to push for a unified Macedonia within this federation, a move Stalin also sanctioned (Hammond 1983).

The Bulgarians of Pirin Macedonia, however, did not receive well Tito's dangerous imperialism and Dimitrov's capitulation on the Macedonian issue at Bled. Public protests and great demonstrations took place with people declaring, "We are Bulgarians, not Macedonians." Also, the Bulgarian people and their deputies in the Bulgarian parliament representing Pirin were not inclined to allow Tito to Macedonize the Bulgarians. "We are pure Bulgarians," they declared, "and have no relations with the Yugoslavs," insisting that even the so-called Macedonians in Yugoslavia are pure Bulgarians (*Kathimerini* 1996; Vattis 2002).[23]

Vafiadis was also present in Bled during the Tito-Dimitrov discussions (Averoff-Tossizza 1978). It is not known whether he actually attended the discussions, but according to Averoff-Tossizza, he renegotiated agreements he had made at Petric in December 1945. In exchange for promises of help to the KKE in its armed struggle against the Greek government, Vafiadis agreed in Bled to place DAG under Yugoslavia's protection and to participate in the formation of a "joint Balkan headquarters," which was to include DAG.[24]

Two points are worth stressing here. First, it is believed, but not proven, that Zachariadis, who was in Yugoslavia with Vafiadis and other members of the KKE Politburo during the Bled meeting, tacitly consented to the decisions taken by the two top Balkan communists (Kofos 1995). From a series of articles published by the leftist newspaper *Avgi* in Athens from December 1979 to January 1980, it seems that Zachariadis knew what was going on at the meeting and acted accordingly. The second important point is that before the Bled meeting Zachariadis notified Vafiadis that the first and foremost strategic objective of the civil war in Greece was Macedonia, with Thessaloniki, the weakest and most desirable area, to be taken (Kofos 1995, p. 308). He also met with Tito and presented the same views to him in a memorandum dated April 22, 1947, revealing his plans that "northern Greece was the monarcho-fascists' weakest — and most important — territory from a social, economic, political, national, military, and geographic viewpoint." DAG was to concentrate its efforts on that area. Tito and the Soviets approved the plan. The Third Plenum of the KKE Central Committee also approved of Zachariadis's plan in October 1947.[25]

Right after the Third Plenum of the KKE's Central Committee, Zachariadis asked again for a meeting with Tito and Vafiadis (Smith 1995).[26] Vafiadis initially denied that such a meeting was ever held. He revealed years later (1984), however, that a secret meeting indeed took place immediately after the Third Plenum. Tito advised the two top Greek communists not to engage in a stationary war of positions, but to continue the guerrilla-type war, contrary to the decision made by the KKE's Third Plenum. Interestingly, Zachariadis failed to inform the Central Committee members about Tito's views.

Kofos (1995, p. 307, note 89) claimed that he had "privileged information" from Bulgarian sources about a secret protocol that Tito and Dimitrov had signed concerning Greek Macedonia. In 1949, Tito admitted that indeed he and Dimitrov "had decided to definitely solve the Macedonian Question *as a whole.*" They also agreed that "the Macedonian people, not only in the Vardar but in Pirin, and the 'Aegean' Macedonia, would receive their rights, and they alone will decide on their future." There is nothing concrete in Kofos's article, however, about direct Greek communist participation in the Bled discussions. There has been an absence of reaction, an "strange silence," from the KKE leaders from 1947 to this day on the Bled Agreement. The Athens government, however, suspected that Zachariadis and the KKE leadership had agreed with the Bled decisions on the cession of Greek Macedonia to the People's Republic of Macedonia with Skopje as its capital.

The effect of the Bled Agreement on the Macedonian Question and on the relations between Yugoslavia and Bulgaria, and between Greece and the two communist countries, was profound. Greece was isolated from its northern neighbors by the agreement, a naked real threat to Greek Macedonia (Kofos 1995). Without Greece's knowledge, the two neighbors had made decisions in Bled that prescribed solutions for the fate of Greek Macedonia and its more than two million Greeks, a sinister plot to wrest from Greece its ancestral Macedonian land. In December 1947, a month after the Bled Agreement was signed, Yugoslav-operated Radio Free Greece, located in Tito's living compound, announced the formation of the "provisional democratic government" on Mount Grammos (more in the last section of this chapter). The Bled Agreement also ratified the so-called Macedonian "history," altered by Skopjan revisionists, and transferred the altered concepts from the historical to the political and ethnic arenas. After Bled, politicians in Athens and elsewhere believed that if DAG won the war, detachment of Macedonia from Greece was unavoidable. Even the Turks were apprehensive about the possibility of a communist Slav Macedonian state in the middle of the Balkans to their west (Averoff-Tossizza 1978).

The Tito-Stalin Split and Its Effect on Macedonia

The Balkan past is strewn with many political and military wrecks and dramatic events that turned the peninsula into one of the most unstable world spots. But no other post–World War II event changed the Balkan maelstrom and affected the Macedonian Question as much as the split between Stalin and Tito. The incredible communist break caused tremendous shock waves and set off one of the most bitter and dramatic disputes between two major communist countries (Banac 1995). Tito's expulsion from Cominform on June 28, 1948, came as a shock to the Balkan communist leaders and to the KKE. His authoritarian regime came under severe criticism, and Dimitrov's newly gained favoritism by Moscow became Stalin's stinging rebuff to the autocratic ruler of Yugoslavia. As the gunfire of the Greek Civil War continued ringing south of the Iron Curtain, Dimitrov's star and influence with Moscow skyrocketed. The excessive egotism of Tito, dreaming and planning to become the Stalin of the Balkans, became Dimitrov's target after the split. In a May 1948 letter to Molotov, the Soviet Union's minister of foreign affairs, Dimitrov wrote that the Communist Party of Yugoslavia must exit from the impasse to which it was dragged by its egomaniac, sick, ambitious, and naïve leaders (Kouzinopoulos 1999, from Dimitrov's secret diary, pp. 23–24).

The first casualty of the split was the Bled Agreement, which collapsed immediately. The Bulgarian communists, Stalin's allies, were the first in the Balkans to denounce Tito at the end of August 1948, accusing him of imperialist designs and using the pretext of a confederated Macedonia "to take away Pirin Macedonia's and Aegean Macedonia's freedom and independence" (Averoff-Tossizza 1978). They repudiated the theory of the "Macedonian nation," expelled the Yugoslav commissars from Pirin Macedonia, and declared that a pure Bulgarian population had inhabited the Pirin section for as long as Bulgarians had lived in the Balkan peninsula. The Bulgarians never forgot that Tito had pressed Dimitrov to recognize the Bulgarians of Skopje as Macedonians and agree to the annexation of Pirin Macedonia as part of a united Macedonia in the Yugoslav federation. Also, the Bulgarians never agreed with the Macedonization of a large part of their population, history, and cultural heritage (*Kathimerini* 1996). Their temporary wise behavior not withstanding, the Bulgarians resurrected their own dreams of the late 1800s and early 1900s for an independent and united Macedonia under their hegemony.

In retrospect, the signing of the Bled Agreement between Tito and Dimitrov had relatively little effect on the Macedonian issue. Nonetheless, it offered a glimpse into how Greece's two strong communist neighbors were intrinsically bound in intrigue, conspiring to impose brutal solutions at Greece's expense. Looked upon it in a different way, one might ask what would have been the fate of Greek Macedonia and Greece if DAG had won the civil war. The tragic events following Yugoslavia's dissolution at the end of the twentieth century, and the bloody conflict in Bosnia and Kosovo, must awaken the Greek people to reflect with trepidation on the consequences the sinister Bled arrangements and Skopje's irredentism would have had on their country.

The split between Stalin and Tito was very painful for Zachariadis, who faced enormous problems in the conduct of the war in Greece. It forced him to face the dilemma of either untangling himself from Stalin, his life-long mentor and supporter, or splitting with Tito, the strong neighbor whose military aid he needed more than ever before. Zachariadis, a doctrinaire Stalinist, made again the wrong choice. He remained in Stalin's orbit and cut all ties with Tito against Vafiadis's advice, an unmitigated disaster. Everything — the organization of DAG's struggle in Greece, its most impor-tant bases, instructors, hospital supplies, and even the KKE's radio station — was in Yugoslavia. The most important DAG leaders had been trained in Yugoslavia, and most of the high-echelon DAG commanders, including Vafiadis, maintained a pro–Tito position to the end. Vafiadis's "Titoism," however, cost him his position and threatened his life (Gage 1983).[27]

Zachariadis's reckless decision to side with Stalin forced the KKE to face two serious problems: how to treat the large slavophone minority within DAG and how to replace Yugoslavia as a supplier of military aid (Kofos 1995). He "solved" the problem of the slavophone minority by returning to and supporting the idea of Macedonian autonomy favored by Bulgaria. To consolidate his position, he removed the pro–Tito Slavomacedonians from NOF and from important DAG and KKE positions and replaced them with trusted Bulgarophile Slavomacedonians (Kofos 1995; Koliopoulos 1995). Zachariadis's courting of the Bulgarians, however, did not amount to much because the majority of NOF's cadres favored Tito and the Yugoslavs. Even the increased military assistance from Bulgaria was useless. It did not delay the inevitable — DAG's demise.

After the Tito-Stalin split, Zachariadis's reaction was swift. Openly defying Tito, he directed the KKE to align its policies immediately with those of Cominform and attempted to use NOF as a weapon against Tito. To accomplish this, he had to make more concessions to NOF's slavophones: DAG's 11th Division was renamed the Macedonian Division, and on March 17, 1949, five months before the defeat, a new organization, the Commu-nist Organization of Aegean Macedonia, favored by NOF's leaders, was formed. Had there been any lingering doubts concerning the path Zachari-adis would follow, they would have been erased when, as the undisputed party leader, he assumed the post of the president of the War Council while remaining general secretary of the party. To secure Bulgarian military sup-port, Zachariadis committed another error with grave consequences for the party. He reshuffled the communist government of the mountains, giving top positions to the following Slavomacedonians, members of the revolu-tionary NOF: Paschali Mitrofsky, NOF president, minister of supply; Van-geli (Gelo) Koitsev, member of the DAG Supreme War Council; and Stavro Kotsev (Kostopoulos), undersecretary of minorities (Averoff-Tossizza 1978; Vattis 2002).

The impetuous Zachariadis was able to control the revolutionary movement in Greece, neutralizing Tito's "treason" with these desperate but futile actions. But the outcome of his manipulations and encouragement of the anti–Tito slavophones did not produce the desired results. Instead of extirpating the "Macedonian" nationalism ingrained in the minds of a number of slavophone villagers after years of distorted "historical" misinformation, Zachariadis had chosen the wrong approach: by placing trusted slavophones in vital DAG, NOF, and KKE positions (and later in the communist government), he raised their level of expectation to a point where they considered the formation of an autonomous Macedonia a sure thing if DAG won the war.

While Zachariadis secured and even increased access to the Bulgarian bases for military help, it hardly needs to be pointed out that NOF, as SNOF before, could not be trusted even with all the concessions made to it. Both organizations were mixtures of Bulgarian nationalism and Yugoslav socialism with a good dose of chauvinist opportunism (Shoup 1968). Observers could envision the irreconcilable gap existing between the KKE and NOF on the Macedonian Question: autonomy for the Macedonians for the KKE and immediate annexation by the People's Republic of Macedonia for NOF. Eventually, DAG's cadres in Macedonia not affiliated with NOF were the minority: a deplorable situation for a Greek Bolshevik army, half of which was composed of foreign agents, Tito sympathizers, and Bulgarian autonomists, fighting a revolution in Macedonia and in the remainder of Greece against the government (Banac 1995, p. 266; Vafiadis 1992).

The Fifth Plenum of the Communist Party of Greece

As it turned out, from December 1924 to the spring of 1949 the KKE changed its strategy and tactics on the Macedonian Question several times. The most dramatic change occurred at the Fifth Plenum of its Central Committee held on January 31, 1949, near Lake Prespa in northern Greece, seven months before the party's catastrophic defeat. The change in strategy was dramatic, because the plenum's decision resurrected the Third Special Congress's decision (December 1924) "for an independent Macedonia and Thrace" and the Third Plenum's platform (December 1931) that "the KKE declares for Macedonia and Thrace the principle for self-determination ... and the right to separate themselves from Greece." The united and independent Macedonia was to include the Greek, Bulgarian, and Yugoslav sections of Macedonia, not with Yugoslavia this time, but within a Balkan communist federation under Bulgarian hegemony (Antonakeas 1993; Vattis 2002). It just so happened that the KKE consented to the secession of

Greek Macedonia to the communist world three times from 1924 to 1949: to the Balkan Communist Federation in 1924 and 1931, a communist organization dominated by the Communist Party of Bulgaria; to Tito's Yugoslavia in 1946 with the secret agreement between Tito and Zachariadis; and finally to the Bulgarians again with the KKE's Fifth Plenum of 1949.

It is not unreasonable to suggest that the KKE fell deeper into the trap, irreversibly one might say, when Zachariadis forced the Fifth Plenum to declare that the "hard-fighting slavophones," spilling their blood on the frontiers of Macedonia, must find their complete ethnic restitution and freedom within an independent and united Macedonia. Once again, the KKE's position at the critical Fifth Plenum gave a conclusive impetus to the separatist-prone Slavomacedonians' dreams, increasing their demands for Macedonia's unification. The new KKE position on Macedonian autonomy (i.e., loss for Greece), coinciding with the Bulgarian views and plans, startled many Greek communists and NOF leaders alike who were looking to Yugoslavia for a solution to the Macedonian Question and their "restitution" (Woodhouse 1976). With the Tito-Stalin split, the Slavomacedonians became the tools in the struggle between Bulgaria and Yugoslavia, this time with Bulgaria gaining the upper hand as Stalin's strongest remaining satellite in the Balkans. With the Fifth Plenum's resolution, Zachariadis came along and offered Macedonia to Dimitrov, not to Tito (Vafiadis 1992).

The excerpts below from the KKE's Plenum declaration demonstrate Zachariadis's ultimate gift to a contemplated Balkan communist federation dominated by Bulgaria— *donation of Greek Macedonia and its two and a half million people to the communists of the north.*[28] It took the party's leadership twenty-five years to return to its 1924 anti–Hellenic decision on Macedonia supporting the annexationist plans of Greece's communist neighbors, selling Macedonia with Thessaloniki for a few pieces of silver— military supplies to continue a war already lost by the beginning of 1949. The Plenum declared: "In northern Greece the Macedonian people gave everything for the struggle and fight with heroism and self-sacrifice, deserving admiration. No one should doubt that with DAG's and the people's revolution's victory the Macedonian people, offering today their blood, will achieve their complete ethnic restitution.... With their blood [the Macedonian people] will gain the right for a free and independent life.... There must be no doubt that as a result of the victory of the people's revolution in Greece, the Macedonians will acquire the right ... for a free life and existence" (Vattis 2002).[29]

On March 1, 1949, the radio station of the Provisional Democratic Government (the communist government of the mountains) announced the decision of the Second Plenum of NOF's Central Committee held on February 4, 1949, to call the Second NOF Congress in March to announce officially the unification of the three sections of Macedonia as the United Macedonian Republic, an independent state, not with Tito's Yugoslavia, but with the People's Democratic Balkan Federation (Kofos 1995; Nikoloudis 2002). It would have been an official declaration climaxing the KKE's monumental decision at its Fifth Plenum. The announcement had been ordered by Moscow as a rebuff to Tito, boasting of the formation of a new coalition inimical to his plans, and a call to the Slavs to fight against Greece, assisting DAG and the KKE. Because Zachariadis had overextended himself with the plenum's earth-shaking decision, however, surprising even the Bulgarians and the Yugoslavs, the Second NOF Congress avoided any mention of the plenum's decisions.

The anti–Hellenic Fifth Plenum's resolution drove the last nail into the coffin of cooperation between the KKE and Tito's Yugoslavia and caused great confusion and consternation among the KKE's Greek cadres. Quite apart from its disastrous effects on the KKE-CPY relations, the plenum was also characterized by many communists and noncommunists as a "moment of ethnic treason" (Nikoloudis 2002). No one knows what made Zachariadis offer on a platter most of Greek Macedonia to the Bulgarians. Numerous remarks were made in books on the pro–Bulgarian Fifth Plenum decision that dealt DAG's Greek guerrilla forces a serious moral blow when their party announced the formation of an "independent Macedonia" under Bulgarian hegemony (Kontis 1984). In 1956, six years after the civil war, the Sixth KKE Plenum, held behind the Iron Curtain, renounced the Fifth Plenum's decision, characterizing it as a "mistake," and returned to the equality concept of all the minorities in Greece (Gregoriadis 1984). The KKE's 1956 change of platform, however, came too late to improve the party's image. Greece's enemies still use the Fifth Plenum's decision to show the world that a sizable part of the Greek people had agreed twice during the 1940s with the separatist Slavomacedonian demands for a united Macedonia under Yugoslav or Bulgarian hegemony.

After the Tito-Zachariadis acrimonious split and the pro–Bulgarian tilt of the KKE's Fifth Plenum, Tito did not turn the other cheek to Zachariadis's bashing. By August 1949, he declared in Skopje: "The KKE must know that, because we respect the Greek democratic movement, we cannot follow the example of those [in the KKE] and reveal things that will not be very complimentary for Zachariadis.... The Greek people's struggle forces us to shut our mouths. One day the Greek and the Macedonian people will learn the truth" (Vattis 2002).

The KKE's answer to the accusations was published almost immediately: "Continuing the treasonous activities, the gang of Keramitziev-Gotse installed in Skopje refers to the 1946 unwritten agreement and accuses the KKE of violating the agreement to muddy the waters and cover its treason.

With the agreement, the KKE was only aiming at neutralizing the CPY's efforts to undermine the KKE.... The unwritten agreement provided equality to the Macedonians as far as their participation in the Democratic Army was concerned" (Vattis 2002).

The breakdown of the secret, unwritten agreement between Tito and Zachariadis raises numerous questions: What were the uncomplimentary "things" for Zachariadis? What was the truth behind the agreement that was kept secret from the Greek people? What kind of "equality" had Zachariadis promised the Slav-speaking Macedonians in Greece? The decisions of the Fifth Plenum of the KKE Central Committee held in the Grammos mountains in January 1949, six months before DAG's final defeat, revealed some of the "things" Zachariadis promised the Slavs.

Another way of looking at all this is based on material from books written by Greek communist leaders after the civil war. In many ways, they reflect a biased perspective and an audacious attitude exhibited by defeated communist ideologues who had nothing to lose or gain in exile by exposing their party's mistakes on the Macedonian issue and the link between the age-old controversy with the Greek Civil War. Most of the key players, however, remained sphinxlike on the issue at best, or blamed others for grave errors at worst; bluntly speaking, they ignored their involvement in and responsibilities for the Macedonian problem.[30]

The Fifth Plenum's decision was Zachariadis's last desperate gamble giving credence to the suspicions that the Macedonian Question and the struggle for Macedonia were shaped by sinister forces and interests directed from the communist world abroad (Kofos 1995). It was a big gamble for Zachariadis because it irrevocably tied the Macedonian Question with the fortunes of the KKE's desperate struggle to win the civil war. It also forced the vacillating Greek politicians and the Greek people to realize how close Greece had come to losing its territorial integrity if the KKE had won the struggle. The plenum's decision tied together, once and for all, the sinister external forces and interests on Macedonia's fate and the seditious propaganda by a fraction of Slavomacedonians. It also meant, as the entire political spectrum of the Greek government camp knew, that a communist victory in the civil war would lead to the loss of Macedonia for Greece (Kofos 1995). Deciphering this into simple terms, it meant that the civil war in Macedonia was no more than an armed movement of a fraction of Slavomacedonians demanding Greek Macedonia's union with Bulgaria or Yugoslavia (Vafiadis 1992).

The KKE's general secretary belatedly expressed his *mea culpa* when he admitted to DAG Colonel Papaioannou in Sorgout, Siberia (where he was exiled by the Soviets after Stalin's death), about his inner feelings on NOF: "There was a group of Slavomacedonians in Skopje with autonomist, chauvinist tendencies. They had formed NOF demanding separate armed bands, which were sent to Greece. They influenced the Slavomacedonian people of the Vitsi [territory], doing underground, autonomist work among the Slavomacedonian fighters. It was a job done by Skopje.... They also sent spies and organized desertions from the Democratic Army to Yugoslavia" (Papaioannou 1986). The bottom line is that Zachariadis was aware of the sinister plans at Greece's expense, as he admitted; sadly, he not only chose to go along with the anti–Hellenic plans, but he also expended considerable efforts to sustain them.

The communist intrigue within and outside Greece did not daunt the Greek people, because they knew Greece was not fighting an internal war, but an international communist conspiracy aiming at converting Greece into a Stalinist satellite with the loss of Macedonia, an unacceptable grave injury following the political insult. Instead, it strengthened the resolve of the people, the national forces, and the Sofoulis government for a final, decisive victory over communism and their communist neighbors' machinations. The victory was finalized by the end of August 1949. The Greek people in general and many Greek communists were convinced that under Zachariadis's disastrous leadership, the KKE and the Bulgarian and Yugoslav communists were planning all along to split Macedonia from Greece and attach it to Yugoslavia or Bulgaria.[31] The story was repeating itself seventy years after the Treaty of San Stefano and fifty years after the Macedonian Struggle of the early 1900s.[32]

It is interesting to note here how some Greek leaders both of the Right and Left felt after the end of the Greek Civil War of 1946–1949 with respect to the Macedonian issue. Antonakeas (1993), a general of the Greek national army, pointed out that the civil war was the last communist offense to complete the original plan of detaching Macedonia from Greece, annexing it to the People's Republic of Macedonia. Zachariadis's policies were also criticized forcefully in public statements and books written by several communist leaders who escaped to the Eastern Bloc at war's end and lived in exile for more than thirty years. Upon return to Greece with the restoration of democracy in 1974, they felt that Stalin used DAG's partisans to rearrange Greece's northern frontier. They saw the decisions of the KKE's Fifth Plenum and NOF's Second Congress as nothing more than a sinister camouflage to cover naked Slavic irredentism for the secession of Greek Macedonia, a plot also condoned by the KKE's general secretary and some of his communist generals (Papaioannou 1990). The second most powerful Greek communist, DAG Commander Markos Vafiadis, wrote in his memoirs (vol. 5, 1992): "The civil war was not a revolution of suppressed democratic civilians ... or a spontaneous manifestation of self-defense against suppression by British and Greeks. The main reason for the decision to fight the war against

Greece was the Macedonian Question." Yiannis Ioannides (1979), the number two man in the KKE Politburo, also wrote after the end of the civil war: "Tito attempted to use the KKE guerrillas for his own irredentist aims against Greek Macedonia."[33]

A hard-nosed examination of how Tito revived and intensified the Macedonian problem with Stalin's urging and his Byelorussian example of how to create a new nation leads us to conclude that if DAG had won the Greek Civil War, two and a half million Greek Macedonians would have been detached from Greece to become slaves to a strange, paranoid, and dangerous ideology under Tito's or Dimitrov's hegemony, depending on which communist leader might have Moscow's favor at the time. When communism fell in the Balkans and in Europe in the early 1990s, it would have been almost impossible for a mutilated Greece to recover a land that would have been altered by ethnic cleansing during fifty years of communism.

World Reaction

The Greek people were not the only ones who adversely reacted to the communist machinations to detach Macedonia from Greece with the false and unacceptable pretense of forming a united and independent Slavic Macedonia.

The Balkan intrigue and communist conspiracies impelled various world organizations (e.g., the United Nations), news media (the *Washington Times,* the *Boston Globe,* the *Economist,* the *Christian Science Monitor, Le Monde, Il Giornare, El Mundo, Die Zeit,* etc.), and individuals (President Truman, the pope, etc.) to protest vehemently the outrageous and callous behavior of sovereign communist states against their noncommunist neighbor to the south.

The *New York Times* wrote on July 16, 1946, that "during the [German] occupation ... a combined effort was made to wrest Macedonia from Greece — an effort that allegedly continues ... the main conspiratorial activity appears to be directed from Skopje." On August 16, 1946, the *Times* wrote again that "a secret meeting [the Petric meeting] was held in southern Bulgaria ... to draw up plans with the ultimate objective of incorporating the region with Thessaloniki in an autonomous Macedonia under Yugoslav hegemony." Almost fifty years later, the *Times* wrote again on May 7, 1992, under the headline "Macedonia Insists," that the Greek KKE leaders in Yugoslavia during the civil war promised to deliver Greek Macedonia to the Balkan Communist Federation dominated by Yugoslavia and Bulgaria (Giannakos 1992).

The Balkan communist machinations and Tito's scheming relationships in the Balkans at Greek Macedonia's expense did not escape the U.S. State Department's attention. Secretary of State Stettinius in the Roosevelt administration declared in his Circular Airgram (H868.014/26 December 1944) to the American embassies and consulates:

> The Department has noted with considerable apprehension increasing propaganda rumors and semi-official statements in favor of an autonomous Macedonia, emanating principally from Bulgaria, and also from Yugoslav Partisan and other sources, with the implication that Greek territory would be included in the projected state. This Government considers talk of Macedonian "nation," Macedonian "Fatherland," or Macedonian "national consciousness" to be unjustified demagoguery representing no ethnic nor political reality, and sees in its present revival a possible cloak for aggressive intentions against Greece.... The approved policy of this government is to oppose any revival of the Macedonian issue as related to Greece. The Greek section of Macedonia is largely inhabited by Greeks, and the Greek people are almost unanimously opposed to the creation of a Macedonian state. Allegations of serious Greek participation in any such agitation can be assumed to be false. This government would regard as responsible any Government or group of Governments tolerating or encouraging menacing or aggressive acts of "Macedonian Forces" against Greece [Martis 2001].

Former Secretary of State Henry Kissinger endorsed Stettinius's views forty-eight years later. Asked at the annual meeting of Management Centre Europe, held in Paris in 1992, about his views on Skopje's authority to use the word "Macedonia" as the name of the new republic, he said: "I believe that Greece is right to object and I agree with Athens. The reason is that I know history which is not the case with most of the others, including most of the government and administration in Washington.... The strength of the Greek case is that of the history which I must say that Athens has not used so far with success." Unfortunately, the explicit directive on Macedonia by one secretary of state and the views on history's importance by another were not heeded by Washington in the 1990s as good examples of sensible policy on the Macedonian Question.

The Western Europeans also noticed the communist scheming to detach Macedonia from Greece with the pretext of unifying the "Macedonians" in an independent Macedonia. The news agency Reuters broadcast the following on March 1, 1949 (Vattis 2002): "The communist NOF will attempt next month during its congress to incorporate Greek Macedonia as an autonomous country together with Bulgarian Macedonia and Yugoslav Macedonia, to obtain later its incorporation in the Slavic Balkan

Federation.... The proposed new state will be connected with Bulgaria, whose prime minister, Dimitrov, is trusted by Moscow more than any other leader. The formation of this state would have meant shrinking Greece's northern borders ... perhaps as far south as Thessaly."

7

The Struggle for Macedonia After 1950

Our name is our soul
—*Odysseus Elytis*

When the guns in Greece became silent at the end of August 1949, almost ten years of war, occupation, and civil war finally ended, but the Macedonian Question remained unresolved. Tito was not willing to give up the struggle for Macedonia despite several major setbacks and his inimical relations with Moscow. One of the civil war's major consequences was the mass flight of Slav-speakers from Greece who had collaborated with the occupation forces, expressed anti–Hellenic feelings, or performed anti–Hellenic acts as communist guerrillas from 1940 to 1950. About 35,000 slavophones left the Kastoria, Florina, and Pella districts for Yugoslavia. An unknown number fled to other Eastern Bloc countries, together with their defeated Greek comrades, lived in exile for more than thirty years as far away as Tashkent, Uzbekistan, and became involved in intraparty ideological struggles that split the Communist Party of Greece (KKE) into two inimical fractions (Yiatroudakis 1998). The flight of these people, reneging their Greek citizenship or taking arms against their country, "rendered Greece free from the foreign-loving minority that actively threatened [Greece's] security and internal peace" (Kostopoulos 2000). According to the 1951 Greek census, 35,894 slavophones remained in Greek Macedonia and about 47,167 in all of Greece.

Post–Civil War "Macedonian" Activities

The systematic campaign launched in 1944 to change history, promoting the view that the ancient Macedonians were not Greeks, and Greek Macedonia and Pirin Macedonia would eventually be reunited with the Yugoslav Macedonia under Yugoslav hegemony, continued unabated after the end of the Greek Civil War. To replace the historically and archaeologically documented view that the ancient Macedonians were Greeks (see chapter 5), Skopje continued promulgating the politically motivated concept that the Macedonians descended from non-Greek people whose descendants are the present Balkan Slavs and Albanians (Marinos 1997). These views were supported by a few academics and politicians whose intent was, and still is, to alter historical facts with baseless genetic theories and unsubstantiated historical analysis. The misinterpretation of Macedonian history during the tumultuous 1940s perpetuated the injustice done with reference to Hellenic Macedonia even after the Greek Civil War.

In the Paris Peace Conference (1946) after the end of World War II, for instance, Tito's Yugoslavia brought back to the forefront the Macedonian Question, demanding unification of the "Macedonian nation" and restitution of the "ethnic borders of Macedonia" (Nikoloudis 2002). The People's Republic of Macedonia (renamed Socialist Republic of Macedonia in 1953) in the Yugoslav federation in the meantime worked feverishly to stabilize the young republic, expediting the Macedonization of its polyglot conglomerate. Hoping to mold the districts bordering Greece as a solid "Macedonian nation," communist Yugoslavia accepted the Slav-speaking refugees from Greece and, recognizing their anti–Hellenic actions in Greece from 1941 to 1949 as legitimate military service performed during the Greek Civil War, granted them Yugoslav citizenship, "Macedonian" identity, free housing, honors, and military pensions (Vattis 2002).

It is impossible to give a precise picture of demographic changes in Greek Macedonia in the 1940s, but one thing is certain. There were several kinds of refugees from Greece to Yugoslavia: self-exiled Bulgarophiles, Tito-prone annexationists, and DAG recruits and sympathizers thrown out of the Greek territory along with the defeated DAG forces. DAG also forced a small number of Greek-speaking and Slav-speaking civilians from villages near the border to cross the border, together with the defeated communists (Gage 1983). Tito made great efforts to attract Slav-speaking DAG fighters (*machites*) from all parts of the communist world, including the Soviet Union, Romania, and Bulgaria.

The Yugoslav accommodations to the slavophone refugees from Greece, many of them collaborators of the Bulgarian, German, and Italian occupiers during World War II, and later SNOF or NOF members, were granted under strict terms: settle only in the Skopjan district, find employment, change ethnicity to "Macedonian" and personal names and names of villages and towns of Greek origin to Slavic names (e.g., Topourkas to Topourkofski) (Vafiadis 1992). The Greek state in the meantime abolished the Greek citizenship of the Slav-speaking renegades, defectors, and forced refugees and confiscated their land, houses, and all their belongings.[1]

Because of all the above reasons, and Tito's demanding that Greece recognize the slavophone remnants in Greece as a "Macedonian minority," the Yugoslav-Greek relations were extremely poor after the civil war.[2] In 1959 the two countries finally signed an agreement. But even then, Yugoslav communist provocations and accusations against Greece continued. A very good example is Tito's visit to the United States from September to October 1960 to attend the United Nations General Assembly meeting. During a dinner in his honor given by Slavic organizations in New York, he said: "The Macedonian people, ethnically free, and [free] in every other respect, gladly rebuilt their country. Unfortunately, not all Macedonians are free today" (Vattis 2002). Also, on November 13, 1961, the prime minister of the Socialist Republic of Macedonia declared during a press conference: "Certain measures of the Greek government toward the Macedonian minority are very disturbing.... The pressures on the Macedonian element intend to destroy the ethnic consciousness of the Macedonian minority."

The Greek-Yugoslav friction on the Macedonian issue did not subside with Tito's death and Greece's falling into the hands of dictators in 1967. The Yugoslav communist leadership never stopped proclaiming Tito's wishes on the Macedonian problem. The continued hammering of Greece on this issue coincided with Yugoslavia's rapprochement with the new Kremlin leadership after Stalin's death, and with that, the attacks against Greece increased in frequency and intensity. In 1962, two communist Slavomacedonians from western Macedonia, Greece, held ministerial portfolios in Skopje: Naoum Pejov, minister of justice, and Paschali Mitrofsky, minister of agriculture. Another 1940 EAM and KKE member, Antonefsky, previously active in the Edessa district, became professor of history and "Macedonian" language in Skopje. As editor of the newspaper *Aegean Voice*, he traveled abroad repeatedly lecturing on the unification of Macedonia (Vattis 2002). Even the Bulgarian Gotse, who had fled to Yugoslavia, was honored by Tito and appointed minister of welfare in the Socialist Republic of Macedonia's government in Skopje.

Convinced that the safest and wisest ways to a settlement on the Macedonian problem remained those of friendly relations and negotiations, communist Bulgaria took a refreshingly different position after 1950 on the Macedonian problem. On October 5, 1953, Greece and Bulgaria signed a commercial agreement and on December 30 a border agreement between the two countries. In 1954, with Bulgaria's initiative, the two countries restored their diplomatic relations (Vattis 2002). Bulgaria strongly opposed Belgrade's propaganda on the existence of a "Macedonian" ethnicity and a "Macedonian" language (Palmer and King 1971). It steadfastly adhered, however, to the line that the slavophones of the former Vardar Province and those in northern Greece, speaking a Bulgarian dialect, should be granted minority status as Bulgarians. Even the Slav-speakers who objected to the idea of a Greater Bulgaria, preferring an independent Macedonian state, never disputed the prevailing Bulgarian character among the Slav-speaking population of Vardar Macedonia (MacDermott 1978). Gotse-Delcheff, for instance, the "hero" of the Ilinden uprising of 1903, referred to the Slavs of Macedonia as Bulgarians.

The Macedonian Question was a sensitive issue till 1991— and more so today—for the Bulgarians who insist there is no Macedonian ethnicity in Pirin Macedonia. Bulgarian scholars and politicians continue accusing Skopje's "Macedonians" of using their ethnic heroes and the Bulgarian civilization. A Bulgarian official, for instance, declared in Belgrade in 1962: "For Bulgaria there is no question of a Macedonian race. The so-called Yugoslav Macedonians are Bulgarians." Almost at the same time the Bulgarian ambassador in Athens expressed the following views to Greek Foreign Minister Stephanopoulos: "My government is against Yugoslavia on the Macedonian [issue] and supports [the view] that there is no such thing as Macedonian minority. Those considered by Yugoslavia as belonging to the Macedonian nation are Bulgarians." The Bulgarian communist Prime Minister Zifkov also declared: "Bulgaria has no claim over Greece." He also elaborated in 1975: "Certain [people] speak about minorities insisting they exist. I do not see any and have no intention to search [for them]" (Kostopoulos 2000).

More than anything else, from its first days in power, the Bulgarian communist regime turned its wrath against IMRO, the rightist organization of the old regime and its leaders. It forced Mihailov, IMRO's leader, to transfer the organization's offices to Rome and eventually to the United States, where he established cooperative relations with several "Macedonian" patriotic organizations. These groups have now organized "Macedonian" societies in the United States, Canada, Western Europe, and Australia (Vattis 2002).

It may be useful at this point to discuss certain slavophone "Macedonian" agitations in Greece that began after the end of the civil war, especially within the favorable climate for dissension created by the European Union's strong stand on human rights and the European Treaty of Maastricht, which Greece also signed. For the first time in April 1981 a "new" group of slavophones in Greek western Macedonia demanded respect for the language and cultural traditions of the local "Macedonians" (Kostopoulos 2000).

Proclamations were circulated in the Florina, Pella, and Drama districts and in the Thessaloniki railroad station urging the "Macedonians" to state their ethnicity and speak their "Macedonian" language. The proclamations were signed by EAMO (National Macedonian Liberation Organization). Three years later, another group, KOE-MAD (Central Organizational Committee for Macedonian Human Rights), mailed to newspapers, political parties, and local authorities a manifesto addressed to the Greek parliament, demanding recognition of their "human and ethnic rights" and freedom for the "Aegean Macedonians" within Greece's borders. It also demanded repatriation of the "Macedonians" living abroad (in FYROM and countries of the former Eastern Bloc) and free use and teaching of the "mother language of the Macedonian people" (Hotzides 1997).

The movement stagnated in the next five years, but the manifesto is still being used by "Macedonians" abroad, Amnesty International, the British Helsinki Human Rights Group, the Minority Rights Group, and others as the beginning of new slavophone activism in Greece. Both the organizations and the few remaining slavophones in Greece believe they are "Macedonians" and not Greek Macedonians. Pretending to abhor the name "Slavomacedonians," the "new" group of Slav-speaking activists made great efforts to create and project a separate ethnic identity — simply, the people of the group wanted to project themselves as a separatist national clan, organized as a separate political party with the name Rainbow Party. The group claims to have its own popular traditions, separate language,[3] and separate social orientation. Its claims pose two questions: Does the new slavophone group consider itself separate from the Greek nationality? And if so, what is its relationship with FYROM's Slavs? There are no answers to these questions.

The Rainbow Party participated for the first time in the elections for the European Union's parliament and collected 7,263 votes, an event advertised by its members as a great victory (Hotzides 1997), "demolishing the politico-teleoptic myth that there is no 'Macedonian' element in Greece" (Kostopoulos 2000). The "great victory" encouraged the leaders of the movement to continue their activism in subsequent elections, believing they would pull off a great electoral victory. But events disappointed them. In the Greek parliamentary elections of September 1996, the Rainbow Party, together with OAKKE (Organization for the Reconstitution of the KKE) received 4,464 votes in all of Greece. It lost even bigger in the 2000 Greek elections, with OAKKE's representative receiving 1,139 votes. All attempts of the new "Macedonian movement" in Greece during the last ten years of the twentieth century to show to the world that the "appreciable" Slav-speaking minority is suppressed by the Greek state fell into a vacuum.

The irony surrounding the Rainbow Party members is that they do not belong to a national "Macedonian" minority — strange indeed since they claim to be "Macedonians"— and do not accept the ethnicity of FYROM's inhabitants (Hotzides 1997). While actively engaged in demonstrating their special "independent Macedonianism," the Rainbow Party members appear to be reactivated FYROM Slavomacedonian followers in Greece under a different mantle (Kofos 2003b, p. 239). Perhaps to camouflage its future intentions and plans, the group asked the Greek government to recognize it as a national minority and as a small separate linguistic community of slavophone Macedonians.

In the meantime, the defeated KKE, which was in exile from 1949 to 1974, found out that the ethnological composition in Macedonia had changed even more since 1935 to reflect the views of the overwhelming majority of Greek-speaking people living in Macedonia. Heretofore, it returned to its 1935 platform on the "equality of the minorities" within Greece. In 1957, eight years after the defeat, the KKE Central Committee's Seventh Plenum, held in Budapest, approved the new platform on the Macedonian Question dictated by Moscow on the equality of the minorities— a glaring contrast to Zachariadis's Fifth Plenum decision handing Hellenic Macedonia to the Bulgarians (Vattis 2002). The Eighth Plenum of the KKE's Central Committee held in Bulgaria in 1961 slightly corrected the party's platform on the issue to read as follows: "Beginning with democratic principles for recognition of full equality of the national minorities, the KKE has sided with the principle of equality of the ethnic minorities that live in Greece, including the Slavomacedonian minority."

After the civil war, the entire Greek political spectrum, including the KKE, insisted that there is no "Macedonian minority" in Greece. Most of the slavophones who remained in the country after 1950 speak a Slavic language, but they are Hellenes in their beliefs and feelings. Former KKE General Secretary Charilaos Florakis declared in Thessaloniki in 1988 that "for the KKE a Macedonian minority does not exist in Greece" (Nikoloudis 2002). After the dictatorship's fall in 1974, the Greek governments did not recognize the so-called "Macedonian" language and did not accept official papers from Yugoslavia written in this language. Yugoslavia continued in the meantime its chauvinist policies at Greece's expense and kept repeating the view of "the existence of a Macedonian minority" in Greece.

Formation of the Autocephalous
Church of "Macedonia"

Continuing efforts to sever the link between the newly created "Macedonians" and the other Balkan Slavs and Bulgarians, and to boost the

Macedonian consciousness (Palmer and King 1971), the government of the Socialist Republic of Macedonia, with CPY's support, formed the Orthodox Church of "Macedonia" in 1967 with Skopje as the seat, despite protests by the Serbian Patriarchate. None of the other five Yugoslav republics had an autocephalous church. It was the only church formed by a communist regime, whose motto in the past was Lenin's dictum: "Religion is the opium of the masses." The Autocephalous Church of "Macedonia" broke the religious ties of the Socialist Republic of Macedonia's Slavomacedonians with the Serbs and Bulgarians. Little by little everything became "Macedonian" in the Socialist Republic of Macedonia: history, culture, heroes, monuments, music, events, locations, language, even the Greek Civil War of 1946–1949 (which they renamed the "Macedonian National Liberation War") and, finally, the church in 1967. By playing with the two meanings of the name, the ethnic and the geographic, history revisionists in Skopje constructed an artificial "Macedonian" nationality from Serbs and Bulgarians and created such confusion among unsuspecting foreigners who were unable to distinguish between the two meanings,[4] assuming that everything Macedonian must belong to the Slavs of the Vardar Province or "Macedonia."[5]

The formation of the independent Church of "Macedonia" solved the religious affiliation problem faced by the diaspora Slavic emigrants. From the beginning of the twentieth century to 1967 slavophone immigrants in the United States, Canada, and Australia attended the Macedono-Bulgarian Orthodox Church affiliated with the Bulgarian Exarchate. After 1967, however, the members of the Macedonian Patriotic Organization (MPO) split into two groups, the Bulgarophiles, who still attend the Macedono-Bulgarian Orthodox Church, and the Skopje-oriented slavophones, who attend the Autocephalous Church of "Macedonia."

The Autocephalous Church of "Macedonia" was formed in violation of the rules of the Orthodox Church to strengthen Macedonia's autonomy vis-à-vis Serbia — autonomy expressed with the slogan "one state, one church, one nation" (Papastathis 1967). The independent "Macedonian" Orthodox Church also founded an extremely active bishopric in America and propagandized extensively on the Macedonian Question as a CPY tool. The church's intense "Macedonian" activism in the United States and Canada is supported by about thirty thousand Slav-speakers who continue to stir provocatively the Macedonian problem. The slavophones in America, mostly of Yugoslav origin, who emigrated after 1950, became the most vociferous people on the Macedonian issue, with their activism continuing unabated today in the press, on television, and on the Internet.

The Former Yugoslav Republic
of Macedonia (FYROM)

During the last twenty years of communism in the Balkans, Greece's relations with its three communist neighbors were still strained by old unresolved contradictions and new Cold War political problems. Since the bloody 1940s, improvements occurred in Greece's relations with Bulgaria, but problems still existed in its relations with Yugoslavia and Albania. In Skopje intrigue was rife with intense rumors of impending developments, and Albanian irredentists were feverishly conspiring against the Socialist Republic of Macedonia. IMRO's ideological descendants in Skopje, the VMRO-DPMNE (Internal Macedonian Revolutionary Organization/Democratic Party of Macedonian National Unity), were extremely inimical to the small republic's Albanian minority and to Greece, Serbia, Albania, and Bulgaria for "suppressing the unredeemed Macedonian people living in these countries" (Hassiotis 1992).[6]

In the mid–1980s, a new deceptive, nonmilitary, but highly dangerous threat to Greece became evident among knowledgeable Greek people and more so among the diaspora Hellenic Macedonians (Kofos 2003, p. 157). During the last few years of declining communism, a well-organized, persistent propaganda offensive, perpetrated by Slavomacedonian nationalists and die-hard Marxist operatives, became a real threat aiming at eroding the Hellenic Macedonian cultural identity and historical heritage. Utilizing all available means of mass communications (radio, TV, book publishing, magazine articles, public performances, etc.), the ill-defined but real threat to Hellenic Macedonia became pervasive before great political, demographic, and military events were about to happen in the Balkan Peninsula.

We know now that the collapse of one of the two Cold War ideological superpowers and the return of democracies in the Balkan states energized various ethnic groups suppressed by the communists or the precommunist regimes. A classic example was the awakening of various ethnicities that comprised the federated state of Yugoslavia. These were inactive but not dead under Tito's authoritative government (Papaconstantinou 1992). The territorial dismemberment that followed Yugoslavia's collapse was a historical upheaval not only for its people awakening one day in a disastrously messy situation, but also for the rankling problems it created for its immediate neighbors. The collapse also contributed to border changes and readjustments and the rise of various conflicts in the Yugoslav republics.

An unusually disturbing event that came out of Yugoslavia's breakup, especially for Greece, was the conversion on September 17, 1991, of Tito's Socialist Republic of Macedonia to an independent state with the name "Republic of Macedonia" (*Republika Makedonija*). All of a sudden, Greece was confronted with a new multiethnic, fragile state to the north that inherited many of Yugoslavia's political and economic problems. The new state's constitution, approved by Skopje's parliament on November 17, stated in its preamble that the country's charter was inspired by the ideals of the Republic of Krushevo (the center of the Bulgarian *komitadjides*' Ilinden uprising of 1903) and Tito's 1944 antifascist Assembly of Macedonia that had loudly announced the goal of "liberation of Macedonia from the Greeks, Serbs, and Bulgarian conquerors."[7] Immediately after its secession from Yugoslavia, the new republic, beguiled by the foolery of age-old distorted historical misinformation, revealed in the first draft of its constitution its irredentist aspirations. Specifically, articles 3 and 49 of the constitution's preamble heralded to the world that the boundaries of the new state also included Greek Macedonia. Following Greece's loud protests, the new republic toned down the key flashpoint somewhat in January 1992, deleting the reference to Greek Macedonia in the second draft of its constitution. It included, however, in the final draft an appeal to the "Macedonians" of Greece and Bulgaria to continue their struggle for union with Skopje, an inclusion implying a camouflaged threat against Greece's and Bulgaria's territorial integrity (Tarkas 1995).

While differing perceptions on this point are inevitable, there was never any doubt that Greek Macedonia was at first on Skopje's target list. The constitution's irredentist character was also obvious from three of its articles on border adjustment with Skopje's neighbors. The struggle over the future of Macedonia between Greece and the southern Slavs that began in 1862, exacerbated by communism's overtures over the same land, made Greece understandably suspicious of the plans of its new neighbor, which half a century earlier had harbored some of the most important bases, including one in Skopje, to support the KKE's sedition against the Greek government. It was obvious that the Macedonianism of the Greeks, an integral part of their identity, pride, and culture, was targeted for a future verbal, political and diplomatic assault. To put it bluntly, the new state broke into the world like a lamb with no economy and army, but roared like a lion. In retrospect, it is clear that *Republika Makedonija*'s administration was determined to stir up political and demographic problems from its first day of secession from Yugoslavia.

What forced the Slavomacedonians of the Socialist Republic of Macedonia to separate from Yugoslavia, going their own way in 1991? There are weighty reasons to believe that self-preservation and the need to cultivate their own ethnicity — any ethnicity other than Bulgarian or Serbian and cultivate it as their own — prompted them to push for independence. They had no other way to go when they sensed Yugoslavia's breakup than to split into three ethnic parts, each joining one of the three neighboring countries,

Albania, Bulgaria, or Serbia. Perhaps it would have been a better solution in the long run. Only time will tell. To enhance their chances for survival in the midst of all the happenings in the Balkans with Yugoslavia's dissolution — ethnic transformations, name changes, war — they had to claim something, anything. In this case, they chose the "Macedonian" name and the "Macedonian" history, church, language, literature, heritage, custom, origin, and civilization, fully aware that the name and its dervatives belonged to another nation, another civilization, for thousands of years. Tito had established the foundation for them to continue history's alteration.

There were also other fundamental reasons for Skopje's reformed communist politicians to separate from Yugoslavia with the name "Macedonia" (Koppa 1994): (a) the need to build a new ethnicity, the "Macedonian" ethnicity, to offset the Bulgarian claims about the Socialist Republic of Macedonia's inhabitants being Bulgarians; and (b) the desire to counteract the increasing influence of the Muslim/Albanian element. Finding refuge in an ethnically neutral and glorious "Macedonian" ethnicity permitted FYROM's Slavs to express their differences from the Albanians, Bulgarians, and Serbs (Kofos 1964). If they did not, they would have run a great risk of Albania's awaking at the same time with Yugoslavia's breakup. VMRO's grip on FYROM's Slavs is too strong for them to disregard the Albanian threat.

Regarding the small republic as western Bulgaria and claiming its people are Bulgarians, speaking a Bulgarian dialect, did not deter Bulgaria from being the first country to recognize Skopje as a state, not as a "Macedonian nation," ostensibly to protect the large Bulgarian population of the small republic.[8] Bulgaria, however, refused to recognize the so-called "Macedonian" language spoken by the inhabitants of the new state. The new Yugoslavia also refused to recognize its frontier with the breakaway republic; and the Serbian Orthodox Church denied the status of the Orthodox Church of "Macedonia."

The new landlocked state with the name *Republika Makedonija* (Republic of Macedonia, Tito's forty-seven-year-old People's Republic of Macedonia without the socialist-tinted word "People's") found at the outset its bid for recognition by the European powers and the rest of the world blocked when it decided to maintain the word "Macedonia" in its name. Greece, in particular, whose northern province has been known as Macedonia since antiquity (the center of ancient Macedonia with Pella, the capital, and many other historical sites representing 75 percent of Philip's historic Macedonia) challenged the new republic's status, its constitution, the design and symbol on its national flag, and the name conveying indirect but nonetheless implicit claims on Greece's northern territory and its 3,000-year-old heritage. Greece was not about to relinquish its strong objections and grant recognition to the small state as "Macedonia."

Present-day Macedonia. A large part of present-day Former Yugoslav Republic of Macedonia (FYROM), above the dotted line, never belonged to historic
Macedonia.

The Greek adverse reaction to the name "Macedonia," exacerbated by
Greece's phobia of its northern neighbors, ridiculed by some American
politicians, stemmed from the fact that the name itself hid territorial claims
at Greece's expense, which owns a province with the name "Macedonia"
almost one and a half times the size of the new republic (Zaikos 2003).
Specifically, Greece stated that granting sovereignty to FYROM with the
name Macedonia was bound to create new problems in the Balkans, adding
new dimensions and unacceptable complications to an age-old complicated
issue. Simply, it would grant FYROM a monopoly, an unwritten "patent" on
the name "Macedonia" and its derivatives and a strongly implied legitimacy
to pursue future unification of the three parts of Macedonia. It would also
grant support to the small polyglot conglomerate's nationalism to pursue
the dreams haunting the Balkans since 1870 when the Bulgarian Exarchate
was formed. Greece believed that in the light of overwhelming Balkan realities, the rush to the seceding republic's recognition with the name "Macedonia" would undoubtedly provide a new spark to inflame the already hot
Macedonian issue.

While a few contemporaneous sources reproached Greece's position
on refusing to recognize Skopje with the name "Macedonia," arbitrarily

assumed by Skopje, the Greek people never forgot Tito's communism next door and his camouflaged and not-so-camouflaged attempts to use the Socialist Republic of Macedonia as a ploy and a bridgehead to annex Greek Macedonia to his Balkan Empire two years before the beginning of the Greek Civil War and during the war. Neither did they forget that Skopje's leaders were Tito's protégés and collaborators, every one of them (Troebst 1989) or the avalanche of war material and men pouring down to Greek Macedonia and Epirus from bases in Yugoslavia, Bulgaria and Albania, including several of them in what is FYROM today, during the Greek Civil War. Though FYROM's neighboring countries deny the existence of a separate Macedonian nation (Perry 1988), and Greece advances convincing historical, ethnic, archaeological, and geographical arguments to prove Macedonia's Hellenism (Mylonas 1991), what is to prevent Skopje on some future day from committing itself to an alliance with another Balkan country to liberate the "unredeemed Macedonian" brothers, threatening Greece's security, especially because the world is allowing the small republic to usurp a name and its derivatives that did not belong to it?[9]

On December 16, 1991, the Greek government submitted through the Foreign Ministers' Council of the European Economic Community [EEC, now European Union (EU)] three conditions to Skopje demanding acceptance of all three if the new republic were to be recognized: (a) discontinue using the name "Macedonia," a practice that would be interpreted as having territorial claims over Greek Macedonia; (b) denounce any territorial claims on Greek Macedonia; and (c) recognize that there is no "Macedonian" minority in Greece (Kofos 2003b, p. 160; Tarkas 1995).

All Greece's demands for recognizing the new republic were related to its security: avoid establishing a new state to the north as a future base against Greece (as happened in 1946–1949), discontinue stirring the old argument of "Macedonian minorities" in Greece, and stop pressuring Greece to allow the Slavomacedonians who renounced their citizenship and defected from their country in 1949 to return to Greece. The Greek foreign minister Antonis Samaras said this at the EEC Foreign Ministers' Conference in Lisbon on February 17, 1992: "If Skopje is allowed not only to usurp, but also as an independent state to monopolize the [Macedonian] name, old disputes will resurface and new extensive conflicts [will take place] in the entire region." The name will become "a vehicle of expansionist dreams, not only for territory, but also for the Macedonian inheritance through the ages" (Kofos 2003b, p. 160).[10]

Greece scored a partial success on the problem with the EEC Council of Foreign Ministers, who adopted the Greek foreign minister's proposal not to recognize the Slavic state unless it renounced any territorial claims in its constitution against its neighbors, discontinued its unsupported inimical minority claims against Greece, and refrained from using the Hellenic name "Macedonia." Gligorov, shaken at the outset by the decision made by the foreign ministers on December 16, 1991, accepted the first two terms but not the third on the republic's name, propelling the problem to interminable meetings and deliberations in Europe, in the United States, and at the United Nations (Tarkas 1995; Tsalouhides 1994). The Greek pressure also caused a great crack in the Skopje leadership. The ultranationalist VMRO dissociated itself from President Gligorov's policies when Gligorov made it known that he was ready to accept the Greek demands. VMRO's leader Ljupko Georgijevski immediately resigned as vice president in the Gligorov government.

On April 1–13, 1992, Portuguese Foreign Minister Z. Pinheiro, chairman of the EEC's Council of Foreign Ministers, proposed in Lisbon a plan including the name "Nova Macedonia" for the new republic. Samaras and the council of Greek party leaders, with the consent of President Constantine Caramanlis, rejected the proposed name which, according to Kofos (2003b, p. 165), was a "positive international conciliatory suggestion for Greece."[11]

On May 1 the German foreign minister informed the Greek prime minister that Germany had decided to establish a consulate in Skopje, de facto recognizing the small republic with the name "Republic of Skopje." The German proposal on the name was immediately rejected by the British, French, and Italian foreign ministers. Following the British-French-Italian rejection, the United States announced that Skopje must be recognized as the "Republic of Macedonia" to avoid war and partition of the small state.[12]

In June 1992 in Lisbon, the EEC foreign ministers recognized Skopje, but without the name "Macedonia," a decision rejected by the Skopje parliament. Almost at the same time (July 6, 1992), the White House disagreed with the Lisbon decision and urged Athens and Skopje to resolve their problem bilaterally. Gligorov, in the meantime, encouraged by the American-British attitude, petitioned the United Nations, requesting recognition of the small state as the "Republic of Macedonia." The unexpected U.S. decision, coupled with Great Britain's similar approach, hardened Skopje's attitude on the name and forced the Europeans to begin looking for ways to disengage from the thorny problem. Three months later, the European ministers buried the Lisbon plan and welcomed the U.S. decision to send a small army contingent to the republic's border with Yugoslavia.

On April 7, 1993, the United Nations Security Council accepted Skopje as a member with an awkward name, the Former Yugoslav Republic of Macedonia (FYROM). Had the EEC Council of Foreign Ministers acted decisively from the very beginning, considering the historical facts on Macedonia and the lessons from the vacillating European diplomacy at the end of the nineteenth century, it could have solved the Macedonian Question by insisting that Skopje respect Greece's sensitivities and the historical and ethnological rights on Macedonia. In their haste to dismantle Yugoslavia, the European diplomats made the same mistakes as their predecessors from 1878 to 1908, despite overwhelming evidence that the ancient Macedonians were Greeks.[13]

Even after Skopje's recognition by the U.N. as FYROM, the rankling problem did not end. On October 10, 1993, the socialist party Panhellenic Socialist Movement (PASOK) won the elections in Greece. A month later the Greek foreign minister informed the U.N. secretary general that Greece "froze" the dialogue with FYROM, because Skopje continued using the name "Republic of Macedonia." Four months later, on February 16, 1994, the PASOK government imposed a total embargo on FYROM, excluding food and medicine. The embargo put Greece on opposite sides with the United States and the EEC countries and caused great economic damage to both FYROM and Greece.[14]

The Interim Accord — Effects on Bilateral Relations

After the Athens-Skopje enmity smoldered for four acrimonious years, both sides of the quarrel thought that interim concessions by FYROM and Greece could create conditions favoring negotiations and normalize relations between the two neighbors: a normalization more easily accepted by Athens since Skopje's extreme party of the Right —VMRO-DPMNE— was no longer in Gligorov's government. The positive thinking, coupled with pressure from the United States and EEC, brought back Athens and Skopje to the negotiating table under U.N. auspices. Richard Hollbrook and Christopher Hill brokered a deal in which Andreas Papandreou, Greece's prime minister, called off FYROM's blockade, and Gligorov promised to remove the Sun of Vergina from the flag (Brown 2000). To protect Greece's historic inheritance, the U.N. Security Council immediately directed Skopje to remove the Sun of Vergina from its national flag.

On September 13, 1995, the two countries signed a so-called Interim Accord, whereby Greece lifted the embargo, recognized FYROM as an independent and sovereign state, and agreed to establish diplomatic relations with Skopje. FYROM removed the Sun of Vergina from its flag and public buildings and agreed that nothing in its constitution can or should be interpreted as constituting, or will ever constitute, the basis of any claim by FYROM to any territory not within its existing borders, or to interfere in the internal affairs of another state to protect the status and rights of any persons in other states who are not citizens of FYROM. The small republic was thus bound by the Interim Accord not to refer to its constitution in its international relations and never to raise irredentist claims on its neighbors or to intervene in affairs that do not pertain to its own citizens (Zaikos 2003, pp. 38–39). The U.N. Security Council decisions 817 (1993) and 845 (1993) did not introduce an agreement on the name, but directed the two parties to find an amicable solution.[15]

It may seem to be a taboo to continue the rhetoric of delineating the early violations and the irredentist proclivities by the new republic, but nonetheless we will return to a symbolic violation corrected by the Interim Accord. In addition to the name, the early Skopjan leaders committed an act unheard of in world historical annals, this time using an ethnic Hellenic symbol. In the 1970s, Manolis Andronikos, professor of archaeology at the Aristotelian University of Thessaloniki, and his colleagues excavated what is now accepted as the tomb of King Philip II at Vergina, about forty miles west of Thessaloniki and ten miles from Pella, the ancient capital of Philip and Alexander the Great. Among many striking findings unearthed, exhibited now at the Archaeological Museum of Thessaloniki and in Vergina, Andronikos found inside a brilliant tomb a shield engraved on a gold chest, the so-called sixteen-ray Sun of Vergina (Touratsoglou 1995).

The striking sun has been one of the most disputed symbols in the conflict between Athens and Skopje. As soon as FYROM declared its independence, the Gligorov government placed the finding on its first national flag and on government buildings as a Macedonian symbol, presumably to connect the new "Macedonian nation"—FYROM's population conglomerate — with the ancient Macedonians. In their desperation to make such a connection, the Skopjan leaders committed the morally unforgivable act of using without permission a symbol belonging to another nation, another culture, another civilization. The usurpation pointed to FYROM's desperate struggle for international legitimacy with symbols from an ancient glorious civilization that belonged to a neighbor.[16] It is therefore not rhetoric or "shrill" confrontation when a small country (Greece) mobilizes its resources to protect its history, its inheritance, and its rights to an exclusive ownership of symbols and territory that belong to it. "The question of the flag did not just illuminate a quarrel between two history-obsessed Balkan states," wrote Brown (2000, pp. 122–23). "Rather, it pointed to the struggle for internal legitimacy that was already in train within the new state."[17]

Andronikos interpreted the Sun of Vergina as the symbol of the Macedonian royal family, an emblem of the Macedonian dynasty, an interpretation disputed by a few historians, who suggested that the Sun of Vergina was an ethnic symbol, not an emblem of the royal family. Historical and archaeological evidence shows that the sun goes back to the glory of ancient Greece, used before Philip's period as an important decorative item. It is found in at least four classical temples in Athens: Theseum (built 449 B.C.), Parthenon (437–432 B.C.), Temple of Nemesis (436 B.C.), and the Acropolis Propylaea (435 B.C.). It is also found in Eleusis, dating back to the middle of the fifth century B.C., fifty years before Philip II was born (Tsalouhides 1994). The sun expresses the universality and completeness of the Greek spirit. It was natural for it to be adopted by the Macedonian kings who considered themselves Greeks.

By signing the Interim Accord, Greece made substantial commitments without gaining any benefits and set the stage for future concessions to FYROM. If we look carefully at all the factors involved, Greece was the real loser because it lifted the embargo in return for Skopje removing the Sun of Vergina from its flag, a symbol that did not belong to FYROM to begin with. The irredentist clauses in FYROM's constitution and Skopje's promise not to interfere in the internal affairs of its neighbors had already been decided by the EEC Foreign Ministers in 1991. Greece had imposed the embargo to force Skopje to remove the word "Macedonia" from its name, not its flag decoration. The two parties agreed to disagree on the name and promised to continue negotiations till a mutually satisfactory agreement could be reached on FYROM's name; no agreement has been reached yet.

The Interim Accord was and still is a significant political event that had an ameliorating effect on the fourth phase of the Macedonian Question brought about by the sudden secession of the small republic from Yugoslavia (Coufoudakis 1998). It successfully laid the foundation and the prerequisites for peaceful cooperation and development between the two governments and promoted several constructive constitutional changes in FYROM, including economic cooperation in the private sector of the two countries easily approved by the respective governments and the public (Kontonis 2003, p. 69). It marked the beginning of a dramatic improvement in Athens-Skopje relations, shifting them from the political arena to international law, with Greece recognizing FYROM as an "independent and sovereign" state with a temporary name (Zaikos 2003, p. 65). Skopje, however, misinterpreted from the very beginning the base of the agreement as a legal document between Greece and the "Republic of Macedonia," an unintentional or deliberate misinterpretation of the agreement that actually had been signed between Greece and the Former Yugoslav Republic of Macedonia.

What seems certain now is that the benefits to FYROM from the Interim Accord were many and the price it paid was none so far. First and foremost, the accord permitted FYROM to participate as a full member in various international organizations and prepared the ground for profitable relations with Greece (Kontonis 2003, pp. 108–9). One of the most important economic developments to benefit FYROM was Greece's announcement of a five-year Greek Plan of Economic Reconstruction of the Balkans for 550 million euros. On July 30, 2002, FYROM signed an agreement with Greece whereby the small republic was accepted in the Greek plan, with FYROM to receive 75 million euros from 2002 to 2006. Twenty percent of this stipend will be contributed by Greece's Ministry of Economic Development (Zaikos 2003, pp. 62–63).

The positive attitude in the bilateral relations that emerged from the Interim Accord between the two countries is also indicated by the Greek parliament's approval on May 27, 2003, of allowing FYROM to enter the Stabilization and Association Agreement with the European Union, a positive event favorably greeted by the FYROM government and the Skopje political world as an expression of concrete support of the "Republic of Macedonia" (Kontonis 2003, p. 95).[18] High-ranking FYROM politicians characterized Greece-FYROM bilateral relations as "excellent and especially significant," given the fact that Greece is the "most important strategic partner of FYROM" (Kontonis 2003, p. 87).[19]

From 1995 to 2002 Greece has invested more than 400 million dollars in FYROM and on November 16, 1995, supported FYROM's entering NATO's initiative known as NATO Partnership for Peace (PfP) (Kontonis 2003, p. 87). Cooperation between the two countries was not restricted to NATO's PfP. On December 14, 1999, an agreement of military cooperation was signed between Greece and FYROM which allowed high-ranking FYROM military leaders to participate in the multiethnic Center of Military Training in the Greek city of Kilkis. Scholarships were also granted by Greece to FYROM military personnel to attend military schools in Greece, and the Greek Department of Defense granted 580,000 euros in 2001 for the construction and renovation of dilapidated public buildings in FYROM.

But even from the outset of the Interim Accord's implementation, bilateral relations between the two countries have not always been smooth, despite the unilateral political and economic support given by Greece. Attitudes diverging on the name of the new republic and on interpretations attached by the two countries on historical and archaeological findings pertaining to ancient Macedonians' ethnicity, are too deeply rooted in Greece and FYROM to be softened in Skopje by the Greek economic and political support. The Skopjans, for instance, habitually dispute the authenticity of archaeological findings unequivocally showing the ancient Macedonians' Hellenism.[20]

The worst confrontation between FYROM and Greece occurred immediately after the two countries signed the Interim Accord (Tziampiris 2003, pp. 271–73). FYROM's Foreign Minister Ljubomir Frckovski initiated a confrontational policy with Greece so hostile that it reminded neutral observers

of the Cold War years. In contrast to Gligorov, who pursued a policy of
"compromise" with Greece, at Greece's expense of course ("Greece could
use any name it wished"), Frckovski followed a reckless policy opposite that
of Simitis, the PASOK leader and Greece's prime minister, disregarding many
articles of the Interim Accord. He also pursued an uncompromising policy
outside the United Nations to delete the temporary name FYROM, hoping
that as the time passed, Skopje would win de facto the name *Republika
Makedonija*.

Although FYROM's constitution, amended on January 6, 1992, specifies
that FYROM will "take effective measures to prohibit propaganda by state-
controlled agencies," its Academy of Sciences and Arts, a state-controlled
institution, published a memorandum with government support mentioning again the existence of a "Macedonian minority" in Greece (Zaikos 2003,
p. 65). When the Interim Accord was signed, the prominent Skopje newspaper *Nova Makedonija* predicted the end of the Bucharest Agreement of
1913 and expressed the view that by signing the Interim Accord, *Republika
Makedonija* made the last concession (Vlasidis 2003, p. 305). No sooner
had FYROM become a member of the European Council in 1995 after signing the Interim Accord that it surreptitiously used its membership status
to promote its nationalist aims, including "redemption" of the "Macedonian minorities" in Greece and recognition of the "Macedonian language"
(Kontonis 2003).[21]

The Struggle for a Name

On October 13, 2002, the Interim Accord expired and was renewed
automatically since none of the two countries withdrew, but parts of the
old Vardar Province still remain officially with a temporary, impractical
name that no one uses except Greece.[22] This is not to say that the Interim
Accord did not have an impact on the conflict between Athens and Skopje.
Among other things, it removed Greece's concern about security and
certified the inviolateness of FYROM's frontier, but it did not include any
decision on FYROM's name other than to suggest that the two governments continue the dialogue to find an amicable solution. The fact that
no decision was made on the name when Andreas Papandreou, Greece's
prime minister, and Kiro Gligorov, FYROM's president, affixed their signa-
ture on the Interim Accord paper indicated that both politicians did not
wish to endanger their image as leaders of their people if they had agreed
on a name unacceptable by their respective countries (Kontonis 2003). Even
when Gligorov signed the Interim Accord making no concessions on the
name, his action, favorable to FYROM, did not please his enemies, who

attempted to assassinate him in Skopje in October 1995 (Kofos 1999, pp. 247–56).

To many knowledgeable Greek observers the concessions made by Greece in the Interim Accord are bound to lead to a de facto recognition of the small republic with the name "Macedonia." This view is enhanced by the well-known fact that the EU and, especially, the United States continue to press the Greek government to find a solution on the name even if it is unacceptable to the Greek people. The silly justification given is that Greece must swallow its ethnic pride, surrendering to the demands, because the name "Macedonia" would stabilize the new republic and its people, who feel that their neighbors are enemies coveting their land. The world forgot that the Greek people sacrificed everything in the 1940s fighting for ten years to thwart communism's advance from its extensive bases in Yugoslavia, Bulgaria and Albania to the Aegean Sea and the Mediterranean. Unbiased analysts of foreign and military policy would also argue that those "unfortunate" people are the same ones who welcomed the Bulgarian fascists (German allies) as liberators in 1941 in the streets of Skopje and who, during Greece's difficult years in the 1940s, connived, conspired, assisted the Greek communists, and eventually succeeded in using a historical name that does not belong to them (see Chapters 4 and 6).[23]

The Greek concerns and position on FYROM, simply put by Kofos (1995), is that "Greece does not dispute the existence of a nation, a language or a republic after 1944, but rather refuses the legitimacy of the appropriation of the Macedonian name for defining a Slavic people." What specifically Greece disputes is the naming of the seceded small state from Yugoslavia as "Macedonia" on the basis of geography, a clever act by FYROM's former communist leaders because it would seem natural to the world that the other two sections of Macedonia, one belonging to Greece and the other to Bulgaria, must eventually be liberated and united with the Republic of Macedonia, first to be redeemed from foreign (Serbian) occupation. Viewed in another way, if Greece finally were to accept a neighbor with the name "Macedonia," it would automatically condone Skopje's aspirations, tacitly legitimizing its expansionist dreams and intentions for territorial expansion at Greek Macedonia's expense. Greece therefore must realize that accepting the use of a Greek name by a neighboring state would automatically transform the new state into a future territorial threat to one of Greece's most precious territories.

Greece also realizes that adoption of the name "Macedonia" by Skopje constitutes another equally serious threat to Greece, a threat to its national identity and cultural heritage.[24] Use of the name "Macedonia" by Skopje, which Greece had used since Alexander the Great for one of its largest districts south of the new republic, representing 75 percent of King Philip's historic Macedonia, conveys the impression that monopoly of the name inadvertently will lead to a monopoly of everything Macedonian: history, culture, symbols, art, traditions, all the expressions that define the concept of Macedonian Hellenism's national identity and pride (Kofos 1962). The Greek suspicions were fortified by the efforts of FYROM's leaders to hold together their cultural and ethnic groups by projecting several irredentist clauses in their constitution, unmistakenly betraying what their future struggles would be: convince the world of the existence of a "Macedonian nation" and the need to protect their "Macedonian" brethren in Greece and Bulgaria. FYROM's expansionist policy, supported by its constitution, and supported by Skopje's maps hanging on school walls, depicting Hellenic Macedonia under Greek occupation, was as clear a threat to Greece as Tito's irredentism against Greek Macedonia in the 1940s.

That the new republic begins to control all things Macedonian also becomes clear from Skopje's insistence on using nationalistic Macedonian tenets while its politicians and educators struggle to inculcate in the younger generations the defunct communist expansionist tendencies.[25] Within this framework, the Skopje propaganda machine circulated — and still does in FYROM and abroad — irredentist maps depicting "Greater Macedonia" with slices of eastern Albania, southwestern Bulgaria, and northern Greece (equal to one-fourth of the Greek mainland, including Thessaloniki);[26] printed and circulated "commemorative" bank notes showing the famous White Tower of Thessaloniki and currency with the figure of Alexander the Great; and declared that the leaders of the Greek revolution against the Turks in Halkidiki, Greek Macedonia (Karatasos, Papas, Yiannakis, Tsamis, Zafeirakis, etc.) were "Macedonians."[27]

The shrill controversy over these issues, and the rift over the name "Macedonia" for the small enclave and "Macedonians" for its polyglot con-glomerate (Slavs, Bulgarians, Albanians, Turks, Vlachs, Serbs, Romanians, gypsies), was exacerbated by politicians, NGOs, and eager anthropologists. Several countries, especially in the Third World, established diplomatic relations with FYROM with the name "Republic of Macedonia."[28] The plain name "Macedonia" wrongly prevailed also among NGOs and even Ameri-can and European officials. Even the U.N. Secretary-General Kofi Annan felt obliged to excuse himself in Skopje when he as a diplomat had to use the U.N.-accepted name "FYROM" instead of *Republika Makedonija* in an official speech (Kofos 2003b, p. 186). All these well-meaning groups and individuals began using FYROM's constitutional name before the name issue was settled, some of them feverishly diving into studies of Macedonianism and the "Macedonian" ethnicity with human experimental samples from Greece's border districts harboring a small group of slavophone inhabitants, ignoring the majority of Greek Macedonia's inhabitants, and especially the indigenous Hellenic Macedonians (IHMs), who have lived in Macedonia for many generations. Although FYROM has not been recognized as the "Republic of Macedonia" by the United Nations, when the news media offer news from Skopje, for instance, the word "Skopje" at the beginning of the first column is always followed by the word "Macedonia," giving the reader the impression that recognition has already been given to Skopje to monopolize the name "Macedonia."

Because of intentional or unintentional support given to FYROM by individuals, NGOs, academia, and a few countries, calling it "Macedonia" before an acceptable name was officially chosen, and for other reasons to be discussed later, FYROM displayed a naked intransigence during the seven years of the Interim Accord (1995–2004) in its dealings with Greece and the U.N. representatives attempting to negotiate in good faith the country's name with Greece. Simply, *the spoiled child* [29] took advantage of the Greek diplomacy's "condition of self-disarmament" (Kofos 2003b, p. 255) and of the unrelenting, one-sided attempts by some influential outsiders to bend Athens to submission as if Greece were responsible for apprehending a name that did not belong to it. During the same period Greece demonstrated a reasonable compromising stand for a just solution.

Greece's intense official campaign against the new republic's bid for recognition with the name "Macedonia" was considered unrighteous by NGOs, not to mention the unjustified accusations of Greece's being "Balkan" rather than European, or even the preposterous allegation of Greece's harboring irredentist aspirations on the new republic. Knowledgeable members of the NGOs (Gelb 1992; Hitchens 1994), however, discerned the falseness of the charges and wrote that Greece's preoccupation with history and the past was justified because FYROM's constitution and the propaganda emanating from Skopje raised legitimate concerns about the new republic's chauvinism.[30]

People around the world and some politicians in Europe and Washington may think that names and symbols are only of minor significance and, therefore, not worth preserving. This thinking, replete with shortcomings, does not consider the threat to Greece's security and cultural-historical heritage that must be seen against an intricate Balkan historical background rife with dangers. Failing by imposed circumstances to preserve the cultural-historical heritage is tantamount for Greece to failing to keep alive the *power of Hellenic Macedonian ethnic identity, culture, and pride,* one of the paramount tenets in people's lives defining Macedonian Hellenism.[31] The power of Macedonianism among the Greek Macedonians originates from many things, including the feeling and pride of being Hellenic and from what Durant wrote so eloquently about Greece (1939, vol. 2, p. 668): "Our literature could hardly have existed without the Greek tradition.

Our alphabet came from Greece through Cunea and Rome; our language is littered with Greek words; our science has forged an international language through Greek terms; our grammar and rhetoric, even the punctuation and paragraphing of this page are Greek inventions. Our literary genres are Greek — the lyric, the ode, the idyl, the novel, the essay, the ovation, the biography, the history, and above all, the drama."

After four centuries of suppression by the Ottomans, the power of ethnic pride and culture, manifested as an intense and deep awareness of history and pride in the culture by the people, which the West fails to understand, surfaced stronger than ever after Macedonia's liberation from 1912 to 1913 and communism's repugnant intrusion into the Balkan peoples' mentality and life. It surfaced even stronger as the fourth phase of the struggle for Macedonia reemerged after FYROM's independence, capturing the interest of the Greek people and world politicians, NGOs, academics, and anthropologists. According to Cowan and Brown (2000, p. 2), Macedonia emerged "not only as a geographical area, but also as a discursive space of global significance" (see chapter 5).

History may be irrelevant to some people, but not to people in the Balkan nations who experienced numerous upheavals and fought so many wars. History played a great part in the politics of the Macedonian Question and must not be irrelevant to politicians in the West dealing with issues of war and peace; nor to the press and NGOs, which must know history's falsification is bound to perpetuate conflict; and, certainly, not to the people of Greece, where the legends of Alexander the Great still reverberate in the air from the pillars of Hercules to the pyramids of Egypt and the Hindu Kush (Alexandrou 1991). As we stand on the side attempting to understand Balkan history, we can predict that FYROM's constitution and its name will involve, sooner or later, Greece's security. Hitchens (1994) wrote from Skopje: "His [Gligorov's] is a republic with no economy, no tradition, no identity and no standing except that conferred to it by others. An imagined provisional entity is the best he can do.... Only those who have contempt for questions of language and history can continue to find the Greek concern about names and symbols in at least bit funny."

Greece's dispute with FYROM over the use of the name "Macedonia," and FYROM's Slavs' claiming descent from the Macedonians of antiquity, and of the existence of a distinct "Macedonian" nation with its people being separate from Bulgarians, Greeks, and Serbs, deeply disturbed the Greek Macedonians. Equally disturbing to the Greeks was FYROM's claim of the presence of "unredeemed" brothers in Greek Macedonia and Bulgarian Macedonia, whose national aspirations the new republic promised to fulfill (Zahariadis 1996).[32] The answer to the claims by FYROM's Slavs that they descended from the Macedonians of antiquity, absurd as it may sound to a historian, was given by FYROM's first president, Kiro Gligorov, who, in a moment of repentance, declared the following in Rome on October 31, 1991 (Tsalouhides 1994): "It is inconceivable to think that today's Slavomacedonians are descendants of Alexander the Great." Later in Skopje he said to a group of Greek correspondents: "We do not insist we are descendants of Alexander the Great or the ancient Macedonians."[33]

Despite admitting the truth about the Slavomacedonians' descent, Gligorov was not in a position to make concessions about symbols, the name, and history. At a rally in Skopje he was shouted down when he admitted that his republic's Slavic people did not descend from Alexander the Great (Hitchens 1994), a daring admission that did not please the FYROM politicians and historians who struggled hard to link the present-day Slavs of their country with the glorious Macedonians of antiquity, hardly camouflaging their brazen efforts in using the name "Macedonia" for their multiethnic country. As if this were not enough, FYROM renamed the Hellenistic Age as "Macedonian," appropriating its civilization, undermining the fundamental principles of European history and civilization. Many people know of Alexander's attempt to civilize Asia and its aftermath in the Hellenic world that followed his death: the conquering of Macedonia by the Roman Empire and its division; the prevailing Hellenism of the eastern half of the empire under Byzantium that included Macedonia; and Hellenism's survival in Macedonia for more than four hundred years under the Ottomans.[34]

The historical guilt for launching a new state with a name that did not belong to it must first and foremost burden those who created it. They could have written a constitution friendly to their neighbors, making an auspicious beginning by choosing a neutral name that was not offensive to their neighbor. The historical guilt also belongs to the Europeans and Americans who, to expedite Yugoslavia's dissolution, embraced the fledgling country with a historic name expropriated from the long past of one of its neighboring countries, which possessed a much larger territory with the same name. The Europeans and Americans did it for expediency, ignoring three thousand years of history.[35]

The guilt also belongs to the Greek political world. Despite a few, limited collective or individual initiatives, inefficiencies, selfish reasons, histrionics, vacillations, and flip-flopping dominated the Greek politicians' actions on this vital issue for Greece. During the first two years (1991 and 1992) after the Socialist Republic of Macedonia declared its independence from Yugoslavia with the name "Republic of Macedonia," the Greek government leaders, with a few exceptions, faced the Skopje problem with timidity and disarray (Tarkas 1995). Athens had no concrete, unified national policy on Skopje's aims and the still-unresolved Macedonian crisis simmering under a communist camouflage (Kargakos 1992). Greece appeared in the eyes of the world, especially among EEC's foreign ministers and in Washington, as a weak, inept, vacillating country, most of the time running behind events, always waiting and acting or reacting (Kollias 1995; Tsalouhides 1994). Instead of assuming responsibility with one unwavering voice to show the world that a neighboring enclave had given itself a historic name that had always belonged to Greece, the Greek politicians' attitude ranged from hostility to this important ethnic problem to indifference, fatalism, or submission and obedience.

The first enthusiastic burst of ethnic pride in 1991 and 1992 in Greek politics was mostly the result of the Greek people's exuberant reaction to the Macedonian problem facing Greece. There followed a political numbness, exacerbated by an uncoordinated, unexplained defeatism as if Greece were the guilty party that had appropriated a name from one of its neighbors; as if Greece were a new republic with an irredentist constitution, claiming territories right and left, north and south; as if Greece were the country that appropriated a foreign emblem (the Sun of Vergina) and placed it on its national flag. Simply, the attitude of several Greek politicians on this critical ethnic problem was inexcusable. During the political storm following Yugoslavia's collapse none like Pavlos Melas, Metropolitan Germanos Karavangelis, Ion Dragoumis, or Lambros Koromilas could be found on the Greek political horizon.

The historical guilt in handling the Macedonian problem also weighs heavily on the Communist Party of Greece (KKE), particularly for the old sins that provided ammunition to support Skopje's claims today. Articles in *Rhizospastis*, the official KKE newspaper, for instance, were used repeatedly by Skopje to show that there "always existed a Macedonian nation," which received the complete support, recognition, and help from a segment of the Greek people represented by the KKE. Yugoslav documents, KKE archives, and the *Rhizospastis* articles were compiled by Skopje into a two-volume document to show to the world the Yugoslav and the KKE writings favoring Skopje's views on Macedonia.[36] Mertzos's book (1984), *The Ten Deadly Sins of the KKE*, pointed out the KKE's most serious mistakes favoring the Slavic demands on Greek Macedonia.

The uncoordinated, feeble actions of the Greek politicians and the vacillating, often seditious policies of the KKE, especially its decision at the Fifth Plenum of the Central Committee in 1949, contrasted sharply with the resolute, clever, and one might say audacious efforts of Gligorov and other Skopjan redressed communist leaders. Gligorov was successful indeed in convincing the world to sanction the expropriation of a name that belonged to another country for a thousand years before his ancestors descended upon the Balkans. Not surprisingly, the Skopjan leaders, well versed in communist dialectics, cleverly handled the ensuing deliberations on the name of their small republic, culminating in the unheard-of situation: Skopje, with no historical and ethnological rights to the name "Macedonia," was the victor and Greece the guilty party.

In a murky political and military situation created by the ever-increasing pressure on FYROM's Slavs by the large Albanian minority, George Papandreou, Greece's foreign minister, and Ljupko Georgijevski, FYROM's prime minister, met repeatedly to find a compromise on the name under conditions favorable for Greece. The two politicians made an honest effort to overcome the difficulties for a compromise, finding a name that could be used for all national and international dealings by both countries. *Nova Makedonija* and *Gorna Makedonija* were proposed and discussed. The leader of FYROM's opposition party, Branco Tserbenkovski, endorsed the name *Gorna Makedonija*. The Albanian insurrection and Georgijevski's fall from power terminated the effort (Kofos 2003b, p. 199). In 2002 the new FYROM Prime Minister Branco Crvenkovski and President Boris Trajkovski supported the so-called double formula: *Republika Makedonija* for FYROM's consumption and international dealings and a different name (still containing the word "Macedonia") for Skopje's dealings with Greece. This proposal was rejected by Greece. The continuing procrastination in finding an acceptable name is disadvantageous to both countries: for Greece, no acceptable name is tantamount to a "solution by forgetfulness"; for FYROM, the disagreement delays the ratification by the Greek parliament of eighteen agreements and protocols favorable to FYROM and jeopardizes its entrance into NATO and the European Union (Kontonis 2003).

Greece and FYROM procrastinated in finding a solution on the only issue not resolved by the Interim Accord—a final name for Skopje acceptable to both sides—but for different reasons: Greece to avoid "the political cost of compromise" and FYROM "to harvest the gains procrastination could offer" (author's translation of the quotations from Kofos 2003b, p. 250). Athens believed that the Greek economic penetration of FYROM would strengthen FYROM's political and economic independence and create a climate for negotiations pointing to a road of compromise on the name. Time proved, however, that the Greek carrot without a stick was thoroughly ineffective. In fact, it gave the impression to the Slavs that Athens was always negotiating from weakness. Greece, unable to obtain concessions, found itself under great pressure from outsiders to compromise in order to please the Slavomacedonians as a reward for good behavior and for making concessions to the Albanian insurrectionists (Kofos 2003b, pp. 203–4). The PASOK government failed to see—or had no choice but to act with timidity—that improvement in relations with Skopje after the Interim Accord was signed increased Skopje's intransigence.

It is not only Greece's mishandling of the name problem that brought about the thirteen-year-long impasse.[37] It is also Skopje's unreasonable stance and its arrogant attitude stemming from a myth promulgated by the West that FYROM is "a place of stability in the Balkans" and "a good example of respecting the minority rights" (Kontonis 2003, p. 75). But the myth collapsed and FYROM's "important" geostrategic position in the Balkans, overestimated by Skopje's reformed communist politicians, was greatly eroded by the precipitous events of 2001–2002 (Kofos 2003b, p. 197; Kontonis 2003, p. 75): the fall of Serbia's Milosevic, Montenegro's crisis, and especially the dramatic entrance onto the murky scene of the military posture of the significant Albanian minority.

In 2001, the fear of the Albanian insurrection becoming an all-out war, which could have resulted in a dramatic Balkan destabilization, led the United States and the EU to press Skopje to make concessions to the Albanians (Carpenter 2002), forcing FYROM's Slavic majority to a spectacular recoiling, seriously curtailing Skopje's arrogance. These events were better expressed in the so-called Ochris Agreement signed by the Albanians and the Slavs on August 13, 2001.[38] Greece, witnessing the magnitude of the crisis in FYROM, and despite the pressures by its people, especially by the Hellenic Macedonians in the country and abroad, to take advantage of FYROM 's weakness to promote its views on the name, chose to support Skopje's government, a decision that impressed the Skopjan politicians and the West (Kofos 2003b). However, Greece's magnanimous behavior, supporting the embattled FYROM's Slavic government in a period of serious crisis, failed again to produce results on the name.

The bottom line is: enough is enough even in politics. Greece has made more than enough concessions during the seven years of the Interim Accord: provided enough carrot without brandishing a stick; allowed FYROM's commerce to move through the port of Thessaloniki; helped FYROM enter several international organizations, including the all-important Stabilization and Association Agreement with the EU, a preliminary but important step for FYROM's future acceptance by the EU; allowed FYROM military officers to be trained in a Greek city; and stood politically and financially by the FYROM government during its nationalist clash with the local Albanian minority, endangering its good relations with the Albanians. No other state in the world has done so much for FYROM in such a short period of time as Greece. Exhausting its reserves of goodwill toward Skopje, Greece succeeded only in reducing the pressure by the West, with the subject of an acceptable permanent name being now in a condition of a "free fall" (Kofos 2003b, p. 251); but the Skopjan politicians remained unmoved on their pedestal of unyielding posture on the name "Macedonia" that did not even belong to them to begin with.

FYROM has every right to remain free, democratic, and prosperous. Everyone must agree on that. But it has no right to use the names "Macedonia" and "Macedonians" to promote the idea of liberating the "unredeemed" brethren in Greek and Bulgarian Macedonia. But is it politically wise for the Greek government to continue supporting financially a state that has no intention of arriving at an amicable solution on the name? "It is inconceivable and self-destructive for Greece to pursue a policy that promotes the creation, survival, independence, and a close alliance with a state that with the name [it selected] expresses its enmity against Hellenism and declares with its constitution its unshakable intention for further inimical acts." Every word of this statement by Mertzos (1993) holds true today.

In the light of such relentless inflexibility, any further concessions by Greece, accepting a name with the word "Macedonia" or a second name to be used only in Greece's bilateral dealings with Skopje, would be tantamount to a reckless destruction of Greece's national dignity, including the destruction of the *power of Hellenic Macedonian ethnic identity, culture, and pride.* Any Greek politicians or political group selling the country's dignity "for thirty pieces of silver" would be remembered forever in the pages of history tinted with national shame. Kofos (2003b, pp. 253–55) rightly pointed out that if a compromise on the name acceptable to the Greek people, and especially to the three million Hellenic Macedonians in Greece and the diaspora, cannot be found, Greece must stop coddling FYROM, offering incentives in advance, and withdraw from the Interim Accord. Should Skopje still be uncompromising, Greece must never support its entrance into the European Union irrespective of consequences. If Skopje insists on using the name *Republika Makedonija*, no one will be the winner in the end.

In light of such compellingly diverse views on FYROM's name, any solution to the ongoing conflict must address the historical truth, the historical background, the essence of which has been the attempt to apprehend a name that Greece used for more than two thousand years and still uses for one of its largest territories adjacent to FYROM. The former communist regime in FYROM, reformed now as democratic, is an extreme example, supported by peace-seeking but history-insensitive politicians elsewhere, of what dominant forces can achieve for unknown reasons. Simply, the entire affair is a case of apprehended identity. The Skopjan regime is using Macedonian Hellenism's name and symbols, leaving thousands of IHMs unrecognized by the world media. FYROM, with Tito's legacy behind it, accomplished what Bulgaria was unable to do during so many previous Macedonian crises. By assuming the name "Macedonians," the people of FYROM's multiethnic conglomerate preempted the same name from and eclipsed the Macedonian identity of Hellenic Macedonia's Greek-speakers. Barring military or terrorist attacks, in the pages of modern history no other offense is more serious than appropriating an individual or group's identity and pride.

Future Prospects

From the very beginning of FYROM's independence, Greece declared it had no claims on FYROM's territory. Greece's only serious grievance was, and still is, the use by FYROM of the name "Macedonia" and its derivatives (Kofos 1995; Woodhouse 1992). Greece presented its case as follows: The People's Republic of Macedonia — renamed *Republika Makedonija* in 1991— was a Tito invention to be used as a bridgehead for the virtual annexation of the northern Greek territory with the name Macedonia. Tito's "Macedonia" did not exist as an independent state till 1991 and as a province with the word "Macedonia" in its name on any map before 1944. After the small federated republic's formation in 1944, Tito announced the Slavic people's desire to form a Greater Macedonia that would include the People's Republic of Macedonia, Greek Macedonia, and Bulgarian Pirin Macedonia. (He did not ask the Greek Macedonians, the overwhelming majority in historic Macedonia.) To achieve his goal of a Greater Macedonia, he used his state-controlled propaganda, not to mention his scheming relationships with the communist leaders of Greece and Bulgaria, Nikos Zachariadis and Dimitrov, respectively. If he had succeeded, Greater Macedonia would have been established under his hegemony with Thessaloniki as its capital.

In the postexpiration phase of the Interim Accord, it is perhaps appropriate to ask whether it is in Greece's advantage for the small country to survive in the long run. The answer to this question must unequivocally be positive. It is to be hoped that Skopje's political leaders understand Greece's contribution and assistance toward that end. Skopje must realize that in the long run the key to solving finally the name problem is its decision to delete the word "Macedonia" from its name. Skopje must also understand Greece's sensitivity on this issue, because for more than fifty years the name problem has always been used as a pretext to create an independent and united Macedonia, which, if it had been achieved, would have meant the shrinking of Greece's territory and the loss of the precious Macedonian inheritance.

The Europeans and the Americans have not been very helpful on this matter. They never seriously considered the fact that the People's Republic of Macedonia was the only Stalin and Tito achievement that the West declared preservable, though there is no blame for declaring the small enclave viable. The blame is for disregarding facts, brushing aside the available historical data to punish Greece, as if Greece were the instigator of this vexing Balkan event. If history had meant anything to the Europeans and Americans, they should have discouraged Skopje at the outset from using the name "Macedonia."

It is now thirteen years since the Socialist Republic of Macedonia seceded from Yugoslavia and declared its independence. The small, landlocked country survived Greece's, Serbia's, and Bulgaria's objections; frictions among its numerous political parties and ethnic groups; border incursions and armed confrontations between police and citizens and government scandals; an embargo imposed by Greece; and insurrections by armed bands of Albanian secessionists from Kosovo and FYROM's own Albanian minority (Mertzos 1993).[39] At present, FYROM appears stable on the surface, thanks to the presence of the United Nations Kosovo Force (KFOR) and NATO elements that keep an acceptable, ephemeral normalcy in the country. Its instability, however, stemming from ethnic rivalries, especially between Slavs and Albanians, is simmering under a superficial calm. The only thing that keeps relative peace in the landlocked country is foreign interference that ended a six-month conflict between FYROM security forces and Albanian guerrillas of "Macedonia's" National Liberation Army (NLA). Many consider this group of secessionist Albanians an offshoot of the Kosovo Liberation Army (KLA) (Carpenter 2002).

Although a lull prevails at present, it is not a secret that both Albanian organizations have spread their tentacles into FYROM, looking for an opportunity to strike again against the Skopje government. Georgijevski, leader of the VMRO-DPMNE, voted out of the government for corruption and mishandling the 2001 conflict, accused the Albanian minority of planning to split the country apart. "It is only a matter of time when they [the Albanians] will opt for their next action," declared Georgijevski (Wood 2003).[40]

Founded on June 17, 1990, the political party VMRO-DPMNE now has branches in Australia, the United States, Canada, and Germany (Koppa 1994). The party is the façade behind which stands the real power, VMRO (Internal Macedonian Revolutionary Organization), representing the extreme nationalist views and positions in Skopje that contributed to the inimical relations between Skopje and Athens. During the party's First Congress, Georgijevski provocatively declared that "the next Congress will convene in the real capital of Macedonia, Solum" (Thessaloniki). The VMRO-DPMNE's platform is anticommunist, anti–Albanian, nationalist, and strongly anti–Serbian.[41]

To restore allegiance of the Albanian minority to the FYROM government, the West pressured Skopje to make concessions to the country's largest minority. This strategy had a double undesirable effect: it weakened the government's authority without restoring the Albanians' allegiance or securing a peaceful future. The concession imposed by the West gave NLA de facto control of a large territory in the Tetovo-Kumanovo districts, near Kosovo, a strategy doomed to failure, because NLA is not interested in cooperating with the central government (Carpenter 2002). Its ultimate objective, coinciding with the KLA's objective, is to "liberate" the area populated by Albanians and attach it to an ethnically pure Greater Albania. True to the Albanian irredentists, a Greater Albania will include not only Kosovo and Albania, but also Montenegro and parts of FYROM, Serbia, and even Greece. The danger to FYROM comes from the Albanians, and this danger will become a crisis again when the international force departs Skopje.

"Unfortunately, because of the myopic policies pursued by the United States and its European allies," wrote Carpenter (2002), "that goal [a Greater Albania] is no longer a pipe dream." The Americans and Europeans brushed aside the mounting evidence that the KLA-NLA was a collection of fanatic nationalists, unchanged communists, and common criminals. Carpenter nonetheless addressed the danger from the two organizations, stating there is now good evidence of almost a ten-year connection between international terrorism and Albanian nationalism, an event more disturbing than the drive to form a Greater Albania. "An estimated six thousand Islamic fighters from various Arab nations (as well as such places as Turkey and Bosnia) [are now] in Macedonia [FYROM]."

FYROM's long-range survival will depend not only on its neighbors. The Skopjan leaders must accept the reality that FYROM's multiethnic conglomerate population, not really "Macedonian" (Gligorov already admitted that), is in itself the key to FYROM's survival. It is difficult to speak of a Skopjan nation representing a coherent collection of individuals—too many ethnic, religious, and cultural groups (a miniature Yugoslavia)—as the dominant ethnic majority, the Slavs, will be overwhelmed by Muslims in a relatively short period of time. High Islamic population growth rates will bring increasing pressure on overcrowded cities and towns; and the demographic changes in western and northwestern FYROM have often been accompanied by violence. Islamic militancy, coupled with FYROM's proximity to Albania and Kosovo, will eventually haunt FYROM as it did Kosovo. Everybody knows it, including the European Union, NATO, and the United States. Do the Skopjan politicians realize it?

The Albanian minority, "the incurable tumor of Greater Albania" (according to Kole Casule), is of greater threat to Skopje than its neighbors, if we take into account that most Albanians inhabit areas close to Albania that have high Albanian population. In a few years the Albanian Muslim population will be the majority in FYROM because they multiply two to three times faster than the "Macedonian" majority. Difficult-to-control Muslim forces will have the will, the numbers, and the power to topple the Slav-dominated government, creating another Balkan crisis.[42] The next ten to fifteen years will be crucial and may well determine the fate of the tiny conglomerate Balkan country. The potential maelstrom presents a big challenge to the neighboring countries, especially Greece and Bulgaria. The Bosnian experience has shown how powerless the outside world can be in managing events in the Balkans.

Another fundamental problem that needs to be stressed is FYROM's relations with Greece. Although the reformed Skopje communist leaders threw off Titoist-inspired attitudes, pretending at least to be democratic, they have been unable to shake off their irredentist mentality demonstrated by their keeping the name "Macedonia" and condoning the ongoing unrelenting anti–Hellenic propaganda by the Slavic organizations in the United States, Canada, and Australia.[43] Because it is unlikely that changes in such long-cherished attitudes will be forthcoming soon, the Macedonian problem will continue. It is unlikely that FYROM leaders will see the dangers looming for their country to agree on the name with Greece, the only country that has no territorial claims on FYROM. In the not too distant future, the choice for alliances may depend on tomorrow's majority, the Albanians. Time, demographic changes, and the Slav majority's stubborn adherence to a name that never belonged to it are FYROM's worst enemies.

If Skopje were to opt for steady, friendly relations with its neighbors, it should be opting above all for continuing the good relations with Greece, with which only one word, "Macedonia," prevents it from having excellent, mutually beneficial relations with its neighbor to the south. Sooner or later instability will force it to opt for a compromise on the name with Greece. Relations with the other three neighbors are complicated, involving territorial claims, demographic problems, minority problems, etc. The plethora of historic, demographic, religious, ethnic, and geographic factors combined make FYROM the most ethnically heterogeneous, politically unstable state in Europe and especially in the Balkans, where heterogeneity and instability are the rule.

It is the purpose of this brief, last section of the book to dwell on the dysfunctional effects from Skopje's attitude: the absurd claim by the Slavs that the name "Macedonia" belongs to them, and only them. The Slavs' ultranationalist attitude emanates from their age-old dream for an independent state of their own, kin to a glorious past, not shared with anybody else. This is exactly their own Achilles' heel, because they ignore reality and the basic principle that multiethnic countries such as the United States, Canada, and Australia have successfully used names for their countries encompassing all their multiethnic groups, excluding none. To them the Albanians are just a minority (30 percent or more), not Macedonians. The FYROM Slavs have no intention of recognizing the Albanians as citizens of the republic equal with them. With this attitude, FYROM jeopardizes its chances of surviving as an independent republic, given the Albanians' fierce desire for independence.[44]

The new world realities are prompting a rethinking of the concept and the methods of how to create a new nation-state. The early 1920s have gone forever, when the Soviets created Byelorussia from scratch in defiance of international opinion and with the absence of a separate ethnic legitimacy. In contrast, the world perspective in the beginning of the twenty-first century suggests that a new state may not survive for long if its formation is based on a wrong historical footing. As the Athens Academy and Senate pointed out (Kargakos 1992), "It [FYROM] does not have the right to acquire, by international recognition, an advantage enjoyed by no other state in the world: to use a name which of itself propagandizes territorial aspirations."

Cappelli (1997), discussing the Bosnian question, appropriately pointed out that "international recognition by no means necessarily endows a state with legitimacy, especially when the recognition has been granted in such an impetuous manner in the midst of a crisis and if legitimacy is held to have any connection with a common history and a sense of common destiny as characteristics of the state's population, without which no state can survive." Every word of this statement on Bosnia applies to FYROM.

Appendix: A History of FYROM (or Balkan) Slavs Compared to the History of Greek Macedonians and Albanians

by Marcus Alexander Templar

The history of the Slavs of the Former Yugoslav Republic of Macedonia (FYROM), compared to the history of their Hellenic and Albanian neighbors, is very recent. It began approximately during the fifth century A.D. Originally, the southern Slavs were called *Venedi*, but the Byzantines changed their name to *Sklavini* when they migrated to the south part of the Balkans where they established alliances or unions amongst themselves known as *sklavinije*. The *sklavinije* asserted as their commanders a regular hierarchy of princes such as Hatson, Akamir, and Prvud. In the middle of the fifth century the southern Slavs crossed the Carpathian mountains and settled in the former Roman provinces of Panonia (modern-day Hungary) and Dacia (modern-day Romania). The first Slavic and Turkic tribes of the Bulgarians also began attacking the Balkan areas jointly in the fifth century. In the beginning they robbed the Byzantine population, devastated the countryside, and returned to their bases.

Lasting settlements of Slavs in Macedonia began at the end of the sixth century. Up to the middle of the seventh century, the Slavic tribes, namely Draguviti, Brsjaci (or Bereziti), Sagudati, Rinhini, Strumljani (or Strimonci), Smoljani, Velegeziti, Milingi, Ezedrites, Timocani, Abodrini, and Moravijani, formed tribal unions, thus turning into an important political and ethnic factor in the history of the Balkans. They are the ancestors of FYROM's current Slavic population, and originally they inhabited parts of the territory from the River Nestos to Thessaly, and from Thessaloniki to mountains Shar, Rila, and Osogovska. As time passed, the trapped Thraco-Illyrian population was either pushed to the mountainous region or assimilated at a later time by the Slavs.

The paragraph below is written in the Military Encyclopedia of the Titoic Yugoslavia, part of which is the present-day FYROM. Its Slav inhabitants never objected to such published truths in their own federal state:

> Due to its strong culture and multitudinous population the Hellenes could not be assimilated [by the Slavs], but stayed intact. Areas with strong Hellenic presence remained Hellenic. Though Slavic and Bulgarian elements were living in Macedonia and Thrace, the main bulk of the populace was Hellenic. The Illyrian lands that form today's Albania and its neighboring areas were too distant to Slavic and Bulgarian reach.

In brief, this means two things: (a) The Slavs imposed their language and culture on the Hellenized Paeonians, distributed sparsely in certain areas of the Balkans, and to other people they encountered in the area; and (b) the inhabitants were actually Hellenes, because the word "Macedonians" does not appear in the text. Instead, the encyclopedia uses the word "Slavs."

The Slavs continued to exist in culturally separate communities along with the Hellenic communities, but their Slavic mass was in the area of the FYROM. In the same area a notable minority of Hellenes existed until communism managed to Macedonize them. Since Slavic communities were attached to the Bulgarian populace from the time of their appearance in the Balkans, they behaved as Bulgarians and were identified as Bulgarians. Alleged "Macedonian" consciousness did not exist as is demonstrated copiously in the most important document, the Manifesto of the Krushevo Republic (see Chapter 1), which the Slavs invoked later as "Macedonian." The individuals who wrote the manifesto considered themselves Bulgarian and not "Macedonian." In addition, the document, considered a historical Declaration of Independence of Geographical Macedonia, was directed toward all inhabitants of Macedonia, regardless of faith, nationality, sex or religious conviction; and furthermore, it was written in perfect Bulgarian.

The Slavs' assertion that by occupying lands that were parts of the ancient Kingdom of Macedonia, and mixing with Macedonians, they themselves became Macedonians, and their country's name must be Macedonia, is simply baseless.

Firstly, FYROM's land today was the land of the Paeonians, a Thraco-Illyrian tribe Hellenized by the Macedonians by the time of King Philip V's reign (238–179 B.C.). FYROM professors Fanula Papazoglou, Ivan Mikulcic, Eleonora Petrova, Victor Lilcic, Vera Bitrakova-Grozdanova, Vojislav Sanec, and Fanica Veljanovska, and the publications "Macedonian Heritage" (1996), "The Art in Macedonia" (1984), and others have attested to that fact. When the Macedonians Hellenized the Paeonians and made them Hellenes like them, all Paeonians disappeared.

Secondly, it is a known fact that Philip II and Alexander III, the Great, expanded the ancient Kingdom of Macedonia to present-day Bulgaria, Asia Minor, Egypt, the Middle East, and Central Asia, all the way to the River Hindus. It is also known that it was the custom of the ancient Macedonians to give to the lands they conquered the name "Macedonia" or as historians call it, the "Macedonian Empire." Based on the above, there is no convincing reason for the FYROM Slavs to demand and be granted the name "Macedonia," and be recognized internationally as such, when the piece of land occupied by FYROM is only a tiny portion of the total area of what was once referred to as Macedonia. Such recognition would grant a definite monopolization of the name Macedonia and its derivatives to the Slavs.

Thirdly, when the Slavs occupied Paeonia and conquered its people, everything Paeonian (or even Hellenic) disappeared. That is why FYROM's people, with the exception of the Albanians and other minorities, who settled in that area after the Slavs, are Slavic and speak a Slavonic language.

Fourthly, if we regress in time as the Slavs aspire, taking into consideration that the Paeonians were already Hellenized, to agree with the Slavs' theory, the Slavs were also Hellenized, accepting the Hellenic language, religion and culture of the Macedonians. Therefore, with their own criteria, the Slavs must consider themselves Hellenes.

One thing that people usually overlook is the fact that some of the descendants of the Macedonians who followed Alexander the Great almost 2,300 years ago have returned and keep returning to Greece, speaking Hellenic and claiming Hellenic ancestry. Thus far, nobody has returned from countries conquered by the Macedonian army claiming other Macedonian ancestry, and absolutely no one arrived speaking the so-called non-Hellenic "ancient Macedonian" language. If the ancient Macedonians did not consider themselves Hellenes after so many years, one would expect at least one person to claim his/her rightful ancestry.

The Kalash, for instance, one of the tribes descending from the ancient Macedonians, recognize Shalakash (Seleucus, Alexander's general and later King Seleucus I Nicator of the Seleucid Empire) as their ancient leader. The

Kalash is a tribe that still exists in the northern Himalayan region of the Hindu Kush mountains. Even though their language has been influenced by Muslim languages of nations surrounding the Kalash, it contains many elements of the ancient Greek language. They greet their visitors with "*ispanta*" from the Greek verb "*ασπάζομαι*" (greet) and warn them about "*Heman*" ("*χειμών*," winter). The Kalash sing song reminding people of the age-old music from northern Greece (Hellenic Macedonia) and dance in circles in the Greek way. These indigenous people still believe in the Olympian gods and their architecture resembles the Macedonian architecture (see "Quest for Alexander's Lost Tribe," *Reader's Digest*, July 20, 2000; also "A School in the Tribe of Kalash by Greeks," *National Herald*, October 11, 1996).

The FYROM Slavs advocate that the occupier takes the identity of the occupied. If we apply this logic, then the FYROM Slavs are Hellenized Paeonians. In the same context, the Turks would be called Hellenes, or even Byzantines, and their language Hellenic. Let us not forget that contemporary Turks are Turks only in a political sense. Ethnologically, they are a mixture of Turks and all the other people who were living in Anatolia, such as Hellenes, Slavs, Kurds, Persians, Armenians, Arabs, Georgians, Circassians, etc. The Ottoman population has lost its Turanian characteristics, showing a uniform anthropological type that evolved from a Hellenic substratum. The founder of the Republic of Turkey, Mustafa Kemal Ataturk, who in a speech he gave to the Grand National Assembly declared, "ben Turkum" (= I am a Turk), was blond with blue eyes, a far cry from the effaced Turanian type, traces of which rarely have been seen.

According to Plutarch (Alexander 47:6), while in Asia, Alexander the Great selected thirty thousand young Persians to join his army and "he ordered to teach them the Hellenic letters and the Macedonian weapons." The word "letters" means education. He did not impose a Macedonian education because it was the same education shared by the rest of the Hellenic world, but he considered the Macedonian weapons, training and tactics superior to the ones of the southern Hellenes. One must not forget that those weapons and tactics proved superior to those the southern Hellenes possessed during that time. Furthermore, when Alexander came across a foreign inscription, "he read the inscription and then ordered to write under it a translation to the Hellenic language" (Plutarch 69:4).

In order to accomplish international recognition, the Slavs attempt to alienate everything Hellenic from the ancient Macedonians, citing books by Eugene Borza and Ernst Badian. However, both Borza and Badian accept that the Macedonians were Hellenized and spoke a Hellenic dialect from the fifth century B.C. onward. Their thesis is that since we do not know anything about the Macedonians' origin, we cannot identify their ethnicity or specify their language. However, such a thesis is very true regarding other peoples, not only from within the Hellenic family of nations, but also from other nations, i.e., Slavic, Germanic, Latin and so on. In most cases, we do not know when the different languages spoken today were separated from one another or from their mother language.

Casson in his *Macedonia, Thrace and Illyria* (1926) was concerned with "whether there is any evidence to show that the Macedonians were not of the same stock as the Hellenes of recorded history." Interestingly, however, Casson agrees with Hoffman and Hatzidakis that the ancient Macedonians were of Hellenic stock since the artifacts of Macedonians living in Pateli and Kalindoia were identical to those found in Sparta, Olympia, Delphi, Aegina, Argos, and numerous other Greek sites. What kind of language or dialect the ancient Macedonians spoke is a matter of how one comprehends the issue. If we examine the Macedonian dialect, we will gather that it is a member of the *centum* (pronounced "kentum") subfamily of the Indo-European family of languages. It uses words or glosses of the roots that remind us of Doric- and Aeolic-based speech.

It is true that the Macedonian language included words of Thracian and Illyrian roots. However, considering the geographic location of Macedonia and the history of the Hellenic peninsula as a whole, we should understand the above reality. As for the Phrygian toponymies in ancient Macedonia, they can be explained by the fact that the Macedonians had displaced and occupied the lands of the Phrygians. Occupation is a common phenomenon even today. Toponymies such as Skopje (Scupi), Stip (Stypeon, Astibus), and Veles (Vylazora) are good examples. Alexander's expansion to Central and South Asia also brought words from Tocharian, Farsi, Gedrosian, Median, etc., into the language of the Hellenic soldiers.

Some people claim that conclusions not based on scientific research are assumptions, contending that unless we can find convincing archaeological evidence dated before the fifth century B.C. proving that the ancient Macedonians spoke a Hellenic dialect, their ethnicity is debatable. Thus far, archaeologists have found pottery, coins, monuments, frescoes, stelae, etc., proving that Macedonia was part of the Hellenic world. Etymologically, Hellenic toponymies that existed in ancient Macedonia and even in southern Paeonia and the vast majority of recovered words point to the reality that the Macedonians spoke a Hellenic dialect.

If we examine the Macedonian speech from a broader perspective, its similarities and differences from other Hellenic languages and dialects are the same as the similarities and differences of Ionic to Attic, Attic to the Doric family, Arcadian to Cypriot, the Doric family of languages to the Aeolic family of languages, etc. Linguists use the Doric family of languages to compare Hellenic to Latin. What is interesting is that all Hellenic tribes were influenced by and accepted words from proto-Hellenes such as Pelasgians, Leleges, and others. If we compare the Ionic speech to its closest relative, Attic, we will be amazed how different these two languages were; and yet both were Hellenic.

The argument that the ancient Macedonians did not speak a Hellenic dialect was defeated by a fourth century B.C. papyrus of Mygdonia found in ancient Ephyra, present-day Derveni (Langada, Central Hellenic Macedonia), written in pure Hellenic. Fanula Papazoglou reveals in her book *The Central Balkan Tribes in Pre-Roman Times* that Miculcic showed her a plaque found on the side of a church in the town of Oleveni near Bitola (FYROM), exhibited now in the Archaeological Museum of Skopje. Papazoglou has published her own copy along with Nikola Vulic's copy of the plaque, dated from the second century B.C. with a text in pure Hellenic. The areas of Bitola, Struga, Resen, and Ochris have many written ancient monuments that archaeological guides point out to tourists as ancient Macedonian, but the guides themselves are unable to read the texts, all of them written in Hellenic.

The FYROM public schools hardly teach the history of their own Slavic ancestors; rather, they concentrate on the history of Macedonia, which is being taught in a twisted and slanted manner. The truth is that hardly anyone knows about his or her own ancestors. FYROM's educational system methodically and continually aims toward a complete Macedonization of their Slavic pupils in a way that a direct line of ancestry has been established and accepted by politicians and educators alike.

Some contemporary countries, for reasons of expediency and even anti-Hellenism, work very diligently to reward FYROM's Slavs with the name "Macedonia" and its derivatives as a prize for their subservient demeanor. Their prevailing philosophy is that FYROM's Slav inhabitants feel insecure by not having a name; that it is very important for the stability of their state to be called "Macedonia." The same countries argue that their insecurity may become the reason for FYROM's disintegration and not the irredentism of the Slavs that creates ethnic antagonisms and animosity between Slavs and Albanians.

In actuality, after their country's independence from Yugoslavia, the Slavs refused to alter the philosophies they had developed while they were simple citizens or politicians of FYROM or they served in the Yugoslavian People's Army. The most rational decision they could make is to seek two names: one for their own Slavic history as their own ethnic name and its derivatives, and one for their country as a whole and its derivatives. Regarding the latter, the Slavs must consider the fact that FYROM by any standards is a multiethnic and multicultural country and it should remain, develop, and be named as such.

Unfortunately, some people do not understand that the reason for the conflict between the two FYROM ethnic groups, the Slavs and the Albanians, is the monopolization of the state mechanism by the Slavs as if it were monoethnic and monocultural country. It is indeed a miniature Yugoslavia. The philosophy has given rise to a very incongruous axiom that the conflict exists because the Slavs do not officially have the name "Macedonia." The philosophy also ignores the fact that a neighboring state, Greece, has had a province called "Macedonia" for at least three thousand years with a population calling itself "Macedonian" from the very beginning of Macedonia's existence. Therefore, if FYROM permanently assumes the name "Macedonia," the action (sanctioned officially by the United States recently) will permanently jeopardize peace in the Balkans.

In the middle of the nineteenth century, Prussian historian J. G. Droysen, using the term *Hellenismus* from the Hellenic verb *hellenizein* (= to spread Hellenism), which derives from the word "Hellenes," coined a new word, "Hellenistic." Adding the word "era" gives rise to perhaps the most glorious period of Hellenistic history, the Hellenistic Era; the era that followed the conquest of the then known world and spread Hellenic civilization and culture to all humankind. It is the era that united all Hellenes under the brilliant leadership of the greatest general the world has ever known, Alexander III, the Great.

Chapter Notes

Chapter 1

1. According to Grant (1988, p. 259), Macedonia's court was Hellenic and its monarchs claimed descent from the Argos dynasty founded by Heracles's descendants in Peloponnesus. They called themselves "Argeads" and believed in Zeus and the other Olympic gods.

2. Alexander's successors (*diadochi*), all Macedonian chieftains, divided the empire into five parts: Antipater took Greece including Macedonia, Lysimachus Thrace, Antigonus Asia Minor, Seleucus Babylonia, and Ptolemy Egypt (Durant 1939, vol. 2, p. 558).

3. Ancient Macedonia's mountaineers and peasants were related to Dorians who conquered the Peloponnesus. The ruling aristocracy spoke a Greek dialect and claimed Hellenic lineage from Heracles. "Near the sea was Pydna," wrote Durant (1939, vol. 2, pp. 69–70), "where the Romans would conquer the conquering Macedonians and win the right to transmit Greek civilization to the Western world."

4. Cowan and Brown (2000, p. 2) defined Macedonia "not only as a geographical area, but also as a discursive space of global significance."

5. Philippoupolis in Eastern Rumelia was a pure Greek city until 1819. By 1859 the city had only eighteen Bulgarian families (Vavouskos 1993).

6. In Serbo-Croatian, *sklavinija* means a condition of gathering, a tribal union. The etymology of the word *Slav* derives from the word *sklavinija* and *Serb* from the word *servus*.

Procopius and other Byzantine writers of Chronicles considered the name *sklavinija* as the Slavs' collective name, Sklavinoi or Slavinoi. Because the Slavs were working for the Byzantium government in the mines, but also for landowners and for very low compensation, the term *Sklavinos* or *Slavinos* became *sklavos* or *slavos*, eventually taking the meaning of *doulos*, a Greek word for a slave. Something similar happened much later when the Byzantines gave the Serbs the name of *servus*, a servant from the Latin adjective *servus-a-um*. From the term *sklavinija* the various European languages adopted the words *sklavos, slave, Slav,* and *Serbian* (Marcus A. Templar, personal communication).

7. In Lettera Ostrolica's *Egregiae Virtutis*, cited by Martis (2001), pp. 57, 71. The Macedonian Patriotic Organization (MPO), a Slavic propaganda organization in the United States and Canada, claimed in 2002 on the Internet that the Cyrillic alphabet was used by ancient Macedonians, an irresponsible propaganda claim. The alphabet was created by Cyril in the tenth century A.D., about thirteen centuries after the death of Alexander the Great.

8. Alexander had been dead for seven years when twenty-four small settlements were united in 316 B.C. by Cassandros and named Thessaloniki in honor of his wife, Alexander's half sister. She was named Thessaloniki for Alexander's victory in a battle in Thessaly (*nike* = victory) (Mitsakis 1973).

9. Besides the Greeks, Serbs, and Bulgarians there were also in Macedonia small numbers of Jews, Albanians, Armenians, Turks, Wallachians, Vlachs, and gypsies (Dakin 1966;

Vattis 2002). None of these groups identified itself as "Macedonian."

10. Cited by Dakin (1966, p. 12). Professor Kyriakides (1955) pointed out ironically that Rakowski did not go far enough to claim that St. Paul's letters to the Philippians and Thessalonians were written in Slav.

11. Declared separatist (defector) by religious decree.

12. The author's designation of Greek-speaking Macedonians whose forebears' roots were in Macedonia for countless generations, always speaking Greek (see Chapters 5 and 7).

13. As the Russian forces moved southward in January 1878, the local Muslim population was terrorized by the troops, Bulgarian volunteers, and local Bulgarian inhabitants. About 260,000 Muslims perished, and more than 500,000 refugees abandoned their houses and fled with the Turkish forces (Hupchick and Cox 2001, p. 27).

14. One of Istanbul's sections, San Stefano today is called Yesil Koy (Green Village).

15. Russia was a good friend of Greece during Greece's War of Independence from Turkey in 1821–1828. In the first Russo-Turkish War the Russians forced the defeated Turks to accept Greece's independence won in 1828 by the Greeks with the assistance of England, France, and Russia. In 1846, however, the Russians attempted to forestall future territorial expansion of Greece because its weakening would have assisted their plans to reach the Aegean Sea, bypassing the Dardanelles. They changed policy in 1846 after the Greek Prime Minister Kolettis declared the dogma of Megali Idea (Great Idea). Disappointed with Greece's new policy and King George's pro-British stand, and seeing their influence in Greece waning, the Russians brought the Bulgarians into the picture, a new element in the Balkans (Vavouskos 1995).

16. In the Ottoman Empire the millet (religious) affiliation defined ethnic groups, with the glossological characteristic not always corresponding to religion. A Christian with Bulgarian or Hellenic sentiments could speak Greek, Albanian, Slavonic, or Vlach, but not Turkish (Mackridge and Yiannakakis 1997).

17. Avgerinos, a Greek activist, asked a few Macedonians whether they were Greeks or Bulgarians. "What do you mean Greeks or Bulgarians, we are Christians," they replied. Christianity was the important thing to them, not the language. Many attended church services in Greek and spoke Slavic. By the end of the nineteenth century and at the beginning of the twentieth century, these peoples' nationalism flourished, and after the beginning of the 1920s communism and fascism exacerbated the enmities and intensified the bloodshed (cited

by Mazower 2000). No one up to that time mentioned "Macedonians" or a "Macedonian nation" (author's comment).

18. See note 5 of this chapter.

19. General Lyndon Simmons, a British delegate to the Congress of Berlin, announced at the congress that Hellenism was the only power capable of stopping the Russians. The population of Epirus, Thessaly, and Macedonia was basically Greek and had the highest cultural level in the Balkans (Martis 2001). Also in Berlin, Lord Salisbury, British Foreign Minister, declared that "Macedonia and Thrace are just as Greek as Crete." The Congress of Berlin gave Thessaly and the Arta district to Greece and for the first time recognized Macedonia as an entity with the name "Macedonia" (Vavouskos 1995).

20. During the last decades of the Ottoman rule, the slavophones of Macedonia became the "apple of discord." The Greeks claimed them as Greeks based on religion (they were Greek Orthodox, Patriarchist) and their ethnic beliefs and convictions; the Bulgarians claimed them as Bulgarians first, and the Serbs later as Serbs on the basis of their language. The ethnic identity of the Macedonian slavophones and the Greek and Bulgarian influence on their ethnic identity became the hot issue of the Macedonian Struggle between Hellenism and Bulgarism (Koliopoulos 1995).

21. Many slavophones were so strongly ethnic Greek that their Bulgarian opponents called them Grecomans (Vakalopoulos 1987). Nikoloudis (2002) quotes from Vakalopoulos (1993) a Bulgarian leader: "Their [Grecomans'] language, their customs and manners, their clothes, their house habits, all scream Bulgarian origin. And yet, they remain attached to the Patriarchate and Hellenic ideas like oysters." The two Slav-speaking andartes who died fighting for the Hellenic cause during the Macedonian Struggle of 1904–1908, Kotas and Vangelis, were good examples of Grecomans. Dakin (1966, p. 66, note 83) refers to the early Slav-speaking individuals with pro-Hellenic sentiments as Grecomani.

22. Mount Athos, the spectacular mountain that rises like a pyramid on the easternmost finger of Halkidiki, in Greek Macedonia, is considered a bridge between God and the monks of twenty or so Orthodox monasteries of several Orthodox Christian countries, including Russia. It is an inseparable part of the Greek state. Foreign monks who live in the Mount Athos monasteries automatically become Greek citizens and must obey the Greek constitution.

23. The slogan "Macedonia for the Macedonians" meant no particular Macedonian ethnicity, just Macedonia for the entire polyglot conglomerate of people who lived in Macedo-

nia under the Ottomans (Papakonstantinou 1992). A politically motivated, communist-supported mention of a "Macedonian" ethnicity appeared for the first time in the early 1920s and was officially sanctioned in 1943–1944 with the formation of the Communist Party of Macedonia (CPM), Vlahov's and Tomov's naming as "Macedonians," and the formation of the People's Republic of Macedonia by Tito.

24. IMRO, operational in Macedonia under a central committee in Sofia, was supported by Bulgarian officers' clubs in Bulgaria that provided financial help and war materials. In spite of the apparently disparate aims of IMRO and the Vrchovists, the ulterior motive of both committees was Macedonia's annexation by Bulgaria, the only difference being that IMRO wanted to do it in two steps: autonomy first followed by annexation (AHD 1979; Dakin 1966). IMRO's dictum "Macedonia for the Macedonians" (as a first step to annexation) was a deceptive approach to convince many uncommitted slavophones to join IMRO, avoiding European resistance.

25. Gotse-Delcheff, one of IMRO's leaders and an agent of Prince Ferdinand (Dakin 1966), was a close friend of Boris Sarafoff, a Vrchovist leader. The latter adopted the autonomy-for-Macedonia concept later, believing that autonomy was only the first step to annexation as it had occurred with Eastern Rumelia.

26. Villages in Macedonia were forced by Slavic bands to join the Exarchate. After Greece was defeated in the Greco-Turkish War of 1897, with the Turks punishing only the Hellenic Macedonians, to avoid persecutions, many villages went to the Exarchate. This was a temporary victory for IMRO (Dakin 1966).

27. The proposal to organize an uprising was supported largely by factions of the Bulgarian committees (IMRO and the Vrchovists), but they themselves took no part in the uprising (Dakin 1966).

28. IMRO agents did everything possible to implicate in the uprising the two Vlach-speaking villages Kleisura and Nymfaeon, both belonging to the Diocese of Kastoria, by organizing celebrations and freedom declarations to draw the Turkish army's wrath. Turkish reprisals were prevented at the last minute by the intervention of Germanos Karavangelis, metropolitan of Kastoria (Museum of the National Struggle, Doc. 60, 1993).

29. The epicenter of the uprising was the Vlach town of Krushevo, where the Greek population and the Vlachs were slaughtered and their properties destroyed. The American consul Pericles Lazzaro wrote to the Consulate General and the American embassy in Constantinople (Museum of the Macedonian Struggle 1993, pp.100–101): "One hour before sunset on the 12th Bahtiar Pasha entered the town and his troops began a systematic looting of the place under the eyes of their officers confining themselves to the Greco-Walachian quarter fine houses.... The soldiers roughly stripped the women of all money, garments.... Many wives and daughters were treated in the most shameful manner. Details which are not fit for reproduction, I personally secured from eye witnesses and sufferers ... 368 residences and 290 shops were burned. The large Greek church was polluted, rifled and burned.... The extraordinary part is that not a Bulg[arian] was touched and soldiers did not even enter the B[ulgarian] quarters.... The case of Krushevo is typical, because it shows that the tactics of the B[ulgarians] consist in compromising Greek towns, and that the Turks [have] neither learned anything, nor forgotten any of their own tricks."

30. Brailsford's (1971, originally published in 1906) statement that "proof of their courage is that they rose at all" (cited by Dakin 1966) merely assumes there was an uprising when there was only a flight to the mountains.

31. Comintern was founded in 1919 by Lenin to organize the communist parties throughout the world and to foster revolutions. Communist parties sent delegates to congresses, usually held in Moscow. It was dissolved by Stalin in 1943 as a goodwill gesture to his World War II allies and reestablished by Stalin in 1947, at the beginning of the Cold War, as Cominform (Communist Information Bureau).

32. As with other symbols and historical facts, Skopje discovered half a century after Ilinden that the uprising in July 1903 was staged by "Macedonians," not by the Bulgarians (Vavouskos 1993).

33. According to the 1905 statistics by the Ottoman Inspector General of the three Macedonian vilayets, Hilmi Pasha, when many slavophones claimed Bulgarian, not "Macedonian" nationality, there were 373,227 Greeks and 207,317 Bulgarians in the Thessaloniki vilayet (Dakin 1966, p. 20, note 63). With the population exchanges between Bulgaria and Greece, thirteen years later, the numbers of Greeks increased dramatically and by 1928 the Bulgarian numbers decreased to about 81,984, many of whom were slavophone Hellenic Macedonians.

34. The English journalist Brailsford (1971, originally published in 1906) wrote from Macedonia: "You may see him any day toward noon — a handsome figure with a black robe, black beard, flowing locks, and chiseled features, prancing up the main street [of Kastoria] on his white horse to his own palace on the top of the hill. He has been dictating policy to the Turkish Kaimakan" (cited by Dakin 1966).

Dakin also wrote, "He showed himself in the villages; he rallied the wavers; he encouraged the faithful to maintain staunch resistance."

35. Dakin (1966, p. 122) gives the following account of a meeting between Kotas and Karavangelis that resulted in bringing Kotas back to Hellenism. The metropolitan said to Kotas, "You were Greeks from the time of Alexander the Great: the Slavs came and enslaved you. Your features are Greek, and the soil you tread is Greek. That is proved by the statues which lie hidden in it. Those too are Greek, and the coins which we find are Greek, and the inscriptions are Greek... Bulgaria had no idea of freeing herself, but the Russians freed her. And do you now expect them to free Macedonia? And do you think it is never possible for European diplomacy to incorporate Macedonia in Bulgaria?"

36. On June 22, 1904, Kotas, perhaps betrayed by former associates, was caught by the Turks and imprisoned in Monastir. After trial, he was condemned to death and hanged on September 27, 1905. He shouted before he died, "Long live the nation" (Dakin 1966, p. 183, note 135). That was the tragic end of this *Grecoman*, who did so much for Macedonia's Hellenism.

37. Dakin (1966, p. 127) relates an interesting conversation between Vangelis and Bulgarians that shows how deep Hellenism was rooted in his heart. Asked to become a committee chief of Strebenko and two other adjoining villages, Vangelis replied that he would do it if they also included the villages of Lehovo, Kleisura, Losnitsa, and Kostarazi, and later the Korestia villages. Popoff, the organizer, reminded Vangelis that "the inhabitants of these Greek and *Grecoman* villages were not wanted in the movement." Vangelis replied, "But are not these people slaves and enemies of the Turks? Do we not get arms from Greece, and do we not tell the world that we are fighting for the cross and freedom — without distinguishing between Greeks and Bulgars.... I don't understand."

38. *Ethniki Amina*, with 3,200 members, superceded the Greek government in many fields of national endeavor: It embarked on a hectic program of raising funds, organized arms caches, sent armed bands to enslaved Greek territories, and supported financially local organizations in occupied territories such as Macedonia, Epirus, Thessaly, and Crete (AHD 1979).

39. The island of Crete remained under Ottoman administration until the late 1800s. Most of the people on the island were Christian in faith, Greek in speech, and Hellenes in sentiment. After the Ottoman departure, Great Britain, France, Italy, and Russia agreed to allow Prince George of Greece to serve as governor of Crete. The island became part of

Greece soon after the Balkan Wars of 1912–1913 (Dakin 1966).

40. By 1904 Metropolitan Karavangelis plunged into the struggle with such enthusiasm and determination that Russia demanded (through its ambassador in Constantinople) his removal from Kastoria. The Patriarch rejected the first request. The pressure on the Patriarch, however, became ruthless, and in 1907 the leader of the Greek Orthodox Church recalled Karavangelis to Constantinople and appointed him to a diocese in Pontos, Asia Minor (Museum of the Macedonian Struggle 1993).

41. On August 31, 1905, near Lake Ochrida, the Bulgarian External Organization (Vrchovist) came to blows with IMRO, and several members from both sides were killed (Dakin 1966).

42. Almost a century later, in 1992, when FYROM took the name "Macedonia" as its own name and copied King Philip's symbol found in Vergina near Pella in Greece for its flag decoration, a few politicians in Europe and the United States blamed Greece for irredentism (see Chapter 7).

43. Even villages in the periphery of the struggle epicenters also suffered financially. The author's village, Krimini in western Macedonia, had to prepare meals regularly for Greek *andartes* for four years and dispatch the food to secret meeting places.

44. Translation of Paillarès's statements from Greek into English by the author.

45. Macedonia was privileged to hear the first Christian messages in Greek from Saint Paul, who preached to the people in Philippi, Thessaloniki, and Veria, where he founded vigorous Christian churches.

46. Hellenism triumphed against Bulgarism in Macedonia because hardly any of the Slavs cared for what to the Greeks was the very essence of life—"liberty to be, to think, to speak, and to do. The Greeks were people believing with reason, not content to live in slavery" (Durant, vol. 2, 1939).

47. Dakin (1966, p. 475) pointed out that "the incoherent mixture of sheer terrorism, social revolution and religious propaganda, combined with the heavy exactions imposed upon the villages, destroyed the gains which over the years had been made by more peaceful means.... By 1907, if not before, the Bulgarian-Macedonian cause was thoroughly discredited."

Chapter 2

1. The underground forces that blew up the Thessaloniki-Veria railroad line were under Constantine Mazarakis, the former officer

attached to the Thessaloniki consulate, and later "Akritas," the leader of armed bands in the Veria-Thessaloniki district during the Macedonian Struggle (Dakin 1966).

2. Immediately after Katerini, Mount Pangeon was liberated by *capetan* Dukas and Nigrita by *capetan* Vlachbei, the two Greek *andartes* who fought with their guerrillas in the Serres-Halkidiki district.

3. The dates cited are based on the Julian calendar. Prince Boris and General Petrov of Bulgaria were six miles from Thessaloniki. When they asked for the city's surrender, the Turkish Governor replied: "I have only one Thessaloniki, which I have already surrendered." Dragoumis raised the Greek flag at the bishop's palace (Dragoumis 1914). With this symbolic act, the Macedonian city that had fallen to the Turks in 1430 was returned to Greece (Karvelis 1996).

4. On June 1, 1913, Greece and Serbia, suspecting secret Bulgarian preparations for further military adventures at their expense, signed an agreement of mutual military support in the event one of the countries was attacked by a third country in the Balkans or if one of the two partners was engaged in war with a third non-Balkan country, meaning an Austrian attack against Serbia (Vattis 2002).

5. These percentages do not correspond to the division of historic Macedonia, but to the area liberated by the four allies, considered as "Macedonia." In reality, Greece's portion approved by the Treaty of Bucharest corresponds to 75 percent of Philip's historic Macedonia. Almost half of today's FYROM is not part of historic Macedonia.

6. When the Soviet army entered Bulgaria in 1944, the Soviets appointed Georgiev as the new Bulgarian prime minister. As governor of the Greek city of Serres from 1916 to 1918, he had committed numerous atrocities against the Greek people of the Serres district (Kargakos 1992).

7. The staggering number of Greek civilians reported lost was perhaps due, in part, to displacement of populations because of the war. About 270,000 civilians were displaced, and only about 140,000 returned to eastern Macedonia and Thrace after the war (Limber 1997).

8. The Bulgarian King Boris and Premier Stamboliiski had no choice but to sign the Treaty of Neuilly (November 27, 1919), accepting its severe punitive terms: extensive military limitations; large war indemnity; and loss of all lands acquired since 1912, including western Thrace (Hupchick and Cox 2001).

9. Nystazopoulou-Pelekidou (1988, p. 29) and Mitsakis (1973, p. 53) reported that 60,000 Bulgarians moved from Macedonia and Thrace

to Bulgaria, and 250,000 Greeks moved from Bulgaria to Greece.

10. The Treaty of Lausanne, signed in 1923 at Lausanne, Switzerland, stipulated a compulsory exchange of populations that ended conflicts between Turkey and the countries of Europe. Turkey gave up the Aegean islands and western Thrace to Greece. Greeks were ordered out of Turkey and Muslims out of Greece, with the exception of Greeks in Constantinople and Muslims in the prefectures of Rhodopi and Xanthi.

Chapter 3

1. In 1885 Bulgarian writers were complaining that the largest part of Pirin (Bulgarian) Macedonia had not developed an ethnic [Macedonian] consciousness (Dakin 1966).

2. For details on Ochrana and Kaltsev see Chapter 4.

3. For details on the resistance encountered by Serbs to Serbianize the Vardar Province see Palmer and King, (1971), pp. 14–15 and 56; also Kofos (1974), p. 6.

4. The Serbian army, defeated by the Austro-Bulgarian pincer, was forced to cross the Albanian mountains, reaching the Adriatic Sea, and then the Greek island of Corfu. According to a different version of Serbia's odyssey (Limber 1997), King Constantine of Greece opposed the Serbs' crossing neutral Greek territory to join the entente allies who had landed in Thessaloniki. France, disregarding Greece's neutrality, allowed the Serbs to settle in Corfu.

5. The Balkan Communist Federation (BCF) was organized in Sofia on January 15, 1920, by the communist parties of the Balkan countries under Comintern's guidance. The BCF's goals were (a) social revolution in the Balkans, and (b) liberation and self-determination of enslaved Balkan people. The reasons for founding BCF left no secret as to its aims: to serve the political aims of Comintern in the Balkans and prepare the ground for the formation of an autonomous Macedonia, with BCF as the Macedonian problem's protagonist. The BCF's Central Committee was composed of three Bulgarian communists (Dimitrov, Kolarov and Kirkov), one Yugoslav, and one Romanian. The KKE and the Turkish Communist Party were not represented in the Central Committee.

6. Translation from Vattis's Greek book by the author.

7. Stamboliiski's postwar Agrarian Union government, an alternative to Lenin's Bolshevism, alienated the Soviet Union, the Bulgarian communists, and the commercial and

professional classes of his country. The communists in particular considered Stamboliiski's Agrarian Union with its socialist reforms as their political enemy. His lack of interest in national territorial expansion won the entente countries' appreciation and a membership in the League of Nations in 1920, but his harsh treatment of IMRO and his socialist reforms provoked its leaders and the nationalist military officers, two decisions that spelled his doom (Hupchick and Cox 2001, p. 39).

8. From 1934 on, IMRO turned into a "racketeering-gangster operation extorting money from Macedonian immigrants in southwestern Bulgaria." It also became involved in illegal drug manufacturing and smuggling, owning and operating numerous opium refineries (Hupchick and Cox 2001, p. 39).

9. Before the ultranationalist IMRO aligned its Macedonian policy with Comintern, much blood was spilled in Bulgaria. In May 1924, a meeting was held in Vienna under Comintern's auspices with IMRO and Bulgarian communist leaders, with Soviets also participating. Comintern proposed that IMRO cooperate with the CPB, a proposal accepted by Tsaoulev, but not by the anticommunist Protogerov and Alexandrov of IMRO. Tsaoulev murdered Alexandrov and fled to a foreign country, but thirty of his followers were arrested by the government and executed. Protogerov resumed IMRO's leadership with the government's blessings, but he was also murdered by Michailov, who immediately assumed IMRO's leadership. Further strife and bloodshed in the two factions after IMRO's split reduced its ability for clandestine work in Greece and Yugoslavia (Vlasidis 1997, 2003).

10. In 1923, a communist attempt to overthrow the Bulgarian government failed, and Kolarov and Dimitrov escaped to Moscow. Soon thereafter, Dimitrov was appointed Comintern's general secretary and Kolarov BCF's general secretary (Vattis 2002).

11. Serafim Maximos went to Greece in 1918 from Thrace and joined the KKE. Of dubious ethnicity, he appeared pro-Bulgarian in his beliefs and actions. In retrospect, it was found that he was a Bulgarian communist agent within the KKE (Vattis 2002).

Chapter 4

1. General Ioannis Metaxas became Greece's dictator in August 1936 and died in January 1941.

2. Germany, Italy, and Japan entered into the Tripartite Pact during World War II. The pact bound the three powers to assist one another in case of attack by a power not yet engaged in the European or Asian war.

3. Upon his return to Belgrade, Cvetkoviae declared triumphantly: "We have secured Thessaloniki; it is a great opportunity and an excellent chance for our country" (Amperiadis 1998).

4. In a speech after Greece's capitulation, Hitler said about his gift to the Bulgarians: "We salute the fact that now at last our allies are in a position to satisfy their national and political aspirations.(We are particularly touched that the injustice once inflicted on Bulgaria is now redressed" (Stassinopoulos 1997). With these few words, Hitler revived the dormant Macedonian problem.

5. The heroism and self-sacrifice of the brave Greek soldiers on the Greek-Bulgarian border April 6–9, 1941, caused enormous admiration among the attackers. The German commandant who took the fortress *Rupel* after three days of bloody fighting congratulated the Greek commander, declaring that it was an honor for the German army to fight against such gallant opponents. Other commanders, including Hitler, also praised Greek valor. But the Nazis showed their harshness and barbaric behavior even as they were praising their opponents. On the first day at the front, when Sergeant Dimitri Intzos's artillery battery surrendered for lack of ammunition after a hard fight all day, the German commander congratulated him and then shot him in cold blood (Stassinopoulos 1997).

6. Even the Nazi Germans described the Bulgarian occupation as "a regime of terror which can only be described as "Balkan'" (Poulton 1995, p. 109).

7. As shown by the examining committee of the War Criminals Service (Amperiadis 1998).

8. Eight men survived the massacre by pretending they were dead on the ground among the bodies (Amperiadis 1998).

9. Marinov, a fascist turned communist after Bulgaria surrendered to the Allies in 1944, served as the Bulgarian ambassador in Paris after the war. The Greek government accused him of war crimes against the Greek people, but he was never tried because Bulgaria, supported by the Soviets, refused to extradite him to Greece.

10. Immediately after his release, Tzimas was appointed secretary of the Athens KKE by the party's General Secretary Siantos, a post he held for less than a year (Mazower 1993).

11. *Ellenikos Laikos Apeleftherotikos Stratos* (ELAS), Greek People's Liberation Army (see next subsection of this chapter).

12. The attachment of the slavophone Greek Macedonian population to Orthodoxy and the Patriarchate and its unique antityranny attitude enhanced its Hellenic beliefs. Unfortu-

nately, it took a long time for the Greek government to realize the innate resistance to servitude of the xenophone Greeks of Macedonia. The fact that they spoke another language was a good reason in the eyes of the government for persecutions (Tsaparas 1996).

13. *Ochrana*, a Slavic word, appeared for the first time in 1903 as the name of the Russian czar's secret service. It was organized by the Russian minister of the interior, murdered by Ochrana a year later. It is said that Ochrana murdered forty thousand Greeks in Macedonia and western Thrace during World War II (Karvelis 1996). More on Ochrana in the next sub-section.

14. After the war, Ravali was arrested and tried in 1946 in Thessaloniki for war crimes committed in the Kastoria District (Koliopoulos 1964).

15. The presence of Kaltsev and his men at the Kleisura massacre was substantiated by witnesses during his second trial in May 1948, who testified that Kaltsev was responsible for turning the Nazis against Kleisura (Koliopoulos 1995, p. 232, note 64).

16. By October 1944, Germans and Italians, with or without the help of Bulgarian *komitadjides,* partially or thoroughly destroyed 250 villages of western Macedonia west of Aliakmon (Papavizas 2002).

17. According to Patrick Evans, a British officer and a Slav sympathizer, there were four kinds of *komitadjides*: (a) those who liked neither Bulgaria nor the conquerors, (b) those who were forced to be armed by the Italians, (c) those who took up arms because they were afraid of ELAS, and (d) the fanatic Bulgarians, who comprised only a small fraction of the total number (FO 371/43764/R14551, August 7, 1944, cited by Koliopoulos 1995).

According to a KKE leader, the 1,800 to 2,000 *komitadjides* of the Kastoria district were divided into three categories: (a) communists; (b) fascists, Bulgarian sympathizers; and (c) nationalists. In reality, there existed many degrees of cooperation among the groups and even among members of the same family. Confused communist slogans and Bulgarian promises encouraged jumping from the *komitadjides* to Tito's partisans, to ELAS and KKE, and later to the communists of the Democratic Army of Greece (DAG).

18. According to George Papandreou, the Greek prime minister during liberation, the KKE was the brain and the spine of EAM and ELAS, a fact known by the majority of the Greek people (Haritopoulos 2001).

19. Farakos (2000), former general secretary of the KKE, wrote about a conversation between Siantos and Ioannides (KKE Politburo member), revealing that behind their sincere war efforts against the occupiers loomed their desire and intentions of seizing power in Athens at war's end.

20. Beginning in the summer of 1943, the KKE Central Committee began degrading EAM's status, which it had worked so hard to organize (Haritopoulos 2001). "From then on, where there is EAM, read KKE," Haritopoulos wrote. From 1943 on, the KKE Central Committee, not EAM's Central Committee, led the resistance in Greece.

21. The Yugoslavs and Bulgarians always use the phrase "Aegean Macedonia" instead of "Greek Macedonia."

22. Quoted in Tsola Dragojceva's *Macedonia: Not a Cause of Discord but a Factor of Good Neighborliness and Cooperation,* pp. 57–58 (cited by Kofos 1995, p. 282, note 18). Italics by the author for emphasis.

23. According to Hammond (1983), the Soviet plan for the Balkans was to create a Soviet-type republic, the Republic of Macedonia, in which Greek Macedonia, Yugoslav Macedonia, and Bulgarian Macedonia would be amalgamated into a non-national republic. People of various ethnic backgrounds, speaking a multitude of languages, would be under one flag, that of a new Soviet satellite.

24. Veremis (1997) reserves the term "Slavomacedonians" for the largest ethnic group in FYROM. Mackridge and Yiannakakis (1997) use the term "Slav-speakers," or Slav-speaking inhabitants of Macedonia, and Koliopoulos (1997) uses the term "Slav Macedonians." In his book *Plundered Loyalties* (1995), Koliopoulos suggested that the term "slavophone Greeks" would be more accurate than the term "Slavomacedonians." The first indicates their probable origin and the second their place of dwelling. In this book I use the term "slavophone Greek Macedonians" for Greek citizens whose political, ethnic, and national affiliations and sentiments are Hellenic.

25. According to studies by the Greek military in 1925, the slavophones could be divided into three categories: (a) slavophones, fanatic Greeks; (b) slavophones, fanatic Bulgarians; and (c) slavophones without an ethnic consciousness (Koliopoulos 1995). This group became the target of Hellenization and Bulgarization. The Greek government's official criterion of ethnic identity was not the language, but the people's sentiments and religion. The Greek government did not consider as Slavomacedonians the inhabitants of Greek Macedonia with Hellenic beliefs and Greek Orthodox Church affiliation; it considered them as slavophone Greek Macedonians (the term used in this book). In contrast, the KKE called all the slavophones Slavomacedonians. At the beginning of World War II the inhabitants of

Greek Macedonia that disagreed with the government position were about eighty thousand.

Of about fifty thousand slavophones living now in Greece, only five thousand declared themselves ethnic Slavs. Greece enacted laws guaranteeing equal rights to all citizens of the country, but refused to recognize the five thousand as "Macedonians." If it did, what then would the almost three million inhabitants of Greek Macedonia call themselves?

26. See Banac 1995, p. 260, note 6.

27. According to Kofos (1995, p. 293, note 47), the real threat to Hellenic Macedonia during the *Dekemvriana* was reported by Brigadier Maclean to the Foreign Office, February 1, 1945, FO371/48181, and by Ajanovski-Oce (1975), pp. 139–45.

28. General Tempo's mission in western Macedonia was a complete failure, with all his proposals rejected by the Greek ELAS leaders, all of them born in Greek Macedonian villages and towns (Hammond 1983).

29. According to Haritopoulos (2001), Tempo wrote in his report to Tito: "These [the Greek communists] annulled the agreement [for the joint Balkan headquarters] ... and especially disagreed on the Macedonian Question.... They refused to recognize the right of our detachments, which entered Greek Macedonia, to speak for an independent Macedonia which, after victory, will acquire complete freedom and the right for autonomy."

30. Instead of approving the formation of a joint Balkan headquarters to coordinate the war against the Germans, proposed by Tempo, Tito backed out of Tempo's outrageous demands and proposed that Greece recognize the slavophones of Greek Macedonia as "Slavomacedonians," without changing the borders (Kofos 1989).

31. George Papandreou, prime minister of Greece during liberation, wrote in his book: "The KKE is not only responsible for the civil war in the mountains; it is also responsible for the terrorization and the dynamic occupation of the country. The country moans from the violence of the KKE organizations. The political opponents are persecuted, not the enemies of the country.... The wind of freedom does not blow in the areas liberated from the Germans. New occupation, just as harsh as the Nazi occupation, is installed by the Communist Party of Greece" ... cited by Giannopoulos 1999....

32. After the war, Tito appointed Vlahov, the Bulgarian-named-Macedonian, president of the parliament of the "People's Republic of Macedonia" in Skopje (Kouzinopoulos 1998).

33. This was the first time a prominent Balkan communist leader admitted publicly that the "Macedonians" were really Slavs, since he proposed to include them in the South Slav federation.

34. Translated from *Otecestven Vestnik (Sofia Daily)* (Martis 2001, p. 101). Italics by the author for emphasis.

35. Reversing a decision by the pre-Tito Yugoslav nationalist government that Vardar Macedonia's inhabitants lacked a clearly defined national Macedonian character of their own, Tito founded the People's Republic of Macedonia, promising "to unite [within Yugoslavia] all parts of Macedonia that the Balkan imperialists (Serbs, Bulgarians, Greeks) occupied in 1913 and 1918" (Woodhouse 1976). To support Tito's plans, Stalin said to a Bulgarian delegation (Dimitrov, Kolarov, and Kostov) in June 1946 that cultural autonomy must be granted to Pirin Macedonia within the framework of Bulgaria as a first step toward the unification of Macedonia.

36. EDES (*Ethnikos Demokratikos Ellenikos Syndesmos*, or the National Republican Greek League) was the second largest resistance group in Greece during the occupation. This nationalist group, organized by Colonel Napoleon Zervas, predominated in Epirus. In 1942 EDES, in cooperation with British saboteurs and an ELAS unit under Aris Velouhiotis, destroyed the Gorgopotamos railway bridge after a hard fight against the Italian troops guarding it and disrupted the railway line between Athens and Thessaloniki. It was the first and last cooperation between the two resistance groups.

D.G. Kousoulas pointed out in his book *Revolution and Defeat: The Story of the Greek Communist Party* (1965) that the ELAS *capetan* Orestis told him [Kousoulas] that Siantos justified the attack by Velouhiotis against EDES during the *Dekemvriana* as an attempt to prevent an attack against EDES by Yugoslav partisans and avoid their entry into Greece (see also Zachariadis's report to the KKE Central Committee, 7th Olomeleia).

37. IMRO has been revived in Skopje under the initials VMRO (*Vatresna Makedonska Revolutionna Organizacija*). Today VMRO appears democratic, but to FYROM's neighbors "Nomen est omen" (the name is a pledge).

38. Ioannides (1979), a member of the KKE Politburo, denied he ever signed an agreement with the CPB. Kofos (1964) also stated that there is no evidence that such an agreement was ever signed. Vattis (2002, p. 241), however, reported that a copy of such an agreement was published for the first time in the German newspaper *People's Observer*.

39. According to Koliopoulos (1995), the Slavomacedonian leaders' demands for autonomy were opportunistic but stronger than their communist beliefs or Bulgarian affiliations.

Their attachment to Yugoslavia after 1943, as their attachment to Bulgaria before, was the last resort of this Greek slavophone group to avoid the harsh treatment by the Metaxas government or by other Greek governments. Unfortunately, foreign observers who visited Macedonia mistook the vacillating tendencies of the slavophones for autonomy as true, unshaken beliefs.

40. Ochrana, and even IMRO members, joined the KKE or the CPM and fought as SNOF guerrillas with ELAS or Yugoslav partisans. Other Ochranists and IMRO members joined the Gotse battalion organized by the KKE Slavomacedonian guerrillas (Michailides 2000).

41. According to Patrick Evans, British liaison officer with ELAS, the purpose of SNOF (a variation of EAM) was to attract the Slavomacedonian element into EAM's orbit, a partially successful movement. At the beginning SNOF did a good job, penetrating areas hitherto held by the Germans, not only for the benefit of ELAS, but also of the allies (cited by Koliopoulos 1995). The Greek authorities and ELAS, however, suspected Evans of encouraging the autonomists in western Macedonia (Hammond 1991; Rossos 1991).

42. On the surface, the German-supported Ochrana (Voluntary Battalion) was unrelated to the ultranationalist Bulgarian Ochrana.

43. According to Koliopoulos (1995), there appeared to be a connecting force among the Slavic organizations, the desire for autonomy of a fraction of Slavomacedonians, inspired by Bulgarians or Yugoslavs, operating freely within the Greek communist resistance. Ochrana (like the Komitet before) and SNOF were undoubtedly branches of the same tree. Several observers believed Ochrana and SNOF, opposite on the surface, were actually connected by a secret agreement.

44. We will see him again in Greek Macedonia during the Greek Civil War of 1946–1949. In 1949 he was appointed by the KKE General Secretary, Nikos Zachariadis, Minister of Supply in the communist government of the mountains (Averoff-Tossizza 1978).

45. The turning of the tide was evidenced by the overthrow of Mussolini (July 25, 1943), the invasion of Sicily by the Allies (July 10, 1943), and the signing of an armistice between Italy and the Allies (September 3, 1943).

46. The Germans arrested Kaltsev on September 9, 1944, immediately after Bulgaria declared war against Germany and incarcerated him in a concentration camp in Skopje. When the Germans left Yugoslavia, he was handed over to the pro-Nazi Albanian partisans, who delivered him to *capetan* Ourdas, commissar of a Slavomacedonian battalion of the 30th ELAS Regiment. Before defecting to Yugoslavia, Our-

das delivered him to ELAS after the German withdrawal from Greece. After the Varkiza Agreement in March 1945, ELAS delivered him to the British. In his second trial in Thessaloniki by a Greek court, he was found guilty for war crimes and executed (Koliopoulos 1995, p. 224, note 31).

47. ELAS allowed formation of Slavomacedonian battalions within its regiments, one battalion per regiment, such as Gotse's battalion within ELAS's 28th Regiment, 9th Division, with Gotse as commissar; and a second battalion in the Kaymaktsalan area. Both of these Slavomacedonian battalions crossed the border and joined Tito's partisans from October 15 to early November 1944.

Chapter 5

1. Milovan Djilas, Tito's righthand man and a Yugoslav vice president, said in an interview (see newspaper *Ta Nea*, February 21, 1994): "Formation of the People's Republic of Macedonia was the choice of the times and an effort to neutralize the Bulgarian irredentism.... It is foolishness and megalomania [for Skopje] to use Philip's symbols." Djilas also remarked in his book *Conversations with Stalin* (1962, p. 36): "But I do not believe that even he [Dimitrov] adhered to the viewpoint that the Macedonians were a separate nationality."

2. Feigenbaum (1997) wrote that "the Skopjans will have a hard time in the future to reconcile an ethnic integration in a polyglot conglomerate with nation building."

3. *Vardarska Banovina* (Vardar Province, South Serbia) included the present area of the FYROM, Kosovo Polje i. Metohija, and the territory that lies south of Nis to FYROM's border. The People's Republic of Macedonia received only a part of Vardar Province, not all of it (Templar 2002).

4. Tito wrote to Tempo on December 6, 1943: "The Macedonian people have the right to self-determination, and even to secession.... the Macedonian people have the right to join the federal community of other peoples. This is what they, in fact, should be doing today by joining the common struggle of the peoples of Yugoslavia against the German conquerors and Bulgarian occupiers." From Josip Broz Tito, *Sabrana djela* (Collected Works), 1977–1984 (cited by Banac 1995, p. 261, note 7).

5. Dimitar Vlahov was a Bulgarian who exchanged the crown of his country for Bulgarian communism, and later for the Slavomacedonian red star (Kouzinopoulos 1999).

6. It is clear from his diary that the Bulgarian communist leader did not believe there ever existed a Macedonian ethnicity in geographi-

cal Macedonia: just Greeks, Bulgarians and Serbs.

7. Poulton (1995, p. 116) remarked that as soon as the People's Republic of Macedonia was established (1943–1944), its new authorities realized that the new "nation" needed a written language. The communist authorities selected the spoken dialect of the northern section of the Vardar Province, but because this dialect was too close to the Serbian, they began using the Bitola-Veles dialect, which Sofia insists is Bulgarian.

8. Details about the language of ancient Macedonians appear in the subsection of this chapter titled "Who Were the Macedonians?"

9. Feigenbaum (1997), writing about the French national integration, said: "The dominant characteristic of a nation is its language. Historically, language seems to have generated more intense bonds of solidarity than geographic proximity or even race."

10. In April 1994 the Bulgarian Education Minister Todorov refused to sign the protocol recognizing the new Skopje language as "Macedonian," declaring that the language in Skopje is a Bulgarian dialect (Vattis 2002).

11. The 1991 FYROM census showed 474 Greeks, whereas independent observers raised the number to 20,000 Greeks and 1,370 Bulgarians (see *Economikos Tachydromos*, December 25, 1993, to January 7, 1994, p. 18). In 1989 the Bulgarians in a conference in Copenhagen announced that the time had arrived to find out what had happened to one million Bulgarians in the People's Republic of Macedonia (Kathimerini 1996).

12. During World War II, when the Bulgarian army (Hitler's allies) occupied Vardar Province, the population welcomed the Bulgarian army of occupation with great enthusiasm: fireworks, Bulgarian flags, etc. The people had not yet been bent to restorative visions of Macedonian grandeur by the Yugoslav communists or been told they were "Macedonians," not Bulgarians (Vattis 2002).

13. The Albanian minority in the People's Republic of Macedonia is outnumbered by the "Macedonian" majority, an artificial group created for political purposes by Serbia, composed of Slavs, Karakachani, Vlachs, Jews, Greeks, Turks and gypsies. The Slavic population is predominantly Bulgarian by ancestry, according to Feldman (1992).

14. It is to be regretted that we have very limited information on Cominform's and Stalin's manipulations of the Macedonian issue.

15. According to the book *Documents on the Struggle of the Macedonian People for Independence and a Nation-State*, vol. 2, (University of Cyril and Methodius, 1985), "In 1939 about 100,000 Macedonians [Slavomacedonians] lived in Greece." According to this volume, p. 167, in 1985 200,000 to 250,000 Slavomacedonians lived in Greece! The actual number in 1939 was 99,000, many of them slavophones with Hellenic consciousness. In 1985 about 47,000 slavophones lived in Greece, a country of eleven million people (Tsalouhides 1994). Of the 47,000, only about 1,800 voted for the Rainbow Party, a new political Slavomacedonian organization in Greece. The reduction from 99,000 to 47,000 is due to emigration of a large number of communist Slavomacedonians to Skopje, to self-exile behind the Iron Curtain when DAG lost the civil war, and to losses because of the war.

16. A very good example of this is the work of the brothers Konstantin and Dimitar Miladinov, *Boulgarski Narodni Pesni* (Bulgarian Ethnic Songs) printed in Zagreb in 1861. The popular songs were reprinted in the 1980s in Skopje as *Makedonski Narodni Pesni* (Macedonian Ethnic Songs) (Nystazopoulou-Pelekidou 1988).

17. The historically established term *Hellenistic Age* was renamed "Macedonian Period" (i.e., Slavomacedonian Period) by Skopje history revisionists who want the world to forget that Alexander's conquest changed the course of history by fusing the Greek and ancient Middle Eastern civilizations (Ferrill 1988).

18. If history accepts that ancient Macedonians and other inhabitants of Macedonia were Slavicized following the Slav migration to the Balkans in the sixth century A.D., as the Skopjan historians want the world to believe, we must admit they ceased to be Macedonians; they became Slavs (according to the amalgamation theory). In the same context, if history accepts Borza's (1990) contention that the ancient Macedonians were Hellenized by the middle of the fifth century B.C., then we must admit they ceased to exist as a hypothetical non-Greek ethnic group prevailing before the fifth century; they became Greeks.

19. "The present-day Hellenic nation is the result of social, civic, and linguistic amalgamation of more than 230 tribes (including the Macedonians) speaking more than 200 dialects that claimed descent from Hellen [and Orseis], son of Deukalion," wrote Templar (2003).

20. *Hellenismus* is a concept encompassing the Greek city-states' culture, including that of the Seleucid parts of western Asia and Ptolemaic Egypt, summarized in one word by Droysen (1877–1878). For modern Hellenic Macedonia, *Hellenismus* reflects the power of Hellenic Macedonian ethnic pride, culture, and identity (see the next subsection of this chapter).

21. There are exceptions to this rule. For instance, the so-called *Grecomans* of modern

times, speaking Slavic, have been known to have strong Hellenic consciousness (Dakin 1966).

22. The five centuries following the collapse of the Mycenaean civilization between 1200 and 1100 B.C.

23. See Pandermali-Poulaki (2003).

24. We know from inscriptions that the Magnetes (Magnes's descendants) spoke an Aeolic dialect of the Greek language. Therefore, we presume that the early Macedonians, even as far back as the Greek Dark Ages, also spoke an Aeolic dialect of the Western group (Hammond 1989, pp. 12–13).

25. According to Herodotus, the Dorians moved to southern Thessaly and southwest Macedonia before the Trojan War. After the Trojan War this Greek-speaking tribe, known as "Makedoni," moved south to the Peloponnesus (Poulton 1995, p. 12).

26. Hammond (1986) supports Herodotus and Thucydides (Thuc. Pelop. II.99) on the Argos-Macedonia connection. Theopompus (Theop. in F.H.G. fr. 30, 12, 283) gave a different, but equally convincing account of the Temenid-Macedonian connection. He mentioned Ceranus (Caranus, or Karenos, Ionic form of Karanos), brother of the king of Argos, who abandoned the city and went to Macedonia, defeated several opposing clans, and settled in Aegae, where he became king in the ninth century B.C. Herodotus's and Theopompus's stories agreed on one thing: that there was a Macedonian-Temenidae connection. Daskalakis (1965) believes that Ceranus founded the Macedonian dynasty about two centuries before Perdiccas.

27. Italics for emphasis by the author.

28. Over the years, Macedonia had several names (Templar 2003): At first it was called *Emathia* after its leader Emathion (*amathos* = sand). Later it was called *Maketia* or *Makessa*, and finally *Makedonia* (Macedonia). The word *Makedonia* is derived from the Doric/Aeolic word *makos* (in Attic *mekos* = length) (see Homer, *Odyssey* VII.106). According to Mitsakis (1973), the name "Makedonia" derives from the very ancient Greek adjective *makednos* (= tall), found for the first time in the Homeric poems as "μακεδνής αιγείροιο" (= tall poplar tree).

29. Interestingly, the Macedonians' Hellenism and use of a Hellenic dialect by the ancient Macedonians had not been disputed before the establishment of communism in the Balkans in the 1940s.

30. The Macedonian state included the city-states of Imathia, Pieria, Bottiaia, Bisaltia, Odomantis, Edonis, Mygdonia, Crestonia, Sintiki, Elimeia, Orestis, Eordea, Almopia, Lyncestis, Pelagonia, and Macedonian Paeonia. The latter is the part of Paeonia that lies south of the narrow pass at the area of Demir Kapija (FYROM) (Templar 2002).

31. Some other well-known dialects were Attic, Cypriot, Arcadic, Aetolic, Acarnanic, Macedonian, and Locric. Livy (*History of Rome*, XXXI. 29) wrote: "The Aetolians, the Acarnanians, the Macedonians, men of the same speech, are united or disunited by trivial causes that arise from time to time" (Templar 2003).

32. In his book *The Genius of Alexander the Great,* Hammond stated: "The cities [built by Alexander in Asia] spread Greek skills in agriculture, land reclamation and capitalism, and a knowledge of the Greek language, which was the official medium of all cities. The language, known as *koine,* was based on the Attic dialect modified by Alexander and his staff."

33. All inscriptions on artifacts, including on those found in Trebeniste and Oleveni near Bitola, are in pure Greek. Non-Greek names are found only in the expansions of Macedonia such as Paeonia, Thrace, etc. (Templar 2002). The National Research Center of Athens has collected five thousand Greek inscriptions and names of common people from Macedonia and published them as a book (Martis 2003, p. 72). Also, archaeological evidence from Aegae, the first Macedonian capital, showed that the common Macedonian people had Hellenic names (Nystazopoulou-Pelekidou 1988, p. 22). It was easy for the ancient Macedonians of the fifth century B.C. to adapt to the Attic (Athenian) dialect during Philip's reign because they were already speaking a Hellenic dialect of the Aeolic group.

34. The *Military Yugoslav Encyclopedia* (1974, Letter M, p. 219), an anti-Hellenic publication, states: "u doba rimske invazije, njihov jezik bio greki, ali se dva veka ranije dosta razlikovao od njega, mada ne toliko da se ta tva naroda nisu mogla sporazumerati." (At the time of the Roman invasion their language was Hellenic, but two centuries before it was different enough, but not as much as the two people [Macedonians and the other Greeks] could not understand one another; see Templar 2003.)

35. One of the most convincing linguistic arguments proving the ancient Macedonians' Hellenism was brought forth by Hatzidakis, who showed that the Greek dialects spoken by both the ancient Macedonians and the other Greeks belonged to the Indo-European language group called "centum." In contrast, the ancient non-Greek Thracians and Illyrians spoke a language that belonged to the group called "satem," a linguistic group completely distinct from "centum," a fact proving that the so-called Macedonian dialect could not have been a Thraco-Illyrian dialect (Hatzidakis, discussed by Mitsakis 1973).

36. Herodotus wrote that in 513 B.C. King Alexander I executed the Persian emissaries because they had offended the palace women and sent this message to the Persian king: "Tell the king who sent you here [to Macedonia] that a Hellene received you well and offered you gastronomic pleasures" (Herodotus V. 20, 22; VIII. 137; IX. 45).

37. The historian Herodotus (V. 22), speaking about Perdiccas I, the first Macedonian king, and his descendants, affirmed that "Ἕλληνας δὲ εἶναι τούτους τοὺς ἀπό Περδίκκεω γεγονότας" (= Hellenes are those people who are descendants of Perdiccas).

38. The Macedonians and the Illyrians did not speak the same language. Polybius in book XXVIII, paragraphs 8 and 9, stated that the Macedonians were using translators when they were communicating with the Illyrians. Perseus, the Macedonian king, sent Adaaeus of Berroia (who spoke only Greek) and Pleuratus, the exile Illyrian living in Perseus's court, as a translator (because he spoke the Illyrian language) on a mission to the Illyrian King Genthius (169 B.C.). The Illyrians and Macedonians were vicious enemies (Templar 2003).

39. Hammond explained in his book *The Macedonian State* (1989, p. 13, note 29) the reason why Badian did not consider the ancient Macedonians Greek. He also stated that Badian in his *Greeks and Macedonians* (1982, pp. 33–51) disregarded the evidence as stated in *The History of Macedonia* by Hammond and Griffith (1979, pp. 39–54) because it was against his beliefs and convictions (Templar 2003).

40. In contrast, Wilcken (1967, p. 23) pointed out that the ancient Macedonian state institutions were similar to those of the Mycenaean and Spartan institutions.

41. The way of life of the Molossians, Chaones, Thesprotians, Acarnanians, Aetolians, and Macedonians also differed in many ways from the Athenian way of life (Errington 1990, p. 4).

42. Borza (1990, p. 5) pointed out that "Only recently have we begun to clarify these muddy waters by realizing the Demosthenes corpus for what it is: oratory designed to sway public opinion at Athens and thereby to formulate public policy. The elusive creature, Truth, is everywhere subordinate to its expressive servant, Rhetoric."

43. The renowned historian Will Durant wrote (Volume 2, *The Life of Greece*, 1939, p. 437): "Under [King] Archaelaus (399 B.C.) Macedonia passed out of Barbarism and became one of the powers of the Greek world: good roads were laid down, ... a handsome new capital was built, Pella, and many Greek geniuses, like Timotheus, Zeuxis, and Euripides found welcome."

44. When the author was a student at the Tsotyli High School (*Gymnasion Tsotyliou*) in Greek western Macedonia, the entire school body had picnics and history excursions in a nearby village. The four hundred students were asked to comb the area of a quarter square mile, searching through the scrub or digging the ground superficially, looking for artifacts from an age long past: the Greek Macedonian era before and after the early Macedonians abandoned Argos Orestikon near the modern city of Kastoria, crossed the mountains of Upper (western) Macedonia, and colonized the fertile plains west and southwest of present-day Thessaloniki. Searching year after year, the students had accumulated an interesting coin collection exhibited in the high school building. All coins had Greek inscriptions, easily read by the students.

45. "His [Alexander the Great's] belief in the validity of the Greek outlook of his time was not modified by his acquaintance with Egyptian, Babylonian and Indian ideas.... Alexander believed that the best way to spread Greek culture and civilization was by founding cities throughout Asia" (Hammond 1997). Durant (vol. 2, 1939) also wrote: "At the same time [Alexander] drafted 30,000 Persian youth, had them educated on Greek lines, and taught them the Greek manual of war."

46. The Macedonian King Alexander I was named Philhellene by the Theban poet Pindaros for the same reason Jason of Pherrae was called Philhellene, which is why Alexander the Great did not touch Pindaros's house when he ordered his soldiers to burn Thebes. The title *Philhellene* in antiquity meant *philopatris* (lover of the homeland or a patriot) (see Plato, *Politics* 470E) (Templar 2003).

47. Carelessly using the word "Macedonian" to describe the Slavs, Albanians, Bulgarians, and other smaller ethnic groups in FYROM, as some anthropologists, NGOs, and other organizations do, enhanced the Skopjan politicians' intransigence, arrogance, and unwillingness to cooperate in solving FYROM's name problem.

48. By July 2003 the legislation of twelve U.S. states (California, Florida, Illinois, Louisiana, Massachusetts, Michigan, Missouri, New Hampshire, Ohio, Pennsylvania, Rhode Island, and Texas) passed resolutions signed by the governors recognizing that the ancient Macedonians were Hellenes and the inhabitants of the northern province of Greece, Macedonia, are their Hellenic descendants. Many other examples ascribing Macedonianism to the Greeks of Macedonia have been cited in this book's pages.

49. In 1960 a group of Greeks invited by the Yugoslav government to visit the Lake Ochrida district was entertained by a Yugoslav scientist who exhibited several archaeological findings

with Greek inscriptions. When the Yugoslav attempted to inform the Greeks that the inscriptions were written in Slavic, one of the Greeks retorted: "I, a Greek, can read the inscriptions; you, as a Yugoslav, can you do it?" (Vattis 2002).

50. Only athletes of Hellenic origin could participate. The Macedonian kings Alexander I (498–454 B.C.), Perdiccas II (454–413 B.C.), and Archaelaus (413–399 B.C.) won the Olympic Games (Herodotus V. 22). King Philip scored victories in three successive Olympics (356, 352, and 348 B.C).

51. The Skopje theorists claim that no Greek inscriptions are found to have been written before the fourth century B.C. That is not correct. Macedonian coins with Greek inscriptions from the fifth century are now exhibited in the Archaeological Museum of Thessaloniki: Octadrachm of Alexander I, 478 B.C.; the ring of Sindos, 480 B.C.; and coins of King Archaelaus, 413 B.C. Also, ten years ago a silver decanter dated back to 500 B.C. was found in Vergina bearing the name *Peperias* inscribed in unmistaken Greek characters (Tsalouhides 1994, p. 307).

52. The historian Koliopoulos (1997, p. 47) commented negatively on the anthropological forays into Greek Macedonia: "Deconstructionist anthropological forays into the Greek Slav Macedonian past, in particular, have gone a long way towards establishing generally held notions about Greece's Slav Macedonians on the basis of weak but seldom questioned evidence.... [R]egularly recycled 'evidence' [is] drawn from sources produced by the misinformation machine of the communist regime of the Yugoslav Republic of Macedonia...."

53. Shea (1997, p. 270) reported that students at the University of Skopje demonstrated against the Albanians with the slogan "Let the damned *schiptars* [ethnic slur for Albanians] know the Macedonian name never dies."

54. Several modern historians pointed out that only communism could provide the theoretical base and the necessary force to push for a separate "Macedonian nation."

55. "The claims to Greek national identity of people who were born in Greece but who speak Macedonian [Slavonic] and not Greek are just as legitimate as the claims to Macedonian national identity of people who earlier in their lives identified themselves as Greeks," wrote Danforth (2000). Such people must admit they are Greek Macedonians whose ancestors learned to speak a Slavic dialect.

56. The *prosfyges* are descendants of ancient Greeks, including ancient Macedonians, who either colonized various areas of what presently are Russia, Ukraine, Georgia, Bulgaria, Turkey, and the Middle East or followed Alexander the

Great. These Hellenes simply came home after at least two and a half millennia of spreading the Hellenic spirit, culture, language, and civilization. They had every right to return home, just as the Jews did, and they are still doing so (Templar 2003).

Chapter 6

1. After Stalin made a tick on the paper where the future of the Balkans had been decided, Churchill remarked: "Might it not be thought rather cynical if it seemed we had disposed of those issues, so fateful to millions of people, in such an offhand manner? Let us burn the paper." "No, you keep it," said Stalin (Churchill 1953, pp. 227–28).

2. Evans was referring to the Slav-speakers of western Macedonia as "Slavs of Greece," "Slavomacedonians," "Macedonians," and "Slavophone minority" (Evans's report of August 1944, cited by Koliopoulos 1995).

3. Though he was invited by the Communist Party of Greece, the Soviet Marshal Tolbukin refused to cross the Greek-Bulgarian border into Greece (Kofos 1989).

4. For the British pressure on Bulgaria to withdraw from the occupied territories see Stoyan Rachev, *Anglo-Bulgarian Relations During the Second World War (1939–1944)* (Sofia: Sofia Press, 1981), pp. 189–204.

5. PAO, the largest Greek nationalist organization in the Bulgarian-occupied territories and an implacable enemy of the KKE, fought valiantly against two enemies: the Bulgarian occupiers that remained in Greece even after the Germans left and the ELAS communists who repeatedly assisted the Bulgarian fascists-turned-communists (Papathanasiou 1997, pp. 623–27, 641–52).

6. PEEA was EAM's government of the mountains during the occupation.

7. According to Vattis (2002), some Bulgarian army troops assisted ELAS during the fighting in Athens.

8. "The fierceness of the Greek Civil War in the second half of the 1940s can be understood only in the light of the Communist Party's association with sedition in Greek Macedonia," wrote Koliopoulos (1997, p. 46).

9. For a summary on Yugoslavia's role in the Greek Civil War of 1946–1949, see Nicholas Pappas, "The Soviet-Yugoslav Conflict and the Greek Civil War," in *At the Brink of War and Peace: The Tito-Stalin Split in a Historical Perspective,* ed. W.S. Vucinich (New York: Brooklyn College Press, 1982).

10. After thirty-nine days (December 3, 1944, to January 11, 1945) the vicious fighting in Athens between ELAS and the Greek

government forces and the British stopped with the defeat of the ELAS forces. The ELAS and KKE leaders finally capitulated and signed the Varkiza Agreement on February 12, 1945. ELAS was to disarm and the KKE was to become a legal party in Greece (Averoff-Tossizza 1978).

Not surprisingly, the Left and Right violated many of the articles of the Varkiza Agreement even before the ink had dried on the paper where the signatures were affixed. While a handful of KKE leaders were negotiating the practical implications of the agreement, other KKE leaders were secretly engaged in concealing ELAS's best arms and ammunition, working closely with trusted and loyal EAM leaders (Averoff-Tosizza 1978). Preparations for the new civil war had begun before the fighting in Athens was officially over (Papavizas 2002, pp. 136–38). The Right, on the other hand, immediately after the agreement was signed, launched the so-called White Terror, the indiscriminate terrorization of the Left by clandestine right-wing gangs and paramilitary groups tolerated or encouraged by the governments (Smith 1995, pp. 91–92; Stassinopoulos 1997, pp. 214–16, 248–59). Churchill, who had suggested the 90 percent agreement with Stalin, had lost interest in honoring it (for details see also Papavizas 2002, Appendix 1).

11. During the Seventh Plenum of the KKE Central Committee held behind the Iron Curtain after the communist defeat in Greece, the party members learned for the first time their leader, Nikos Zachariadis, was first a Soviet communist and second a Greek communist.

12. During Zachariadis's absence, Giorgos Siantos was the KKE's general secretary, but in reality, Ioannides made the important decisions. Siantos was used later as a scapegoat for Ioannides's mistakes. He was removed from the party and accused of being a British spy. He was reinstated in 1957 (Averoff-Tosizza 1978).

13. Lavrenti Beria was considered in glasnost-era sources "as one of the most loathsome monsters of a loathsome system" (Thurston 1996).

14. The Second Plenum of the KKE Central Committee, held on February 16, 1946, decided that armed conflict was the most probable course to solve the political problem in Greece (Smith 1995).

15. After the war, Markos Vafiadis, the DAG commander, admitted in his book Democracy and Totalitarianism that he had met at Petric with Bulgarian and Yugoslav communists leaders who encouraged the Greek communist leaders to organize the Greek communist guerrillas and promised lavish military support. Vafiadis entered Greece from Bulkes in the fall of 1946. During a meeting of high-echelon KKE leaders in the Hassia mountain range on October

18–20, 1946, with Vafiadis presiding, it was decided to form a "Supreme Command of the Rebel Forces" and officially name the KKE guerrillas the "Democratic Army of Greece" (AHD 1980).

16. Gagoulias (2001), a communist leader, shed new light on life at Bulkes. He painted a bleak picture of the terrorization of comrades by OPLA (Organosi Perifrourisis tou Laikou Agona, Organization for the Protection of People's Struggle) thugs who, under Ioannides's and Roussos's thumb, forced Stalinist orthodoxy and the hard dictatorship of the proletariat on comrades who expressed the slightest criticism of the system. Bulkes became a dreaded place, a "hell on earth," where Zachariadis's "draconian orthodoxy" was strictly enforced.

According to Yiatroudakis (1998), a communist who spent thirty years in exile in Tashkent, Uzbekistan, disgrace, suspicion, terror of snitches, humiliation, and torture were the order of each day at Bulkes. Scores of communists were thrown into the Danube River and many perished at Devil's Island on the Danube.

Zachariadis visited Bulkes on April 12–14, 1946, after he returned from Crimea, where he had met with Stalin (Stassinopoulos 1997). He spoke to the veteran communists announcing the beginning of a new phase in the conflict: "You have to make up your minds that you will return to Greece with your rifles at the ready, because the monarcho-fascist regime there has planned civil war."

17. Thirty-five years later, Vafiadis wrote in his memoirs (1992) that with Ioannides's orders, Bulkes' administration began a real slaughter, murdering communists for the slightest rule violation. The bodies were dumped in a well in the camp. More than four hundred bodies were thrown in the well.

18. In his memoirs, Markos Vafiadis (1992) also pointed out that Zachariadis never changed his mind about his intentions to hand Greek Macedonia to the Bulgarians with the Fifth Plenum's decision. Zachariadis said on October 14, 1950, after the defeat: "The KKE recognizes the right for autonomy, and even separation, for the Slavomacedonian people of Aegean Macedonia. The Fifth Plenum acted correctly voting for the separation."

19. Markos Vafiadis, Tito's friend, born in Asia Minor and living in Thessaloniki, fell into a trap, presumably to please his friend. He committed the same error for which he blamed Zachariadis years later. His remarks condoned Tito's falsification of history about the Slav-speakers being "Macedonians." By doing so, he condemned the Greek Macedonians, the overwhelming majority in Macedonia, whose ancestors lived in Macedonia for hundreds of

generations, depriving them of their Greek Macedonian ethnicity and pride.

20. One of the reasons the KKE lost the civil war was its inability to recruit large numbers of men and women to offset the more numerous national army. That is why the party decided on forceful recruitment of people (both Greek-speaking and Slav-speaking young men and women) every time DAG occupied a village or a town for a short period of time. The reason that 45 percent of DAG's fighting force consisted of Slav-speakers is not because all were separatists with anti-Hellenic feelings (except for a small percentage subjected to NOF's propaganda), but simply because their villages, being near the border, were subjected to occupation and forceful recruitment by DAG.

21. Italics by the author for emphasis.

22. Direct quotation from Kofos 1995, note 90, p. 307.

23. The Greeks and the Bulgarians believe that a separate non-Greek Macedonian ethnicity does not exist. Also, most world-renowned historians believe that the Skopjan theory of two separate people, Slav "Macedonians" and Greeks, contradicts a very important fact curiously ignored by many anthropologists: there are millions of indigenous Hellenic Macedonians, speaking only Greek, who have lived in Macedonia for countless generations. In contrast, FYROM Slavs, who live in parts of geographical Macedonia, lack racial or linguistic unity and speak a dialect claimed by a neighbor to be Bulgarian (see Chapter 5). The small slavophone minority in Greece is a linguistic group and not an ethnic minority. Many of the slavophones consider themselves Greeks (Zotiades 1961), often called "Slavophone Greeks" (Barker 1950).

24. Averoff-Tossizza (1978) offered no proof that Markos Vafiadis had indeed renegotiated agreements previously made at Petric in 1945 or agreed to place DAG under Yugoslavia's protection.

25. It became evident from available KKE documents that in 1947 the KKE's strategy had concentrated on "liberating" an area in northern Greece, including Thessaloniki (Smith 1995). These plans must have been made by the KKE leadership before Zachariadis's talks with Stalin and Tito. Vasilis Bartziotas (DAG major-general) was ordered to organize armed bands to support the operation against Thessaloniki. Promises of Yugoslav aid for the operation were given to Vafiadis through Ioannides, a KKE Politburo member (see the leftist paper *Avgi*, December 9 and 12, 1979, on Ioannides's telegram to Markos and the Moscow talks). The British legation in Sofia had also learned that inclusion of Thessaloniki in Zachariadis's plans

would undoubtedly receive Soviet support (Kofos 1995, p. 291).

26. The Third Plenum, held in Yugoslavia in September 1947, was a call to arms by the KKE (Smith 1995). Its resolution, which openly supported DAG and approved the Politburo's decision of February 17, 1947, to escalate the war, ended the KKE's legality in Greece. Zachariadis sacrificed the privilege of his party's legality, and by September 1947 he ordered full mobilization of the KKE's forces.

27. On February 4, 1949, the DAG radio station announced a decision made unanimously on January 31 by the KKE Fifth Plenum, thoroughly controlled by Zachariadis, to relieve Markos Vafiadis of all party responsibilities on the grounds he was gravely ill. At the same meeting, Zachariadis accused Vafiadis of defeatism. Many believe today that only Vafiadis's prestige saved him from execution. Others insist that Vafiadis, who escaped to Albania, was saved by the death squad sent by Zachariadis to assassinate him (Gage 1983). After his flight, he disappeared behind the Iron Curtain. He survived and returned to Greece in 1975.

On the same subject, the KKE political commissar Gagoulias reported in his book (2001) that at the Third KKE Conference in Bucharest in 1950, after the KKE's defeat, Zachariadis branded Vafiadis "a corrupt adventurer and an enemy agent."

28. Italics for emphasis by the author.

29. According to Papaioannou (1990), the communist colonel who interviewed Zachariadis in Sorgout, Siberia, after the war, the Party told the slavophones of Macedonia that they were neither Greeks nor Bulgarians. They were Slavomacedonians who would be equal with the Greeks if DAG won the war. Papaioannou also revealed that Zachariadis committed a "treasonous" act in 1949 when he went a step further, pressing the Fifth Plenum to change the platform from "equality of the minorities" within Greece to detachment of Macedonia from Greece. The pressure by Zachariadis was a "tragic" mistake.

30. Kofos (1995, p. 276, note 3) cited Petar Galabov's *Cominform's Discrimination and Francolevantistic Intimations* (Skopje: Iselenicki Kalendar, 1982), pp. 79–85, for his remarks on the silence by the KKE's leaders on the Macedonian issue.

31. Regrettably, the world forgot the rivers of blood spilled by the Greek people to thwart communism's advance into the Balkans during the terrible 1940s and condoned the use by the communist perpetrators of the Macedonian name that never belonged to them.

32. Nikos Zachariadis, whose implacable malice and misguided military strategy led to disaster for the KKE, disappeared behind the

Iron Curtain. The Sixth Plenum of the KKE Central Committee in 1956 removed him both as general secretary and from the Politburo. The Seventh Plenum in 1957 branded him a traitor and removed him from the party altogether. He died under mysterious circumstances in Sorgout, Siberia, in 1973 (Papaioannou 2001).

33. Dimitri Vlantas, KKE Central Committee member, wrote in his book *Civil War, 1945–1949* (1981): "Zachariadis acted like he was a slave of the Russian leadership." In his first book, *Betrayed Revolution* (1977), he wrote: "The second basic reason for the defeat was the CPSU's leadership [Stalin]. From March 1946 he pushed the KKE toward civil war to serve Russian interests.... It would have been unthinkable to imagine that ... the KKE leadership would have started an armed struggle without the Soviet leadership's promise for aid."

Chapter 7

1. Loss of Greek citizenship and confiscation of property was applied to all who fled to Yugoslavia, regardless of language. When Greece allowed the return of the self-exiled refugees, for those in Skopje who had changed ethnicity and name, it was a matter of identification before reentering Greece. The Slav-speakers who fled to the other Eastern Bloc countries were repatriated, together with other DAG communists after 1974 (Vattis 2002).

2. If Greece had capitulated to Tito's demands recognizing the 35,894 slavophones remaining in Greek Macedonia as "Macedonians," what would then be the ethnicity of millions of indigenous Hellenic Macedonians?

3. The historian Koliopoulos (1997, p. 39) addressed the language problem as follows: "By the time the dispute [over Macedonia] is over, it is most likely that those who could credibly be described as Slav Macedonians will not fit the image fashioned for them by those who have been striving to discern an identity different from that of the rest of the present-day Greeks.... Instead of caring for their vanishing Slavonic idiom, they will be employing tutors from England, Germany or France to instruct their progeny in one of the languages of these European countries, as many other Greeks are doing these days."

4. Skopje removed every Greek and Byzantine achievement and famous artist from their natural environment and treated the achievers as Hellenized "Macedonians" (Vlasidis 2003, p. 347). For instance, Skopje converted Ioannis Koukouzelis, the Byzantine composer, to "Macedonian" because he was born in Divri, now in FYROM. It also dissociated Byzantine paint-

ings from Byzantium and redressed them with "Macedonian" ethnic and cultural notes. Skopje even converted the heroes of the Naousa revolt against the Turks in 1822, who blew themselves up instead of surrendering, to "Macedonians." Of course they were Macedonians, Hellenic Macedonians.

5. A few years ago Skopje organized a touring exhibition of superb Byzantine icons from Macedonia, most of them with Greek inscriptions and Greek artists' names on the back. The exhibit impressed many people all over the world, but only a few experts discerned Skopje's efforts to usurp the identity of the painters when they read the painters' Greek names on the back of the icons (Martis 1983).

6. According to Poulton (1995, p. 174), the news agency Tanjug reported on September 2, 1990, that the communist authorities in the Socialist Republic of Macedonia suspected VMRO-DPMNE of provocations toward the Serbs, accusing them of favoring a "Bulgarian nation." Also, the Society of Bulgarians in the Vardar Province condemned the Skopje-promulgated "Macedonian" concept, insisting that all Macedonians in Yugoslavia and Greece are Bulgarians.

7. FYROM (the Former Yugoslav Republic of Macedonia) presented itself as a product of the Ilinden uprising, originally known to be a Bulgarian uprising, its ethnological tenets subsequently usurped by the "Macedonians" of Tito's People's Republic of Macedonia, and now by FYROM. As a gesture of goodwill to the new republic, Bulgaria sent the body of Gotse-Delcheff—the leader of the Bulgarian Ilinden uprising—to Skopje, but in 1948 it reverted to its old nationalist views, prohibiting the use of the "Macedonian" language (Vattis 2002).

8. Todor Zhivcov, communist leader and president of Bulgaria, decided not to recognize a separate Macedonian nationality (King 1973, pp. 188–89). He declared on January 21, 1992: "If we examine the problem of Macedonia on official documents I possess, we can see that Tito pressed Stalin to recognize the Yugoslav federation, including Macedonia. During my presidency, 58 percent of the Republic of Macedonia is Bulgarian.... I cannot accept the ethnic substance [of FYROM] and the existence of such a state" (Tsalouhides 1994).

9. Let us assume a hypothetical scenario: If in the future the FYROM Albanian minority becomes the majority, and FYROM allies itself with Greater Albania (including Kosovo), what is to prevent Greater Albania from making territorial demands on Greek Macedonia and Epirus?

10. Translation of Samaras's speech excerpts from Kofos's Greek text (2003b, p. 160) by the author.

11. A year later, on May 14, 1993, Cyrus Vance and Lord Owen proposed "Nova Macedonia" again, but the name was rejected by both sides (Kofos 2003b).

12. While an American secretary of state, Stettinius, had declared in 1944 that "the Government considers talks of Macedonian 'nation,' Macedonian 'Fatherland,' or Macedonian 'national consciousness' to be unjustified demagoguery," another secretary of state disapproved of the name "Republic of Skopje," supporting an ex-communist country, destroying all the goodwill toward America among the Greeks (*Kathimerini* 1996).

13. The Macedonians of ancient times were Greeks, spoke the Greek language, believed in the same gods as the remainder of the Greek states, and were just as distinct from the Athenians as the Spartans, the Corinthians, the Thevans, the Thessalians, etc. It would be impossible to believe that the ancient Greeks would think their gods lived on a non-Greek mountain on a non-Greek country. Olympus to them in Macedonia was Greek country (see also Chapter 5).

14. See *Kathimerini* (Athens newspaper), *Seven Days, Skopje: The Adventure for a Name*, special edition, April 19, 1996.

15. According to this agreement, Greece recognizes FYROM as an independent and sovereign state and the two countries will establish diplomatic relations; confirm their common existing borders and respect the sovereignty, territorial integrity, and the political independence of the other country; FYROM declares that nothing in its constitution can or should be interpreted as constituting, or will ever constitute, the basis of any claim by FYROM to any territory not within its existing borders, or to interfere in the internal affairs of another state in order to protect the status and rights of any persons in other states who are not FYROM citizens; each Party shall take effective measures to prohibit hostile activities or propaganda by State-controlled agencies and to discourage acts by private entities likely to incite violence, hatred or hostility against each other. The Interim Accord also includes several articles on economic cooperation, water resources management, movement of people or goods, capital investment and industrial cooperation, avoidance of dangers to the environment, improvement and promotion of business and tourist travel, and cooperation in the fight against organized crime, terrorism, economic crimes, narcotics crimes, illegal trade, and offenses against air transport and counterfeiting.

16. Would the American public, for instance, accept with cheerful equanimity a hypothetical usurpation of its ethnic symbols, the bald eagle or the stars and stripes, by Mexicans or Canadians?

17. Brown (2000, p. 136) also pointed out that "because the remainder of the paper deals primarily with the FY Republic of Macedonia, and there is thus little risk of confusion, I henceforward refer to the republic as Macedonia." Reference to the republic as "Macedonia" is against the United Nations' acceptance of the name FYROM until a permanent solution can be reached. Also, rushing to recognize FYROM's inhabitants as "Macedonians" before a final settlement has made the FYROM Slavs arrogant and uncompromising, believing that the names "Macedonia" and "Macedonians" have been reserved for them. Brown also admits that "the objectival form 'Macedonian' presents greater possible confusion. It has both (a political meaning connected to the republic and a cultural meaning referring to a particular language and sense of identity deriving from the 'assumed givens' of language, religion, kin connection and social practice."

18. The approval by the Greek parliament of FYROM's entering the Stabilization and Association Agreement was severely criticized by Martis (2003).

19. Eighty percent of FYROM's commerce moves through the port of Thessaloniki (Zaikos 2003).

20. FYROM Slav archaeologists, for instance, visited the Vergina tombs in Greek Macedonia and after a brief stay, they returned to Skopje and declared that the interpretations of Greek and foreign archaeologists were a Greek trick (Vlasidis 2003, p. 315, from the Skopje newspaper *Dnevnik*, December 21, 1996).

21. Propaganda against Greece emanating from Slavic organizations in the United States, Canada, and Australia continues even as this book is being written. In February 2003, for instance, several attempts were made on the Internet to dispute Alexander the Great's Hellenism.

22. This has changed somewhat during the last few years. Several organizations recognize Skopje as FYROM: NATO, the EU, and the U.N. FYROM's representative in the U.N. sits between Thailand and Togo. In contrast, a few other countries signed economic agreements with FYROM using the name "Republic of Macedonia." A good recent example is Israel, which signed an economic agreement with the "Republic of Macedonia" (see "FYROM and Israel Strengthen Their Cooperation," Macedonia Press Agency, Internet News, July 9, 2004).

23. According to Poulton (1995, p. 101), the exuberant welcome extended to the fascist Bulgarian army (Hitler's allies) in 1941 was a spontaneous popular reaction of Vardar Macedonia's

population, who had suffered greatly under the Serbs.

24. "Greece ... challenged the republic status by interpreting its constitution, new flag and very name as expressions of extraterritorial ambitions" (Cowan and Brown 2000, p. 4).

25. As the pages of this book are written, students in FYROM are taught ancient history laced with historical falsifications and inaccuracies to de-Hellenize the ancient Macedonians of the Philip and Alexander era and the Hellenistic Age, which FYROM's schoolbooks have renamed the Macedonian Period, undermining the basic principles of European civilization and history (Vlasidis 2003). The Skopjan young generation is educated today to believe that the Greeks usurped the Macedonian history. Students are also encouraged to be resentful and vindictive against the Greeks. And while all this propaganda is going on, Greece keeps an unexplained silence, as if it were Greece that usurped a name that did not belong to it (Martis 2002).

26. According to Vlasidis (2003, pp. 336, 338), in every FYROM schoolroom there are two maps on the wall. The first depicts FYROM with its present frontier; the second the entire geographical Macedonia, suggesting to the students that large areas belonging to Greece and Bulgaria actually belong to FYROM. The presence of the two maps is a powerful irredentist stimulus, teaching the young generation that a large part of their "country" is still occupied by foreign powers. The FYROM schoolbook contents and the maps are in violation of the Interim Accord, which stipulates that each party must take the necessary measures to prevent inimical acts and propaganda against the other by government organizations and private individuals.

27. All this agitation created a big problem: how to differentiate legitimate concerns about FYROM itself from the illegitimate or non-government-supported propaganda in the United States, Canada, and Australia, and whom to blame for history's great alteration (Kofos 1964).

28. Two days after the 2004 U.S. presidential elections, the U.S. State Department officially recognized FYROM as the Republic of Macedonia to provide "stability" in the small country. It was an out-of-place, thoughtless foreign policy announcement which will undermine the bilateral negotiations between Athens and Skopje on the name issue.

29. Characterization and italics by the author.

30. Before he became deputy secretary of state in the Clinton administration, Strobe Talbott wrote in a *Time* magazine editorial, "Greece's Defense Seems Just Silly" (April 30,

1995), that "the Skopjan constitution explicitly disavows any such [territorial] claims.... Partly because the Greek position is so preposterous, the suspicion persists that the complaint about the name camouflages a revival of Greece's own age-old expansionist ambitions." Greece never expressed any territorial claims on FYROM.

Also on April 30, 1995, former Secretary of State James Baker wrote in the *Washington Times*: "The most serious threat to the stability [in the Balkans] comes not from the Serbs but from the aggressive policy toward Macedonia being pursued by our ally, Greece."

31. Quotation and italics by the author.

32. The issue of the "unredeemed" brothers in Greek Macedonia does not deserve an elaborate explanation. It suffices to say that the 1951 Greek census showed 47,157 Slavomacedonians in all of Greece, a nation of eleven million. A reported 35,894 of them live in Greek Macedonia, a province with about three million people. Moreover, most of them harbor Hellenic sentiments.

33. Gligorov also declared later: "But we are Slav Macedonians. That's who we are! We have no connection to Alexander the Great and his Macedonians.... Our ancestors came here in the fifth and sixth century" (*Toronto Star*, March 15, 1992).

FYROM's ambassador to Canada, Gyordan Veselinov, stated during an interview with the *Ottawa Citizen* (February 24, 1992): "We are not related to the northern Greeks, who produced leaders like Philip and Alexander the Great. We are a Slav [people], and our language is closely related to the Bulgarian. There is some confusion about the identity of the people of my country."

Also, on January 22, 1999, FYROM's ambassador to the U.S., Ljubica Achevska, stated: "We do not claim to be descendants of Alexander the Great. We are Slavs, and we speak a Slavic language" (Templar 2003).

34. The peak period of Greece's internal flourishing coincides with Pericles's period; the peak period of Greece's external flourishing coincides with the reign of Alexander the Great (Marx-Engels, in Kargakos 1992).

35. Presidential candidate Bill Clinton expressed the following views to AHEPA (American Hellenic Progressive Association) on August 20, three months before the 1992 elections: "If this southern former Yugoslav democracy wishes to be recognized by the United States, it must first accept the Helsinki principles to satisfy its neighbors and the international community that its intentions are peaceful and to comply with the decision of the European Community that rejects the use of the name 'Macedonia.'" On February 9, 1993, Clinton reneged on his promises to AHEPA,

granting full diplomatic recognition of the small republic as FYROM.

When the Pan-Macedonian Association (USA) protested the use of the name "Macedonia" by President Clinton, the State Department replied that the name "Macedonia" is used unofficially for brevity and assured the Pan-Macedonian Association that "the United States continue to support the use of the name FYROM" (Kofos 2003b, pp. 186–88).

36. The second volume, entitled *The KKE and the Ethnic Question, 1918–1974*, translated into Greek, contains 250 KKE documents supporting Skopje's policies on the Macedonian issue (Vattis 2002).

37. A new disturbing perception appeared recently online with respect to "repatriation" to Greece of about one hundred thousand "Aegean" Slavomacedonian exiles from the period of 1941–1949 from FYROM (Kofos 2003a). Implementation of this act by the Greek government would be tantamount to transplanting a Trojan horse among the patriotic people of the sensitive Macedonian frontier districts. "Repatriation" of thousands of Slavomacedonians with deeply entrenched Slavic consciousness and attitude, including thousands of young Slavs well indoctrinated to hate the Greek "usurpers" of their "Macedonian" ancestry, would be a great disaster, not to mention the certainty of a new bitter war between the fervently nationalist "Aegean Macedonians" and Hellenic Macedonians for the prize of history, culture, and the name "Macedonia."

38. "The Framework Agreement," Ochris; see Kofos 2003, p. 197, note 68.

39. During an incident between government forces and Albanian extremists, VMRO-DPMNE politicians accused President Gligorov of orchestrating the incident to bring FYROM back to Serbia (Shea 1997, p. 209).

40. Kole Casule, a Skopje intellectual and an ex-communist, told Hitchens (1994): "The project of a Greater Serbia has within it the incurable tumor of Greater Albania. And this cancer will metastasize in Macedonia." He also told Hitchens of the "party of fear" that dominated the parliament in FYROM's first general elections in 1990. The nationalist VMRO's aim is to create an ethnically pure nation-state in which there must be only one ethnic group. VRMO considers the existence of Albanians in FYROM a significant threat to FYROM's future. Even FYROM's Slavic majority worries about the presence of a thriving and rapidly multiplying Albanian minority.

41. During FYROM's 1994 presidential elections, Georgijevski minimized the Albanian influence within the small republic with this remark: "We will let the eagle fly, but we will cut off its talons first" (quoted by Brown 2000, p. 133).

42. If the KFOR and NATO elements leave FYROM, a new breakdown in relations between the Slavs and Albanians could cause an internal collapse. Should this happen, three of FYROM's neighbors, Albania, Bulgaria, and Serbia, may attempt to intervene and fill the vacuum. On the other hand, if Skopje and Athens compromise on a name, what would the VMRO do? Would it revert to its terrorist history, acquiring assistance from extreme foreign elements from within or outside the country?

43. Slavic organizations in North America and Australia continue their destabilizing propaganda and distorted diplomacy. For instance, during the winter of 2002 a relentless disinformation campaign via mass media (TV, Internet, books, etc.) depicted the ancient Macedonians as non-Greek and used provocative symbols to offend or denigrate Greece.

44. Vasil Topourkovski, a Skopjan politician (his father was *capetan* Voulkan, an NOF leader from the village of Trigono, in the Florina district of Greek Macedonia), stated recently in Washington that FYROM's future is uncertain.

Selected Bibliography

Ajanovski-Ocer, Vangel. *Egejski Buri*. Skopje, 1975.

Alexandrou, Dimitris N. *Kalas, the Greeks of the Himalaya* (in Greek). 5th ed. Trapezous, Thessaloniki: n.p., 1993.

Amperiadis, Panayiotis. *Eastern Macedonia in 1941 and the Drama Uprising* (in Greek). Thessaloniki: Ekthosis Kyriakides, 1998.

Anarhistov, Kiril, ed. *Glas na Makedoncite*. Vol. 6, nos. 28–29 (August-November 1982). Australia: Kogana, NSW.

Anastasoff, Chris. *The Tragic Peninsula: A History of the Macedonian Movement for Independence Since 1878*. St. Louis: Blackwell, 1938.

Andonovski, Hristo. "The Ancient Macedonians and Alexander the Great." *Macedonian Review* 8 (1978): 10–15.

Andriotis, N. *The Federative Republic of Skopje and Its Language* (in Greek). Thessaloniki: Trohalia, 1992.

Andronikos, Manolis. *Vergina: The Royal Tombs and the Ancient City*. Athens: Ekdotike Athenon, 1984.

Angelopoulos, A. "Review of *British Documents on the History of the Macedonian People (Britanski Dokumenti Istorijata na Makedonskiot narod)*, ed. H. Andonov-Polianski, Vol. 1, 1797–1839. *Institute of Balkan Studies* 9 (1968): 559–61.

_____. "Population Distribution of Greece Today According to Language, National Consciousness and Religion." *Balkan Studies* 20 (1979): 123–32.

Antonakeas, A. *Guerrilla War, Not Civil War* (in Greek). Athens: Nea Thesis, 1993.

Army History Directorate. *The Macedonian Struggle and Events in Thrace* (in Greek). Athens: Greek Army History Directorate (AHD), 1979.

_____. *The Greek Army During the Anti-Guerrilla War (1946–1949): The Second Year of the Anti-Guerrilla War, 1947* (in Greek). Athens: Greek Army History Directorate, 1980.

Averoff-Tossizza, E. *By Fire and Axe*. New Rochelle, N.Y.: Caratzas Brothers, 1978.

Bacid, Jacques. *Macedonia Through the Ages*. New York: Columbia University Press, 1983.

Badian, E. "Greeks and Macedonians." In *Macedonia and Greece in Late Classical and Early Hellenistic Times*, Studies in the History of Art, eds. B. Barr-Sharrar and E.N. Borza, vol. 10: 33–51. Washington, D.C.: National Gallery of Art, 1982.

Banac, I. *The National Question in Yugoslavia: Origin, History, Politics.* Ithaca, N.Y: Cornell University Press, 1984, 1992.

_____. "The Tito-Stalin Split and the Greek Civil War." In *Greece at the Crossroads*, eds. John O. Iatrides and Linda Wrigley, 258–73. University Park, Pa.: Pennsylvania State University Press, 1995.

Barker, Elizabeth. *Macedonia: Its Place in Balkan Power Politics.* London: Oxford University Press, 1950.

_____. *British Policy in South-East Europe in the Second World War.* London: Macmillan, 1976.

Barr-Sharrar, B., and E.N. Borza, eds. *Macedonia and Greece in Late Classical and Early Hellenistic Times.* Studies in the History of Art, vol. 10. Washington, D.C.: National Gallery of Art, 1982.

Barth, Fredrik. *Ethnic Groups and Boundaries.* Boston: Little, Brown, 1969.

Berar, V. *La Turquie et l'Hellènisme Contemporain.* Paris, 1896.

Borza, Eugene N. "The Macedonian Royal Tombs at Vergina: Some Cautionary Notes." *Archaeological News* 10, no. 4 (1981): 73–87.

_____. *The History and Archaeology of Macedonia.* In *Macedonia and Greece in Late Classical and Early Hellenistic Times*, Studies in the History of Art, eds. B. Barr-Sharrar and E.N. Borza, vol. 10, 17–30. Washington, D.C.: National Gallery of Art, 1982, 1992.

_____. *In the Shadow of Olympus: The Emergence of Macedon.* Princeton, N.J.: Princeton University Press, 1990.

Brailsford, H.N. *Macedonia: Its Races and Their Future.* New York: Arno, 1971. First published in London, 1906.

Bramos, Costas. *Slavocommunist Organizations in Macedonia* (in Greek). Thessaloniki: n.p., 1953.

Brewer, D. *The Greek War of Independence.* Woodstock, N.Y.: Overlook, 2001.

Brown, K. S. "In the Realm of the Double-Headed Eagle: Parapolitics in Macedonia, 1994–1997." In *Macedonia, the Politics of Identity and Difference*, ed. Jane K. Cowan, 122–39. London: Pluto, 2000.

Cahill, Thomas. *Sailing the Wine-Dark Sea: Why the Greeks Matter.* New York: Anchor Books, 2003.

Cappelli, V. "The Bosnian Question and the Great Powers." *Med. Quart.* 8, no.1 (1997): 92–114.

Carpenter, T. G. "Kosovo and Macedonia: The West Enhances the Threat." *Med. Quart.* 13, no. 1 (2002): 22–37.

Carter-Norris, F. *The Changing Shape of the Balkans.* London: University College, 1996.

Cartledge, Paul. *Alexander the Great.* Woodstock & New York: The Overlook Press, 2004.

Casson, S. *Macedonia, Thrace and Illyria.* Oxford, 1926; Westport, Conn.: Greenwood, 1971.

Centre for Macedonians Abroad, Society for Macedonian Studies. *Macedonia: History and Politics.* Athens: Ekthotiki Athenon, 1994.

Chatzis, Thanasis. *The Victorious Revolution That Was Lost* (in Greek). Athens: Ekthosis Papazisi, 1977.

Chrysochoou, Athanasios T. *The Occupation in Macedonia* (in Greek). 6 vols. Thessaloniki: Society for Macedonian Studies, 1952.

Churchill, Winston S. *The Grand Alliance.* Vol. 3, *The Second World War.* Boston: Houghton Mifflin, 1950.

_____. *The Grand Alliance.* Vol. 6, *The Second World War.* Boston: Houghton Mifflin, 1953.

Coufoudakis, Van. "Greece and the Problem of Macedonia: Myths and Realities" *Journal of Modern Hellenism* 15 (1998): 1–29.

Cowan, Jane K. "Idioms of Belonging: Polyglot Articulations of Local Identity in a Greek Macedonian Town." In *Ourselves and Others: The Development of a Greek Macedon-*

ian Culture Since 1912, eds. Peter Mackridge and Eleni Yannakakis, 153–71. Oxford: Berg, 1997.

_____, ed. *Macedonia: The Politics of Identity and Difference*. London: Pluto, 2000.

Cowan, J.K., and K.S. Brown. "Introduction: Macedonian Inflections." In *Macedonia: The Politics of Identity and Difference*, ed. Jane K. Cowan, 1–27. London: Pluto, 2000.

Dakin, D. *The Greek Struggle in Macedonia, 1897–1913*. Thessaloniki: Museum of the Macedonian Struggle, 1966.

Danforth, Loring M. *The Macedonian Conflict: Ethnic Nationalism in a Transnational World*. Princeton, N.J.: Princeton University Press, 1995.

_____. "How Can a Woman Give Birth to One Greek and One Macedonian? The Construction of National Identity among Immigrants to Australia from Northern Greece." In *Macedonia: The Politics of Identity and Difference*, ed. Jane K. Cowan, 85–103. London: Pluto, 2000.

Danopoulos, C. P. "Toward Cooperation in Post–Cold War Southeastern Europe." *Med. Quart.* 12, no. 2 (2001): 101–18.

Daskalakis, A. *The Hellenism of the Ancient Macedonians*. Thessaloniki: Institute for Balkan Studies, 1965.

Daskalov, Giorgi. *The Drama Revolt* (in Bulgarian). Sofia, 1992. Quoted in P. Amperiadis, *Eastern Macedonia in 1941 and the Drama Uprising*, pp. 4, 9, 10, 12, 23, 35, 84, 122, 193, 333. Thessaloniki: Ekthosis Kyriakides, 1998.

Djilas, Milovan. *Conversations with Stalin*. Translated by Michael B. Petrovich. New York: Harcourt, Brace & World, 1962.

Dragnich, A.N. "Yugoslavia in Historical Perspective." *Med. Quart.* 3, no. 3 (1992): 5–19.

Dragojceva, Tsola. *Macedonia: Not a Cause of Discord but a Factor of Good Neighborliness and Cooperation*. Sofia: Sofia Press, 1979.

Dragoumis, I. *Blood of Heroes and Martyrs*, 2nd ed. Athens, 1914.

Droysen, Johann Gustav. *Geschichte des Hellenismus*. 2 vols. Gotha, 1877–1878.

Dumont, A. *Souvenirs de la Roumelie, Revue de Deux Mondes*, Vol. 95, 1871. Quoted in the Army History Directorate, *The Macedonian Struggle and Events in Thrace*, p. 42. Athens: Greek Army History Directorate, 1979.

Durant, Will. *The Story of Civilization II: The Life of Greece*. New York: Simon and Schuster, 1939.

Durant, Will and Ariel Durant. *The Lessons of History*. New York: Simon and Schuster, 1968.

Errington, R.M. *A History of Macedonia*. Translated by Catherine Errington. Berkeley: University of California Press, 1990. Originally Published as *Geschichte Makedoniens*. Munich, 1986.

Farakos, G. *ELAS and Power* (in Greek). Athens: Ellenika Grammata, 2000.

Feigenbaum, H.B. "Centralization and National Integration in France." *Med. Quart.* 8, no. 1 (1997): 59.

Feldman, H.J. "The Balkan Dimensions of the Yugoslav Crisis." *Med. Quart.* 3, no. 3 (1992): 20–25.

Ferrill, Arther. "Alexander in India: The Battle at the Edge of the Earth." *Quart. Jour. Military History* 1, no. 1 (1988): 78–84.

Fleischer, Hagen. "The National Liberation Front (EAM), 1941–1947: A Reassessment." In *Greece at the Crossroads*, eds. John O. Iatrides and Linda Wrigley, 48–89. University Park, Pa.: Pennsylvania State University Press, 1995.

Gage, N. *Eleni*. New York: Random House, 1983.

_____. "Usurping a Name." *The Boston Globe*, November 6, 1992.

Gagoulias, G.D. *The Hidden Side of the Civil War* (in Greek). Athens: Iolkos, 2001.

Gelb, Leslie H. "'Macedonia' for Greece." *New York Times*, December 6, 1992.

Giannakos, S.A. "The Macedonian Question Reexamined: Implications for Balkan Security." *Med. Quart.* 3, no. 3 (1992): 26–47.

Giannopoulos, E. *The National Resistance of the Greeks Against the German, Italian, and Bulgarian Occupiers, 1941–1944* (in Greek). Athens: Ekthosis Tsiverioti, 1999.

Gounaris, Basil C. "Reassessing Ninety Years of Greek Historiography on the 'Struggle for Macedonia 1904–1908.'" In *Ourselves and Others: The Development of a Greek Macedonian Cultural Identity Since 1912*, eds. Peter Mackridge and Eleni Yannakakis, 25–37. Oxford: Berg, 1997.

Grant, Michael. *The Rise of the Greeks.* New York: Scribner's, 1988.

Green, Peter. *Alexander of Macedon, 356–323 B C.: A Historical Biography.* Berkeley: University of California Press, 1991.

Gregoriadis, Solon. *December: Civil War, 1944–1945.* Athens: Ekthosis Kapopoulos, 1984.

Hammond, Nicholas G.L. *A History of Macedonia.* 3 vols. Oxford: Oxford University Press, 1972–1988.

_____. *Migrations and Invasions in Greece and Adjacent Areas.* Park Ritz, N.J.: Noyes Press, 1976.

_____. *Venture into Greece: With the Guerrillas, 1943–1944.* London: William Kimber, 1983.

_____. *The Macedonian State. Origin, Institution and History.* Oxford: Oxford University Press, 1989.

_____. *The Allied Military Mission and the Resistance in West Macedonia.* Thessaloniki: Institute for Balkan Studies, 1993.

_____. *The Genius of Alexander the Great.* Chapel Hill, N.C.: University of North Carolina Press, 1997.

Hammond, N.G.L., and G.T. Griffith. *A History of Macedonia, 550–536 B.C.* Vol. 2. Oxford: Clarendon Press, 1979.

Haritopoulos, D. *Aris: Leader of the Irregulars* (in Greek). Athens: Exantas, 2001.

Hassiotis, I.K. *Landmarks and Principal Phases in the History of Modern and Contemporary Macedonia.* Thessaloniki: Ekthosis Paratiritis, 1992.

Helmreich, E.C. *The Diplomacy of the Balkan Wars, 1912–1913.* Cambridge, Ma.: Harvard University Press, 1938.

Hitchens, Christopher. "Minority Report: Skopje/Tetovo, 'Macedonia.'" *Nation*, April 18, 1994.

Hotzides, Angelos. "Articulation and Structure of Speech: The Example of Moglenon and Zora." In *Identities in Macedonia* (in Greek), eds. Vasilis Gounaris, I. Michailidis, and G. Angelopoulos, 143–70. Athens: Ekthosis Papazisi, 1997.

Howard, Harry. *The U.N. Commission of Investigation Concerning Greek Frontier Incidents.* U.S. Department of State Bulletin 17, July 6, 1987.

Hupchick, Dennis P., and Harold E. Cox. *The Palgrave Concise Historical Atlas of the Balkans.* New York, N.Y.: Palgrave, 2001.

Iatrides, John O. "Greece at the Crossroads, 1944–1950." In *Greece at the Crossroads*, eds. John O. Iatrides and Linda Wrigley, 1–30. University Park, Pa.: Pennsylvania State University Press, 1995.

Institute for Balkan Studies. *The Treaty of Bucharest and Greece: 75 Years from the Liberation of Macedonia.* Thessaloniki: Institute for Balkan Studies, 1990.

Ioannides, Yiannis. "Memories." In *Problems in the Policies of the KKE in the National Resistance, 1940–1945* (in Greek), ed. P. Papapanagiotou. Athens: Themelio 1979.

Kargakos, Sarantos I. *From the Macedonian Question to the Skopje Entanglement.* Athens: Gutenberg, 1992.

Karvelis, Nikos K. *Macedonia.* Athens: Ekthosis Pitsilos, 1996.

Kathimerini. Seven Days, Skopje: The Adventure for a Name. Special edition, 32 pages. Athens, April 19, 1996.

King, Robert. *Minorities Under Communism: Nationalities as a Source of Tension Among Balkan Communist States.* Cambridge, Ma.: Harvard University Press, 1973.

Kofos, Evangelos. "The Making of Yugoslavia's People's Republic of Macedonia." *Balkan Studies* 3, no. 2 (1962): 375–96.

_____. *Nationalism and Communism in Macedonia.* Thessaloniki: Institute for Balkan Studies, 1964, pp. xxi, 251; 2nd ed., New Rocheller, N.Y.: Aristide D. Caratzas; 1993.

_____. *The Macedonian Revolution in 1878* (in Greek). In *Reports of the Consuls,* Unpublished Consular Documents, IMXA, 1969.

_____. *Macedonia in the Yugoslav Historiography.* No. 24 (in Greek). Thessaloniki: Society for Macedonian Studies, 1974.

_____. "The Macedonian Question: The Politics of Mutation." *Balkan Studies* 27 (1986): 157–72.

_____. "The Macedonian Struggle in the Yugoslav Historiography" (in Greek). In *Records on the Macedonian Struggle,* 279–317. Thessaloniki: Museum of Macedonian Struggle–IMXA, 1987.

_____. "The Balkan Dimension of the Macedonian Question During the Occupation and the Resistance" (in Greek). In *Greece from 1936 to 1944: Dictatorship, Occupation, Resistance,* eds. H. Fleischer and N. Svoronos, Annals, First International Conference on Contemporary History. Athens, 1989.

_____. *The Impact of the Macedonian Question on Civil Conflicts in Greece, 1943–49.* Athens: Hellenic Foundation for Defense and Foreign Policy, Occasional Papers 3, 1989.

_____. *The Vision of Greater Macedonia* (in Greek). Thessaloniki: Museum of the Macedonian Struggle, 1994.

_____. "The Impact of the Macedonian Question on Civil Conflict in Greece, 1943–1949." In *Greece at the Crossroads,* eds. John O. Iatrides and Linda Wrigley, 274–318. University Park, Pa.: Pennsylvania State University Press, 1995.

_____. "Greek Policy Considerations Over FYROM's Independence and Recognition." In *The New Macedonian Question,* ed. J. Pettifer, 247–56. London: Macmillan, 1999.

_____. "Unexpected Initiatives: Towards the Resettlement of a Slaw-Macedonian Minority in Macedonia?" www.macedonian-heritage.gr/Opinion/comm_20030710Kofos.html, 2003.

_____. "The Unresolved 'Difference over the Name': The Greek Perspective." In *Athens–Skopje, Seven Years of Symbiosis (1995–2002),* eds. E. Kofos and V. Vlasidis, 155–264. Athens: Ekthosis Papazisi, 2003b.

Koliopoulos, John S. *Plundered Loyalties: World War II and Civil War in Greek West Macedonia* (in Greek). 2 vols. Thessaloniki: Ekthosis Vanias, 1995.

_____. "The War Over the Identity and Numbers of Greece's Slav Macedonians." In *Ourselves and Others: The Development of a Greek Macedonian Cultural Identity Since 1912,* eds. Peter Mackridge and Eleni Yannakakis, 39–57. Oxford: Berg, 1997.

Kollias, A. *1991–1994: Greece in the Trap of Serbs of Milosevic* (in Greek). Athens: Thamyris, 1995.

Koneski, Blaze. *The Macedonian Literary Language.* Balkan Forum No. 4. Skopje, Former Yugoslav Republic of Macedonia, September 1993.

Kondis, B. *Anglo-American Policy and the Greek Problem, 1945–1949* (in Greek). Thessaloniki: Paratiritis, 1984.

Kontis, V., and S. Sfetas. *Civil War: Documents from Yugoslav and Bulgarian Archives* (in Greek). Thessaloniki: Paratiritis, 1999.

Kontonis, Haralampos. "The Bilateral Relations of Athens–Skopje and FYROM's Course Toward International Organizations." In *Athens–Skopje, Seven Years of Symbiosis (1995–2002),* eds. E. Kofos and V. Vlasidis, 69–112. Athens: Ekthosis Papazisi, 2003.

Koppa, Marinela. *A Fragile Democracy* (in Greek). Athens: Ekthosis Papazisi, 1994.

Kordatos, Yiannis. *History of Modern Greece* (in Greek). Vol. 12, *On the Macedonian Question. Athens,* 2001.

Kostopoulos, Tasos. *The Prohibited Language* (in Greek). Athens: Mavri Lista, 2000.

Kousoulas, D.G. *Revolution and Defeat: The Story of the Greek Communist Party.* Oxford: Oxford University Press, 1965.

Koutsonikos, Georgios. *Grammos–Vitsi: Places of Tragedies* (in Greek). 2 vols. Thessaloniki: Ekthosis Meandros, 2000.

Kouzinopoulos, Spyros. *Pages from the Secret Diary of Giorgi Dimitrov* (in Greek). Athens: Ekthosis Kastanioti, 1999.

Kyriakidis, S. *The Northern Ethnological Boundaries of Hellenism.* Thessaloniki: n.p., 1955.

Kyrou, Achilleas. *The Conspiracy Against Macedonia, 1940–1949* (in Greek). Athens: Ekthosis Delos, 1950.

Ladas, S. *The Exchange of Minorities: Bulgaria, Greece and Turkey.* New York: Harvard University and Radcliffe College, Bureau of International Research, 1932.

Limber, T.P. *Hellenika.* River Vale, N.J.: Cosmos, 1997.

MacDermott, Mercia. *Freedom or Death: The Life of Gotse-Delchev.* London: Journeyman, 1978.

Mackridge, Peter, and Eleni Yannakakis. "Introduction." In *Ourselves and Others: The Development of a Greek Macedonian Cultural Identity Since 1912,* eds. Peter Mackridge and Eleni Yannakakis, 1–22. Oxford: Berg, 1997.

Makris, Petros. *The Anatomy of a Tragedy* (in Greek). Athens: Ekthosis "Angyra," 2000.

Margaritis, Giorgos. *History of the Greek Civil War, 1946–1949* (in Greek). 2 vols. Athens: Bibliorama, 2002.

Marinos, Yiannis. *Truth and Distortion: The Cultural Identity of Macedonia, History vs. Propaganda.* Athens: Oikonomikos Tachydromos, January 30, 1997.

Martis, Nikolaos K. *The Falsification of Macedonian History.* Athens: Athanasiades Bros., 1983.

_____. *The Macedonians and Their Contribution to Western Civilization.* Athens: Society for the Study of Greek History, 2001.

_____. "On the Border of Ridicule and Insult." www.macedonian-heritage.gr/Opinion/comm_20020104Martis.html, 2002.

_____. *FYROM, The Anti-democratic Residuum in Europe and the Problematic Stabilization and Association Agreement with the EU.* Athens: The Society for the Study of Greek History, 2003.

Mavrogordatos, George. *Stillborn Republic: Social Coalitions and Party Strategies in Greece, 1912–1936.* Berkeley, Ca.: University of California Press, 1983.

Mazarakis-Ainian, A. *Historical Studies, 1821–1897 and the War of 1897.* 2 vols. Athens: Memoirs, 1950.

Mazower, Mark. *Inside Hitler's Greece.* New Haven, Conn.: Yale University Press, 1993.

_____. *The Balkans.* New York: Modern Library, 2000.

McNeill, William H. *The Greek Dilemma: War and Aftermath.* Philadelphia: Lippincott, 1947.

Mertzos, N.I. *The Ten Deadly Sins of the KKE* (in Greek). Athens: Ekthosis Sideris, 1984.

_____. *Extension of Ilinden or a Modern State* (in Greek). Thessaloniki: Macedonian Life, 1993.

Michailides, Iakovos D. "On the Other Side of the River: The Defeated Slavophones and Greek History." In *Macedonia: The Politics of Identity and Difference,* ed. Jane K. Cowan, 68–84. London: Pluto, 2000.

Mihailoff, I. *Macedonia: A Switzerland of the Balkans.* Translated by C. Anastasoff. St. Louis: n.p., 1950.

Miller, Marshall L. *Bulgaria During the Second World War*. Stanford, Ca.: Stanford University Press, 1975.

Mitsakis, K. *Macedonia Throughout the Centuries*. Thessaloniki: Institute for Balkan Studies, 1973.

Morgenthau, E. *I Was Sent to Greece*. Constantinople: Estia, 1928.

Museum of the Macedonian Struggle. *The Events of 1903 in Macedonia*. Thessaloniki: Museum of the Macedonian Struggle, 1993.

Mylonas, Polys A. *Macedonia's Hellenism* (in Greek). Athens: Ekthosis Nea Synora, 1991.

Myrivilis Stratis. *Life in the Tomb*. Hanover, N.H.: University Press of New England, 1977.

Nikoloudis, Georgios N. *The Greek Slavophones in Macedonia* (in Greek). Thessaloniki: Ekthosis Herodotos, 2002.

Notaris, Yiannis. *The Macedonian Question as Seen by "Yiannis" Kordatos* (in Greek). Athens: Ekthosis Dodoni, 1985.

Nystazopoulou-Pelekidou, M. *The Macedonian Problem* (in Greek). Athens: Greek Committee for Studies in Southeast Europe, Center for Studies in Southeast Europe, 1988.

Paillarès, M. *L'Imbroglio macédonien*. Paris, 1907. Reprint, *I Makedoniki Thyella. Ta Pyrina Chronia 1903–1907*. Translated by B. Kardiolaka. Athens: Trohalia, 1944.

Palmer, S. *The Macedonian Front and the Greek Split*. Athens: Ekthosis Bergadi, 1977.

Palmer, S.E., and R.R. King. *Yugoslav Communism and the Macedonian Question*. Hamden, Conn.: Archon, 1971.

Pandermali-Poulaki, Efi. "Olympus." www.macedonia.com/english/olympus, 2003.

Papadimitriou, Roula. *The Church in the Macedonian Struggle* (in Greek). Thessaloniki: Ekthosis Apostolikis Diakonias, 1991.

_____. *The Macedonian Struggle* (in Greek). Athens: Ekthosis Sakkoula, 1995.

Papadimitropoulos, D. *Greece in the Balkan Crisis* (in Greek). Athens: Polis, 1994.

Papaioannou, Achilleas. *The Testament of Nikos Zachariadis* (in Greek). Athens: Glaros, 1986.

_____. *Giorgis Giannoulis* (in Greek). Athens: Ekthosis Glaros, 1990.

_____. *The Forbidden Image* (in Greek). Athens: Filistor, 2001.

Papakonstantinou, Michalis. *Macedonia After the Macedonian Struggle* (in Greek). Athens: Ermias, 1992.

Papastathis, Ch. "L'Autocéphalie de l'Église de la Macédoine Yugoslave." *Balkan Studies* 8 (1967): 151–54.

Papathanasiou, A. *The Slavic and Communist Conspiracy and the Macedonian Resistance* (in Greek). Thessaloniki, 1950.

Papathanasiou, P.I. *For the Greek North, 1941–1945: Resistance and Tragedy*. Athens: Ekthosis Papazisi, 1997.

Papavizas, George C. *Blood and Tears — Greece 1940–1949 — A Story of War and Love*. Washington, D.C.: American Hellenic Institute Foundation, 2002.

Papazoglou, Fanula. *The Central Balkan Tribes in Pre-Roman Times (Triballi, Autariatae, Dardanians, Scordisci and Moesians)*. Amsterdam, 1978.

Pavlowitch, Stevan K. *Tito: Yugoslavia's Great Dictator, A Reassessment*. Columbus: Ohio State University Press, 1992.

Pentzopoulos, D. *The Balkan Exchange of Minorities and Its Impact on Greece*. Paris: Mouton, 1962.

Perry, Duncan M. *The Politics of Terror: The Macedonian Liberation Movements, 1893–1903*. Durham, N.C.: Duke University Press, 1988.

Poulton, Hugh. *Who Are the Macedonians?* Bloomington and Indianapolis: Indiana University Press, 1995.

Rallis, Georgios. *Looking Back* (in Greek). Athens: Ekthosis Ermias, 1993.

Rodakis, Perikles. *The Siantos Report for the Dekembriana* (in Greek). Athens: Ekthosis Glaros, 1986.

Rossos, Andrew. "The Macedonians of Aegean Macedonia: A British Officer's Report, 1944." *Slavonic and Eastern European Review* 69, no. 2 (1991): 288–309.

Rothchild, Joseph. *The Communist Party of Bulgaria: Original Foundation (1883–1936)*. New York, 1959.

Shea, John. *Macedonia and Greece*. Jefferson, N.C.: McFarland & Company, 1997.

Shoup, Paul. *Communism and the Yugoslav National Question*. New York: Columbia University Press, 1968.

Smith, Ole L. "Communist Perceptions, Strategy, and Tactics, 1945–1949." In *Greece at the Crossroads*, eds. John O. Iatrides and Linda Wrigley, 90–121. University Park, Pa.: Pennsylvania State University Press, 1995.

Society for Macedonian Studies. *Macedonia: History and Politics*. Athens: Ekthotiki Athenon, 1994.

Stassinopoulos, Costas. *Modern Greek*. Washington, D.C.: American Hellenic Institute Foundation, 1997.

Svoronos, N. *Survey of Modern Greek History* (in Greek). Athens: Themelio, 1976.

Tarkas, Alexandros G. *Athens–Skopje: Behind Closed Doors* (in Greek). 2 vols. Athens: Labyrinth, 1995.

Templar, Marcus A. "Replies to the 'MPO' (Macedonian Patriotic Organization) Letters." *Macedonia* 48, no. 1 (2002): 14.

_____. *Fallacies and Facts on the Macedonian Issue*. 2003, n.p.

Thurston, Robert W. *Life and Terror in Stalin's Russia*. New Haven, Conn.: Yale University Press, 1996.

Touratsoglou, Ioannis. *Macedonia: History, Monuments, Museums*. Athens: Ekthotiki Athenon, 1995.

Troebst, Stefan. "The Action of 'Ochrana' in the Prefectures of Kastoria, Florina, and Pella, 1943–1944." In *Proceedings of the International History Congress: Greece 1936–44, Dictatorship, Occupation, Resistance*, 1989.

Tsalouhides, Yiannis. *Macedonia and the Historical Guilt* (in Greek). Thessaloniki: Ekthosis Kyriakidi, 1994.

Tsamis, P. *The Macedonian Struggle* (in Greek). Thessaloniki: Society for Macedonian Studies, 1975.

Tsaparas, Stephanos. *Macedonia and the Macedonian Problem* (in Greek). Athens: Ekthosis Livani, 1996.

Tziampiris, Aristotle. "The Topic of the Name in FYROM After the Signing of the Interim Accord." In *Athens–Skopje, Seven Years of Symbiosis (1995–2002)*, eds. E. Kofos and V. Vlasidis, 265–96. Athens: Ekthosis Papazisi, 2003.

University of Cyril and Methodius. *Documents on the Struggle of the Macedonian People for Independence and a Nation-State*. 2 vols. Skopje, 1985.

Vafiadis, Markos. *Memoirs* (in Greek). 5 vols. Athens: Ekthosis Papazisi, 1984–1992.

Vakalopoulos, A.E. *History of Macedonia, 1354–1839* (in Greek). Thessaloniki: Ekthosis Sfakianakis, 1973.

_____. *History of Thessaloniki, 316 B.C.–1983* (in Greek). Thessaloniki: Ekthosis Kyriakidi, 1997.

Vakalopoulos, Constantinos. *The Macedonian Struggle, 1904–1908* (in Greek). Thessaloniki: Barbounakis, 1987.

_____. *Macedonia within the Balkan Politics, 1830–1986* (in Greek). Thessaloniki: Barbounakis, 1987.

_____. *The Macedonian Question*. Vol. A, *1856–1912* (in Greek). Thessaloniki: Paratiritis, 1989.

_____. *The Foreign-Speaking Macedonians, Backbone of Defense* (in Greek). Thessaloniki: Macedonian Life, Emfietzoglou, 1993.

Vattis, Kiron. *MPAM Presents the Conspiracy Against Macedonia*. Thessaloniki: Ekthosis Orias, 2002.

Vavouskos, Constantinos A. *Historical and Ethnological Basis of Ilinden* (in Greek). Thessaloniki: Macedonian Life, Emfietzoglou, 1993.

_____. "The Macedonian from an International Perspective" (in Greek). In *Macedonia, Shield of the Nation*, no editor. Thessaloniki: Federation of Western Macedonian Societies in Thessaloniki, 1995.

Veremis, Thanos. "The Revival of the 'Macedonian Question,' 1991–1995." In *Ourselves and Others: The Development of a Greek Macedonian Cultural Identity Since 1912*, eds. Peter Mackridge and Eleni Yannakakis, 227–34. Oxford: Berg, 1997.

Vesilind, Priit J.. "Whose Macedonia?" *National Geographic*, March 1996, 118–139.

Vlantas, Demetrios. *Betrayed Revolution* (in Greek). Athens: Georgios Evangelou, 1979.

_____. *The Civil War, 1945–1949* (in Greek). Athens: Grammi, 1979, 1981.

Vlasides, Vlasis. "Macedonia's Autonomy: From Theory to Practice." In *Identities in Macedonia* (in Greek), eds. V. Gounaris, I. Michailidis, and G. Angelopoulos, 63–87. Athens: Ekthosis Papazisi, 1997.

_____. "Us and the Others: Greece's Image in the Press and the FYROM Educational System." In *Athens–Skopje, Seven Years of Symbiosis (1995–2002)*, eds. E. Kofos and V. Vlasides, 295–366. Athens: Ekthosis Papazisi, 2003.

Vontitsios-Gousias, Giorgos. *The Reasons for the Defeats, for the Break of the KKE, and the Greek Left* (in Greek). Athens: Na Iperetoume to Lao, 1977.

Vukmanovic-Tempo, Svetozar. *Borba za Balkan (Struggle for the Balkans)*. Zagreb, 1981.

Waller, John H. *The Unseen War in Europe*. New York: Random House, 1996.

Wilcken, Ulrich. *Alexander the Great*. Trans. G.C. Richards, ed. Eugene N. Borza. New York: W.W. Norton, 1967.

Wilkinson, H.R. *Maps and Politics: A Review of the Ethnographic Cartography of Macedonia*. Liverpool: Liverpool University Press, 1951.

Wood, Nicholas. "Stability is Still a Struggle in Macedonia." *Washington Post*, January 25, 2003.

Woodhouse, C.M. *The Apple of Discord: A Survey of Recent Greek Politics in Their International Setting*. London: Hutchinson and Co., 1948.

_____. *The Struggle for Greece, 1941–1949*. London: Hart-Davis, MacGibbon, 1976.

_____. "Recognizing 'Macedonia' Defies History." *Christian Science Monitor*, October 28, 1992, pp. 31–32.

Yiatroudakis, Stelios. *Tashkent: 30 Years of Exile* (in Greek). Athens: Ekthosis Diogenis, 1998.

Zafeiropoulos, Demetrios. *The Anti-Guerrilla Struggle* (in Greek). Athens: Ekthosis Mavridi, 1956.

Zahariadis, Nikolaos. "Is the Former Yugoslav Republic of Macedonia a Security Threat to Greece?" *Med. Quart.* 5, no.1 (1994): 84–105.

Zaikos, Nikos. "The Interim Agreement Between Greece and FYROM" (in Greek). In *Athens–Skopje, Seven Years of Symbiosis (1995–2002)*, eds. E. Kofos and V. Vlasides, 21–67. Athens: Ekthosis Papazisi, 2003.

Zotiades, Georgios B. *The Macedonian Controversy* (in Greek). Thessaloniki: Institute for Macedonian Studies, 1961.

Index

Orpheus/Orphic hymns 32
Orthodox Church/Orthodox Christians 117, 217
Orthodox Church of "Macedonia" 217, 220
Ossa, Mount 163
Otto von Bismarck 37, 38
Ottoman 1, 5, 23, 25–28, 30, 32–35, 37, 38, 40, 41, 43, 44, 48, 49, 53, 60, 61, 67, 73, 76, 79, 83, 85, 92, 125, 145, 146, 175, 232, 233
Ottoman Empire 5, 11, 28, 30, 33–35, 37, 39, 42, 44, 46, 53, 54, 69, 70, 75, 93, 146, 179
Ottoman occupation 26, 28, 29, 16
Ottoman-occupied Macedonia 37, 74

Paeonia 244, 245, 247
Paillares, M. 71, 73
Palangurski, M. 29
Palmer 85, 92, 214, 217
Pandermali-Poulaki 165
Panhellenic Liberation Organization (PAO) 123, 124, 129, 184
Panhellenic Socialist Movement (PASOK) 224, 228, 235
Panitsa 103
Panslavic Komitet 43
Panslavism 31, 33, 34, 36
Papadimitriou, R. 64, 65
Papaioannou, A. 129, 206, 207
Papakonstantinou, Michalis 96, 130, 155–57, 218
Papandreou, Andreas 224, 228
Papandreou, George 235
Papas 230
Papastathis 217
Papathanasiou 119, 123, 129
Papavizas, George 45, 110, 120, 123, 129, 135, 147, 185, 191
Papazoglou, Fanula 245, 248
Papoulias, Anastasios 62
papyrus of Mygdonia 247
Paris Peace Conference 1946 212
Patriarch 63, 82
Patriarchate/Orthodox Patriarchate 31, 34, 37, 39, 41, 45, 53, 57, 58, 64, 65, 67, 70, 74, 91, 152
Paul (prince of Yugoslavia) 108
Pausanias 163
Pavlov, P. 29
Pavlovitch 125
Pelagonia 63
Pella 4, 16, 169, 174, 176, 211, 215, 220, 225
Peloponnesus/Peloponnesian War 22, 163–65
Pentalofos 14, 28, 127
Pentzopoulos 85
People's Democratic Balkan Federation 205
People's Republic of Macedonia 3, 12, 13, 15, 42, 143, 148–55, 157–59, 161, 178, 185, 187, 194, 197, 198, 200, 203, 207, 212, 220
Perdiccas I, King 162, 165, 169
Perdiccas II, King 169
Perlepe 67, 912

Perry 159, 222
Perseus 23
Persia 170, 171
Petra Pass 166
Petric 189, 190, 192, 199, 208
Petroff 41
Petrograd 40
Peyov, Naoum 128, 138, 140, 141, 182, 213
Philellene 172
Philip II 2, 4, 7, 8, 11, 16, 21–27, 34, 42, 53, 65, 95, 132, 148, 157, 167, 169, 171, 173, 174, 176, 177, 220, 225, 226, 229, 245
Philip V 245
Philippi 4, 27, 174
Philippoupolis (now Plovdic) 27
Pieria/Pierian coastal plain 77, 163, 164, 166
Pindar 163, 164
Pindus mountains 21, 24, 81, 163, 164
Pinheiro, Z. 223
Pirin (Bulgarian) Macedonia (*Pirinska Makedonija*) 124, 132, 133, 137, 141, 149, 173, 174, 190, 198, 201, 212, 214, 238
Plastiras government 182
Plato 3, 72, 73, 176
Plutarch 87, 168, 246
Political Committee for National Liberation (PEEA) 184
Polygyros 77
Pouliopoulos 96, 100
Poulton 48, 80, 83, 96, 125, 148, 157, 162, 176, 177
Prague 192
Prespa Lake 25, 30, 35, 126, 203
Principality *see* Bulgarian Principality
Prohor Pcinjsky 148
prosfyges (refugees) 179
Proti 184
Proto-Dorians 163, 164
Proto-Hellenic language/dialect 163, 169
Provincia *Macedonia* 23, 25
Provisional Democratic Government/communist government of the mountains 200, 204
Ptolemais 50
Pydna 4, 23, 174

Rachment Bey 70
Rainbow Party 215, 216
Rakoski 32
Rallis, Georgios 103
Rankovic 133
Ravali, Jovanni 118–20
rayah 26, 28, 75
Reader's Digest 246
Realpolitik 15
Reat V 69
Red Army/Soviet Army 183
Republic of Krushevo 219
Republic of Macedonia (*Republika Makedonija*) 3, 6, 14, 15, 218, 220, 223, 224, 226–31, 233, 235, 237, 238, 239
"Republic of Skopje" 223